The Expansion of Prophetic Experience

The Expansion of Prophetic Experience

Essays on Historicity, Contingency and Plurality in Religion

By

Abdulkarim Soroush

Translated by

Nilou Mobasser

Edited with Analytical Introduction *by*

Forough Jahanbakhsh

BRILL

LEIDEN • BOSTON
2009

Cover illustration: Hamid Nouri

This book is printed on acid-free paper.

Library of Congress Cataloging-in-Publication Data

Surūsh, ʿAbd al-Karīm.
    [Bast-i tajrubah-ʾi nabavi. English]
    The expansion of prophetic experience : essays on historicity, contingency and plurality in religion / edited with analytical introduction by Forough Jahanbakhsh ; translated by Nilou Mobasser.
        p. cm.
    Includes bibliographical references and index.
    ISBN 978-90-04-17105-3 (hardback : alk. paper) 1. Muhammad, Prophet, d. 632—Prophetic office. 2. Islam—Doctrines. I. Jahanbakhsh, Forough. II. Mobasser, Nilou. III. Title.
    BP166.55.S8713 2008
    297.2—dc22

                                                                    2008035400

ISBN 978 90 04 17105 3

PRINTED IN THE NETHERLANDS

CONTENTS

Preface ix
Introduction xv

PART ONE

Chapter One   The Expansion of Prophetic Experience 3
Experiential Nature of Prophethood 3
Evolutionary Nature of Prophetic Experience 9
Dialogical Nature of Prophetic Experience 13

Chapter Two   The Last Prophet—1 25
On the Meaning of "Finality" 25
The Relation of Finality to the Prophet's Persona 37

Chapter Three   The Last Prophet—2 45
End of Religious Legislation or End of Religious
   Experience? 45
The Seal of Prophethood, Not the Seal of Interpretation 52

Chapter Four   Essentials and Accidentals in Religion 63
Relationship Between the Essential and the Accidental 63
Distinguishing the Essential from the Accidental 69
   Arabic Language and Arabic Culture 70
   Conceptual Limitations 76
   Scientific Knowledge of the Age 78
   Fiqh: Essential or Accidental? 83
   Ijtihad: Cultural Translation of the Accidentals 89
Conclusion 90

Chapter Five   Maximalist Religion, Minimalist Religion 93
Maximal View of Religion 93
Fiqh: Minimum "Necessary" or Maximum "Sufficient"? 96
Science and Religion 102
Ethical All-inclusiveness? 104
Minimal on Theological Issues 107

What Does the Expandability of Religious Knowledge
   Tell Us? 109
Minimalist Religion and Everlasting Continuity 111
Minimalist, not Maximalist Guidance 112
On the Perfection of Religion 113
On *Ijtihad* 114
Excessive Expectations of Religion 115

Chapter Six   Straight Paths—1. An Essay on Religious
   Pluralism; Positive and Negative 119
Positive Pluralism: Irreducible Plurality 120
   Diversity of Understandings of Religious Texts 120
   Diversity of Interpretations of Religious Experience 123
   John Hick and Noumena/Phenomena Distinction 131
   An Alternative Explanation: Formless within Forms 134
   Immersion of Truth within Truth 135
Negative Pluralism: Diversity Explained via Negativa 137
   One Destination, Different Paths 137
   Exclusivity of God's Guidance? 140
   Inextricable Mix of Truth and Falsehood 142
   Compatibility of All Truths 146
   Pluralism of Values and Causes 147
   Religiosity is Caused not Reasoned 149
   Pluralistic Society versus Ideological Society 152

Chapter Seven   Straight Paths—2. A Conversation on
   Religious Pluralism 155
Critical Rationalism or Relativism 155
Cause versus Reason 158
Faith and Certitude 162
"Truth" and "Truth for" 165
Nominalism and Pluralism 168
Truth and Salvation 171
Plurality of Meaning and Text 175

PART TWO

Chapter Eight   Types of Religiosity 181
Pragmatic/Instrumental Religiosity 182

Discursive/Reflective Religiosity 186
Experiential Religiosity... 190

Chapter Nine   The Prophet Present 193
Prelude 193
The Essence of Religiousness 195
Religious Experience: the Quintessence of Religion 202
Rituals 205

Chapter Ten   Prophets Unheard 209
The Paradoxical Nature of Prophetic Mission 211
Following the Prophet Is More than Following His
     Commandments 217

Chapter Eleven   Faith and Hope 225
Religious Faith 225
Religious Experience: Cause or Reason for Faith 228
Forming the Formless 230
Doubts and Criticisms 232
Need for Religious Experience 239
Relation of Legal Precepts to Formless Experience 241

Chapter Twelve   Spiritual Guardianship and Political
     Guardianship 245
Ghadir and Some of Its Consequences 245
Sense and Essence of Spiritual Guardianship 247
Wilayat and Imamate in Shi'ism 258
Confusing Spiritual Guardianship and Political
     Guardianship 264

APPENDICES

Appendix One   The Word of Mohammad. An Interview with
     Abdulkarim Soroush, by Michel Hoebink 271

Appendix Two   Ayatollah Sobhani's First Letter 276
An Experience Like Poets' Experiences 279
The Prophet is the Qur'an's Creator and Producer 280
Meanings from God, Words from the Prophet 282
Conditions of the Prophet's Life Produced the Qur'an 282

Appendix Three   *Bashar* and *Bashir*. Soroush's First Response
   to Sobhani   288
   Muhammad's Word, Muhammad's Miracle   289
   Secondly, the Tale of the Poetry   292
   Thirdly, Appealing to Rumi   292
   Fourthly, as for "Humanness" Implying Idle Passions and
      Desires   293
   Fifthly, the Possibility of the Qur'an and the Prophet's
      Knowledge Containing "Flaws"   297
   As for Apparent Incongruities between the Qur'an and
      Human Findings..   298

Appendix Four   Ayatollah Sobhani's Second Letter   303
   The Nature of Revelation in this Interview?   304
   Muhammad, Peace Be Upon Him, Is Human   307
   Notion of Speaker and Loudspeaker   308
   Prophet, Not Scientist?   309
   Anything That Comes into Being is Preceded by Material
      Potentiality and Time   312
   Inconsistency between the Surface Appearance of the
      Qur'an and Human Science   313
   Chasing Away Devils with Meteors   316

Appendix Five   The Parrot and the Bee. Soroush's Second
   Response to Sobhani   319
   Faith Weakening!   320
   Learning, Not Sinning   322
   Revelation as a Natural Phenomenon   324
   Dialogical Nature of the Qur'an   326
   The Parrot and the Bee   329
   The Formless and the Form   330
   "The Phenomenon of the Qur'an"   335
   Gabriel within the Prophet   337
   Some Metaphysical Considerations   338
   Conflicts of Science and Scripture   340
   Pluralistic Islam versus Monolithic Islam   343

Bibliography   345

Index   349

PREFACE

About the Author and the Book

Abdulkarim Soroush (b. 1945) is one of the most eminent, influential and controversial intellectual figures of contemporary Iran. In the mid-1970s, equipped with a degree in pharmacology from Tehran University, Soroush left for London to study analytical chemistry and philosophy of science. By the late 1970s, he had made a name for himself through publications that revealed his wide range of interest in philosophy of science, philosophy of history and traditional Islamic metaphysics. Upon his return to Iran a few months after the 1979 Revolution, Soroush became a public intellectual figure thanks to his extraordinary talent and philosophical knowledge, which he continued to demonstrate through publications, university teaching and public lectures on various subjects, including Rumi's mysticism and the best philosophical defence of Islam against the contesting Marxist and materialist ideologies of the time. While holding his academic position as chair of the department of Islamic culture in Tehran's Teachers' College, he was appointed, along with several other academic and intellectual figures of the time, as a member of the Advisory Committee on Cultural Revolution. He resigned from these positions within four years and devoted himself exclusively to teaching and research at the Academy of Philosophy and the Research Center for Humanities and Social Sciences.

The remarkable combination of intellectual influences and disciplines of thought that shaped Soroush's mind have made him a hybrid intellectual with profound knowledge of both classical Islamic intellectual tradition and modern Western philosophical tradition and critical thinking. During his teaching in the post-revolutionary period, Soroush found himself deeply engaged in what he often refers to as an "unabated intellectual struggle." On the one hand he was armed with an understanding of philosophy of science that had taught him of the collective and competitive nature of science and knowledge. On the other hand, he was witnessing the dramatic adaptation of religion to a political ideology that demanded exclusivity and dogmatism. He was becoming increasingly cognizant of the inherited challenges lying ahead in the relationship between religion, humanity, science and social institutions in the modern age—challenges that he addressed in his innovative course, Modern Theology (*Kalam-e Jadid*), offered at the divinity school in Tehran University. He was also equally intrigued by what he had learned through his classical Islamic education, namely, the existing diversity and multiplicity of interpretations of religion thanks to mystics, jurists, philosophers, and Ash'ari and Mu'tazili theologians. The combination of all these contending ideas and disciplines guided his interest towards the field of philosophy of religion. So it was under the influence of the theories and ideas of some of the best minds of the West and the East, such as Wittgenstein, Kuhn, Quine, Lakatos, Popper, al-Ghazali, Shah Wali Allah of Deli, Sadr al-din Shirazi (Mulla Sadra), Rumi, Ibn Arabi and others, that Soroush began to explore the field of philosophy of religion. The pinnacle of his intellectual production in this area finally appeared in the late 1980s in a trilogy of articles later republished in book form under the title "The Contraction and Expansion of Religious Knowledge." This is an epistemological/hermeneutical theory about understanding religion that accounts for the collective and human nature of religious knowledge, treating it like other forms of knowledge and thus making it fallible, constantly evolving and interactive with other human learning. The implications of this theory were far reaching for the clerical monopoly over religion and their exclusive right to its interpretation. It was soon after the publication of this theory, but more particularly when Soroush began publicly applying it to the given socio-political and religious context of Iran when talking about democracy, freedom, human rights and religious pluralism, that he began to face severe criticism and even personal aggression. Soroush's theory posed an obvious challenge to the theological, philosophical and political foundations of the ruling Islamic regime. For almost a decade, while Soroush's popularity as a dissident intellectual continued to increase among his growing and enthusiastic audience in universities and intellectual circles, so did the vehemence of his critics. His lectures were often violently interrupted, while organized extremist gangs called for his assassination accusing him of heresy and treason. He was called for questioning by the officials. His publications came under severe censorship and were periodically banned. He was fired from his academic post and finally barred from any teaching and lecturing in Iran. He was gradually forced into exile. Since the year 2000, Soroush has taught as a visiting professor at Harvard, Yale, Princeton, Columbia and Georgetown universities and has been a senior fellow at the Wissenschaftskolleg zu Berlin, the Free University of Amsterdam and The International Institute for the Study of Islam in the Modern World in the Netherlands. In spite of his physical absence, his popularity and influence have not diminished among his Iranian audience and his ideas and writings continue not only to inspire followers but also to instigate new waves of intellectual debate, even among his opponents in the religious seminaries. His striking audacity and selflessness in the face of all these restrictions and deprivations speaks volumes of his uncompromising intellectual commitment to advance the frontiers of Islamic thinking to new horizons beyond the boundaries set by traditional orthodoxy. Soroush's influence has been manifold, yet it is his role as a reformer that will be considered as his unique and enduring contribution. This was acknowledged when Soroush, along with two other contemporary Muslim scholars, won the prestigious international Erasmus Prize (2004) for religion and modernity. He was also chosen one of the 100 Most Influential People in the World by Time Magazine (2005).

Soroush is a very prolific thinker. He has penned close to thirty books and numerous articles. Some of his writings were first made available to English readers in his *Reason, Freedom, and Democracy in Islam* (Oxford, 2000) and in some of the studies written about him in a variety of western languages. Several of his writings have also been translated into other languages such as Turkish, Arabic, Indonesian, etc. Many of his lectures, articles and interviews are also posted on his webpage, *www.drsoroush.com*, in both Persian and English. The present book is the second published collection of his writings rendered into English.

Between 1997 and 2001 Soroush delivered several lectures both outside and inside Iran thanks to the relative freedom afforded to him by the reformist government of President Muhammad Khatami, although neither his official restrictions nor the unofficial harassments were eliminated. These lectures, which were later on published in book form, marked the beginning of a new phase in his intellectual trajectory and his treatment of religion—as will be explained later in the introduction to this volume. The hallmark of this new phase was his theory about the contraction and expansion of religion itself. His discussions on the historicity of the Prophet Muhammad's revelatory experience and the human and contextual aspects of religion were mostly captured in his book entitled *Bast-e Tajrubeh-e Nabavi* [The Expansion of Prophetic Experience]. The present volume retains the same title because it reflects the core of this intellectual endeavour. However, it is not a full-length translation of that book. It presents a collection of twelve articles selected from a total of three books: eight chapters from *Bast-e Tajrubeh-e Nabavi* [The Expansion of Prophetic Experience] (Tehran: Serat, 1999); two from *Seratha-ye Mostaqim* [The Straight Paths] (Tehran: Serat, 1998); and one from *Akhlaq-e Khodayan* [The Ethics of Gods] (Tehran: Tarh-e Nou, 2001). Moreover, this collection presents for the first time some further arguments put forward by Soroush in 2008 in elaboration of certain of his ideas that have recently come under bitter attack by a number of ayatollahs. The gist of these critiques and Soroush's responses to them—that resulted in a theological debate—are captured in the appendices to this volume.

Readers should be reminded that Chapter One, "The Expansion of Prophetic Experience," is not alone sufficient to understand Soroush's theory about humanness and the historicity of religion. Rather, in order to obtain a full view of his theory, at least Chapter One, materials in the Appendices and Chapters Four and Five—if not the whole of Part One of the book—should be read together.

In this book some articles have gone through substantial reorganization even though the main text is faithful to the original Persian. For instance, "Faith and Hope," which was originally in interview format, has been restructured and shortened. "Straight Paths (2)" is an abridged version of the article "Truth, Reason and Salvation" in *Seratha-ye Mostaqim*. Finally, certain others, like "The Essentials and Accidentals of Religion," have been shortened here by eliminating inconsequential material.

As for the quotations of Persian verses—or at least the ones retained here—those taken from Rumi's *Mathnawi* are given in the rendering by Reynold A. Nicholson (Ed., Bouteh Research Institute and the Center for Dialogue Among Civilizations. Tehran: Nashr-e Bouteh, 2002). Throughout the book the translations of Qur'anic verses are taken mainly from A. J. Arberry's translation, in some cases slightly modified by that of M. Dawood.

Over the years of preparing this book, I received much encouragement from several scholars and individuals who showed great interest in seeing another collection of Soroush's work made accessible to his non-Persian readers. I am very grateful to all of them. Special thanks are due particularly to John Hick and Jose Casanova for their invaluable support and encouragement at various stages of the work. Their continuous enthusiasm and constant reminders of the book's significance have been a source of tremendous encouragement and support. I am also deeply appreciative of Casanova's positive feedback and insightful suggestions after reading the manuscript in its almost final stage. I would also like to thank the anonymous readers of Brill for their constructive advice and important support.

At Brill, I would like to thank Joed Elich, the Publishing Manager, and Trudy Kamperveen, the senior assistant editor, whose keen interest and wise advice were particularly instrumental in bringing this book to publication. I am also sincerely grateful to Stephen Milliere at McGill University's Islamic Studies Library for his helpful and friendly assistance in the preparation of the introductory chapter.

Some notes on the translation are in order here. The articles in this volume were rendered into English by Nilou Mobasser, whose mastery in translating Soroush's sophisticatedly complex and highly poetical language should be congratulated. Both the author and the editor are very grateful to her for dedicating her talent and time to this project. The translations were then read by the editor against their original Persian in order to make sure that the intricacies of the author's style and the technicalities of the subject matters were conveyed as closely as possible. Inquiries and recommendations for change were then discussed with the author himself and applied to the text afterwards.

During long hours of discussion and rereading of these passages with Soroush—whenever he could find time in his busy schedule and wherever I could reach him (Harvard University, 2000–2002; Princeton University, 2003; London, Tehran and Berlin, 2001–2006, New York and Washington D.C. 2007–2008)—I learned an enormous amount and came away with many invaluable gains. The most precious of these was, however, the assurance that the content of this book presents the closest possible rendering of Soroush's thought in another language. This would simply have been impossible without his generous help. My most sincere thanks go to him for graciously entrusting me with the editorship of this manuscript.

In the year 2006, when the first draft of this manuscript was prepared Soroush turned sixty years old. It is in honour of his sixtieth birthday that this work is dedicated.

Forough Jahanbakhsh

INTRODUCTION

Abdulkarim Soroush's Neo-Rationalist Approach to Islam

For over two centuries Muslim societies have been experiencing the challenges of modernity and modernization. During this time their response in terms of thought and practice has swung like a pendulum between premature or even "radical" secularization (in the name of modernity) and the extreme reactionary trends of religious revivalism and fanaticism (in the name of religion). Now, at the dawn of the twenty-first century, it is only natural to expect that this pendulum should begin to find its balance. It is at this balance point that gradually, but surely, the pieces of a reformed Islam are coming together. The Islam that is emerging draws upon a rich religious, ethical and intellectual heritage and is responsive, in a positive and serious sense, to the imperatives of modern human values.

This book offers its readers an overview of certain substantially important dimensions of this reformed Islam, which I would call "Neo-Rationalist Islam." In order to explain the features of Neo-Rationalist Islam, it seems necessary to situate it first in the broader context of Muslim responses to modernity. Much has been written on the latter subject, and several categorizations and taxonomies applied in an attempt to differentiate the types of Muslim responses to modernity. One commonly used model is the bipolar category of fundamentalist/militant/political/ideological Islam versus a moderate/non-militant/modernist/liberal Islam. If we broadly accept this notion of fundamentalist vs. liberal poles as indicators of the two ends of a very wide and heterogeneous spectrum, Neo-Rationalist Islam certainly does sit on the liberal side of the divide inasmuch as it is a reaction to the opposite pole and departs from traditional orthodoxy on a number of points as well. Nevertheless, it also differs from its other siblings under the overall umbrella of reform/liberal Islam. Among the features of a liberal presentation of Islam there are: a call for the rereading of religious texts, rejuvenation of the Islamic intellectual and ethical traditions, a greater role for reason, social and legal improvements (particularly for women), public participation in politics and reopening the gates of *ijtihad*. Surely almost all representatives of liberal Islam have called for at least one or a combination of a few of these themes. Therefore, it can be said that there have been as many liberal Islams as the number of individual reformists who have supported one or more of the above issues. This is not to suggest that anything is wrong with this diversity of focuses and different degrees of emphasis; indeed, it may reveal an existing dynamism for change among Muslims. However, a crucial question inevitably imposes itself: Why is it that, despite all these attempts at religious reform and modernization, no fundamental or comprehensive change has yet occurred that could take root and grow systematically from that soil? Some might provide social and political explanations that could partially, I think, account for the situation. Nevertheless, it would be somehow misleading to place all the blame on the unfavourable political and economic conditions of Muslim societies.

From an intellectual perspective, at least, the question invites a critical examination of all these disjointed efforts on a grander scale to discover possible shortcomings. Have these efforts fallen short of bringing about substantial changes in Muslim thought and societies because they engage with the wrong questions in the first place? Have they misperceived the nature and depth of the challenges posed by modernity? Have they addressed the "effects," so to speak, and not the "root causes," thus improvising provisional and incomplete solutions? Or, has it been so because of a lack of theoretical depth, harmony and/ or a matrix? Fortunately, it seems that the modern Muslim intellectual trajectory is entering a stage of self-examination that will allow it to overcome its past shortcomings and where its discourse will soon leave behind its habit of addressing disparate and circumstantial issues. It is at this critical stage of intellectual maturity that Neo-Rationalist Islam presently stands, calling for systematic approach to reform through rethinking the underpinnings of the tradition.

Islamic thought, like any other intellectual tradition, has gone through a period of development and will surely continue to do so. Contemporary Muslim intellectuals, along with their societies and regardless of ethnic, linguistic and sectarian differences, have come a long way and have learned some hard and often costly lessons to reach this point. Whatever the achievement of the next phase of this evolving intellectual maturity, it will undoubtedly be the result of their cumulative and collective endeavours. To cite but a single example, the contributions of Iranian religious intellectuals in this regard have been substantial. One practical reason (among others) for this has been their experience of the politicization and ideologization of Islam during the 1970s and 1980s that culminated in the establishment of an Islamic regime. Islamic rule posed for them tremendous first hand challenges, and yet, in the last twenty years or so, a few outstanding reformist thinkers have emerged in Iran, each contributing to one dimension or another—depending on their areas of specialty and training—in shaping a non-political, Neo-Rationalist reformed Islam. The very eminent and one of the most influential figures among them has been Abdulkarim Soroush, whose consequential ideas have set in motion new religious discourse and intellectual trends in contemporary Iran. It would indeed be no exaggeration to say that this point of religious reform might never have been reached so soon without the contribution of Abdulkarim Soroush. He is undoubtedly one of the most systematic architects of the Neo-Rationalist Islam, and one whose ideas have introduced a paradigm shift in Muslim religious thought.

Towards a New Theology

The systematic and comprehensive nature of Soroush's approach to religious reform is mirrored in his own intellectual trajectory. In the course of his intellectual development, Soroush has dealt with issues related to the three interrelated realms of "religion," the "interpretation of religion/text" and the "practical application" thereof. Since the late-1980s he has proposed two ground-breaking theories.[1] The first of these was his seminal hermeneutical and epistemological theory known as the "Contraction and Expansion of Religious Knowledge" (1987–1989), which deals with the "interpretation/understanding" of religion. The second was his theory of "Expansion of Prophetic Experience," a theory about "religion" that he presented between 1997 and 1999. Since then, drawing upon these two grand theories, he has been addressing some of the most pertinent practical issues in Muslim societies—issues such as religion and democracy, religious pluralism and religion and human rights. In his earlier phase, which began with the "Theory of Contraction

---

[1] For an account of his other public activities and a very comprehensive intellectual autobiography of Soroush see his book: *Reason, Freedom, and Democracy in Islam*, trans. and ed. Mahmoud Sadri, Ahmad Sadri (Oxford: Oxford University Press, 2000), Introduction and Chapter One. Forough Jahanbakhsh, *Islam, Democracy and Religious Modernism in Iran (1953–2000): From Bazargan to Soroush* (Leiden: Brill, 2001), Chapter Five.

and Expansion of Religious Knowledge," he dealt mainly with the historical evolutions and devolutions that occur in the "understanding of religion," offering a hermeneutical and epistemological theory to explain this phenomenon.[2] Later on, without essentially departing from that path, Soroush moved on to a more challenging venture: that of analysing the contraction and expansion of "religion" itself due to the role of human agency and historical contexts. In his theory of "The Expansion of Prophetic Experience,"[3] a hallmark of this new phase, Soroush lays the foundations of an Islamic reformed theology. In the process he explores and explains, among other things, issues such as the historical and human nature of religion, religious experience, revelation, the role and place of the Prophet in the prophetic mission, the position of scripture and the interrelation of all these. In doing this, Soroush deploys a host of supporting arguments and ideas drawn from classical Islamic theology, philosophy and mysticism while at the same time adopting analytical rational approaches from outside the domain of religion. This represents an attempt to actualize what he has long been calling for, namely, a new rational theology. Soroush is convinced that a viable and meaningful Islamic reform in modern times is not possible unless it begins systematically at the foundational and theoretical levels, particularly in the realms of ethics and theology. He argues that modernizing Islamic thought and its empowerment does not simply mean posing new/modern questions to an outdated frame of references and working out their solutions by using old concepts. Modernity consists, more than anything else, of new concepts and frames of reference of which rationality is the most substantial. Theology is the realm where fundamental concepts such as God, humanity, revelation, prophethood, etc., can be revised and redefined. Soroush's training in analytical philosophy does not allow him to be content with unsystematic, piecemeal adjustments and changes. His erudition in

---

[2] Abdulkarim Soroush, *Qabd wa Bast-e Te'urik-e Shari'at: Nazariyah-e Takamul-e Ma'rifat-e Dini* [The Theoretical Contraction and Expansion of Religion: The Theory of Evolution of Religious Knowledge], 3rd ed. (Tehran: Sirat, 1373/1994). English readers may find the core arguments of this theory in his book *Reason, Freedom and Democracy in Islam* (Chapter 5) and in his article: "The Evolution and Devolution of Religious Knowledge," in Charles Kurzman (ed.), *Liberal Islam* (Oxford University Press, 1998). An English translation of the book is underway while its Arabic translation is now available under the title *Al-Qabd wa al-Bast fi al-shari'ah*, trans. Dalal 'Abbas (Beirut: Dar al-Jadid, 2002).

[3] This volume presents his essential writings related to this theory (see the Preface for details).

traditional Islamic theology and philosophy, on the other hand, helps him to understand and discern points of both weakness and strength to see what can be built upon and what should be left behind.

Main Features of Neo-Rationalist Islam

Abdulkarim Soroush's Neo-Rationalist project puts forward one of the most comprehensive, systematic, and balanced presentations of a reformed Islam thus far presented by an individual thinker. It is comprehensive in that it deals simultaneously with all three aforementioned aspects of religion: "religion", the "interpretation/understanding" of religion/text and the "practical application" thereof. Unlike other reform projects that usually focus on certain practical issues of modern Muslim life and call for change and reinterpretation in relation only to these matters, Soroush's Neo-Rationalist project takes a more comprehensive approach. This manifests itself in its recognition of the historicity of all three of these realms and in its consequent acknowledgement of the role of reason in them all. As such, this foundational and comprehensive scheme bypasses the typical theoretical problems that usually emerge as a result of only partially rationalized interpretations of religious tradition—problems such as incongruities between proposed solutions and the so-called fixed and ahistorical Qura'nic pronouncements that have so often impeded reform. One of the best examples of such problems is women's rights issues. Regardless of the overall will, public pressure and numerous scholarly attempts at proposing legal improvements in this respect through readjusting shari'ah laws to suit modern conditions, problems persist due to the apparent incompatibility of these efforts with explicit scriptural pronouncements regarding women.

Soroush's Neo-Rationalist reform project is systematic in two senses. It is systematic in itself because it has recognized and defined problems posed by the challenges of modernity at the foundational level, where their root causes are organically connected. That is to say, it does not address disparate or singular problems in a diffused and segmented manner, but rather deals with why and how these problems are generated. It looks into the interaction of theoretical underpinnings of ethical, theological, legal, social and political problems and tries to resolve them at their root. Besides, Soroush's theories about religion and the understanding of it provide a cohesive matrix and frame of reference that allow for working out systematic, logically harmonious and rationally defendable solutions for these problems—as is manifested in his own writings.

The third characteristic of Soroush's Neo-Rationalism is its balanced nature. Faced with the swing of Muslim thought between the two extremes of radical/strong secularization and a maximalist/strongly radical understanding of religion, it successfully creates a zone at the center where a measured secularism and minimalist understanding of religion meet in harmony. It involves secularism by recognizing the role of human agency—that is history and human reason—in the three aforementioned aspects of religion. It is ready to desacralize two of them completely, that is, (a) the understanding/interpretation of religion and (b) the practical application of the latter in the socio-political and legal affairs of a religious society by relinquishing them to reason independent of revelation. However, it upholds the sacredness of "religious experience," the essence of religion, to the extent that it involves encountering the Transcendent, albeit insisting that religious experience itself is influenced by historical and cognitive conditions of the subject as well.[4] The understanding of religion, according to Soroush, is an age-bound and context-bound human endeavour nourished by other fields of human knowledge that are not religious. Similarly, the governance and administration of the practical aspects of life in a religious society are rational in nature and decided by the collective will of its members. The main function of religion is not to offer practical plans for the everyday affairs of the society. Indeed, if anything at all is found in religion of that nature, it is, at best, marginal or even accidental. In other words, religion deserves a very minimal role in the public sphere.

Moreover, ethics in Soroush's view is independent of and prior to religion. If secularism means administering society by the rule of reason independent from revelation, Neo-Rationalist Islam advocates legitimizing reason as the base-foundation and life blood of the social, political and ethical institutions and norms in a community of believers, while at the same time allowing for their expression of religious sentiments. This latter point, however, is subject to an important condition, namely, that it not run contrary to or negate the human rights and values derived *a priori* from reason independent of revelation. In other words, unlike

---

[4] Soroush rejects the typical dichotomy of secular/non-secular and insists that we have secularisms. Allusions to this position can be found in Chapter Eight in this book.

maximal/strong secularism, which rejects outright anything religious in the public sphere, the minimal secularism of the Neo-Rationalist project allows it an examined and rationally measured role in a religious society. By minimal religion (a notion elaborated below in detail in Chapter Five) is meant the desacralizing of everything temporal (like politics), which in fact possesses no transcendental nature and has been wrongly linked with religious faith. Or, to put it differently, it involves minimizing expectations of religion in matters related to public spheres of life. Soroush emphasises "religious experience," which is private by nature though influenced by external circumstance, as the core of religion and religiosity vis à vis the outward practices of one's faith.

A brief exposition of some other distinguishing features of Neo-rationalist Islam is in order here. Neo-rationalist Islam has its roots in the intellectual tradition of the Mu'tazilah, the rationalist theological and semi-philosophical school of thought influential in the 2nd Islamic century (9th century CE). As such it is not an alien construct, being possessed of some indigenous continuity. Soroush's Neo-Rationalism is, in a sense, a reinvention of Mu'tazilite rationalism. Nevertheless, it differs from the rationalist tradition of the Mu'tazilah in that the latter was based on an intellectual world-view of its own time, dictated by the philosophy and science of the 9th century CE. Neo-rationalist Islam, on the other hand, has evolved within the intellectual framework of the modern age and benefits from its philosophical and scientific rationality. The prefix "Neo" points to this difference. However, inasmuch as their rationalism is based on and recognizes a "Reason" independent of "Revelation," they are effectively the same. This recognition, of course, entails some unorthodox theories regarding prophecy, the nature of revelation, the interpretation of scripture, the underlying assumptions of law/shari'ah and, most importantly, ethical beliefs.

The Neo-Rationalist theory of rational ethics is based on the assumption that ethical right and wrong can be ascertained by natural reason independent of the teachings of revelation. This, of course, has a wide range of implications for people's rights, duties, choices and responsibilities, since primary ethical values such as freedom, equality and justice are notions independent of and prior to religion. In other words, this creates a paradigm shift in the traditional orthodox view of the role of religion in both the private and, more significantly, the public sphere. There have been some contemporary Muslim reformers who have moved in this direction, though not always in a comprehensive or systematic manner. Yet while the demand for a greater role for reason has been a recurrent theme in Muslim modernist/liberal literature, at least from the late nineteenth century onward, in almost all cases this role has been conceived of as subordinate to revelation and its exercise still circumscribed by the boundaries of tradition. Consequently, reason has, at best, been restricted in the legal domain to the exercise of traditional *ijtihad*, whose underlying premises in themselves beg independent rational evaluation and critique in the light of modernity.

By contrast, Neo-Rationalist Islam is rationalist not so much in the traditional sense of putting forward a rational defence of religion, but mostly because it is chiefly concerned with the dialectic of faith and reason. It does not apologize for the elements of doubt or questioning since these are inherent components of any critical rational exercise. It welcomes critical rationalism, for this will, in the final analysis, enhance and empower one's faith and render religion and religiosity ever-expandable notions. This of course has implications for notions of belief and disbelief as well, which can sometimes be dramatically at odds with orthodox notions, not the least being recognition of plurality in understanding religion and types of religiosity.

Neo-Rationalist Islam also departs from some other reformist expressions in its approach to the interpretation of scripture. It employs modern "hermeneutical" methods that incorporate rational and historical assumptions and favours critical analysis of texts. This may be compared with some other liberal presentations of Islam in which the treatment of scripture is still mostly subordinate to the "exegetical" standards and parameters set by classical methods. These "exegetical" methods in turn rely heavily on traditional approaches and materials from within the religious tradition, such as *hadith*, biographical literature and classical *tafsirs*.

In a broader sense, one can say that Neo-Rationalist Islam distinguishes itself from other reformist/liberal projects as far as the latter's treatment of "tradition" is concerned. It seems that other liberal presentations have mostly embraced inherited "tradition" and its components—the scripture, history, institutions and ethical system of Islam—in their entirety and have not always been ready to step away from them and analyse this heritage critically from the outside. In other words, their embrace of the tradition leads to limited and often insubstantial criticism. Their fervent desire for reform and modernization is more in the nature of reshuffling the furniture in the house of tradition rather than renovating the structure itself. It is thus with a much more creative attitude that Neo-Rationalism approaches the repository of religious knowledge and the traditional intellectual heritage. In the hierarchy of all religious sciences and doctrines, it assigns priority to foundational ones and begins reform with a rereading at the deepest levels in order to build a cohesive and systematic intellectual edifice more suited to modern times. That is why in the Neo-Rationalist project creating a new theology and new ethical theory is given precedence over legal and jurisprudential reforms. For in the end, the latter without the former will produce only piecemeal and provisional solutions.

However, Neo-Rationalism's treatment of the tradition is neither a total rejection of the old in favour of the new nor a total and an uncritical embrace in the name of "preserving the legacy." Rather, it is a critical adoption of selected elements of this legacy based on a foundational epistemological principle, namely, recognizing the historicity and historical expansion of religion and religious knowledge. In short, it acknowledges the endless possibility for change and creativity even in this domain. Neo-Rationalist Islam interacts with the historical development of religion inasmuch as and in the same critical manner that it engages in dialogue with and borrows from rational achievements outside the tradition. Accordingly, it can reject with authority certain outdated elements and paradigms or create new ones. Thus, for instance, it critically and prudently benefits from the Muslim mystical tradition (of course in the context of discovery and not in that of justification), while at the same time selectively adopting certain western philosophical and rational frames of reference. In sum, one can argue that, if al-Ghazali's *Revival of the Religious Sciences* and Muhammad Iqbal's *Reconstruction of Religious Thought in Islam* have been the iconic moments of past scholarship, Soroush's Neo-Rationalist project is that of the present.

With regard to its treatment of 'modernity,' Neo-rationalist Islam also stands apart from some other liberal reformist projects. Unlike the latter, it is very much cognizant of the epistemological ruptures produced by modernity. It is attentive to the philosophical and conceptual underpinnings of modernity and does not confuse them with its outward products—modernization, so to speak. Rather, it tries to institutionalize, as much as possible, these conceptual underpinnings by weaving them into the very foundation of its new rational theology and rational system of ethics. It has often been due to such negligence or misunderstanding of modernity that Muslim reformers have contented themselves with drawing superficial parallels between the achievements of modernity and various obscure and underdeveloped notions existing in the tradition. This lack of depth is perhaps best revealed in their prevailing discourse on democracy where, for instance, the traditional notions of *shura, bay'ah* and *ijma'* have been over-emphatically equated with the principles of democracy. This is done, of course, at the expense of any substantial discussion of *a priori* human rights such as freedom, equality or sovereignty and by confusing the notions of "rights" and "duties." Another focus of the contemporary Muslim reform project has been legal reform, i.e., modernization of the shari'ah, which has similarly been carried out in an expedient and piecemeal manner (such as in matters related to women's rights). Evidently, only superficial changes can be made to a legal system like the shari'ah as long as its philosophical and ethical underpinnings have not undergone substantial revision and harmonious restructuring.

Principles and Presuppositions

As a basis for a much-needed reformed theology, this book offers a Neo-rationalist theory about religion and its study. It looks at the historicity, humanness and thus expandability of religion/revelation. It rests on certain premises and offers some broad presuppositions useful for understanding religion and interpreting religious texts as well. In doing so:

a. it emphasises a distinction between the internals and externals of the religion (intra-religious and extra-religious elements);
b. it explains the relationship between the two;
c. it clarifies ways in which the externals impact on the internals and vice-versa.

Soroush's aim is to introduce a balance into Muslims' perception of the Prophet, the nature of the revelation and the role of the Qur'an—thus, equilibrium with respect to expectations of religion in general. This balance, Soroush believes, has been lost due to the mystics' emphasis on the celestial, supra-human and spiritual figure of the Prophet on the one hand and the ahistorical dogmatism of orthodoxy on the other, which has reduced the Prophet's role in revelation to nothing more than that of a meta-historical instrument or a mere receiving agent of revelation. This existing imbalance has clouded Muslims' judgment and understanding of their religion, Soroush says, and continues to impair any new interpretation of scripture (especially of the Qur'an), consequently preventing any creative representation of Islam. It also seriously impedes engagement in novel and viable *ijtihad* or reinterpretations of the Shari'ah, to give just one practical example. Soroush cannot emphasise enough, as is evident throughout this book, that contemporary Muslims should be aware of and sensitive toward the existing distinction between those elements in their religion that are "essentially religious" and those that are "accidentally religious" and associated with the essentials in one way or another. He is not claiming that there exists such a thing as "purely religious" by itself, any more than there can exist a pure race or a pure language. He is aware that religions neither take shape nor operate in a vacuum and, more importantly, that there is not even such thing as an "un-interpreted" religious experience. He believes in and explains the inevitability of such a mix when the transcendent comes down to earth and has no choice but to submit to temporal parameters—naturalization of the supernatural, so to speak. What he describes and prescribes is that we distinguish the two domains of the essential and accidental in order to give them their due status and levels of significance when interpreting religious texts or when implementing and practicing religious injunctions.

In order to elaborate the mechanism of the dialogue (to use Soroush's own phrasing) between the inside of the religion and the outside, he propounds certain broad presuppositions/theses. These theses, which are fully elaborated and carefully reasoned, are to be found mostly in Part One of this book. They may be summarized as follows:

1. Revelation is the same as the "religious experience" of the Prophet;
2. Prophetic experience expands as the Prophet's personality expands;
3. The Prophet's personality expands both internally (as his intellectual and spiritual capabilities evolve) and externally (as his societal life and conditions change);
4. Revelation is subordinate to the Prophet's personality and not vice-versa;
5. While the Prophet's message, the formulation of his religious experience, is final (i.e., he is the Seal of prophets according to the Qur'an), it can be infinitely expanded and enriched through the religious experiences of other believers;

6. Religion/scripture includes essentials as well as accidentals, i.e., not everything in the scripture is necessarily religious;
7. Religion/scripture provides the "necessary minimum" guidance for salvation and not the "maximum possible";
8. What is known as the perfection of religion is a minimal and not a maximal perfection;
9. Expectations from religion must be minimal;
10. External, rational, historical presuppositions are everywhere at work either to shape the formless "experience" or afterwards to facilitate the understanding and/or interpreting religion and scripture.

It is in accordance with these presuppositions/theses that Soroush believes contemporary Muslims should try to understand, interpret and, more importantly, adjust their expectations of religion. Soroush's aim is to accentuate the historicity and humanness, the natural side, of the religion by showing the interactive relationship of the Prophet's experience with his community and societal milieu on the one hand—what he calls "external expansion"—and the dialogical relationship of revelation with the Prophet's inner developing personality and intellectual capacities—"internal expansion"—on the other. "In the encounter between all these human elements," Soroush says, "a human religion is gradually born which is in keeping with human beings and an answer to their real circumstances" (Chapter One).

What follows here is to highlight some major points of Soroush's arguments presented in this book, which is divided into two parts. Part One includes subjects mostly related to Soroush's theories on religion (revelation, scripture and prophecy), while the chapters in Part Two include discussions that reflect some practical implications of these theories, particularly in relation to what it means to "be religious."

Part One
Prophetic Experience and the Text

In Chapter One, without negating the divine sanctity and authenticity of the spirit of Islam, Soroush places emphasis on its gradual, historical and experiential genesis. He contends that "Islam is not a book or an aggregate of words; it is a historical movement and the history-incarnate of a mission. It is the historical extension of a gradually-realised prophetic experience." He also puts this in clearer terms, stating that "the Prophet did not adapt abstract experiences to reality." Rather, the actually existing world of his time, with all its problems, questions and intellectual and cultural resources, played a substantial role in the gradual process of a dialogue between heaven and earth. Similarly, the Prophet's gradually burgeoning personality affected the evolutionary process of his inward spiritual experience. The Prophet's personality, Soroush argues, "was both the receptacle and the generator, both the subject and the object of his religious revelatory experiences." Therefore, "[Islam] is nothing other than the condensed sum and substance of his individual and social experiences." What could be some implicit corollaries of these statements are made explicit by Soroush in his further pivotal statement that "revelation was under his [Prophet] sway, not he under the sway of revelation." In fact, he claims that "if the Prophet had lived longer and encountered more events, his reactions and responses would inevitably have grown as well…[and] the Qur'an could have been much more than it is." It would, perhaps, have had a second volume, as he says elsewhere.

These statements place Soroush's views in sharp contrast to the traditional position of Muslim orthodoxy with regard to the Prophet, revelation and the Qur'an. Although Muslim orthodoxy (in compliance with the Qur'anic position) reiterates the humanity of Muhammad, it has always rejected the idea of any influence on his part on the revelatory message. In traditional Muslim religious literature, Muhammad's role in the process of revelation and production of the scripture is reduced to that of being a mere agent of God's Word. Moreover, the insistence of mainstream orthodoxy on Muhammad being unlettered (*ummi*) relates more than anything else to the supremely significant doctrine that the Qur'an *is*, literally speaking, the Word of God. It is an affirmation that the Prophet's personality, mind, and language had no influence whatsoever on God's message. His mind was a pure vessel for the revelation that he simply received and passed on to humanity. Hence, the message, the Qur'an, was not contaminated by any human influence. According to this understanding, the process of revelation, or the Prophet's encounter with the divine, was simply a mechanical one. Absent from this traditional account, however, is any analysis of the role of the person of the Prophet, the only non-divine or human element involved in the process. Likewise, an analysis is missing of the impact on the content of revelation of the society and culture that Muhammad was addressing. And when traditional *tafsirs* (commentary literature) do treat certain episodes in Muhammad's life, or references in the Qur'an to events and personalities in his community, their function is simply to account for the "occasion of revelation" of the specific verses in question.

Nevertheless, there have been some scholars who have tried to explain the mechanism of revelation. They have speculated and expounded on questions such as the nature of revelation, the *kalam-e Bari* (Divine Speech), the angel of revelation, the question of whether the Qur'an was sent down from the *lauh al-mahfuz* (the Heavenly Preserved Tablet) to the Prophet's heart/or mind all at once or in piecemeal, etc.[5] Also, there have been many traditional literary and philological studies of the Qur'an that discern, among other things, the existence of non-Arabic vocabulary in its text, or that explain the etymology of certain ancient Arabic words, etc. Nevertheless, these studies are not concerned with the implications of such occurrences for revelation.[6]

Some Other Contemporary Views on Revelation and the Text

Among other contemporary Muslim scholars who have seriously proposed somewhat non-traditional explanations of the nature of revelation and/or engaged in contextualization of the scripture, one may point to the late Fazlur Rahman (Pakistan, d. 1988) and to the contemporary thinkers Muhammad Arkoun (Algeria, b. 1928), Nasr Hamed Abu Zayd (Egypt, b. 1943) and Muhammad Mujtahed Shabestari (Iran, b. 1924). In what follows the aim is not to compare and contrast the ideas of these scholars in any detail (such a study would require separate treatment), but to show the range of efforts made to explain the historical aspect of the revelation and its understanding that entails and enhances the revival of the Islamic rational tradition in the modern era. It will also help to situate Soroush's ideas in this continuum of efforts. Although there are considerable differences among these individuals in terms of their approaches and conclusions, there are many similarities too.

---

[5] There had been some earlier philosophical speculation on this subject by medieval philosophers like Ibn Sina, Al-Farabi and al-Ghazali, whose ideas were not welcomed by the mainstream orthodoxy. For an exposition of this subject see: Fazlur Rahman, *Prophecy in Islam*, 2nd Ed., (Chicago: University of Chicago Press, 1979).

[6] For a classical approach to these questions see, for instance, the works of Jalal al-Din al-Suyuti (1445–1507); for a modern work see, for instance, Arthur Jeffrey's *The Foreign Vocabulary of the Qur'an* (Baroda, India: Oriental Institute, 1938).

Fazlur Rahman, both as a scholar and as a Muslim intellectual reformist, was concerned about the modern relevance of the Islamic norms and values embedded in the Qur'an. It was this aim, i.e., reformation of Islamic thought and Muslim society, which engaged his interest in literary, philosophical, sociological and hermeneutical discussion of the Qur'an and not vice-versa.

Criticizing orthodoxy and medieval thinkers for their lack of "the intellectual capacity to say both that the Qur'an is entirely the Word of God and, in an ordinary sense, also entirely the word of Muhammad,"[7] Fazlur Rahman developed his theory of "feeling-idea-word" about the nature of revelation. He connected Divine Word to Muhammad's word through first establishing that "the basic *élan* of the Qur'an is moral," and that "the moral law and religious values are God's command."[8] Second, he stated that:

> When Muhammad's moral intuitive perception rose to the highest point and became identified with the moral law itself…, the Word was given with the inspiration itself. The Qur'an is thus pure Divine Word, but of course, it is equally intimately related to the inmost personality of the Prophet Muhammad whose relationship to it cannot be mechanically conceived like that of a record.[9]

Here, Fazlur Rahman is closer than ever to Soroush, who explicitly maintains that the Divine Speech (*kalam-e Bari*) is the same as the Prophet's speech (*kalam-e Payambar*), although he takes a different route to prove it (as we shall see below). Nevertheless, both of them depart from the supernaturalism of dogmatic theology with regard to revelation and emphasise its natural, human aspect. However, Fazlur Rahman's theory of revelation, i.e., that divinely revealed "idea-words" were transformed into the Prophet's "sound-words," remains primarily, if not exclusively, a means of explaining the inner, psychological process of technical revelation—something more or less of the same nature that characterized medieval philosophical and theological debates over the nature of *kalam-e Bari*. Perhaps because recognizing a role for the Prophet in revelation could have tremendous implications for the latter's possible impact on the content of the Qur'an, Fazlur Rahman did not directly link the two in his theory of revelation. Nor did

---

[7] Fazlur Rahman, *Islam*. 2nd ed. (Chicago: University of Chicago Press, 1976), p. 31.
[8] Ibid., pp. 32–33.
[9] Ibid., p. 33.

he pursue it any further in his later work. Nevertheless recognizing the circumstantiality of revelation, he devoted his attempt to develop a theory of Qur'an interpretation known as the "double movement" theory, consisting of two aims: first to decipher the original meaning of revelation within the socio-moral context of the Prophetic era at both the micro (Arabia) and macro (world) levels; and second, to go back to the Qur'an and reread it applying these derived original values and principles to the contemporary context. This hermeneutical method, if applied in its ideal format, can effectively improve legal *ijtihad* since those legal injunctions will be re-interpreted in the light of what Fazlur Rahman called the unified *Weltanschauung* of the whole Qur'an. Fazlur Rahman's interpretive model remains one of the most interesting and cohesive attempts to make the Qur'anic imperatives relevant to the modern world.[10]

While Fazlur Rahman's hermeneutical theory deals with the understanding and interpretation of the content of the Qur'an, Soroush's theory of "The Expansion of Prophetic Experience" searches deeper by examining "how" and "why" certain things would have inevitably found their way into the content of the revelation in the first place. It seems that, while other reformers move from Qur'an's own content to its outside context in order to reconstruct and analyse the history of revelation and the value system behind some of its teachings (inevitably limiting thereby the scope of their investigation), Soroush moves in the opposite direction. He proceeds from the world of externals to the internals of the religion and scripture, since for him, the externals and their impact are much greater both quantitatively and qualitatively. The subjective role in revelation that Soroush's theory ascribes to the Prophet and his societal milieu in general lead him to theorize a "created" nature of the Qur'an far beyond even Mu'tazilite doctrine. It is a position that he confirmed to this author when he said that "yes, the Divine Speech (*Kalam-e Bari*) was created in its very inception and conception in the Prophet's mind." Soroush could not have emphasised the historicity of the revelation more than that. Yet, of course being guided by his religious impulse and his devotion to and love of Prophet Muhammad, he confirms and reiterates that the Prophet's personality

---

[10] It is merited to note that Amina Wadud, the renowned female Muslim scholar and activist, has developed a feminist interpretation of the Qur'an based on Fazlur Rahman's interpretative methodology. See her book, *Qur'an and Women: Rereading the Sacred Text from a Woman's Perspective* (Oxford University Press, 1997).

was an extraordinary one. His was a blessed and divinely inspired and authorized personality (*muʾayyad*). Thus, his revelatory "experience" and his message became divinely authentic, authoritatively binding for others and eternal.

The two other contemporary Muslim scholars of the Qurʾan mentioned above, i.e., Muhammad Arkoun and Nasr Hamed Abu Zayd, pursue their investigation of the human aspect of the Qurʾan primarily through linguistic analysis.

Muhammad Arkoun is, for instance, interested in the historicity of the Qurʾan in terms of its transformation from an initially oral form (what he calls Qurʾanic *discourse*), into a text which finally achieved the status of a "Closed Official Corpus," the Holy Book. Regardless of the theological status of the first enunciation of the message, its passage into a text and its fixation in writing left believers with no choice but to interpret the text, Arkoun contends. This emphasis on the distinction between speech and text is central to his conviction that "the understanding of revelation as a linguistic and cultural phenomenon" through "the pursuit of a modern theory of religious discourse" is necessary prior to the construction of "any theology liberated from traditional dogmas."[11] Beyond these linguistic and literary analyses, Arkoun as a social scientist advocates application of multidisciplinary methodologies derived from the historical sciences, sociology, psychology, anthropology and semiotics in order to understand the theological and historical genesis of "orthodox" dogmas regarding the Qurʾan and all other literature derived from it—what he calls "societies of the Book." The aim is to reveal their ideological and psychological functions, their semantic and anthropological limits and their inadequacies. This process of deconstruction, demystification and demythologization of the phenomenon of the Book will, according to Arkoun, reveal the cultural conditions that enfolded the original message of the revelation, "the novel meaning," and froze it in denotations belonging to the system of signs, symbols, metaphors and myths of that time. Furthermore, it will reveal the triple solidarity that emerged linking the written word (the Book), the state (political power) and the religious orthodoxy (the jurists-theologians), each of which in turn contributed to perpetuating of the others' sacralized, mystified, and transcendentalized positions.

---

[11] Mohammed Arkoun, *Rethinking Islam*. trans. and ed., Robert D. Lee (San Francisco: Westview Press, 1994), pp. 30–39.

It is through the deconstruction of all these complex webs, Arkoun hopes, that the true "meaning" or message will emerge and be differentiated from text and its interpretations.

Hamed Abu Zayd's interest in the historical status of the Qur'an is connected primarily to his educational training in the fields of literary criticism, modern linguistic theories and conceptual analysis. Without entering into a debate about the nature and mechanism of revelation or the original metaphysical status of the Qur'an as the divine speech (*kalam-e bari*), which he apparently leaves to whatever information the Text itself provides, he addresses issues related to the textuality of the Qur'an after its revelation. In his view, any text, religious or otherwise, is a historical and linguistic phenomenon. He argues that "when God revealed the Qur'an to the Messenger, He chose the specific linguistic system of the first recipient, i.e., the Prophet."[12] Thus, linguistic and cultural influences began at this very first stage once the revelation, from the moment of its entrance into history, became humanized and the "divine text" (*nass ilahi*) was made a "human text" (*nass insani*). Hence, by its connection to the Prophet's human intellect, the divine text changed from revelation to interpretation.[13] Abu Zayd's main concern, however, is with the prevailing concept of the Qur'an as a fixed religious text. He addresses the problem that, in his opinion, resulted from the historical transformation of the notion of Qur'an as "discourse" into Qur'an as "text".

Like Arkoun with his linguistic and discourse analysis of the Qur'an, Abu Zayd has also developed a theoretical communication model to explain the existence of a communicative relationship between the Qur'an as a message system and its readers/addresses. This relationship, he states, was very much alive at the time of the Prophet and the first addressees of the message and continued for some time before Qur'an was canonized as a written text. This living communicative relationship allowed the first generation of Muslims to interpret the message and understand its meaning according to their own intellectual horizons and cultural milieu. Abu Zayd aims to revive this pre-text living relationship with the Qur'an, which he thinks lost its flexibility when the

---

[12] Abu Zayd, *Mafhum al-nass: dirasa fi 'ulum al-Qur'an* (Cairo: al-hay'ah al-misriya al-'amah al-kitab, 1990), p. 27.

[13] Abu Zayd: *Naqd al-Khitab al-dini*, 3rd ed. (Cairo: Madbuli), p. 193.

proponents of the prevailing theology began to promote the idea that the Qur'an, as a fixed text, conveyed only one meaning.

Abu Zayd criticizes this rigid attitude for having, in reality, suppressed the "interpretational diversity" that exists within the Islamic tradition and for having limited contemporary interpreters to merely narrating the interpretations of previous generations. It is imperative, in his hermeneutical model, to make a distinction between the concept of Qur'an as the *mushaf*, which is a silent text, and the phenomenon of the Qur'an as a living "discourse" which can move forward in time, producing numerous meanings. It is only then, he states, that Muslims can "re-connect the question of the meaning of the Qur'an to the question of the meaning of life."[14]

While Abu Zayd and Arkoun concentrate their efforts on analysing the historical genesis of the Qur'anic text from linguistic and cultural perspectives and its implications for developing new hermeneutics, Soroush focuses on the historical genesis of the revelation itself at a stage prior even to its early enunciation by the Prophet, a stage that may correspond to the "novel meaning" in Arkoun's language or the "idea" suggested by Fazlur Rahman. Soroush has undertaken this remarkably daring endeavour without any apparent fear of the political or psychological consequences. Perhaps he lost his fear of political repercussions earlier on in the late-1980s when he challenged, through his theory of "Contraction and Expansion of Religious Knowledge," the religious and political establishment of the Islamic regime of Iran. At that time he rejected the exclusivist claims of the ulama to interpretation of religious truth and all the prerogatives that this entailed. Despite the resulting pressure and even severe "punishments," he extended his critical analysis from the realm of interpretation of religion and its scriptures to the very sense and essence of religion and revelation. Intellectually uncompromising as a reformer, he wants to get to the bottom of what he thinks has impeded the progress of much needed intellectual reform in Islam.

Soroush has also handled with apparent ease the psychological challenge of questioning the nature of what Muslim consciousness has long come to believe to be the "Word of God." Given the fact that he is a very devout and observant Muslim, perhaps he derives his courage to do so

---

[14] Abu Zayd, *Rethinking the Qur'an: Towards a Humanistic Hermeneutics* (Utrecht: Humanistics University Press, 2004), p. 11.

from his infinite love and inviolable respect for the Prophet Muhammad. This is something that might be better understood in the light of
his own "experiential" religiosity, a description of which comes later in
Chapter Eight. His boldness in critical analysis can also be explained
by the fact that his erudition in the classical Islamic religious sciences
allows him to draw easily upon and benefit from the great philosophers,
theologians and mystics. It is with such figures as al-Ghazali, Shah Wali
Allah of Delhi, Sadr al-din Shirazi (Mulla Sadra), Ibn Arabi and Rumi
that Soroush identifies both intellectually and spiritually. These iconic
predecessors were courageous enough to speculate on such sensitive
subjects and articulate various daring, unorthodox views. In his own
unique style, Soroush—throughout this book—covers simultaneously
the two terrains of critical rational analysis and the traditional Muslim intellectual heritage without confusing the borders of the two.
Something about the nature of the subject under discussion warrants
this approach and makes it more of a strength than a methodological
weakness.[15] Without compromising the external/rational position that
he takes vis-à-vis religion and without damaging the rational conclusions that he intends to draw from his discussions, he borrows from
these early thinkers whenever necessary. This association is more than
a cautious, tactical move to reduce the risk of charges of heresy and
blasphemy-accusations from which Soroush has never been completely
immune anyway.[16]

---

[15] Soroush respects methodological integrity and he himself is critical to those who
confuse rational and non-rational discussions ('aqli and naqli). Look for instance at
his magnum opus, "The Contraction and Expansion of Religious Knowledge", where
he is entirely into a rational debate, given the nature of the subject, and thus avoids
such intermix.

[16] Surprisingly, in spite of the fact that Soroush first published his theory of "The
Expansion of Prophetic Experience" about a decade ago in Iran, no actual controversy
(barring some mild criticism) came to surround it until quite recently. It was not until
the fall of 2007 that a Persian translation of Soroush's interview with Michel Hoebink
(from Radio Netherlands), after being posted on a Persian-language website, drew the
attention of opponents. Politically motivated polemics, charges of religious innovation
and blasphemy, verbal assaults and death threats against Soroush highlighted on-line
discussions on certain websites. These were not, however, the only responses provided.
Many authors and scholars from various backgrounds, both academics and seminarians
and friends and opponents, published articles expressing surprise, admonishment, advice
and criticism, but all defending the orthodox notions of revelation and the scripture.
Among the more serious respondents were a couple of important ayatollahs, including
the grand ayatollahs Sobhani and Montazeri. Initially, Soroush responded to critics
by writing a short exposé clarifying some of the points of misunderstanding in his
interview. Later on, he welcomed the opportunity of engaging the grand ayatollahs in

Soroush values the intellectual legacy of the past, despite being critical of it. More importantly, he believes that the intellectual achievements of his predecessors—in terms of understanding of religion—have altogether enriched and expanded the collective religious experience of believers in subsequent generations, leading to the historical expansion of religion.

Indeed far from dismissing all traditional intellectual achievements as mere social and historical constructs irrelevant to modern times, Soroush insists that there are valuable teachings in that repository that can shed light on the question of the relationship between the natural and the supernatural. In particular, he relies more on mystical explanations of revelatory experience that somehow equate the human inner self with revelation. Soroush considers mystics to be the closest to prophets since their religious experience is of the same spiritual and revelatory nature, yet points out that, historically, they were more outspoken and could freely describe their experiences due to the fact of their being free from the restrictions of a mission, whereas prophets had to remain silent on this issue. Therefore, the mystical articulations and formulations of their high calibre spiritual experiences still serve as instructive, first-hand testimonies that can better disclose to us the essentially "formless" prophetic experience (*wahy*). Soroush believes that, although the modern critical methodologies of the social sciences and humanities are absolutely useful and necessary tools for solving complicated religious issues, some old debates and intellectual speculations are equally beneficial and necessary to create a comprehensive and workable solution to those complex matters. After all, he says, the world of knowledge and galaxies of thought are full of interrelated complexities with various ramifications. Language, history, spirituality, law, reason, society, politics, etc., are all active participants in these domains and cannot and should not be ignored.

Like Soroush, Muhammad Mujtahed Shabestari, the Iranian reformist cleric, began with hermeneutical discussions about understanding and interpreting religious texts in the 1990s. He likewise came to a similar

---

a theological and hermeneutical dialogue. The result, just as this book goes into print, has been a few public communiqués between Soroush and these ayatollahs that contain not only interesting theological exchanges and further elaborations of Soroush's theory, but also offer a glimpse of the current religious, social and political situation in Iran. The appendices to this volume present these communiqués, which should be read along with the first chapter.

conclusion that the human understanding of religion is context-bound and that as a result there exists no one final understanding of the Qur'an and the Tradition but, rather, a plurality. However, unlike Soroush, Shabestari did not develop a theory extending the claim of the historicity and humanness of understanding the scriptures to the revealed text itself. Although indications could be found in his earlier writings that he would eventually move in this direction, he had not specifically dealt with the issue until very recently in summer 2007.[17] He had sometimes talked about the "anthropological nature of the revealed words (*kalam-e wahy*)," making it synonymous with *kalam-e insani-e payambar* (the Prophet's human words).[18] In his latest interview/essay to emerge since his most recent psychological and intellectual shift, culminating in his self-defrocking of the clerical attire, he presents his more recent views regarding revelation and the Qur'an. While re-emphasizing his argument that the language of the Qur'an is the Prophet's human language, he expounds on what then makes it "divine" and special.

For Shabestari, the Qur'an as a text is *kalam-e insani-e payambar* (the Prophet's human speech) that he could utter only when empowered by God. He argues that the Qur'an is neither a text authored by Muhammad nor is it a word for word revelation—as Muslim orthodoxy has come to believe. Rather, it is the end-product of revelation, namely, the Prophet's expression of his revelatory experience. That is, he was empowered and enabled to speak the words of the Qur'an as a result of what he experienced, though articulated in his human Arabic words. But, what *is* the revelatory experience according to Shabestari? He believes that what Muhammad received during the revelation was nothing but a "*Blick*", as he uses this German term.[19] Thus, the *Blick* [an attitude/outlook] is the content of the revelation, while prophethood is the experience of the *Blick,* and the prophetic mission is to articulate this experience in human language. Explaining what he means by the *Blick*, he insists that the content of the revelatory experience was neither a body of knowledge given to the Prophet nor a secret disclosed to him and certainly not a series of falsifiable propositions that he was asked

---

[17] See the latest issue of the journal *Madreseh* published in Tehran July 2007. *Madreseh* (Vol. 2, No. 6, 2007).

[18] See, for example, his book: *Ta'amulati dar Qara'at-e Insani az Din* [Reflections on Human Interpretation of Religion], (Tehran: Tarh-e Nou, 2004), pp. 83–86; 160–167.

[19] M. M. Shabestari, "*Hermenutiks va Tafsir-e Dini as Jahan*" [Hermeneutics and Religious Interpretation of the World] Interview with *Madreseh* (Vol. 2, No. 6, 2007), p. 87.

to convey to the people. Rather, the *Blick* is an attitude, an outlook on existence—a monotheistic interpretation of existence given to the Prophet by God. Hence, revelation, and by extension its by-product, the Qur'an, are not of an epistemological nature but are, rather, "interpretive."[20] The Prophet was given an interpretation of existence that may be described as a monotheistic outlook. This *Blick*, which is sacred to the Prophet, is what he offered to his audience, asking them to listen and understand existence through its lenses and to behave accordingly. Therefore, the religious text itself, the Qur'an, is an interpretation of the greater text (in its generic sense) of existence, presented to us by the Prophet and expressed in human words. If anything at all is sacred about it, it is only that he received this *Blick* initially from God and that God chose him, commanded him, and divinely empowered him to articulate his experience in words. According to Shabestari, therefore, while the words of the Qur'an are the Prophet's, its source, so to speak, is divine. Shabesteri draws extensively on references from the Qur'an to show that the traditional notion of considering the Qur'anic "*ayat*" (verses) as having been "sent down from heaven" to the Prophet is not acceptable. Instead, he accepts a more theosophical/mystical meaning of the term *ayat*, i.e., God's signs/phenomena. Hence, the content and function of this *Blick* was "sent down" to awaken the Prophet to God's signs. The core message of the *Blick* is that all natural events, as well as all developments in human history and fate, are "phenomena" indicating One Foundational Reality—God—who cannot be understood or known directly but are continuously active in the universe.[21] Consequently, the purpose of the prophetic mission, and accordingly, the message that his Book conveys, is to draw his audience's attention to the existence of One Active Creator God and His involvement in the cosmos and history; hence, to invite human submission to Him. In this vein, it is interesting to note that Shabestari emphatically repeats that the Qur'anic statements are not assertive propositions capable of being verified or falsified. They are simply intended to inform people about what the Prophet saw through the lenses of that *Blick*.

Whatever the theological implications to religious reform this approach may have shown, perhaps the most interesting is Shabestari's

---

[20] Ibid., p. 88.
[21] M. M. Shabestari, "*Qara'at-e Nabavi az Jahan*" [The Prophet's Reading of the Universe]. *Madreseh* (Vol. 2, No. 6, 2007), pp. 92–96.

claim that the Qur'anic laws (*ahkam*) were merely solutions proposed by the Prophet to the religious, social, and moral problems of his day. In other words, as he observed—thanks to his revelatory *Blick* experience—that the moral and social life of his people were contradictory to the active and ongoing will of the One God, he began to invite them to change their lifestyle so as to bring them into harmony with the monotheistic pulse of existence. Hence, he issued laws that would reform or remove these existential incongruities. Shabestari clearly asserts that *ahkam* in and of themselves did not have any direct significance to the Prophet.[22] Thus, all Qur'anic rulings regarding worship and social interactions were pertinent primarily to the religious and social realities of Arabian society in the Prophet's time. As such, "these rulings [as stated in the Qur'an] are by no means applicable to all times and all societies."[23] At the same time, the monotheistic *Blick* and the awareness of the ever present will of God in existence, which was a part of the prophetic experience, should be retained as a frame of reference.

Although Shabestari's view of the applicability of religious laws might be provocative to traditional conservatives, his *Blick* theory of revelation has much validity from the perspective of arguments from within the tradition and might be found very convincing. It seems that he is trying to find a balance between what mainline Muslim opinion is willing to accept and what is necessary to opening a legitimate path towards annulling the application of Qur'anic injunctions. However, theoretical contradictions and weaknesses of logic[24] in his *Blick* theory prevent it from becoming a much needed solid rational theological foundation for legal reform. His theory is, at best, a mystical explanation of revelation. Its mystical qualities are seen not only in the understanding that the prophet Muhammad's was a very subjective experience, but also in that the content of the 'revelation' amounts essentially to a lens through which acts of monotheism that are everywhere at work became evident to him. Muslim mystics have arrived at similar theories, even

---

[22] Ibid., p. 90.

[23] Ibid., p. 97. Shabestari has repeatedly stated this opinion about laws. See, for instance, his previous writings: *Hermenutiks, Ketab va Sunat* [Hermenutics, Book and Tradition], *Naqdi bar Qara'at-e Rasmi az Din* [A Critique of the Official Interpretation of Religion], *T'amulati dar Qara'at-e Insani az Din* [Reflections on a Human Interpretation of Religion].

[24] For a critique of Shabestari in these respects see three articles in the same volume of *Madreseh* by Arash Naraqi (pp. 63–66), Reza Alijani (pp. 67–73) and Soroush Dabbaqh (pp. 76–79).

on a more comprehensive scale, explaining existence through God's *tawhid-e dhati, tawhid-e sefati and tawhid- af'ali.*

Moreover, although in saying that in the process of revelation the Prophet was not given the Book but a *Blick*, Shabestari might sound unorthodox; yet, his theory remains solidly orthodox as far as the place and role of the Prophet as a passive recipient is concerned. The *Blick* theory limits the role of human agency in the process of revelation only to the level of articulation of the experience. It does not allow for any human role in the experience itself. Nor does it specify to what extent, if at all, Muhammad's personal, intellectual, and societal conditions and capacities could have affected his experience and interpretation of what—according to Shabestari—constitutes the Qur'an. "[If] the content of the text [Qur'an] is an interpretive content",[25] is it not then subject to contingencies of the interpreter, that is, to the Prophet? This runs significantly contrary at least to what Shabestari has always insisted on in his previous hermeneutical discussions. Further, the *Blik* theory does not account for any gradualness in the process of revelation. In Shabestari's presentation, this spontaneously given-*Blik* is total and fixed. There is no gradation, increasing or decreasing sequence, or any explanation of Muhammad's capabilities and readiness as a human recipient of this experience. Furthermore, it seems that in order to reconcile the external qualities of the religion with its internal composition, that is to say, resolving the problematic challenges of religion, philosophy, and science, Shabestari takes refuge in a position of antirealism by insisting that the text does not contain assertive propositions capable of being verified or falsified; nor were any such propositions given to the Prophet in the revelation.

What Soroush is trying to achieve in his discussion of prophetic experience is far more than adding further speculation about the technicalities of the nature of revelation. As both an insider and a believer, he adopts an approach from without the religion to examine the impact of the "outside" on the very "inside" of the faith, i.e., the "formless" prophetic experience. The "outside," that which imposes form(s) on the formless, includes: the Prophet's personal psychological and intellectual capacities; his personal private and professional life experiences; his audience; his friends and foes and their capabilities and needs alike; and the broader societal milieu of his times with all its opportunities

---

[25] *Madreseh*, p. 91.

and limitations. Chapter One, The Expansion of Prophetic Experience, reveals not only the dialogical nature of the encounter between heaven and earth and the subjective role of the Prophet in this reciprocal process, but also seeks to prove that religion, by nature, is not a fixed and predetermined phenomenon. History and the humanity of the Prophet, with all its weaknesses and strengths, gave shape to the unformed core essence of the religion, i.e., religious experience. Therefore, there are many elements in the religion, and in its scripture in particular, that are not essentially "religious." This very unorthodox view, with its strong emphasis on fluidity and flexibility in religion, runs also very contrary to the ahistorical view of Islam held by contemporary Islamists/fundamentalists. In its ideological understanding and presentation of Islam, the latter trend abhors history and context. It not only rejects the fact that the totality of Islam as a religio-civilizational tradition is something that has unfolded in history, it presents a perfect, frozen and eternalized image of the Prophet, his message and his time as if everything happened in an utopia outside history. If there is any motive behind this trend of recalling the Prophet and his life, it is to universalize that frozen image of the Medinan period, which is perceived to have been the perfect Islamic society and state besides. References to scripture are cited by them without reference to context or the cultural and historical contingencies related to them. In this monolithic eternalized picture there is no room for interpretation, let alone diversity. It is against this current tradition and the rigid shari'ah-centered tradition of the *fuqaha* that Soroush argues:

> In fact, essentially and fundamentally, to follow the Prophet is to follow his spiritual experiences and not just to obey his commands by doing what he enjoined and abstaining from what he proscribed. (Chapter One)

When he highlights "spiritual experience" as the core of religion and emphasises the historicity of the Prophet and his revelation, he means nothing less than that Islam *is* capable of growth and *can* be improved. He maintains that: "a religion that has a gradual genesis will also undergo gradual movement and development in its subsequent existence" (Chapter One). This "gradual genesis" corresponds to Soroush's usage of the word "expansion" in describing the Prophet's revelatory experience. As for development in its "subsequent existence," however, a further clarification is in order. Besides the historical development of the Islamic disciplines of law, theology, mysticism, exegesis, etc., all of which testify to the gradual growth and enrichment of Islamic tradition, Soroush ventures a more theologically subtle intention. Another connotation of "expansion" in his discourse is that the possibility for undergoing such revelatory experience may be extended to other individuals to varying degrees depending on their abilities. But does this mean that he is challenging the very Islamic doctrine of the finality of Muhammad's prophethood? The answer is both yes and no, depending on what is meant by "finality" and "prophethood."

Finality: Religious Experience or Prophetic Mission?

In Chapters Two and Three, Soroush elaborates that this expandability and extendibility of the prophetic experience after the Prophet does not negate the doctrine of finality in one sense. Granted, its consideration entails flexibility in understanding and interpreting the religion and the acknowledgment of diversity in forms of religiosity. He insists that occurences of esoteric/revelatory experiences did not cease after the demise of the Prophet Muhammad, the Seal of prophethood according to the Qur'an, and may be repeated at any time, as has been manifested in the saintly religious experiences of great mystics or other learned individuals of the past. The more learned and spiritually apt the person, the richer and deeper will be his/her experience and closer to that of the Prophet. Using a mystical language that recalls the thought of Ibn Arabi, Soroush confirms that some of these individuals can even be ranked higher than prophets on the basis of the intensity and richness of their spiritual raptures and their encounters with the divine. Nevertheless, he does perceive fundamental difference between these individuals and the Prophet: the former do not have a "mission" and their experiences will not generate binding results, certainly not legally binding, for others. All the same, their experiences will give them a special perspective in their understanding and interpretation of religion, the articulation of which will enhance, empower, enrich and expand the religious tradition in its ongoing course. Hence, for example, the post-Ghazali, post-Ibn Arabi, and post-Rumi Islam is certainly richer and of a different flavour in that it now opens out onto previously inconceivable horizons.

It is indeed not the first time that a contemporary Muslim reformer has felt it necessary to explain the meaning of the finality of prophethood. For instance, Muhammad Iqbal (d. 1938) argues for the closure of revelation due to the fact that humankind, having supposedly reached a more mature intellectual stage, no longer requires it. Others, like Mortaza Motahhari (d. 1979), have related it to the perfection and completeness of the last Message, as they see it. Soroush discusses the issue from a different angle. Believing that what is essentially "religious" in prophecy is the "experience", he sees no finality to it. Indeed, if there is any finality, he explains, this rests in the distinctive nature of a prophet's religious experience that generates mission and grants legislative authority to him, a unique kind of authority assumed by a prophet in terms of his "charismatic personality" as prophet *per se* (in the Weberian sense of the word). In other words, Soroush separates the mission and non-mission aspects of a revelatory experience. Therefore, from a Muslim's point of view, no one else will claim legislative authority over others merely on the basis of his divinely "authorized and commissioned" personality. Nevertheless, Soroush is aware and acknowledges that any discussion on the finality of prophethood is knowledge of a second order and a discussion from within the religion.

Expectations of Religion

Chapter Four sketches a theory for discerning "the essentials" and "the accidentals" in religion. It provides a theoretical framework that not only sheds more light on the discussion of the expansion of prophetic experience and the nature of religion (preparing the ground for a new theology), but likewise opens many new paths to the interpretation of the Qur'an thereby laying the foundations for a radically new paradigm of *fiqh* and *ijtihad*. Here, again, Soroush's theory of the essentials and accidentals of the religion and the Text stands distinct from some other modernist conceptions by being neither apologetic nor polemic. The novelty of this theory, as reflected in its rather provocative title, lies in its systematically coherent and rationally convincing arguments and in its potential to promote legal change without being pinned down to narrow historical, cultural or grammatical justifications for certain existing Qur'anic injunctions. Nor does it reject them outright as irrelevant, which would be equivalent to antirealism or, from the perspective of believers, to questioning the divine wisdom.

Soroush's theory about the essence of religion consists of these main principles: 1) the Qur'an includes essentials and accidentals; 2) the essentials are the same as "the Prophet's goals" (*maqased-e share'*) while "being a Muslim entails believing in and acting upon the essentials…"; and 3) the essentials, like a precious kernel, are covered in and protected by the thick shell of the accidentals. In order to uncover the essence, the accidentals should be identified and peeled away. The latter is obviously what Soroush attempts here. Inspired by both the mystical classification of *lubb* (the kernel) and *qeshr* (the husk) and I. Lakatos' notion of the protective belt in the philosophy of science, Soroush deals with some major "accidentals" in this chapter. All are products of the "historical, human, evolutionary, interlocutory and dynamic" nature of religion, whose discernment necessitates a "deconstruction of religion's historical body," he says. The chief distinctive characteristic of the accidentals is that they "have local and temporal- not universal and meta-histori-cal- authenticity." Therefore, they "could have been other than they are, unlike the essentials." Among the major accidentals, is one that may sound very shocking to many, namely, "the Arabic language of the Qur'an," and another that generated much criticism from jurists in particular, i.e., "the precepts of fiqh and shari'ah." Also directly related to the previous discussion on the expansion of the prophetic experi-ence is another category of accidentals, viz., the many questions, stories and events mentioned in the Qur'an that have no part in the essentials of Islam. As these have no impact on Islam's message, their absence would be no loss to the religion nor would they lead to weakness in the Scripture. In other words, Soroush maintains: "the Qur'an could have been shorter or longer than it is and still have been the Qur'an, because it is the Qur'an by virtue of its essentials, not its accidentals." Acknowledging that the essences never occur without accidentals, Soroush insists that "confusing the rules that govern them leads to a host of fallacies; therefore, their theoretical distinctions from acciden-tals is an absolute rational imperative." This is imperative not only for contemporary scholars in religious studies, but even more so for the jurists who are involved in *ijtihad*. *Ijtihad*, for Soroush, is not limited to legal *ijtihad* or even to the sort of juridical manoeuvre (within the confines of already set principles) that will bring about only limited, unsubstantial, piecemeal changes. *Ijtihad* for him is "synonymous with the cultural translation" of all accidentals. In other words, *ijtihad* should "transcend" the existing accidentals in the Qur'an and the *sun-nah* by translating them into the accidentals of different cultures and time and "conveying the religion's goals not in form, but in spirit and meaning." This, of course, would be a continuous process of "discover-ing and expounding" accidentals that would not only make *ijtihad* a living process, but would "herald a new order and a new paradigm in the discipline of fiqh."

The contextuality of Qur'anic laws and the pressing need for *ijtihad* have also drawn the attention of other reformist Muslim scholars, although their approaches in resolving the issue are not necessarily hermeneutical or theological. Among those who should be mentioned are Mahmoud Muhammad Taha from Sudan (d.1985), Khaled Abo El Fadl (b. 1963, Kuwait), and Mohsen Kadivar (b. 1959, Iran).

Mahmoud Taha's concern for human rights issues led him to develop a whole new method of interpretation in his book, *The Second Message of Islam*. While restructuring the classical Islamic doctrines regarding the abrogating and abrogated verses in the Qur'an, Mahmoud Taha established an interpretive model of the Qur'an as legal source so as to generate a fresh ethical foundation for a new kind of jurisprudence. According to his interpretive methodology, the Meccan chapters and verses of scripture that include a more universal and generalized moral message should be given precedence—as the foundation of the new jurisprudence—over the Medinan chapters that pertain to specific conditions and contexts of the Prophet's time.[26]

Working from within the Islamic legal tradition, Khaled Abo El Fadl and Mohsen Kadivar—both trained in the classical legal tradition—believe in the relevance and desirability of the Islamic juristic tradition in the present time. Arguing that the divinely ordained laws have been misinterpreted by Muslim jurists, they have set out to overcome what they see as the prevalent methodological shortcomings in contemporary Muslim legal discourse. While cognizant of the need for a new theology and modern hermeneutics, they have not themselves dealt with these subjects. Nor have they opined on the nature of revelation and the prophetic experience. Furthermore, although certain that presuppositions and context are of consequence to interpretation of the Text and convinced that historical circumstances related to certain Qur'anic verses should be taken into consideration, they do not debate the theological implications of the circumstantialities of the revealed verses. They might even disagree with what others like Soroush or Shabestari and Arkoun are saying in this regard. At the same time, they welcome new insights into the analysis of scripture and other doctrinal sources. When one considers the level of engagement and range of reciprocal influence that characterize these contemporary Muslim thinkers and scholars, one can only conclude that theirs is indeed a wholly

---

[26] Theoretical applications of Taha's interperative model to a wide range of human rights issues are best achieved by his accomplished disciple, M. Abdullahi An-Na'im. See, for instance, his book: *Toward An Islamic Reformation* (Syracuse: Syracuse University Press, 1990).

new intellectual trend in the making. Hermeneutical and theological ideas put forward, for instance, by Soroush, Shabestari, Arkoun, et al., provide—welcome or unwelcome—useful theoretical and conceptual frameworks for those involved in constructing a highly technical legal discourse. This is precisely where different, yet complementary components of Neo-Rationalist Islam come together. If Soroush, for example, urges a rational ethics, this should not remain confined to theoretical discourse; it should also be applied in the legal realm, so that changes can be effected to contemporary Islamic practices. Due to their expertise, this is a task that only jurists and scholars of Islamic law can undertake, and there are indeed some who are doing so.[27]

Both Abo El Fadl and Kadivar have been active in investigating and restructuring several authoritative sources of the Islamic legal past in order to deal with a wide range of issues and problems in the modern world. Abo El Fadl in particular has dealt extensively in his writings with the problem of the "abuse of authority in Islamic law." Criticizing puritanical interpretations of Islam more specifically, he has addressed a wide range of critical issues from women's rights to the problem of terrorism and contemporary jihad.[28] Mohsen Kadivar, on the other hand, while engaged in some of the same topics related to human rights, has been trying primarily to expose the abuse or misuse of authority in Islamic law with regard to politics. His re-readings of some doctrinal sources produced by certain authoritative Shi'i jurists of the past has led him to take a position against the religio-political theory of *wilayat-e faqih* (Guardianship of the Jurists) that remains authoritative in Iran.[29]

---

[27] It seems that Iranian religious intellectuals are in a unique position in the sense that proponents of different elements of a Neo-Rationalist reformed Islam (modern hermeneutics, rational theology and new jurisprudence) are engaging in fruitful dialogue, as can be seen in the case of its three most prominent representatives: Soroush, Shabestari and Kadivar. Although each respects the others' differences, they all nourish and stimulate each other intellectually.

[28] See his books: *Conference of the Books* (University Press of America, 2001); *Rebellion and Violence in Islamic Law* (Cambridge Univ. Press, 2001); *Place of Tolerance in Islam* (Beacon Press, 2002); *Speaking in God's Name: Islamic Law, Authority, and Women* (One World, 2001); *The Great Theft: Wrestling Islam From the Extremists* (Harper, 2005).

[29] See his books: *Nazariyehay-e Doulat dar Fiqh-e Shi'ah* [Theories of Government in the Shi'I Fiqh] (Tehran; Nashr-e Ney, 1376); *Hokumat-e Vela'i* [Political Guardianship of the Jurists] (Tehran: Nashr-e Ney, 1377); *Daghdaghehay-e Hokumat-e Dini* [Concerns of a Religious Government] (Tehran: Nashr-e Ney, 1379).

Chapter Five deals with another imperative for Soroush, namely, recognition of the intertwined principles of what religion offers and what its believers should expect from it. In the last century or so the opinion that "Islam is the solution" has become prevalent among Muslims. This has become even more popular due to the contemporary ideologized presentation of Islam. According to this view, all "necessary and sufficient" instructions and guidance for every aspect of life and for all times and conditions are provided by Islam. It particularly emphasizes the perfection and comprehensiveness of Islamic law, or the shari'ah, and does not recognize the need for any other source for achieving prosperity and salvation in this world or the next. This Soroush calls "the maximalist understanding of religion" and/or "the maximalist expectation of religion." In Chapter Five, he identifies this perception of religion as a "maximal source and reservoir," despite its minimal precepts, as "the root cause of serious theoretical and practical problems" in Muslim societies. Here, he analyses almost every possible aspect of the religion—ethics, theology, jurisprudence, etc.—to prove that the guidance offered by the religion is the "necessary minimum" and not the "maximum possible." Nor is it all-inclusive with regard to human needs. He also clarifies some of the confusion and misunderstanding surrounding the Qur'anic notion of the perfection and completeness of the religion. He concludes that if religion is perfect, "its perfection is minimalist and in itself (*maqam-e thubut*), not maximalist and for us (*maqam-e ithbat*)." In other words, "religion is complete in relation to the purpose it was designed for, which is to offer necessary minimal guidance. But it cannot be complete in relation to our every possible and imaginable expectation." Emphasising that placing "excessive burden on religion gradually robs religion of its standing and legitimacy," Soroush explains that it is only through a minimalist approach to religion that one can prevent it from being used as "an instrument of injustice and tyranny, a meal ticket, or a source of superstition and conflict." On the contrary, "in order to be eternal and final," he maintains, "a religion must per force present a central thread and core that is appropriate to every human being in every age and era, and forego certain secondary principles, peripheral issues and unique stances for unique occasions"—what he calls "accidentals" elsewhere.

Religious Pluralism

Chapters Six and Seven present some of Soroush's ideas regarding religious pluralism. As for pluralism in the realm of interpretation of religious texts/scriptures, he had already established his position through his theory of "Contraction and Expansion of Religious Knowledge." There he argued for an inevitable plurality in understanding and interpreting religion and religious texts. The main upshot of his argument—so disturbing to many in the religious establishment—was that there is no "final and official" interpretation and thus no "official" class of interpreters. In Chapter Six he tries to explain the existing plurality of religions; here he is mainly concerned with plurality in interpretation of the "religious experience." He contends that there are two ways to explain religious pluralism: negative pluralism and positive pluralism, as he dubs them. Negative pluralism is based on an *a priori* notion of a unity among religions and is mostly an approach from within religions. Positive pluralism holds an *a posteriori* view of reality and its diversity. Negative pluralism—which in its best form amounts to inclusivism—acknowledges the existence of different paths but still allows one religion to deem itself the perfect, complete, and absolute holder of truth and sole provider of felicity and salvation, and other religions as lacking some of these qualities, being incomplete and less perfect. Critical of those who "unjustifiably" try to "crush pluralities and resolve them into a unity," Soroush insists that "plurality is the norm in this world." In this light and in the wake of his *a posteriori* outlook of positive pluralism, Soroush describes religious pluralism as based on a multiplicity of interpretations/formulations of different religious experiences by prophets/founders that indeed harks back to their different personalities and conditions. Moreover, this multiplicity is also partly due to the multifaceted nature of the experienced Reality itself. His point of departure from others is that, in true nominalist fashion, he subscribes to the idea that prophets'/founders' religious experiences are of a different "species" with only family resemblances. They cannot assume superiority or inferiority in rank or degree, nor should their diversity be subsumed under one alleged whimsical unity. This is a natural diversity reflecting the singularity of each prophet/founder and consequently his experience of the transcendence. Therefore, each religion is in itself unique (*sui generis*) and for its followers the truth, complete, perfect and guide to salvation. This philosophical/theological nominalism is, indeed, the root of Soroush's irreducible pluralism. Being a radical pluralist, he contends that the discussion of religious pluralism is first and foremost an epistemological and extra-religious discussion that can find affinity and support only with and from certain types of religiosity. While a "pragmatic/instrumental" religiosity does not give rise to pluralism, "discursive" and "experiential" religiosities that are based on "reason" and "experience" are by nature pluralistic.[30]

Part Two
Reason, Love and Religiosity

The second part of this book, unlike the first, tends on the whole to avoid presuppositions for the theoretical study of religion and its interpretation. Chapters Eight to Twelve contain mostly a discussion of the sociology of religion, elaborating on the meaning and role of religion and "being religious" in the modern world. Although the chapters in this part have more in common with each other, they are not without some relevance to Part One. Some of them (Chapters Nine, Ten and Eleven) exemplify the practical relevance of some of the theoretical discussion presented earlier in the book. Chapter Eight ("Types of Religiosity") in fact constitutes a borderline discussion, for it provides a typology of religiosity that is a very useful frame of reference for developing both theories about religion, as well as for social and historical studies of religion. "Types of Religiosity" is indeed one of the most interesting of Soroush's innovations and extremely useful for disentangling some of the most complex and complicated subjects pertaining to religion, like pluralism and secularism. In Chapters Six and Seven, he partly demonstrates the application of this typology to the issue of pluralism to show what types of religiosity do or do not allow pluralism. In some of his other theoretical discussions elsewhere he has applied it to the paradoxical issues of secularism and what has been called the decline of religion in modern society. He argues that, when talking about secularism, we should not speak of the decline of "religion" (as an undifferentiated and monolithic notion) but rather of the decline of certain types of religiosity. For Soroush, starting one's analysis with religiosity reveals that, depending on the type of the latter, secularism of some kind can coexist. In this way the difficulties of making sweeping

---

[30] For more on different types of religiosity see Chapter Eight.

judgments about whether we have "secular" or "religious" societies can be prevented in a learned and careful manner. As for social and historical studies of religion, "Types of Religiosity," by categorizing three different religiosities, reveals a kind of pluralism existing within all religious traditions, Islamic or otherwise. In this chapter, Soroush elaborates on the salient features of "pragmatic/instrumental", "discursive/reflective" and "experiential" religiosities and their different implications for some notions fundamental to religion such as God, the prophets, sin, obedience, etc. He also compares and contrasts the relation of each type to passion, reason, ideology, spiritual enlightenment, exclusivism, pluralism, etc. This differentiation between different layers of religiosity is also extremely helpful for believers too, in that it helps them understand where they stand with regard to their faith. For in the modern era in particular, people feel caught between their inclination toward rational investigation of certain elements of their faith, leading to doubt, questions and uncertainty on the one hand, and, on the other, to the existing dogmatic, emulatory presentations of religion that do not satisfy their spiritual expectations.

Chapter Eight also determines the framework of analysis for topics in the subsequent chapters of this part, such as Chapters Nine and Ten, which elaborate on, among other things, the practical meaning of some of the points already made in Chapters One to Three. They reiterate that what constitutes the core essence of religion and religiousness is nothing but the prophetic-like experience of transcendence, and that the continuity and "perpetuation of religion demands the perpetuation of this prophetic experience." Otherwise, "the disintegration and secularization of religion will be certain" (Chapter Nine). After all, in the final analysis, all other ethical, philosophical, social aspects of a religion belong to their respective disciplines outside religion. Those who take the essence of religion to lie in its outward aspects—which are indeed the historical and civilizational achievements of the believers—are non-secular secularists whose efforts neither help to preserve religion nor guarantee the continuing presence of the Prophet. Throughout these chapters Soroush emphasizes that following the Prophet and reviving religion/Islam consist ultimately in following and reviving the Prophet's revelatory experience. He also examines the meaning, possibility and impossibility of such a thing within each of the three aforementioned types of religiosities.

Chapter Eleven ("Faith and Hope") explains the relationship between "religious experience", "faith", "belief" and "practice," all of which fluctuate and vary depending on their operational meaning in different templates of religiosity. The last chapter (Chapter Twelve), "Spiritual Guardianship, Political Guardianship," although having a clear overtone of the Shi'ite doctrine of Imamate and its politicization, sends a fundamental and clear message to all contemporary Muslim shari'ah-oriented revivalists. It warns them against reducing religion and religiosity to fiqh and the legal injunctions of the shari'ah that demand "unquestioning obedience" of the jurists as heirs to the Prophet and his teachings—a fallacy resulting from transferring certain mystical imperatives (such as the master-disciple relationship) into the legal domain for mundane and ideological purposes. All this comes at the expense of neglecting the esoteric and spiritual guardianship of the Prophet—a guardianship over believers' hearts (rather than their bodies) and one that espouses obedience and practice out of the compulsion of love, best manifested in the "experiential" type of religiosity.

Materials in the Appendices were added in the Spring of 2008. Ayatollah Sobhani's letters outline the position of Muslim orthodoxy on issues of revelation and the Qur'an. Soroush's responses are equally important as they put forward an accommodating defence of a Neo-Rationalist Muslim reformer's unorthodox views expressed largely in the language of orthodoxy and the Islamic intellectual tradition. In a broader sense, these four letters are certain to enjoy a lively position in the history of contemporary Islamic thought. They document a critical debate on perhaps the most sensitive issue in the challenge between tradition and modernity.

Forough Jahanbakhsh
Queen's University
Canada

PART ONE

CHAPTER ONE

THE EXPANSION OF PROPHETIC EXPERIENCE

As believers and Muslims deeply immersed in the ocean of prophetic guidance, we rarely reflect on the subject of the prophethood and the prophetic mission. It is incumbent on us to investigate this most important of religious and Islamic concepts. And, to investigate, we must step back and look upon the Prophet with objectivity.

If not for all unquestioning emulators, then surely for all thinking Muslims, constant examination and probing is a precondition for the constant rejuvenation of faith, and a believer's regeneration must be accompanied with the dusting and brushing of the garment of faith. We must not be prepared to see anything reduced to a dusty antique, even faith, even prophetic guidance, even God. They, too, must be reassessed and re-examined. Our understanding of them, too, must be constantly refreshed and renewed. And the prophethood, this vital element of religion and faith, is no exception to this rule.

Experiential Nature of Prophethood

When we look from afar at the Prophet of Islam as a mundane human being, we see an extremely successful leader and reformer who built the edifice he wished to build single-handedly. Even after his death, his project and plan did not come to a halt. On the contrary, it gained momentum and, despite all the hardships and enmities, the pledge God had made to him was fulfilled and realised.[1]

---

[1] Rumi elaborates on this:
> ... They (thy followers), from fear, are uttering thy name covertly and hiding when they perform their prayers;
> From terror and dread of the accursed infidels thy Religion is being hidden underground;
> (But) I will fill the world, from end to end, with minarets; I will make blind the eyes of the recalcitrant.
> Thy servants will occupy cities and (seize) power: thy Religion will extend from the Fish to the Moon.

The Prophet departed from this world, but his purpose and fortune did not depart with him; it flourished, spread and grew. And God's blessing can mean nothing other than this. But there have been other individuals and innovators in history who have achieved great success and whose words and ideas have gained universal currency. Hence, these particular qualities and achievements may not constitute the gauge or necessary condition of prophethood. This is why theologians/metaphysicians have highlighted the "revelatory religious experience of the prophets. They have defined a prophet as someone who can attain unique insights through unique channels, which are out of the reach of and unavailable to others.

Hence, the quintessential constituent of a prophet's personality and prophethood and his unique capital is that divine revelation or what is described today as the paradigm case of "religious experience". In this experience, it seems to the prophet as if someone comes to him and proclaims messages and commands to him and tells him to convey them to the people. And the prophet is filled with such conviction on hearing these commands and messages, he feels such certitude and courage, that he prepares himself to stride forward and carry out his duty single-handedly in the face of even the most bitter attacks, enmities and hardships.[2]

A command came to the prophet Abraham in his dream—which was in fact his religious experience—that he must slay his innocent child; something that not only contravenes the rules of morality but is a violation of any father's natural instincts and sentiments. No father can impel himself to carry out such a deed, even in his imagination, and no man of morality and virtue can, unthinkingly and gratuitously, commit such a crime as to put his hands around his own innocent child's throat with the intention of strangling him. But Abraham's compelling and enlightening revelatory experience filled him with such conviction that

---

Thus He did, and (even) more than He said: he (the Prophet) slept (the sleep of death), but his fortune and prosperity slumbered not. (*Mathnawi*, 3: 1201–1212)

[2] Marun Bak Abud, the learned, contemporary Lebanese poet, for his part, depicts prophethood in the following terms: "Prophethood is wisdom, rebelliousness, inspiration, piety and compassion." He uses rebelliousness here in much the same way as the resolute steadfastness that Rumi attributes to the Prophet: "Every prophet was hard-faced in this world, and beat single-handed against the army of the kings; And did not avert his face from any fear or pain, (but) single and alone dashed against a (whole) world...(*Mathnawi*, 3: 4141–4145).

he was determined to obey and he moved to kill his child. Such is the compelling and enlightening nature of prophets' religious experience, and such is the certitude and boldness that it brings. And it forms the very kernel of their prophetic mission. It is an experience of this kind that prepares them for performing their awesome task in the world.

The difference between prophets and other people who undergo similar experiences is that they do not remain confined within this personal experience. They do not content themselves with it. They do not devote their lives to internal ardour and rapture. Having undergone the experience, the prophet senses a new mission and becomes a new person. And this new person builds a new world and a new people. As Muhammad Iqbal once said in a poem: "This (the Qur'an) is not merely a book. It is something 'completely other'. When it settles in one's heart, the heart will transform; when heart transforms (then) the whole universe transforms."

Abd al-Quddus of Gangoh, an Indian Sufi, found a most graceful way of conveying this difference between Sufi experiences and prophetic experiences. It is recorded that once he said: "the Prophet ascended to the heavens and returned; had I been in his place, I would not have returned."[3] And this is the best description of the difference between someone who remains confined within their own experience and is content with it and someone else who turns into a new person and resolves to build a new world.

It is important to emphasise that religious experience, in itself, does not turn anyone into a prophet, nor does the mere sight of an angel or the hinterlands of the unseen instil one with a prophetic mission. The angel of God appeared to Mary to herald the gift of baby Jesus, but Mary did not become a prophet. The Qur'an tells the tale of Mary's encounter with the angel with great eloquence, of how the sight of the angel frightened Mary, how the angel calmed her and gave her the glad tidings of a child. Rumi, too, with his dazzling elegance and imagination, has recounted the likely conversation between Mary and the angel [the Holy Spirit]. The angel tells her: I am a most mysterious creature. I am both objective and subjective. I am both outside you and within you. I am both a part of nature and beyond nature. And this is why you are so alarmed and perplexed.

---

[3] Muhammad Iqbal, *The Reconstruction of Religious Thought in Islam.* (Lahore: The Ashraf Press, 1958), p. 124.

The Exemplar of (Divine) bounty cried out to her, "I am the trusted
(messenger) of the Lord: be not afraid of me...
"Thou art fleeing from my existence into non-existence (the Unseen
World): in non-existence I am a King and standard bearer.
Verily, my home and dwelling-place is in non-existence: solely my (out-
ward) form is before the Lady (Mary).
O Mary, look (well), for I am a difficult form (to apprehend)..."[4]

In prophethood, then, there is an element of mission, which distinguishes it from the experiences of mystics. This element eventually
comes to an end with the Seal, but the principle of religious experience
and illumination remains.

Al-Ghazali, too, in his historical book *al-Munqidh min al-dalal*,
(Deliverance from Error) which tells the story of his own spiritual
journey, emphasises this same point; that is, religious experience as
the most notable signifier of a prophetic mission.[5]

Al-Ghazali was of the view that the seekers of truth could be divided
into four types: theologians, philosophers, the Batenis and Sufis. As to
himself, at the culmination of his own spiritual and intellectual journeys, he opted for the path of Sufism and, having followed this path, he
sympathetically grasped, in his own words, "the truth of prophethood
and its characteristics". He therefore includes a chapter at the end of
his book about the concept of prophetic mission which, while brief,
has great substance.

He begins by saying that there is no doubt in principle that some of
the knowledge and information possessed by human beings transcends
reason and experience. Did people learn of the characteristics of composite medicines or astrological fortune telling through experimentation? In such instances, there can be no doubt about the presence of
a certain component of divination or a strong, prophet-like intuition.
There are medicines that are only effective if they contain forty or one
hundred different substances in the right dosage. Who ever tested every
possible combination?

Where there is room for doubt is on the question of exactly who is a
prophet. It is in this connection that al-Ghazali says, in order to know
who is a *faqih*, we must either ask the *faqih*s or be an expert in the
field ourselves. In order to recognise a mathematician, we either ask

---

[4] *Mathnawi*, 3: 3768–3779.
[5] Abu Hamed al-Ghazali, *al-Munqidh min al-dalal*, ed. by Farid Jabre (Beirut: Commission Libanaise pour la Traduction de Chefs-d'oeuvre, 1969), p. 44.

mathematicians or we happen to be familiar enough with the discipline ourselves to be able to identify a mathematician. It is the same in the realm of prophethood. If we possess prophetic intuitions and experiences or if we can detect ideas that transcend reason, we can identify a prophet. In other words, we can identify prophets in much the same way as we can identify the followers of any other profession.

But what exactly is a prophetic experience? "Truthful dreams" constitute the lowest level of religious experience. And the higher levels are mystical visions, raptures and illuminations. "It is in this way that you should ascertain prophethood, not through the transformation of canes into dragons and the splitting of the moon", al-Ghazali writes, "because, if no further evidence is found to support these effects, then they may appear to be little more than magical feats or tricks of the imagination".[6]

Hence, when it comes to ascertaining a prophet's prophetic mission, it is not enough to rely on miracles, historical witnesses or documents, or the sheer number of corroborative accounts. First we must establish the essence of prophethood, then look for specific instances. According to al-Ghazali a person who says: "he who works according to what he has learnt, God will grant him knowledge of what he does not know", and "he who rises in the morning and his concern is a just one, God will spare him all the world's concerns", is clearly a prophet. For, these words bear the scent of revelation. They are based on deep, prophetic experience and have clearly been confirmed on countless occasions. In the opinion of al-Ghazali, only people who are familiar with prophet-like mystical experiences, have grasped the meaning of prophetic missions and have confirmed for themselves the truth of these words will recognise their provenance and know who the speaker is and what standing he has.

---

[6] Rumi speaks of astrology and medicine as being products of prophetic revelation. (see *Mathnawi*, 4: 1293–1295). If the idea strikes us as strange today, it is partly because the precepts of astrology are no longer applied and partly because all the sciences including medicine have become conjectural and it therefore seems inappropriate to consider them prophetic and revelational. Nonetheless, the presence of the element of ingenuity and invention in science is undeniable to this day. The theory of relativity or Newton's theory did not spring from either non-empirical premises or experimentation. They sprang out of ingenuity or "of being privy to nature's secrets". And this is what al-Ghazali means when he speaks of a mode beyond the rational mode (inductive, philosophical and experimental).

Hence, the path has been left open for anyone to understand prophet-hood and the Prophet. And the amazing thing is that the Prophet himself has laid this path. Among worldly teachers, you may find some who prevent their students from taking certain paths for fear that they may overtake the teacher and take away his business. But prophets have left the path to prophetic experience open to all their followers. Certain of their own elevated position, they never feared the emergence of any rivals. All the devotional commands that have been set out in religion, such as the night vigils, fasting, prayer and alms giving—headed by the precept "You will not attain piety until you expend of what you love" (3: 92)—are part and parcel of the ways in which the gateway has been left open for people to gain mystical and prophetic experiences, taking them by the hand and showing them the path to prophet-like ardour and rapture.[7]

The Prophet knew full well that those who took this path would not become his rivals or overtake him, but that they would instead come to understand him better and revere him more. He, therefore, encour-aged them to follow this path. If the Prophet ascended to the heavens, he wanted everyone to experience this ascension to the best of their ability. In fact, essentially and fundamentally, to follow the Prophet is to follow his spiritual experiences and not just to obey his commands by doing what he enjoined and abstaining from what he proscribed. The true disciple is he who shares the Prophet's ardour and rapture or experiences them vicariously. This can, of course, only be said of mystical religiosity, not the religiosity of the *faqih*s which is confined to observing the injunctions and prohibitions. It was not without any reason that Rumi encourages Muslims saying: "Come forth to the Ascension, since you are the Prophet's people; kiss the Moon, since

---

[7] Al-Ghazali writes that there are secrets behind the manner in which we have to say our prayers and even their times that, although mysterious to us, cannot be denied or dismissed. In support of his case, he gives the example of a table (Boduh) that was used to ease women's labour pains (the table was written on two parchments and placed underneath the pregnant woman's feet) and tended to be very beneficial. He says: "I do not understand why someone who attests to this cannot attest to the fact that the different lengths of the morning, noon and evening prayers produce benefits that philosophy cannot fathom." (*al-Munqidh*, p. 52)

Ibn Khaldun for his part writes that in the books used by ascetics there are names and words that they recite in their sleep and then see what they desire in their dreams. Then, he mentions six words and he says: "With the help of these words, I have myself had remarkable dream visions, through which I learned things about myself that I wanted to know." See, *The Muqaddimah* (Trs) Franz Rosenthal, p. 84.

you are on the heights (of spiritual honour.)"[8] And yet the Prophet of Islam remains the Seal; that is to say, his absolute illumination and, especially, his mission will never be relived by anyone again.

Hence, prophethood was a kind of experience and illumination. And anyone who undergoes such an illumination and experience brings new gifts and blessings to the rest of the world and, having gained a new personality, lends a new personality to the entire world.

Evolutionary Nature of Prophetic Experience

The above introduction sheds light not only on the essence of prophethood and the way in which a prophet can be identified, but also on the requirements and consequences of viewing prophethood as an experience. If prophethood, in the sense of moving closer to the Hidden and hearing messages from the beyond, is an experience, then this experience can be augmented, enriched and intensified. In other words, just as anyone who gains any experience can become more skilled and more experienced, a prophet, too, can gradually become more of a prophet, in much the same way that a poet can become more of a poet, an artist more of an artist, a mystic more of a mystic and a leader more of a leader. If this idea is difficult to countenance, just take a look at some of the things the Qur'an has said about revelation and the Prophet. On God's command, the Prophet says: "O my Lord, increase me in knowledge." (20: 114) And this revelatory knowledge is embedded in the very essence of prophethood.

Again, when the Qur'an is revealed to the Prophet over a period of time, God tells the Prophet that there is a rationale to it all: "Even so, that We may strengthen thy heart thereby, and We have chanted it very distinctly." (25: 32) He says: We shall reveal the Qur'an to you gradually so that you may gain in confidence, so that you may become sturdier and more resolute, so that you are not overawed and troubled by doubts, so that the opposition and enmity that you face does not undermine your resolve, so that you know that you are Prophet, so that you know that our link with you is constant, so that you know we have not abandoned you, so that you know that our blessings and

---

[8] Jalal al-din Rumi, *Kolliyat-e Shams, ya, Divan-e Kabir* (Tehran: Amir Kabir, 1355/1977), Ghazal # 638 (tras. A. J. Arbery).

supports are always with you, so that you know that this coming and going of the Angel and God's words will continue.

And the Prophet felt a vital and pressing need for this constant link. The perpetuation of his prophetic mission depended on this paced consolidation and constancy. We read in the Qur'an: "And had we not confirmed thee, surely thou wert near to inclining to them a very little; then would We have let thee taste the double of life and the double of death." (17: 74–75)

And so it was that the prophetic experience was constantly renewed. It was not as if the Prophet experienced revelation once and ascended to the heavens once, to then rest on those laurels and spend from that treasure for the rest of his life. No, the blessing of revelation rained down upon him constantly, giving him ever greater strength and flourishing. Hence, the Prophet grew steadily more learned, more certain, more resolute, more experienced; in a word, more of a prophet.

Ibn Khaldun has left us with a very charming and apt observation about the nature of revelation and prophetic experience. He wrote that the Prophet's endurance for revelation gradually grew. Initially, when the verses of the Qur'an were being revealed to him, his endurance would rapidly expire. This is why the Meccan chapters and verses are short, whereas the Medinan chapters and verses are longer. It has even been said by historians that half of the Sura al-tawbah (Chapter 9) was suddenly revealed to the Prophet as he was riding his camel. This is because, with the passage of time, the prophetic experience had become easier for the Prophet. Ibn Khaldun writes:

> It should be known that, in general, the state of revelation presents difficulties and pains throughout. Revelation means leaving one's humanity, in order to attain angelic perceptions and to hear the speech of the soul. This causes pain, since it means that an essence leaves its own essence and exchanges its own stage for the ultimate stage…Gradual habituation to the process of revelation brings some relief. It is for this reason that the earliest passages, surahs, and verses of the Qur'an, revealed to Muhammad in Mecca, are briefer than those revealed to him in Medina. This may serve as a criterion for distinguishing the Meccan surahs and verses from the Medinese.[9]

We even read in Tabari's account how, at the very beginning and after the revelation of the initial verses of Sura al-'alaq (Chapter 96),

---

[9] Ibn Khaldun, *The Muqaddimah*, trans. by Franz Rosenthal (London: Routledge, 1967), p. 78.

the Prophet took fright and could not fully grasp what had befallen him. But he rapidly grew accustomed to it. Moses, too—as the Qur'an testifies—was at first frightened when the cane was transformed into a serpent, but God gently said to him: "Fear not; surely the Envoys do not fear in My presence." (27: 10) Moses, too, grew accustomed to miracles and revelation.

The message of the revelation also changed depending on the context. In Mecca, the Prophet's task was to shake people up, to alarm and awaken them. It was his business to smash the old dogmas. He therefore needed piercing and penetrating sermons and decisive ideological stances. But in Medina, it was time for construction, for following through the mission, for consolidating the teachings. Here, what was needed was legislation and lengthy, all-encompassing explanations and dialogue with the people. Of course, the Prophet's endurance for religious and prophetic experiences had also grown. Hence, the form and content of the message also changed. This is the norm with any experience, that it should grow and mature.

Wherever there is any question of experience, there is also a question of the increasing excellence of the experience. Wherever there is any question of becoming experienced, there is also a question of becoming more experienced. A poet becomes more of a poet by writing poetry. A speaker becomes more of a speaker by delivering speeches. This can be said of any experience: although the essence of the experience does not alter, although its truth is not tarnished, although its validity is not undermined, as the experience endures, so, too, will it gain in excellence.

The Prophet's inward experience was subject to this kind of expansion and evolution. With every passing day, he would become better acquainted with and more discerning about his position, his mission and his ultimate aims; more determined and resilient in the performance of his duties; better prepared and better equipped for achieving his aims; more prosperous and triumphant in his work; and more confident and increasingly certain of success.

There is patently a tight interaction and dialectical relationship between the doer and the deed. The two unmistakably affect one another. Take, for example, a worshipper and his prayers. The more the prayers intensify, the more the worshipper is exalted and the more the worshipper is exalted, the more penetrating and spiritual his prayers become. Now look at the Prophet, whose personality *was* his capital. His personality was both the receptacle and the generator, both the subject and the object of his religious revelatory experiences. And as his personality expanded, so too did his experiences (and vice versa), such that revelation was under his sway, not he, under the sway of revelation. If we were to put it in the language of the mystics, we would say that, as a result of the Prophet's multifarious proximity to God (*qurb-e farayezi* and *navafeli*),[10] he had reached the level that God had dwelled in his sight and other faculties. In so far as the verse reads: "When thou threwest, it was not thyself that threw, but God threw" (8: 17), for him to speak was to speak the Truth. It was not he who was under Gabriel's sway, but Gabriel, who was under his sway. It was he who would make the Angel appear. And, when he wanted to, the Prophet could go beyond the Angel, as the experience of the *mi'raj* testifies.

> If Ahmad should display that glorious pinion (his spiritual nature), Gabriel would remain dumbfounded unto everlasting.
> When Ahmad passed beyond the Lote-tree (on the boundary of Paradise) and his (Gabriel's) place of watch and station and farthest limit,
> He said to him (Gabriel), "Hark, fly after me." He (Gabriel) said, "Go, go; I am not thy companion (any farther)."
> He answered him, saying, "Come, O destroyer of veils: I have not yet advanced to my zenith."
> He replied, "O my illustrious friend, if I take one flight beyond this limit, my wings will be consumed."
> This tale of the elect losing their senses in (contemplation of) the most elect is (naught but) amazement on amazement.[11]

Let me add in passing that viewing Divine Discourse as nothing but the Prophetic discourse is the best way of resolving the theological problems of how God speaks (*kalam-e bari*).

When a genie prevails over (gains possession of) a man, the attributes of humanity disappear from the man.

> Whatsoever he says, that genie will (really) have said it: the one who belongs to this side will have spoken from (the control of) the one who belongs to younder side.
> Since a genie hath this influence and rule, how (much more powerful) indeed must be the Creator of that genie![12]

---

[10] For more on this see the chapter "Spiritual Guardianship and Political Guardianship" in this volume.
[11] *Mathnawi*, 4: 3800–3805.
[12] *Mathnawi*, 4: 2112–2114.

At any rate, the subjective expansion of the prophetic experience of which we have been speaking was accompanied by an outward expansion. As he was becoming more of a Prophet, so his teachings were becoming more robust and sturdier.

Dialogical Nature of Prophetic Experience

Imagine a hermit who sits in a cave and receives certain messages. Compare this hermit to a prophet who lives amongst the people, interacts with them and is faced with dozens of problems every day that he must deal with and respond to the satisfaction of the community and his followers. There is clearly a vast difference between the two.

We can see this, for example, in Jesus' case. Jesus, according to the received accounts of his life, deliberately avoided politics and he never engaged in trade, battles and worldly affairs; nor did he make a family. He passed away rather young, in his mid thirties. This is very different from the case of the Prophet of Islam. First, the Prophet gained his prophetic experience in the full maturity of adulthood, when he was already forty years old. Before then, he had been an honest and abstemious person, who was at peace with solitude. Each year, he would spend some weeks in a cave outside the city; no doubt, reaping great blessings and benefits in this way. He was, at the same time, a merchant and thoroughly familiar with the complexities of social life and its most tempting aspect, i.e., money. But he was not yet a prophet. When, at the peak of adulthood and maturity and being a family man for years, he stepped into the arena of prophetic experience and action, he was totally ripe and ready.

Secondly, he did not restrict himself to solitude and choose to live in isolation in a cave. He came back to the people and considered it his duty to deal with the problems of his day. He encountered great enmity and great friendship, and his outward experiences enhanced his maturity. In other words, they contributed to the expansion and robustness of his teachings.

The Prophet's interaction with the outer world undoubtedly allowed his mission and prophetic experience to expand and flourish. In other words, the religion that we know as Islam did not descend upon the Prophet instantaneously, but had a gradual genesis. And a religion that has a gradual genesis will also undergo gradual movement and development in its subsequent existence.

In comparison to other revelations, that of Moses for instance, the Qur'an was not revealed to the Prophet all at once. It was not as if he was handed a book and told to go to his tribe and guide them with the book. The book itself was revealed and completed gradually and, as it was, religion itself gained in excellence and the Prophet's personality matured and grew. One may ask: did there exist a complete pre-drafted version of the Qur'an to be revealed to the Prophet later on? Or, perhaps it gradually grew as the Prophet's personality developed and circumstances and events unfolded. There are people who believe that the Qur'an was revealed to the Prophet in its entirety over a single night (the Night of Power) and they reject the idea of a gradual genesis. This is a debate that continues to rage and remains unresolved to this day.[13] But perhaps neither theory or both are true. Let us imagine the Prophet stepping into the social arena in much the same way as a lecturer or a teacher steps into the classroom. I describe this relationship as a relationship of interaction or dialogue. When a lecturer walks into the classroom, he knows on the whole what points and material he wants to impart to the students. To this extent, what takes place in the classroom can be foreseen and prepared in advance by the lecturer. But anything beyond this is of the nature of a possibility, not a contingency, and therefore unpredictable, although significant in the teaching and learning process. The lecturer does not know exactly what will transpire

---

[13] The dispute arises from the fact that the Qur'an, on the one hand, speaks of "the month of Ramadan, wherein the Qur'an was sent down" (2: 185) and, on the other, of "a Qur'an We have divided, for thee to recite it to mankind at intervals". (170: 106) These two verses seem contradictory. Hence, some commentators have said that the Qur'an began to be revealed during Ramadan, but was not revealed in its entirety during this month. And they have appealed for support to history, for according to some accounts, the first verses of the Qur'an are said to have been sent down on the Night of Qadr (viz. the verses at the beginning of al-Alaq Sura), not all of it. Other commentators have said that the Qur'an was revealed in its entirety to the Prophet in summation (not in an expanded form) during Ramadan and then unfolded gradually, with the Prophet recalling appropriate verses at appropriate times. These commentators do not explain exactly how that summation actually turned into the expanded form. Our words in the text correspond to and are in keeping with the verse in the Qur'an that states that: "(This is) a Book, with verses basic or fundamental (of established meaning), further explained in detail, from One Who is Wise and Well-Acquainted (with all things)" (11: 1). Given the fact that the Prophet's very personality and prophethood that are divinely approved lent him the authority to make theoretical and practical choices and decisions, it was enough for him to think and to speak and to experience things for the summation of the Qur'an to unfold into the expanded form. This was so because the summation of the Qur'an was potentially engraved in the heart of the Prophet by the very act of his appointment.

in the classroom. What questions will the students ask? What will they misunderstand? What sophistry will the clever students resort to? What excuses will they find for being ill prepared? What rumours will they spread against the lecturer? and so on. These are all variables that the teacher must be generally prepared to contend with.

The relationship between a teacher and his students in the classroom is not a completely unilateral process of inculcation. It is not as if the teacher only speaks and the students only listen. In fact, without forgetting the initial and basic message he wishes to impart, the teacher enters into a dialogue or an interactive relationship with the students. And it is this interaction that shapes the eventual lesson. Occasional digressions and repetitions—even the odd red herring and irrelevancy—the scolding of one student and the praising of another, and interludes in which unexpected questions must be answered are all distinct possibilities. The teacher is faced with bright students and slow students, hard working students and lazy students all sitting in the same classroom. The teacher offers the odd explanation to one and tosses the odd allusion to the other. Adjusting the level of the material to the students' skills and talents is another major variable. And the longer the period over which the lessons are spread, the more likely will be the incidence of the different variables.

The clever teacher will steer the lessons throughout with full mastery and control, without ever losing sight of the overall aims and purpose. At the same time, he is fully prepared to follow through the students' digressions. Far from wanting a passive audience, he encourages the students to take their turn centre stage, so that they may all advance together. This interactive relationship or process of dialogue between the teacher and the students forms the woof and warp of a teaching course over a set period.

Of course, the teacher can entrust to paper once and for all everything that he wishes to teach and distribute it in the form of written lectures. But this is hardly the way to instruct and inspire students. This is authorship, not lectureship. Stepping into the classroom, running lessons, teaching students, taking them by the hand and lifting them higher and higher, pointing out their strengths and weakness, turning a passive audience into confident actors is a much more important task and an altogether different business from penning lectures.

The noble Prophet of Islam was in a similar position among his people. When we say that religion is a human matter, this is not to deny its heavenly spirit. What we mean is that the Prophet steps into the midst of the people and strides alongside them, he sometimes moves this way and sometimes moves that way, sometimes he is drawn into war and sometimes into peace, sometimes he faces enemies and sometimes ignorant friends. And on each occasion he acts in a way that is appropriate to the circumstances in that particular instance. And religion is the totality of the Prophet's gradual, historical deeds and stances. And, since the Prophet's personality is divinely sanctioned and tantamount to revelation, anything he does and says is likewise sanctioned and approved. And this is how it comes about that a holy human being presents a religion that is at once both human and holy.

Islam is not a book or an aggregate of words; it is a historical movement and the history-incarnate of a mission. It is the historical extension of a gradually-realised prophetic experience. The Prophet's personality is the core; it is everything that God has granted to the Muslim community. Religion is woven through and through with this personality. Religion *is* the Prophet's inward and outward experience.[14] Anything that he does is the right thing to do. Anything that he says is rightful guidance, for he never speaks on a whim.

Religion, then, is the Prophet's spiritual and social experience, and it is therefore subject to him. And since these experiences are not arbitrary, but are founded on the Prophet's holy and divinely-sanctioned personality, it becomes binding on all his followers, as well as on the Prophet himself.

With its spirit, its *muhkamat* (unambiguous principles) and indisputable elements remaining intact, the Qur'an was revealed and realised gradually; in other words, it had a historical genesis. Someone would go to the Prophet and ask him a question. Someone would insult the Prophet's wife. Someone would set alight the flames of war. Some would accuse the Prophet of being insane. Some would spread rumours about the Prophet marrying Zayd's wife. Some would overlook their duties

---

[14] Sultan Valad, Rumi's son, offers the following interesting observation about the connection between religions and prophets' characteristics: "The differences between religious laws arise from the differences between prophets; a legal system came into being in keeping with the nature and characteristics of each prophet. Jesus, peace be upon him, had no inclination to marry and was not drawn to women and did not devote time to grooming and cleanliness, and, from these characteristics, emerged his way and his religion...Since Muhammad, peace about him, liked women and grooming and cleanliness, so became his religion...because that which the prophet considers right is acceptable to and cherished by Him, God wants what he wants..." See: Baha al-din Valad, *Ma'aref: Majmu'eh Sokhanan va Mava'ez-e Baha al-din Valad*, compiled by Najib Mayel Heravi (Tehran: Mawla Publications, 1367/1987), pp. 309–310.

during the sacred months. They would kill their sons and daughters for fear of poverty. They would take two sisters as wives. They would observe superstitious rituals over slit-ear she-camels and twin-birth sheep (considering them sacred and refusing to use their milk or meat). And all of this would find an echo in the Qur'an and the Prophet's words. The Jews would do something. The Christians would do another thing.

And if the Prophet had lived longer and encountered more events, his reactions and responses would inevitably have grown as well. This is what it means to say that the Qur'an could have been much more than it is; even perhaps could have a second volume. But, when I suggested this once, some people did not comprehend or countenance it.

If they had not accused Aisha of having an adulterous relationship, would we have the verses at the beginning of the al-Nour Sura (Chapter 24)? If the war of the confederate tribes had never occurred, would we have the al-Ahzab Sura (Chapter 33)? If there had been no Abulahab or if he and his wife had not displayed enmity towards the Prophet, would we have the al-Masad Sura (Chapter 111)? These were all contingent events in history whose occurrence or non-occurrence would have been much the same. But, having occurred, we now find traces of them in the Qur'an. This is precisely the kind of mischief that students get up to in the classroom, forcing the lecturer to give an admonition here, issue a chastisement there. And these admonitions and chastisements become written into religion. And when we say that religion is human and gradual and historical, we mean nothing other than this.[15]

Both the Prophet himself and his experience are human. He is furthermore surrounded by human beings. In the encounter between all these human elements, a human religion is gradually born which is in keeping with human beings and an answer to their real circumstances. Pay earnest heed to the meaning of dialogue and interaction. In a dialogue, the answer is in keeping with the question. And what is said is essentially of the nature of an answer, not of the nature of a unilateral inculcation.

This is why we say Islam was born in the context of these engagements and interactions, and its birth and genesis was a gradual-historical one. It was not as if the Prophet handed a finished book to people and said: see what you make of it and act on that basis. The Qur'an was

---

[15] The accidental and contingent nature of many aspects of religion is explained at length in the chapter "Essentials and Accidentals in Religion" in this volume.

revealed gradually and in keeping with the role played by the people. With the spirit of its message remaining intact, it would take shape in response to events. In other words, day-to-day events played a part in the genesis of religion and, if other events had taken place, Islam could quite possibly have undergone a different genesis (with its main message remaining intact). We would then have been left with a different model and a different society built by the Prophet.

In brief, it is these engagements and interactions that lent Islam its particular structure and composition. To the extent that the Prophet would become embroiled in economics, politics and so on, so Islam would become economical and political. This religion *is* the Prophet's gradually-burgeoning inward and outward experience; a prophet who has a divinely-sanctioned personality and whose experiences are, therefore, embued with divinity and endorsed by God. Rumi says: "Amongst the righteous there is one (who is) the most righteous: on his diploma (is inscribed) by the Sultan's hand a *sahh*."[16]

Many were the events that never occurred during the Prophet's time, so he did not offer any answers to or take any stances on them. For instance, seldom there is any indication about or against Zoroastrianism in the Qur'an. Many, too, were matters that were imposed on him. Motahhari, the contemporary Iranian theologian, was among others who contended that slavery was imposed on Islam. Motahhari believed that, had it been for the Prophet alone and had he lived in a world where there was no slavery, Islam would not have sanctioned it.[17]

There are innumerable phrases in the Qur'an such as, "they ask you about the spirit"; "they ask you about the crescent"; "they ask you about fighting during the sacred months"; "they ask you about the two-horned [Alexander]"; and so on. It is clear that, when a question was asked about the two-horned, then divine verses would be devoted to the subject. If some other question had been asked, we would find some other answer in the Qur'an. This is what a historical genesis and being in keeping with the historical circumstances means. The Prophet of Islam instructed students, created a people and built a city, and this followed from the growth of the Prophet's people in step with revelation and the Prophet himself. The people played a role in the gradual

---

[16] *Mathnawi*, 6: 2622. The Arabic word *sahh*, meaning "it is correct," certifies that the document which bears it is genuine and valid.

[17] Mortaza Motahhari, *Khatamiyat* (Qum: Sadra, 1367/1989), pp. 63–65.

genesis and formation of Islam. And as they played their roles, so their characters were formed. The people were never mere observers, even in the loftiest aspects of religiosity, such as revelation itself.

When we say that Islam is a political religion, we mean that Islam became engaged in politics. If it had not become engaged in politics, it would not have become political, just as Christianity did not. Various figures with various interests stepped onto the stage and engaged the Prophet. And the Prophet did not flee from dealing with these challenges. This is how Islam became embroiled in politics in the course of its historical genesis. It took political stances and left political messages for future generations.

In brief, the Prophet of Islam underwent two levels of "experience" and Islam is a product of both: outward experience and inward experience. Over time, the Prophet became more skilled at both these types of experience. Hence, his religion grew sturdier and more perfected. In his outward experience, he built the Medina, ran the city's affairs, went to war, confronted enemies, cultivated friends and so on. In his inward experience, there was revelation, ascension, reveries, insights and illuminations, and in these, too, he continued to excel and grow increasingly skilled. And, until the actual demise of the Prophet of Islam, this religion, with these characteristics and this nature, continued to perfect and grow.

And the verse that says: "Today I have perfected your religion for you," (5: 4) speaks of a minimum, not a maximum; that is to say, the people have been provided with a necessary minimum of guidance, whereas the feasible maximum will come about through the gradual perfection and historical expansion that Islam subsequently undergoes. We must bear in mind the subtle and important difference between "the necessary minimum" and "the possible maximum".[18]

For religion to become increasingly perfected, it is necessary for the Prophet himself to become increasingly perfected, for religion is nothing other than the condensed sum and substance of his individual and social experiences. Now, in the absence of the Prophet, too, the inward and outward prophetic experiences must expand and grow, thereby enriching and strengthening religion. Mystics, who find vicarious rap-

---

[18] A detailed explanation of the minimal nature of religious guidance in the fields of *fiqh*, ethics and beliefs can be found in the chapter "Minimalist Religion, Maximalist Religion" in this volume.

ture in the Prophet's rapture, who stride lovingly in his shadow and follow the path of the master, enrich our religious experiences and the experience of each and every one of them is unique and singular, and therefore magnificent, precious and laudable.

If Hafez is the most eloquent Iranian poet and his artistic and poetic experience the richest and loftiest of all (assuming this to be the case), this does not imply that we should forego the pleasures of our other poets and fail to view their contributions as an enrichment of "the poetic experience". All our great poets are precious and they all have a place in the history of this exquisite art.

The world of experience is a pluralistic one. The profound, spiritual experiences of Rumi, Al-Ghazali, Shaykh Mahmoud Shabestari, Seyyed Heidar Amoli and other mystics all have something to say and contribute, and they all add to the previous experiences. And if it is incorrect to say that "God's book will suffice for me", it is also incorrect to say "the Prophet's Ascension and the Prophet's experience will suffice for me". The experience of mystical love, for example, has been one of the tender spiritual experiences to have enriched believers' religious practice. We can say much the same about Shi'i belief, which, by taking seriously the idea of religious leadership, has in effect opted for the expansion and perpetuation of prophetic experiences. And this is a precondition for the movement and perfection of a religion that came into being on the bedrock of movement and increasing excellence.

Not only inward experiences, but social experiences, too, have contributed and can contribute to the feasible strengthening and perfection of religion. Through their political achievements, their familiarisation with other cultures, and their development of *fiqh*, theology and ethics, Muslims have in fact enriched religion and transformed it from a potentiality to an actuality. And as long as the way remains open to such experiences, religion will continue to grow sturdier and more perfected.

The coming into existence of numerous Muslim sects must also be viewed in this same light. Seeing the emergence of sects within Islam as a conspiracy and generally attributing major events and great historical developments to intrigues and plots is superficial and simplistic. Was the emergence of different sects not a prerequisite of the religion's historical expansion? Was the coming into existence of Shi'is and Sunnis not a product and corollary of that historical expansion? A religion that has come into being through interaction and conflict will continue to exist and develop through interaction and conflict, thereby adding to the wealth of its experiences. What could be more natural?

Was it not natural that, in the absence of the Prophet, the interactions and engagements, the disputes and disagreements, and the raising of new questions that needed new answers would persist and lead to the theoretical and political division of Muslims? The question here is not their truth or falsehood, which is a theological problem of the first order. What concerns us is their overall historical place and significance. Nothing could be more natural than these divisions and disputes. A religion that comes into being gradually will also mature and grow sturdier and more perfected gradually. And its subsequent existence is dependent on the perpetuation of the initial circumstances.

This religion was not just a book for us to be able to say, if the book endures, the religion will endure, even if it never engages with historical events. This religion was not just a prophet for us to be able to say, if the prophet goes, the religion goes. This religion was a gradual dialogue between heaven and earth, and a lengthy, historical prophetic experience. Muslims will thrive and endure as long as they perpetuate this experience—by taking inspiration from the revelation, relying on the primary sources and allowing the Prophet's personality to serve as their guide—thereby carrying minimal perfection forwards towards maximal perfection. The Prophet's legacy is experience, the book, the city, the tradition and the people, and they must all be taken and understood together.

Let us not overlook the fact that our mystics have enriched our religious experience and our thinkers, enhanced our religious understanding and sense of discovery. We must not imagine that these distinguished people merely explained the previous words and reproduced the earlier experiences. Al-Ghazali made new religious discoveries. So, too, did Rumi, Muhyi al-din Ibn Arabi, Shahab al-din Sohravardi, Sadr al-din Shirazi and Fakhr al-Din Razi. This is exactly how our religion has grown and become perfected. Their experiences, discoveries and ideas are all precious, opportune, beneficial and enriching. They did not just explain things, they discovered things, and this is the key to their greatness. But, unfortunately, from a certain point onwards, our thinkers seemed to confine themselves to explanation and failed to contribute any new ideas and experiences to the logbook of religion. Over the course of history, Islam has grown, developed and matured thanks to new contributions and, as long as this gradual genesis and this historical process of being perfected persists, the religion is sure to endure.

Today, no one's word must be taken as the indisputable truth in religion for us, because the true word and true religious guardianship belonged to the Prophet alone. With the final closure of the prophetic mission and the Seal, no one's personality can suffice to render true their words. Everyone must offer us proof, except the Prophet who is himself the proof.[19] But thinkers, artists, creators and poets may all serve the realm of Islamic culture, thus contributing to the vitality of this gradually-formed identity, repaying their debt to this sacred religion and truly, not figuratively, letting the Prophet serve as their guide.

The era of prophetic mission is over, but the opportunity remains for the expansion of the prophetic experience, both spiritually as well as socially. Following that noble man's path demands that we perpetuate his inner, social and political experiences. While ensuring that the spirit of revelation remains intact, we must embark on an extensive dialogue with the inner and outer worlds. We must act innovatively and courageously and move from the realm of emulation and explanation to the realm of thought and discovery, from the passivity of an audience to the creativity of actors. Let us not fear the emergence of plurality. Let us honour and esteem those who step into this arduous field.

The Prophet's experiences and revelation were answers to questions, solutions to problems, nourishment for minds, and illuminators of hearts and souls in the actually existing world. They were not a mere enumeration of duties and the delivery of a ready-made ideology. The Prophet did not adapt abstract experiences to reality; his whole life *was* experience in the heart of reality.

Today, too, religiosity must become an experience for solving problems, nourishing hearts, untying knots and broadening horizons. It must be as if revelation had been revealed anew and as if reality had become a vital element of religious experience again.

Today, too, religion must be seen as an experience that is nascent, that interacts, that engages (instead of being a closed and finished ideology). And all this, not out of desperation or for fear of the sneers of the sneering, but willingly and out of illuminating experience. And not just in the realm of *fiqh*, but also in the vast arena of religious

---

[19] For an explanation of this point see chapters on "The Last Prophet" in this volume.

knowledge and experience. Just as the Prophet's religious experience interacted and engaged with the actions of the actors of his age, so religious experience today must interact and engage with the actions of the actors of this age. Otherwise, new human beings who feel that they are not addressed by religion and that they are not participants in contemporary religious experience, human beings who find themselves faced with a presumptuous, arrogant, inflexible and patronising religion that demands unquestioning surrender, will not be inclined to submit and accede. A message is only meaningful when there is an addressee. Contemporary addressees must see religion as a message addressed to them. This is the meaning and implication of setting the Prophet as one's guide.

CHAPTER TWO

THE LAST PROPHET—1

The noble Prophet of Islam, peace be upon him, lived to the age of sixty three. Towards the end of his blessed life, he contracted an acute illness. He did not survive the illness, but he left behind an auspicious legacy that formed the bedrock of a civilisation. After his demise, the budding civilisation he had founded took root, grew and flourished, turning into one of the greatest civilisations the world had ever known, a civilisation easily comparable to those of Greece and Ancient Rome and falling nothing short of them in grandeur, a civilisation that enchanted many great hearts and minds, successfully leading them to the lavish banquet of God and enriching their lives and souls with its sweetness and nourishment.

As Muslims believe, the demise of the noble Prophet of Islam brought to an end the abiding dynasty of prophets. The splendid gates of heaven that had been opened to the world were closed for ever more and people were deprived of having a prophet ever again. From then on, people were destined to benefit from the teachings of past prophets and to seek understanding and wisdom at the school of their noble legacies. This is why it is incumbent on us, as the followers of the last prophet and as the disciples of his revelational school, to reflect upon the meaning, implications and mysteries of the ending of the prophetic dynasty and the finality of Muhammad's prophethood.

On the Meaning of "Finality"

Muslims confidently believe that they are the ones to receive the last divine Prophet, that God chose to address his final words to them and that no other sun is ever to rise in the skies of prophethood again; which is why they ignore and disregard invitations from any other claimants. This is an auspicious, liberating and reassuring blessing. But it also raises a number of questions that must be discussed and addressed:

The first question is whether the finality of the noble Prophet of Islam is an intra-religious claim or an extra-religious one. In other words, does belief in the finality of his prophethood have an extra-religious or an intra-religious foundation? Have we recognised that Muhammad is the last prophet of God on the basis of his own teachings and our analyses of his teachings, or are there aspects of his personality and life that point to his being the last prophet even without him having told us?

The fact of the matter is that there is no extra-religious indication or any indication independent of the Prophet's own words to show that he was the last and the Seal. Nor have any of our theologians or philosophers or even our innovative thinkers ever put forward any independent criteria or hypotheses in this respect, such that, had the Prophet not declared that he was the last of the prophets, we would not have recognised it either. Hence, everything that we say by way of an analysis of the finality of Muhammad's prophethood is of the nature of a post hoc explanation. That is to say, having affirmed this finality elsewhere, we then set out to analyse it. We have no independent hypothesis in this respect and we are basing ourselves on the words of the Prophet. These kinds of explanations, which are known as post hoc explanations, have their own particular attributes. One of these attributes is that they have no predictive power and, rather than being scientific-experimental, they are analytical-interpretative. Without going into the whys and wherefores of the claim itself, they probe its meaning and substance. Hence, they are not, strictly speaking, concerned with demonstration, but rather with rationalisation. This is the key to the mystery of why different thinkers have followed different paths in explaining the mysteries of the finality of Muhammad's prophethood. They have done something like trying to understand a language without being able to speak it or construct a sentence in it. Or like trying to guess the cause that led to an effect, under circumstances in which they have no direct or independent access to the cause. Consequently, the reasoning becomes circular and unfalsifiable; like seeing snow and saying something must have happened in the upper layers of the atmosphere to have made it snow. There is no other way of analysing unprecedented and unique historical events, and the finality of the prophethood is one such event.

We read in the Qur'an as part of Zayd's story: "Muhammad is not the father of any one of your men, but (he is) the Messenger of God, and the Seal of the Prophets: and God has full knowledge of all things." (33: 40) And there are traditions citing the Prophet himself to this effect. There is a very well known tradition, reported by Sunnis and Shi'is, in which the Prophet is quoted as saying to Ali: "Your relationship to me is like Aaron's relationship to Moses, with this difference: there will be no other prophet after me". Emphatic statements of this kind made by the Prophet have led Muslims to believe that he is the last prophet. This simply means that no other founder of a religion or a lawgiver will appear to propagate a new faith. And, if such a person does appear, he will be an impostor. Nonetheless, this is not to say that personal prophetic experiences will cease to occur. Mulla Sadra (Sadr al-din Shirazi) recounts an interesting Shi'i narrative in his *Mafatih al-Ghayb* which conveys an elevated, mystical notion: "There are servants of God who are not prophets but rouse the envy of prophets." In other words, there are people who have special links to the world beyond and it may well be that they achieve a loftier status than some of the names engraved in the annals of prophethood. The fact remains, however, that eminent servants of this kind do not have a mission to be the purveyors and propagators of a religion. But the way is never closed to religious experiences and esoteric communications with God, and individuals are always free to emulate the inward/spiritual personality of the Prophet and to attain similar spiritual states of being, ranks and raptures or experience them vicariously. Nonetheless, the burden and responsibility of a prophetic mission will never be placed on anyone's shoulders again.

Jalal al-Din Rumi teaches us to:

> "Come forth to the Ascension, since you are the Prophet's people; kiss the Moon, since you are on the heights (of spiritual honour)."[1]

In other words, the Prophet's experience of Ascension is available to all his followers. And following the Prophet is by no means confined to doing what he enjoined and abstaining from what he proscribed; it can extend to a reproduction of his spiritual experiences. Of course, the Ascension was an elevated, prophetic experience; others can ascend to the best of their abilities.

Second question: Does the finality relate to the religion or the Prophet?

The Seal is an attribute of the Prophet, not the religion. Our Prophet was the last prophet, but religion was the last religion from the start. The Qur'an teaches us that the last religion was the first religion:

---

[1] Jalal al-din Rumi, *Kolliyat-e Shams, ya, Divan-e Kabir* (Tehran: Amir Kabir, 1355/1977), Ghazal # 638 (trs. A.J. Arbery).

> He has laid down for you as religion that He charged Noah with, and that
> We have revealed to thee, and that We charged Abraham with, Moses
> and Jesus. (42: 13)

Or:

> Abraham was not a Jew, neither a Christian; but he was a muslim and
> one pure of faith; certainly he was never of the idolaters. (3: 61)

Contemporary thinkers stress the point that all the principal and essential teachings of religion are in keeping with human nature (*fitrah*) and even arise out of it. They believe that, since human nature is unchanging, religion always remains one and the same; its teachings are not subject to change and movement with the movement of time. *Fitri* religion remains the same because basic nature remains the same. And this is exactly how they understand the following verse:

> The Messenger believes in what was sent down to him from his Lord,
> and the believers; each one believes in God and His Angels, and in His
> Books and His Messengers; we make no division between any one of His
> Messengers. (2: 285)

By "making no division" is not meant only that the prophets are to be respected equally. Rather it implies that they are all purveyors of the same essential message. Of course, one cannot ignore that there are differences between religions' accidentals, the perfections and imperfections of the laws, and different personalities of the prophets: "And those Messengers, some We have preferred above others." (2: 253)

Nonetheless, we see the chain of prophets as a single unified sequence, all conveying the same basic messages, the addressee of which (in the words of the theologians) is that shared core that exists within all human beings and is immutable over time. Of course, prophets would renew and reintroduce these messages, put them at the disposal of the people anew and—depending on the dictates of the age, their personal and collective experiences, and their own particular characteristics—make changes to the outer layers; but the core remained the same. Hence, the Seal means that the need for the reintroduction of religion has been obviated and that it is, happily, no longer necessary, not that the need for religion itself has been obviated.

Third question: Why was it that the Prophet of Islam became the last prophet? And why did it become necessary to end the prophetic succession with his prophetic mission? What was it about his personality, his message or the circumstances of the age that dictated that, after Muhammad and Islam, there should be no other prophet and no other religion, such that God sealed the dynasty of prophets for ever? Many thought-provoking ideas have been put forward on this subject by various thinkers (and I must reiterate that they are all in the nature of post hoc explanations). I will review and assess a number of them:

Muhammad Iqbal was one of the first contemporary Muslim thinkers to tackle this issue from the perspective of a philosopher and a historian, leaving us some astute observations. Mortaza Motahhari's comments on the subject and his disagreements with Iqbal are also worth examining.

Iqbal approaches the issue within a Bergsonian framework.[2] He does not mention Bergson by name here but is clearly speaking under his influence when he says that life progressed by force of instinct until such a time as reason was born out of it. With the coming into existence of reason, life deemed it necessary to curb the instincts and to allow reason to expand and grow. And so it was that a new world and a new era came into being. The sealing of the prophethood belongs to the new age and is necessitated by it.

Iqbal does not mince his words and his contentions on this subject are very clear. He says that we have had two eras: An era in which humanity was under the sway of its instinct and passion and a new era, in which reason has gained the upper hand and people operate more by reason than by instinct. This is not to say that the instinct and passion have been completely quashed, but that a page has turned in the life of humanity and, for the time being, "inductive reason" has the upper hand.[3] Hence, the era of the reign of human instincts—a fertile breeding ground for prophets—has passed. And an era is now upon us that is not prophet-fertile.

From this perspective, the Prophet of Islam stands midway between two worlds. In terms of source and origin, his message belongs to the ancient world, but, in terms of content, it belongs to the new. In the sense that the origin of his message is of the nature of revelation and revelation is, in Iqbal's view, instinctive. But the content of his message is rational. That is to say, it invites people to turn to rationality,

---

[2] Henri Bergson (1859–1941) founded the philosophy of creative evolution (évolution créatrice) and, by raising the idea of "life-force" (élan vital), he attributed a kind of intelligence to life. It was as if life itself had an aim and purpose and surged forward within matter with a mysterious intelligence and élan, brushing some things out of its way and drawing other things to its bosom, travelling through various stages, until it arrives at last at reason and will. Iqbal's words have a Bergsonian ring.

[3] Iqbal, *The Reconstruction of Religious Thought*, Chapter 5.

to apply inductive reasoning, and to consider history and nature as two independent sources of knowledge. And, in effect, the emergence of these considerations and the guardianship of reason leads to the disaffirmation of instinct and termination of revelation as a source of knowledge. In Iqbal's admirable turn of phrase and wise observation: "In Islam prophecy reaches its perfection in discovering the need of its own abolition."[4] In other words, the Prophet himself realised that the time for prophethood was at an end. The era of rationality had arrived and people would henceforth have to adopt a critical approach to revelation and religious experience, and even to all the knowledge they had accumulated in the past. The era of prophets and saints (awliya) who obtained their authority from heaven had thus come to an end.

Iqbal takes things even further than this. He goes on to say that we, Muslims, are the freest people in the world because we believe that prophethood has been sealed. We are not awaiting the arrival of any divine saviour to take our hands like children again and to correct our mistakes.[5] From now on, we are free to criticise, our rationality is awake and alert, and we do not place any verdict or ruling above the verdict of our reason. The abolition of priesthood and hereditary kingship in Islam is further testimony to and a corollary of this same idea of finality. The era of direct guidance and superintendency from above has ended

---

[4] Ibid., p. 126.

[5] Here, Iqbal is responding to Oswald Spengler and the challenges he had raised. Spengler was a writer and thinker in the first half of the twentieth century and of Hegelian persuasion. In a celebrated book after the first world war, he predicted "the decline of the west", introducing this expression into common usage. He presented awesome theories about civilisations and their rise and fall which no one other than Hegelians would have the audacity to do. At any rate, he had things to say about religious civilisations and religions as well, including the suggestion that most of religious civilisations and religions, despite their multitudinous forms, had a common essence and model, viz. magianism, which holds in the existence of the two forces of good and evil, and teaches that ultimate victory belongs to the god of goodness or Ahura Mazda. Thus, these religions are awaiting the end of history when good will ultimately triumph over evil and good people will be rewarded for their sufferings.

It is in response to this that Iqbal denies the idea of an awaited saviour and suggests that, if what he maintains about the finality is right, no such person will ever appear. Iqbal believes that we do not follow the magian model in Islam and are not awaiting a final saviour; that the finality of Muhammad's prophethood brought an end to the appearance of divine reformers; and that no other person with a prophet's stature is ever to appear again to initiate reforms backed by a divine mandate and prophetic authority. It goes without saying that accepting these claims is difficult within Shi'ism, since Shi'is do believe that there is to be a final saviour similar in standing to prophets and with the same mode of behaviour. This is why parts of the fifth chapter of Iqbal's book do not appear in the Persian translation.

and people are now mature enough to determine their own destiny by building on the legacies of the past.

All these points appear in the fifth chapter of Iqbal's important book, *The Reconstruction of Religious Thought in Islam*. In the sixth chapter, entitled "The Principle of Movement in the Structure of Islam", he discusses Islam's capacity to adapt, exhibit flexibility, assimilate and dynamism, and emphasises, in particular, *ijtihad* (independent legal reasoning) as the principal method of renewal and reform. He lists anti-rationalism, Sufism, the Tartar invasion and the fall of the Baghdad caliphate as the causes of the decline of Islamic jurisprudence [*fiqh*], and presents examples of *ijtihad* and ways of dispelling rigidity and reconciling the eternal with change. He mentions *inter alia* the following assessment by Shah Wali Allah of Delhi.[6]

By way of explaining the method and rationale underlying the original ordination of the precepts of *fiqh* and presenting the groundwork for subsequent *ijtihad*, Shah Wali Allah says in *Hujjat Allah al-Balighah* that the Prophet, in his capacity as the founder of a universal religion, could neither grant different peoples the right to legislate laws for themselves, nor legislate different laws for different peoples himself. What he could do was to train a people in a particular way and then call on his followers everywhere else in the world, from any provenance, to consider this people, with its laws and values, as their model. He could tell them: let the precepts of this people serve as a measure for you in deciding what you should do in your own lives and in finding solutions to the problems and dilemmas that you encounter. What Shah Wali Allah is saying here in effect is that the Prophet's words and deeds among his own people was simply intended to serve as model; it was not as if everyone, everywhere was expected to behave in exactly the same way, for ever more. They must be seen and taken as concrete

---

[6] Shah Wali Allah of Delhi was a great Sunni scholar and a master of the Path, who lived in India in the eighteenth century. His book, *Hujjat Allah al-Baligha*, is a major work of Islamic theology. By his own account, Imam Hasan and Imam Hossein [the Prophet's grandsons and the second and third Imams for the hiʿ is] came to him in a dream and presented a pen to him as a token of their grandfather's pen. And Shah Wali Allah was thus inspired to write his book. It is dedicated in the main to the philosophy of Islamic precepts and is an outstanding work of its kind. No other book had been written until then that could bear comparison with it in terms of approach and content. Muhammad Iqbal made extensive use of this great Indian scholar's ideas. (For more on his ideas see "Essentials and Accidentals in Religion" in this volume).

cases of general principles. Different peoples must seek and find the applications of general principles as appropriate for them.

Iqbal subscribes to this view as far as *ijtihad* in secondary rulings (*forou*) is concerned. Nonetheless, he considers formal uniformity within the Islamic nation as a *prima facie* good and believes that no precept (rules and values) should be touched unless absolutely necessary;[7] then and only then does *ijtihad* come into play, whereupon it can proceed on the basis of the assumption that the Prophet's *Sunna* simply serves as a model and nothing more. And this explains how the finality of prophethood leaves us with a religion that has no problem or quarrel with rationality and can adjust to new conditions.

It is worth mentioning that Iqbal's interpretation of the idea of the finality of prophethood is akin to the theory of "the end of history".[8] He believes that the prophetic saying: "no other prophet" amounts to "no other people"; that is to say, no other nation will succeed the Islamic nation; just as Muhammad was the Seal of the Prophets, so, we are to be the seal of nations.

It may be useful for us to look at Motahhari's views now and to assess his critique of Iqbal on this subject. Motahhari first addressed the issue of the finality of Muhammad's prophethood in 1968 in a series of lecturers delivered at the Hosseinieh Ershad cultural-religious centre and then in an article published in the same year in *Muhammad: The Seal of the Prophets*. In the article, which includes the condensed essence of his lectures, he speaks with admiration of Iqbal's approach and, quoting a long section from his work, describes it as a "charming passage".[9] Motahhari's analysis in the article is clearly influenced by Iqbal and, even when he does not refer to him by name, Iqbal's fingerprints are clearly there.

Ten years later saw the publication of two books by Motahhari: *Islamic Movements Over the Past Hundred Years* and *Revelation and*

---

[7] "…The immutability of socially harmless rules relating to eating and drinking, purity or impurity, has a life-value of its own." (See *The Reconstruction of Religious Thought in Islam*, Chapter 6).

[8] "The End of History" is the name of an article and a book by Francis Fukuyama that attracted much attention in the 1990s, especially in the West. The author uses the ideas of Hegel (and Alexandre Kojève's interpretation of those ideas) to show that liberal democracy is history's last stop and port of call and that humanity will not witness any subsequent political system.

[9] *Muhammad: Khatam Payambaran* (*Muhammad: The Seal of the Prophets*) (collection of articles), Vol. 1, the article "End of Prophethood" by Mortaza Motahhari, Hosseinieh Ershad Publications, Tehran, 1347, p. 533.

Prophethood: An Introduction to the Islamic World View (vol. 3), both of which contain criticisms of and even slurs against Muhammad Iqbal, with the harshest criticism reserved for his views on the finality. In these two works, Iqbal is accused of being a westernised thinker and of not knowing much about Islamic philosophy. His theory on the cessation of prophethood is said to lead to the cessation of religiosity. He is said to be of even a lower rank compared to Sayyed Jamal al-din Afghani. And even his "charming passage" is now described as flawed and wrongheaded. We will assess Motahhari's own views on the finality of Muhammad's prophethood below.[10]

Motahhari's own analysis (on the causes of the finality, a post hoc explanation) is that, under the Seal of the Prophets, people reached such a level of mental and social growth and maturity that:

a. They could preserve their scripture intact.
b. They could receive once and for all the full programme for their gradual move towards perfection.
c. They could take responsibility for propagating, promoting and practising religion and fulfilling the duty of enjoining virtue and inhibiting vice.
d. They were, moreover, capable of *ijtihad* now and could extract secondary principles from first principles henceforward.

These capabilities and this level of maturity meant that there was no further need for prophetic missions. And so the era of prophethood came to an end and the book of prophethood was sealed by and in the name of the Prophet of Islam.

The above points can be described as the dispositional aspect of the analysis. In other words, people had developed dispositions and capacities that made the cessation of prophethood possible and necessary (or

[10] As to this new confrontational approach and the about turn in his attitude towards Iqbal, it has to be said that Motahhari's feuds with Shariati and his growing mistrust of non-clerical religious intellectuals in the wake of these feuds, as well as the emergence of the anti-clerical brigade and the "Furqan" group and so on, were not without effect on Motahhari's about turn, lending a particular edge and anger to his words, especially in his book, *Islamic Movements Over the Past Hundred Years.*
[Furqan was a very radical and anti-clerical militant organization emerged after the 1979 Revolution tht took responsibility for assassination of some leading figures of the Islamic Republic regime. It is said that Motahhari himself was finally assassinated by the Furqan.] [Ed.]

made the continuation of prophethood superfluous and unnecessary). But the analysis has a causal efficient (*janbeh-e fa'ili*) aspect as well. That is to say, Muhammad, as the Seal of the Prophets, had a particular personal characteristic that rendered him worthy of being the last: it was that he had scaled all the necessary and possible stations of vision and revelation, such that there was nothing left to be unveiled. Motahhari supports his case with the words of mystics[11] who say: "The Seal is he who has progressed through every station and left no higher station to scale." Motahhari then criticises Iqbal's analysis and verdict, saying:

> His philosophy on the finality of prophethood entails not only an end to the need for further revelations and prophetic missions but an end to any need for guidance by revelation; in fact, it is religiosity that comes to an end, not prophethood.[12]

> It is as if human beings have graduated from the school of prophets and received their diploma, and can henceforth continue their studies by undertaking independent research. In other words, he is suggesting that: The cessation of prophethood means that human beings have attained self-sufficiency.[13]

The post hoc nature of both Iqbal and Motahhari's explanations are already very clear. They both take as read the principle of the finality and then say that humanity must have reached a point that made it possible and necessary, otherwise prophethood would not have ceased. This kind of explanation has absolutely no predictive power. In other words, were it not for the verses of the Qur'an and the words of the Prophet, no one could have said for certain that, since life and humanity have reached a particular point, prophethood must cease and it cannot but do otherwise!

At any rate, with all due respect to a thinker of Motahhari's stature, we have to say that he has not been entirely successful in comprehending and evaluating Iqbal's analysis and has done it injustice. Motahhari's own analysis of the finality is patently needs-based and teleological. That is to say, he seeks to show that, after the last prophet, humanbeings were no longer in need of any prophet. Human beings are portrayed as

---

[11] Mortaza Motahhari, *Vahy va Nabuvat* [*Revelation and Prophethood*] (Qum:Sadra, 1357/1979), see the chapter entitled "Khatm-e Nabuvat" [End of Prophethood], pp. 47–67. See also his article, "Khatm-e Nabuvat" [End of Prophethood] in *Muhammad: Khatam-e Payambaran* [*Muhammad, the Seal of the Prophets*], (Tehran: Hosseinieh Ershad, *1347/1969*), pp. 507–568.

[12] Mortaza Motahhari, *Vahy va Nabuvat*, p. 59.

[13] Ibid.

mature students, who respected the lecturer and did not tear up their lecture notes. They were capable of deducing a hundred new lessons from every lesson. And they had reached a level of mental and social maturity and growth that sufficed for preserving and practising religion, grasping first principles and deriving secondary principles. Even when Motahhari embarks on criticism of Iqbal, he imagines that Iqbal is saying "the cessation of prophethood means that human beings have attained self-sufficiency". Hence, Iqbal's remarks, too, are understood and interpreted in a needs-based or purpose-based way.

A careful look at Iqbal's discussion makes it clear, however, that he was not concerned about needs at all. There is no trace in his treatment of the subject of any intention to prove or disprove a need for revelation and religiosity; nor does it follow as an unintended consequence of his approach. His analysis—quite apart from its correctness or incorrectness—hangs on the idea that, since nature and history were no longer fertile for prophets, prophethood inevitably and naturally ceased. This is why, in our presentation of his views, we used the expression "prophet-fertile", although this particular term is not actually used in his book. Iqbal is saying that the emergence of prophets is only possible in eras when the passions hold sway and when critical, inductive reasoning is not bold and nimble. This is the terrain that allows the emergence of religious experiences, spiritual discoveries and deep inward reflection, and the rise of contemplatives and divine prophets. It is in this soil that a hundred flowers grow and a hundred springs bubble forth in every corner and at every point in the world of humanity. And it is amid these flowers and springs that one or more saplings, stronger, taller and more bountiful than the rest, catch people's eyes, steal people's hearts and become recognised as the apostles of God. Just as, when the study of *fiqh* and philosophy is flourishing, over the centuries and from the ranks of hundreds of philosophers and jurists, several great jurists and philosophers emerge. Or when poetry and music are prevalent and in public favour, great musicians and poets are born. It is not a question here of what these philosophers are needed for or what purpose they are meant to serve (a needs-based, teleological analysis). It is a question of what must occur and what preliminaries must obtain before the emergence of great philosophers becomes likely or possible (or unlikely and impossible) (a causal analysis in terms of favourable conditions).

It is clear that Iqbal's analysis is Kantian in nature. He is trying to shed light on the circumstances in which a human experience becomes possible (or impossible). This is very different from Motahhari's

approach, which seeks to answer the question: would the emergence of
other prophets after Muhammad have served any purpose? And this is
why Iqbal, unlike Motahhari, makes no mention of how scriptures had
been tampered with in the past and of how the Qur'an had not been
tampered with and so on. He does not see these things as relevant to
the analysis of the finality of Muhammad's prophethood.

It goes without saying that Iqbal's cause-oriented approach does not
in any way belie God's will, accord or wisdom or imply that the sapling
of prophethood grew by its own design in the orchard of nature and
history. His analysis does not suggest anything more than that—in view
of the fact that it takes place in the natural world—the emergence of
prophets is a natural phenomenon and, hence, temporal and material.
And there is hardly any need to underline and reiterate the fact that
Iqbal does not claim a complete break with essoteric experiences and
the total displacement of passion by reason; he deems this neither possible, nor desirable. All he says is that:

> The intellectual value of the idea [of finality] is that it tends to create an
> independent critical attitude towards mystic experience by generating the
> belief that all personal authority, claiming a supernatural origin, has come
> to an end in the history of man. This kind of belief is a psychological
> force which inhibits the growth of such an authority.[14]

In other words, it is again a question of the drying up of the springs
that irrigated these saplings.

As to the hurtful suggestion that Iqbal's philosophical thinking is
essentially western: of course, Iqbal was familiar with western philosophy; especially with the ideas of Kant, Hegel, Bergson, Nietzsche and
so on. And he sought their assistance in solving philosophical problems. But to what extent is Motahhari's criticism really merited? In his
Reconstruction of Religious Thought in Islam, Iqbal is actually trying to
extricate Islamic thought from the grip of Greek philosophy. He in fact
complains that, for centuries, Muslims have been viewing the Qur'an
from a Greek perspective. Is Motahhari himself not guilty of this? Is
his philosophy purely Islamic? Or is what is conventionally known as
Islamic philosophy not basically Greek (that is to say, western again)
in structure, essence and spirit? It would seem that, just as Motahhari
did not achieve an accurate understanding of the depth and substance

---

[14] Iqbal, *The Reconstruction of Religious Thought*, p. 127.

of Iqbal's analysis, he is off the mark in his criticism as well. The same can be said of his views of Islamic philosophy and his high estimation of it. If we were to consult great mystics like Jalal al-Din Rumi, Attar and al-Ghazali, they would no doubt tell us that what is known as Islamic philosophy has done Islam more harm than good.[15] Would it not be better, then, to deal directly with the arguments and claims rather than to haggle over the negative and derogatory labels we intend to pin on one another? Iqbal's familiarity with Rumi was by no means less than his familiarity with western philosophers. Hence, if he had a philosophy, it was a composite of eastern and western thought.

The Relation of Finality to the Prophet's Persona

The next important point is that being the last and the Seal relates to the Prophet's *personne juridique (shakhsiyyat-e huquqi)*, not his *personne physique (shakhsiyyat-e haqiqi)*. This makes it imperative for us to know how his *personne juridique* is defined. We need to ask, in other words: now that the principle of the finality is assumed and now that it is an attribute of prophethood and not religion, to what aspect of the Prophet's personality does the finality belong?

The first characteristic of "a prophet" is that he is instructed through the channel of revelation and is in contact with the realm of transcendence or immanence. The other characteristic of a prophet is that he knows things that are hidden. In fact, prophets not only know hidden things, but they also keep this knowledge hidden. In this sense, their lives are extremely difficult and paradoxical. They see things and know things, but they behave as if they do not see and do not know. Living one's entire life in these circumstances demands great endurance

---

[15] Motahhari's assessment of Western philosophy also seems totally unjustified. If we give Motahhari 100 out of 100 for his grasp of Islamic philosophy, we can hardly give him more than 10 in Western philosophy. Motahhari's works give a clear indication of his poor grasp of modern philosophy and, especially, analytical philosophy. A glance at his approach to induction, for example, which is so highly-regarded in Islamic philosophy and which is of such complexity and approached with such caution in modern philosophy shows the scale of the problem.

indeed. Intellectuals and mystics are in a position similar to prophets
in this respect.[16]

Apart from these characteristics, prophets are also revolutionary,
brave, impudent (in Rumi's understanding of the word), kind and
gracious, tranquil and comforting, arbitrators and admonishers, bring-
ers of glad tidings and so on. All these qualities pertain to prophets'
personnes physiques and to their visible behaviour. Prophets also have
a particular way of speaking and expressing themselves that is distinct
in one way: it alerts us to the their *personnes juridiques* and brings us
closer to it.

As a breed, prophets speak imperiously. They speak from a position
of superiority and, generally, do not present any reasons or corroborative arguments for what they are saying. Their manner of expression is
very different from that of other people in this respect. Have a look at
the Qur'an (and any other holy book). You will rarely find any reasoning in it. The language is not the language of theologians, philosophers
and/or sociologists. Reasoning demands that you invite the other party
to present their counter-arguments, leaving the final verdict to a third
party. But speaking like a prophet and from a position of superiority is
very different from this. In this sense, prophets do not conduct conversa-
tions or discussions with us. "Heed me or not," is more their manner.
As we read repeatedly in the Qur'an: "The Messenger's duty is only to
convey the message."[17] This is the refrain and condensed essence of their
mode of speech. Even when they say, "bring me your proof",[18] they
never wait for anyone to present any counter-arguments. They assume
in advance that their words are irrefutable. After all, "the counter-argu-
ment has been refuted by God". This brings us closer to the defining
constituent of a prophet's *personne juridique*, namely, the element of
guardianship. "Guardianship" means that the speaker's personality *is*
his proof and argument. This is precisely the thing that has ceased with
the cessation of prophethood. We do not accept anyone's words now
unless they give us reasons or appeal to a law. But this was not the
case with prophets. *"They"* themselves by virtue of their personality as
prophets were the backing for their words and commands. They were

---

[16] This idea has been explained at length in the article "Intellectuals and Knowledge"
in Abdulkarim Soroush, *Razdani va Rowshanfekri va Dindari* [Knowledge, Intellectuals
and Religiosity] (Tehran: Serat, 1377/1998).

[17] See for instance, Qur'an, 24: 54 or 29: 18.

[18] See for instance, Qur'an, 2: 111; 21: 24; 27: 64.

their own proof. As it were, what a prophet says is: "I am the law, I am the proof, I am the backing for what I am saying". And this effectively marked the beginning of prophetic legal missions, the essential core of which is legislative guardianship. This was why prophets viewed their own experiences as binding on others and believed that they had the right to make decisions that affected other people's honour, life and property. One might say that their religious experience was "transitive", not "intransitive"; it had implications for others as well.

This points to one significant difference between prophetic experiences and mystical experiences. Religious experience can embrace a multitude of things: it can mean "ascension" for some, it can entail subtle spiritual revelations, it can involve the sight of heaven and angels, it can consist of hidden communications with God, and so on and so forth. These are all mystical experiences and they are all "intransitive". But prophets' experiences surpass all of these things. They are "transitive" experiences that create duties and dictate action.

This is in effect the "legislative guardianship" that forms the essential core of prophethood in its legal aspect. As a guardian deriving his authority from God, a prophet constitutes all the proof and force that is necessary to back his own discourse and commands. And it has to be said that considering one's personal experiences as binding on others and viewing this as an adequate basis for making decisions that affect people's lives, property, beliefs, welfare and felicity is a heavy burden to carry and demands tremendous courage. This lies at the heart of prophethood and it is prophethood in this sense that has come to an end. No one will ever appear after the Prophet of Islam whose personality as a prohphet can serve as adequate backing for their words and deeds and impose religious duties on others. But, of course, the possibility of having religious experiences and knowing hidden things has by no means come to an end and the world continues to host saints (*awliya Allah*/ friends of God). I read in a newspaper once that a naive cleric had said: "If I feel a sense of duty, I will malign others." Talking like this indicates delusions of prophethood and demonstrates that the speaker does not believe that the Prophet of Islam was the last prophet. How can anyone say, he must be maligned because I am certain that I am right and feel it necessary to malign him? This amounts to imagining oneself a prophet, pure and simple.

After the Prophet, no one's feelings, experiences or certitudes are religiously binding on others, nor do they constitute the last word. Anyone who wishes to issue a religious judgement that is binding on others must present generally accepted rational or legal arguments, objective evidence, etc. It is inconceivable now of saying that the backing for my judgement is my own self, my experience, my links with the transcendental, my visions, my miraculous powers, my certitude, etc. Here, reasons, laws and evidence are all objective and "collective" affairs. None of them is personal or personality-dependent. The era of personals and particular "personalities" has ended. We must henceforth base ourselves on collectives and universals. Nor can the interpretation of the words of God and the Prophet be personal or personality-dependent. It, too, must be collective and reasoned. An official interpretation is therefore also ruled out and unacceptable.

Hence the fact that Muhammad is the last prophet conveys the following notions in brief:

First notion: The Prophet of Islam will not be succeeded by any other prophet.

Second notion: Islam will not be succeeded by any new religion.

Third notion: History is no longer prophet-fertile and the favourable conditions for the emergence of a prophet no longer obtain.

Fourth notion, which is implied by the first is that: no one is allowed to behave like a prophet any longer. This is the idea that we have just been speaking about. Many people are apparent disciples of the last prophet, but when their baser instincts get the better of them, they start behaving like prophets. Behaving like a prophet means acting merely out of a personal sense of religious duty and considering one's own judgements to be binding on others without any reference to reasoning or laws or objective evidence. This amounts to prophethood and the era of prophethood has come to an end. This is precisely the guardianship that disappeared forever with the demise of the Prophet and was definitively sealed. Moreover, no religious discourse or text can be interpreted in such a way as to grant anyone the right of guardianship in this sense. It is a patent absurdity to suggest that the Seal of the Prophets granted a right to others that would have negated his own position as the Seal.

In brief, we said that the finality and the Seal pertains to the Prophet's *personne juridique* (in other words, his legislative guardianship). This means that it would not have been necessary for or incumbent on the Prophet to provide arguments or evidence or principles in support of what he said. Consequently, the language of religion is the language of guardianship, not the language of reasoning. And this applies to both descriptive and prescriptive affairs. The reason for this is that the presentation of supporting arguments and principles severs the link between one's discourse and revelation, such that the discourse is judged on the merits of the argumentation. For example, it has been said in the *Nahj al-Balaghah* that women have inferior shares (of inheritance), inferior faith and inferior intellects.[19] Reasons have been adduced for these claims and conclusions drawn. What is being suggested here is that, when a discourse includes reasons, the link between the words and the speaker or his personality is severed. All that is left is us and the reasons. If the reasons are convincing, we accept the claim and if they are not, we do not accept it. It makes no difference any more whether the claimant was Imam Ali or anyone else. The discourse is based on the reasoning, not on the venerable speaker. It is inappropriate to say, accept these reasons because they were given by this or that person. A reason's power must lie within itself, not elsewhere. In other words, a reason becomes a curtain between the discourse and the speaker.

By way of another example, the Qur'an presents a reason for the oneness of Almighty God (and this is one of the rare instances of supporting arguments in the Qur'an). It says: "If there were, in the heavens and the earth, other gods besides God, there would have been confusion in both." (21: 22) And since the world has not gone to wrack and ruin, it shows that there is a single master and a single God. It is clear that no one can say, accept this reason because the Qur'an or the Prophet said it. They have to show that the reason itself is adequate and sound. Specialists use this kind of discourse and reasoning; prophets rarely did. They spoke or issued commands on the strength of their personalities and personal experiences. This was dictated by their elevated position. And this is what has ceased now and is never to be repeated.

Let me note here that, when we say the discourse of prophets did not include reasoning, this does not mean that their words were not amenable to reasoning. It means that they themselves did not rely on reasoning to proclaim and convey their message. It was the theologians who subsequently anchored the words of God and the prophets in reasoning. And this is what severed the link between the discourse and revelation. This is also why some people claimed that the disci-

---

[19] Ali Ibn Abi Talib, *Nahj al-Balaghah*, ed. By Feiz al-Islam, Sermon # 80.

pline of theology robs us of religious inspiration. Theologians were not
betraying religion; they were pouring the Prophet's pronouncements
into the mould of rationality and reason. But bear in mind how great
the distance is between this point and that: at one end, we accept the
words because of who the speaker is; at the other end, we accept the
same words because of what the reason is.

Theologians supplied justifications for the Prophet's words. That
is to say, they constructed a rational, human system independent of
revelation which then became a curtain between the message and the
speaker. This was the point at which some mystics instinctively sensed
that theologians were distancing us from the Prophet and moving God
out of our reach. In effect, theologians made religion human. They
severed the link with the personal of the speaker and the receptacle of
revelation. And this is both the cause and the effect of the cessation
of prophethood and the entry of human beings into the arena of the
comprehension and affirmation of religion. Theologians rendered a
service to religion because they turned an unreasoned discourse into a
reasoned discourse and supplied it with rational backing. Nonetheless,
this service had unintended consequences. For example, the discourse
no longer carried the sense and spirit of hailing from a divine guardian.
It cast a shadow over the Prophet's personality, brought the discourse
down to the level of the human mind and locked it into the vice grip
of whys and wherefores.

In sum, the Prophet of Islam was the last prophet, his religion was the
last religion, he was the last person to assume the persona of a prophet's
personne juridique, his era was the last prophet-fertile era and history
will never witness the appropriate fertile conditions again. And, above
all, the Prophet himself constituted the backing for what he said. It is in
this sense that we believe in the finality of Muhammad's prophethood
and embark on independent reasoning (legal or otherwise) within his
religion. We seek assistance from our minds, rationality and reasoning
and the objective evidence at our disposal in order to see his religion
in rational terms. At the same time, we view him as the God's saint
(*wali-e haqq*), place our absolute trust in his apostolic personality and
accept things from him that we would not be prepared to accept from
anyone else other than on the basis of evidence, reasons and laws. We
do not view our personal religious experiences as binding on others,
nor do we consider anyone's personal certitude and sense of duty to
impose duties on anyone else. In this sense, we believe that prophethood and guardianship have come to an end. From now on, everyone

is equal and superiority is only to be sought in piety and rationality. When Iqbal said, "With the onset of rationality, the era of prophethood came to an end," he did not intend to suggest any opposition between rationality and prophethood. What he meant was that the era of personal guardianship has come to an end and that collective rationality will henceforth serve as the collective sovereign, guardian and guiding light for us all.

CHAPTER THREE

THE LAST PROPHET—2

We said that, with the demise of the Prophet, peace be upon him, the book of prophethood was sealed and no prophet is ever to appear again for all eternity. We explored the meaning of the finality of Muhammad's prophethood and explained that, although there are and will continue to be people who are capable of receiving hidden communications and secrets, and to whom God speaks and whispers in the depth of their minds,[1] the difference between these saints of God (*awliya Allah*) and prophets is that prophets have a mission; they have no proof of their mission other than their personality and experience; and they speak to people, issue commands and impose duties on them by the sheer force of their personality. In this sense, they have a different way of operating from philosophers, theologians and thinkers. Thinkers rely on rational justifications and experiences to substantiate their claims and, in so doing, they leave the way open to criticism by others who can, in turn, present alternative rational justifications and experiences. Otherwise, reasoning would become totally pointless; reasoning is always a collective affair and everyone can participate in accepting or rejecting the arguments. But, because of the certitude produced by their religious experiences, prophets believe that what they are saying is the truth; that everyone is duty-bound to accept their words and their commands and to act upon them; and that they have the right to take decisions that affect other people's lives and property.

End of Religious Legislation or End of Religious Experience?

This aspect of prophethood—that is, the fact that one person's religious experience is binding on others, which amounts to the legislative

---

[1] This idea is taken from Imam Ali's words about the *awliya Allah*: "From time to time, in the intervals between prophetic missions, there are servants of God, in the depth of whose minds and thoughts He speaks and whispers." (*Nahj al-Balaghah*, Sermon 220)

guardianship, *wilayat-e tashri'i*—came to an end with the demise of the Prophet of Islam and no one will have duties, rights and experiences of this kind again. Hence, anyone who comes after the Prophet acts within the sphere of his prophethood, their duties flow from his duties and the authority behind their words is validated by his authority, so long as it does not conflict with the substance and logic of the finality. After the prophet, no one's religious conviction, certainty, experience and understanding is on a par with his religious conviction, certainty, experience and understanding or has the same impact. As Muhammad Iqbal puts it in a poem, from now on it falls to us to "serve the wine", whereas the cask is forever his.[2] And, again, in his wise words, we are the freest people on earth because we believe in the finality. Being free is not to say that, with the departure of the Prophet, the age of religion and divine messages has come to an end; it means that we are not dependent on any personality any more. We demand reasons from everyone, our collective reason is the arbiter over everyone and everything, and no one can bind us to a ruling merely on the strength of their own religious experience. This file has been closed forever. From now on, within the framework of religious thinking, a person may be punished or rewarded on the basis of a ruling of *fiqh*, but no one's personal experience or sense of duty can sanction a general law or the censure of any other individual. This falls solely within the purview of a prophet's rights and duties; no one else has or could possibly have such a duty. This is why reason wins outmost freedom with the cessation of prophethood, such that no one's personality can dim the logic of reasoning, experience and the law.

"Being free" means the freedom of the mind from factors that are beyond or beneath it. As a phenomenon that is beyond the mind, prophethood, with its messages and duties, comes to free human beings from all that is base and beneath the mind. Then, with its own cessation, it also does away with all that is beyond the mind and unties the cradle of rationality at both ends, releasing the infant reason—which is now mature and bold—so that it can rise up onto its own feet, stand, walk, run and fly.

The corollary of all this is that, after the Prophet of Islam, no preacher will ever appear; those who are prophets but whose mission is to explain and promote a predecessor's religion rather than to propagate a new

---

[2] Muhammad Iqbal, *Secrets of the Self*.

religion. There have been many such prophets in the past. There was Lot, who followed Abraham, and Joshua, who followed Moses. The following Qur'anic verse clearly substantiates this:

> Surely We sent down the Torah, wherein is guidance and light; thereby the prophets who had surrendered themselves gave judgement for those of Jewry... (5: 44)

But, in Islam and after the Prophet of Islam, the ulema take on this role and, since there is to be no prophet after the Prophet, none of them ever lays claim to prophethood or has the rank, authority and mission of a prophet (even prophets with no new law). And the experiences of mystics are solely for their own theoretical and practical benefit, most certainly not binding on others, and liable to criticism and improvement like any other human product.

This is all to say that no other *personne juridique* with the same impact as that of the Prophet, and no other guardian entrusted with legislative guardianship will ever appear after the Prophet of Islam in view of the principle of finality and the unanimous consensus of Muslims. (This does not apply to *personnes physiques* and the saints, as I have repeatedly said.) This emphatic statements highlights the following question: in this context, what is the role and status of the Shi'i Imams in the propagation and explanation of Islamic precepts and teachings? If we want to ensure that we do not perceive an Imam's status and standing and the extent to which his experiences and words are binding in a manner that would violate the principle of finality,[3] then how should we define his *personne juridique* (quite apart from his *personne physique* and spiritual inward guardianship)? The position of a jurist? An infallible jurist? A spiritual thinker? A chief? An inheritor of the Prophet's knowledge?

Motahhari, too, grappled with these questions. And he arrived at the following answer:

---

[3] In his *al-Tafhimat al-ilahiyah* (Vol. 2, p. 344), Shah Wali Allah of Delhi says that Shi'is' belief in the Infallible Imams of the Household of the Prophet leads to the violation and negation of the finality of Muhammad's prophethood because "they are deemed to be infallible, subject to obedience and in the possession of inner revelation, and this is not very different from prophethood". This is the same Shah Wali Allah who writes elsewhere in the same book that he saw the spirit of the Imams, in the most beautiful form and the most perfect aspect, in a personal mystical experience, and realised that anyone who repudiates them or casts aspersions on them is in grave danger. (*al-Tafhimat al-ilahiyah*, Vol. 1, p. 142)

If, after the cessation, there is no need for a prophet—that is, a person who is inspired, spoken to and backed by God—such that *faqih*s and religious thinkers and scholars can carry out the task of propagating religion...then what need is there for Imams and what can the justification for their presence be from the Shiʻi perspective? This is a very good question...The difference between the Prophet and an Imam does not only lie in the quality of the acquisition of knowledge from the hidden world. Much more importantly, there are also differences in their duties...An Imam does not bring a religion or any laws, nor does he, in being an Imam...have a duty to go to the people, to call them to religion or to propagate religion...What then is an Imam's duty? An Imam is a final authority for the settlement of disputes. He can have the last word in the settlement of the disputes that arise among the ulema themselves....[4]

Muhammad Hossein Tabatabaʼi also believed that the words of Shiʻi Imams carried no independent authority and that the authority of their words was subject to and "dependent on the authority of the words of the noble Prophet".[5] He confined himself to this and did not elaborate on whether an Imam's independent religious understanding and experience had any authoritative force. The authoritative nature of one's understanding of the Qurʼan and the Prophet's discourse is one thing, the authoritative nature of one's achievements independent of the Qurʼan and the Prophet's discourse is another.

The fact that Shiʻis do not consider people who disbelieve in the Imams and disregard their words to be infidels or non-Muslim clearly indicates that the words and experiences of these revered figures are not on a par with the words and experiences of the Prophet, and are not part and parcel of the indisputable components of faith; otherwise this denial, just like the denial of the Prophet, would lead to infidelity and apostasy. What is essential to Islam is the personality of the Prophet, his inner experiences and the dos and don'ts that arose therefrom; experiences that came to an end with his demise, such that anything that occurs thereafter must be interpreted in a way that will not conflict with the firm and immutable principle of finality. And many have been the exaggerators; both those who have raised the *awliya* to the level of God and those who have placed them on a par with the Prophet.

At any rate, it is very important to distinguish between the *personne physique* (*shakhsiyyat-e haqiqi*), on the one hand, and the author-

---

[4] Motahhari, *Khatamiyat*, pp. 50–53.
[5] Muhammad Hossein Tabatabaʼi, *Maktab-e Tashayu* [Shiʻism] (Qum: Dar al-Tabliqh Islami, 1339/1960), p. 77.

ity, mission and legislative guardianship of the *personne juridique* (*shakhsiyyat-e huquqi*), on the other. Individual personalities are not the bearers of religious authority unless they have been bequeathed a mission. There are and have been many divine mystics and thinkers who—their distinguished personalities notwithstanding—are not the bearers of any mission or guardianship. They assist the expansion and evolution of the Prophet's experience, without expanding the scope of his legislative guardianship.

Through their belief in the Imams of the Household of the Prophet, Shi'is have laudably embraced the fine point that the door has not been closed to valid and independent religious experiences, even after the Prophet's demise, and that countless saints may appear and enrich religion with their experiences and discoveries.[6] These saints (*awliya*) may even be of greater stature than some of the prophets (*nabis*) who have preceded them. Nonetheless, this expansion pertains to their *personnes physiques* and cannot, in view of the principle of finality, be extended to their *personnes juridiques*. In Islam, we have no one other than the Prophet, the denial of whose mission and *personnes juridiques* amounts to infidelity.

We took note of Tabataba'i's succinct comment in this connection. Let us now look at the views of the mystic Muhyi al-Din Ibn Arabi—who was himself a claimant of the finality of Muhammadan guardianship (*khatam-e wilayat-e Muhammadiyeh-*) on the difference between a prophet and a *wali* and the scope of a *wali*'s guardianship. He devoted considerable time and space to this subject, for example in the *al-Futuhat al-Makkiyah* (the Meccan Illuminations)., which includes his most extensive and generous mystical-instructive writings. He wrote:

> The *wali*'s vision (*kashf*) does not surpass the contents of the Prophet's Book and revelation. Junayd said that our knowledge is bound by the Book and the *Sunna* and another said, any discovery that is not under-written by the Book and the *Sunna* is false. Hence, the *wali* will not arrive at any discovery that is not of the nature of an understanding of God's scripture…Hence, the *wali* will never utter a precept that violates the precepts of religious law. Nonetheless, on occasion, the inspiration comes to him to place a number of components alongside one another to form an aggregate that was not to be found in religious law, although all the individual components were to be found therein…This level of

---

[6] For more on this point see the first chapter, "The Expansion of Prophetic Experience", in this volume.

law making is permissible for an *wali*…and, if you were to ask specifically where in religion God has granted this right to *awliya* the answer lies in the Prophet's words when he said, if anyone establishes a worthy tradition, he shall be rewarded for it, as will anyone who abides by it until Judgement Day…This is a *wali*'s share of prophethood and it forms a component of prophethood, just as true visions are components of prophethood.[7]

His remarks to the effect that prophethood (*nubuwwat*) is subject to cessation whereas guardianship (*wilayat*) is not are also worth noting. In accordance with his own rubric, he says that *wali* "guardian" is one of the attributes of God and is, therefore, ever present in the form of divinely-appointed guardians, otherwise known as *awliya*; whereas prophethood is not one of His attributes and can therefore cease:

Among the stations of guardianship (*wilayat*) are prophethood (*nubuwwat*) and messengership (*resalat*) of God, which are attained by some people and not attained by others. Nonetheless, no one today may attain the station of legislative prophethood because this door has been closed. But guardianship will never cease to exist in this world or the next…And one of the attributes of God is "the Guardian". But prophet or messenger are not among his attributes; hence, there will be no more prophets or messengers, for they have no roots in the attributes of God. But guardianship has not ceased because God preserves the attribute.[8]

And Imam Ali has the last word on the subject when he is asked:

Are you in the possession of anything from the Prophet's revelation other than the Qur'an? He said: By the God who breaks the seed and creates man, no, there is nothing else; however, on occasion, God grants one of his servants a special understanding of His Book.[9]

But the other important point that needs to be underlined and reiterated is that the concept of the finality is an intra-religious claim, not an extra-religious one. In other words, arguments based on reason and experience cannot prove the necessity of the finality of Muhammad's prophethood; just as the completeness of the religion of Islam cannot be proven on this basis. All that a Muslim theologian can do is to assume the claim itself without question and then to say: (a) maybe the reason

---

[7] *Futuhat Makkiyah* (Meccan Illuminations), Beirut: Sadir Publications, Part 3, Chapter 314, p. 56.
[8] Ibid., Chapter 327, p. 101.
[9] Mullah Mohsen Feiz Kashani, *Al-Safi*, fourth preface.

for this was the appearance of inductive reasoning or (b) maybe it was because people could record the scripture in writing and ensure that it was not tampered with, and many other maybes. These are all rationalisations, not demonstrations or proofs. There is, of course, one definite reason: the completeness of religion. In other words, to reason that since religion is complete, the finality is certain. This reason is fine and correct, but the initial premise is intra-religious and cannot be proven by philosophical or empirical reasoning. Thousands upon thousands of Muslims over the past centuries have believed in the finality without any rational explanation. And the proffered rationalisations are always open to dispute. As to (a), the phenomenon of inductive reasoning, it has practically begun to shine since the Renaissance. Of course, this is not to suggest that inductive reasoning was absolutely absent in the pre-modern time. As to (b), there have been Muslims who have held that the scripture *has* been tampered with. Apart from the scripture, no Muslim is in any doubt that distortions and falsifications have crept into the Prophet's *Sunna* (and the words of the Shi'i Imams). Moreover, if this argument is sound, it would seem more appropriate for the last Prophet to have appeared in the age of film, computers and fax machines so that not a single one of his words could be lost or misplaced, providing indisputable documentation of his words, deeds and pronouncements. Hence, both the maturity and reasonableness of humanity and the suggestion that religion (as combination of the Qur'an and the sunnah) has remained intact can be seriously called into question. There is, in other words, no shortage of counter-arguments against the rationalisations.

All told, although the efforts made by thinkers to shed some light on a tiny corner of the possible mysteries of the finality are laudable, nonetheless, the intellect is incapable of going any further than this. Henceforward, we must focus instead on the message and implications of the finality. Knowing and accepting that there will never be another religion or prophet, and that believers should stop gazing at the sky and expecting another saviour is very useful and liberating information. The mother of the universe cannot beget another prophet. Hence, we must be content with the existing religion (and, in the case of the pluralists, the existing religions) and stop beating on heaven's gate; for, awaiting another religion amounts to longing for the impossible and displaying reprehensible greed.

The Seal of Prophethood, Not The Seal of Interpretation

The Seal of the prophets has been and gone, but the seal of the commentators has not. No one's explanations and interpretations of revelation can be placed on a par with revelation itself. Hence, although we have a final religion, we cannot have a final understanding of religion. And, although we have a perfect religion (an intra-religious claim which is taken to be true because the Prophet is taken to be a true prophet by his followers), we do not have perfect religious knowledge. There is a great distance and difference between attesting to the fact that Islam (intrinsically and in itself) is complete and suggesting that the disciplines of *fiqh*, exegesis, ethics, etc. are all complete; just as there is a world of difference between the flawlessness of nature and the flawlessness of the sciences of nature. Any human discipline, in so far as it is human, is incomplete and impure (and possibly moving towards completion). Kant once claimed that the discipline of logic was perfect. Now, every time there is a new discovery in logic, he turns in his grave. The claim that true *shari'ah* and the true precepts of God (at the level of the in itself) are perfect/complete does not solve the problem in any way or lend any completeness to the discipline of *fiqh* (at the level of the for us). In other words, whilst true *shari'ah* might be final the discipline of *fiqh* (jurisprudence), which is the product of the endeavours of Islamic jurists and is an ongoing collective process entailing truths and falshoods, can by no means be considered final; ditto with any of the other religious disciplines.[10] After all, how can a discipline of *fiqh* that changes with any single change in the *usul al-fiqh* (the logic of jurisprudential inference) be described as complete and final? Hence, any attempt to prove the completeness of the science of *fiqh* and the completeness of the science of ethics and the completeness of philosophy, and, therefrom, to prove the completeness of religion, and, therefrom, to prove the finality of Muhammad's prophethood is futile and doomed to failure. These pretensions will lead us nowhere. The attempt that can be made (by understanding the message of the finality) is to provide a method that will lend fluidity to these religious sciences (and not just to *fiqh*), so that they can absorb both practical *and* theoretical developments

---

[10] I have explained this at length in my book: *Qabz va Bast-e Te'orik-e Shari'at* [Contraction and Expansion of Religious Knowledge].

(and not just purely practical ones), thereby ensuring that they remain vibrant and effective. Only this and nothing more.

The way to produce this fluidity is to throw open the gates of these religious disciplines to every new finding in the realm of knowledge (not just to new practical problems), thus engendering a revolution within them. Hence, the efforts that are made to prove, for example, that the existing discipline of *fiqh* is and has always been capable of answering every conceivable new legal problem are totally inappropriate. In fact, it is incredible that, in their bid to explain (and prove) the finality of Muhammad's prophethood and the perfection of religion, some of our thinkers have focused almost exclusively on the demonstration of the eternal validity of *fiqh*. As if the finality of prophethood had nothing to do with the finality of religious beliefs or ethics, and that nothing needs to be said about their capabilities, and that all the questions that arise ultimately concern the capabilities of *fiqh* alone. This is another instance of incredible and inappropriate oversight. They have first equated the reconciliation of religion and change or eternity and change with *fiqh*'s ability to solve new practical problems; then, they have single-mindedly set out to prove this ability or potential ability.

Amongst our elders and commentators, Fakhr al-din al-Razi has explained the verse "Today I have perfected your religion for you" and the idea of religion's perfection as follows:

> Those who accept the validity of analogy have said that what is meant here by religion being perfected is that God has made known His specific precepts about some actions in the Text, whereas He has made known His precepts about some others by providing us with the instrument of analogy. It is as if God has divided things into two categories: those that have a "direct" precept and those for which the precept must be derived from the first category by analogy. And since God has commanded the use of analogy and made it incumbent on believers to apply it, He has in fact made His precepts clear about all things in advance. Hence, religion is perfect/complete.[11]

Now, remove the word "analogy" (*qiyas*) from the above passage and replace it with the word "independent legal reasoning" (*ijtihad*) (which has a more general meaning and is accepted by both Shi'i and Sunni ulema) and then you will have before you the sum total of what classical and modern commentators have achieved in their attempts to

---

[11] Fakhr al-din Muhammad al-Razi, *Mafatih al-Ghayb* (Beirut: Dar al-fikr, 1978), Vol. 3, p. 358.

prove the perfection of religion. All of Motahhari's endeavours in his discussions of the finality of Muhammad's prophethood, the idea of historical determinism, the particular requirements of the time and so on ultimately amount to this: *ijtihad* can remedy every and any newly emerging sophisticated ills through deriving later particularities from earlier generalities. And herein is said to lie the explanation of the perfection of religion and the secret behind the finality.

Motahhari believed that the religious narrative stating that "what was permitted by Muhammad is permitted until Judgement Day and what was forbidden by Muhammad is forbidden until Judgement Day" is the greatest manifestation of the finality of his prophethood and the eternal validity of religion. And he believes that the most difficult doubts to resolve are those that concern the immutability of the regulations of Islamic law and the precepts of *fiqh* in a rapidly changing world and history. He writes with total conviction:

> Without a doubt, this is the most important problem confronting religions—and Islam in particular—in our age.[12]

In other words, a problem that is totally practical and totally concerned with *fiqh*. Then, he tries to demonstrate that some human needs are unchanging and, therefore, have unchanging rules and precepts, and others are changeable and *fiqh* also has solutions for these, because it is, on the one hand, based on *fitrah* (the innate nature) and on the other hand, has a vibrant dynamism, such that "It can fall into step with the changes in life and even show them the way".[13]

In Motahhari's opinion, the acceptance of the role of reason; religion's all-inclusiveness and scope; the fact that forms are not considered sacred; the existence of unchanging rules for unchanging needs and the adaptation of general principles to meet changing needs; the fact that the beneficial and social an individual interests are taken into account in legislation, as well as allowing the best consideration to supersede the better, and the most important to supersede the important; having overriding principles that have a right of "veto" such as the principle of "no harm"; the extensive powers and discretions at the disposal of an Islamic ruler and state are all features of actually existing Islamic *fiqh* that make up its vibrant dynamism and *fitrah*.

---

[12] Motahhari, "Khatm-e Nubuvat", p. 541.
[13] Ibid., p. 548.

All this is to prove that Islamic *fiqh* has precepts for all things and every state of affairs; that it will not be left behind as human civilisation surges ahead; that it will not be crushed by historical determinism; that it will not be overtaken by the requirements of the age; that new developments will not be left without precepts; and that it is possible to reconcile the movement of history and society with unchanging rules and precepts.

Several observations can be made about this approach to *fiqh* and the cessation of prophethood:

A. If we are determined to prove that the precepts of *fiqh* can include and embrace every eventuality, past, present and future, there is a much simpler way to go about it than this. Razi's pronouncement put it in a nutshell: we can have a series of first principles and decide everything else by analogy. And if there is any flaw in Razi's words, it must lie either in the *adequacy* of the first principles or the *adequacy* of method of analogy. Hence, anyone who speaks of the perfection of *fiqh* and its boundless capacity to answer any legal question that ever arises until the end of history must prove two things (at least): the richness and *adequacy* of *fiqh*'s first principles and raw material, and the *adequacy* of its methods and mechanisms for discovering and deducing new precepts. And neither of these two essential points is to be found in Motahhari's treatment of the subject. He presents no arguments to show that the deductive and theoretical methods currently used by *fiqh* are the most powerful and most comprehensive methods possible. And, in fact, it is impossible to argue such a thing. *Usul al-fiqh*, which is the most important instrument at the disposal of Islamic jurists, has, on the admission of Shi'i jurists themselves, undergone such a vast transformation since Shaykh Ansari's (d. 1864) time and at his hands as to have been inconceivable to earlier jurists like Allameh Hilli (d. 1325) and Shaykh Tusi (d. 1067) and the way remains open for further developments. How is it possible to claim eternal perfection for such a discipline in such circumstances? Unless we were to say that, when these methods are complete, *fiqh* will be complete! Thus, the adequacy of the methods and mechanisms used by *fiqh* to deduce precepts has not yet been proven and is impossible to prove. And if the instruments that are used by *fiqh* are not complete, the discipline of *fiqh* itself cannot be complete; again, unless we say that law is complete quintessentially and as it resides in the divine foreknowledge. Fine, but what we are concerned about here is the discipline of *fiqh* (science of law), that is, the knowledge possessed by Islamic jurists, not quintessential law.

As to the discipline of *fiqh*'s raw material and first principles: Motah-hari himself is one of the people who believe that the precepts of religion were not completed during the Prophet's lifetime and that the general principles of *fiqh* that were set out in his lifetime did not suffice for deducing the answers to every possible question. This was why it was necessary, according to Motahhari, for the infallible successors of the Prophet, the Imams, to appear. And the perfection of religion did not mean the perfection of the raw material in terms of the original precepts (as Fakhr al-din al-Razi maintained) but that *awliya* (saints) would subsequently appear—first and foremost amongst them Imam Ali, peace be upon him—to complete the laws.[14] (And this is effectively Tabataba'i's position in the *Tafsir al-Mizan*, in the commentary he wrote under Verse 5, Al-Ma'idah Sura.) Very well, but how can it be proven that the general principles of religion were completed with the words of the Infallible Imams and lack for nothing? Do we have any rational proof to substantiate this? Not at all. This is an intra-religious claim and it means that, since religion has said that it is complete, we accept that is complete. Only this and nothing more.

In brief, it is neither possible to prove the adequacy of the methods used to deduce precepts, nor to prove the adequacy of the raw material and first principles of *fiqh*. On the contrary, in view of the fact that the *usul al-fiqh* is subject to change and in view of the fact that science of *fiqh* needs and relies on this incomplete and changing *usul al-fiqh*, we can conclude that neither the actually science of *fiqh*, nor the science of *fiqh* at any other time is by any means complete; and that, consequently, the existing human discipline of *fiqh* is incapable of responding to every possible eventuality. In fact, the only thing that one may say is that

---

[14] "The Prophet used every possible opportunity to the full and instructed the people on many things. Nonetheless, in view of the history of Mecca and Medina and the Prophet, and his many problems and concerns, it goes without saying that he did not have enough time to tell the people about every Islamic precept. And it is impossible for such a religion to have been related incompletely. Hence, there had to be some person or persons among the Prophet's companions who learned Islam totally and fully from him and were his worthy pupils, such that they could be on a par with him—after his departure—in terms of explaining and relating Islam, with this differ-ence: that the Prophet spoke on the basis of divine revelation, whereas they spoke on the basis of what they had learned from the Prophet. Later, it is said [by Shi'i ulema] that, since you [Sunnis] did not have any such person and did not consult him, you inevitably gained an incomplete conception of Islam from the start. This is why you raised the idea of analogy..." Mortaza Motahhari, *Emamat va Rahbari* [Imamate and Leadership] (Qum: Sadra, 1364/1986), p. 93.

the *fiqh* that emerges in the future will be able to perfectly respond to every eventuality if it is perfect in every way (in theory and method)! In other words, the fiqh is complete provided it is complete!! Apart from being a tautology, this is something that can be said about any field or discipline; there is no need for all this soul-searching. Let us remind ourselves, moreover, that, according to Motahhari, an Imam is like the Ka'ba; he does not go to the people, the people must go to him to ask their questions. Now, what if they do not go and do not ask? Will this not lead to deficiencies in expounding the precepts by the Imams? No Imam ever drew up a series of generalities to meet the subsequent requirements of jurists. They only answered when they were asked. What guarantee is there that every question that needed to be asked was asked? Did the same problems that impeded the Prophet not impede the Imam's guidance and advocacy? For example, if no one had asked about loan and inheritance, would Ibn-Hanzala's *ravayat* still have come into being and the guardianship of the jurist (the theory of *wilayat-e faqih*) still derived from it?[15] And so on and so forth. Overlooking the historicity of the birth of religion and the human origin/source of the discipline of *fiqh* lead to the baseless claim of perfection.

B. Producing regulations and precepts that embrace all eventualities, past, present and future, is not all that difficult. After all, Sunnis—using that same raw materials plus their method of analogy (*qiyas*), and Shi'is—using the raw material plus their methods of *ijtihad* (which excludes *qiyas*—have until recently been largely successful in responding to new problems. The question now is not whether new individual cases can be brought under the old generalities; this level of *ijtihad* is neither a great art, nor the resolver of any grave problem. The real question now is whether actually existing *fiqh*, with the actually existing instruments, can produce the *best* solutions to the problems of all societies until the end of time. It is this that is difficult, nay impossible to prove. It is a matter of conviction. You can say that, for all eternity, the man has the right to initiate divorce and have custody over the children, thieves hands must be severed, hoarders must be dealt with

---

[15] Reference is to a Shi'ite tradition reported on the authority of the Sixth Imam saying: "I assigned those who report our tradition as ruling judge (*hakem*) among you. They know our injunctions concerning what is permitted and prohibited; thus people should comply with their rulings." (See al-Kulayni, *Usul min al-Kafi*). This tradition was one of Ayatollah Khomein's sources for developing his theory of the Guardianship of the Jurists (*wilayat-e faqih*) that justifies religio-political authority of the 'ulama during the absence of the Imams. [ed.]

in the time-honoured way, apostates put to death, etc. And, on this basis, you can resolve any future marital disputes and so on. This level of comprehensiveness and all-inclusiveness is easy to achieve; new cases can be likened to old cases, analogies drawn, and particular instances brought under the generalities to generate precepts. After all, have our Islamic jurists not already deduced and made known the precepts for prayers, fasting and ablutions on the moon and on Mars? This is not a very sophisticated or significant achievement. What would be significant would be to prove that the discipline of *fiqh* provides the *best* possible solution to problems. And, to do this, it would first have to be proven that *fiqh*'s raw material and first principles comprise the *best*, *most* humane and *most* effective precepts, better than which is unimaginable and inconceivable. Proving this is altogether different from proving the comprehensiveness and all-inclusiveness of the precepts of *fiqh*, which even if proven would not be of much significance. (Quite apart from the fact that it would also have to be proven that the *usul al-fiqh* is the *most* powerful instrument for inferring and deducing precepts.) It is impossible to prove any of this because the science of *fiqh* (not quintes- sential law as it lies in divine's fore knowledge) is a human product and is no different from any other human discipline or product. It consists of an ever changing collective knowledge that includes incongruities and contradictions, truths and falsehoods, suppositions and certainties, which are the product of Islamic jurists' endeavours. To claim that a discipline of this kind (and, indeed, any field or discipline) is the most complete, the best and the most excellent is inappropriate and displays ignorance of the nature of knowledge. And it is always possible that a solution found outside the discipline of *fiqh* may prove better than the solution supplied by *fiqh*. Of course, if we broaden the definition of *fiqh* and jurists' theoretical endeavours to such an extent as to embrace any mental effort, then *fiqh* will certainly become unbeatable, but then it will also become irrelevant!

C. Even if we accept that the precepts of *fiqh* are complete and comprehensive, nay, the most complete and the most comprehensive, this will not take us very far down the road of proving the finality of Muhammad's prophethood and the perfection of religion; because *fiqh* is only responsible for solving legal problems. After all, can it be that all social and human problems are legal? And can it be that a complete and final *fiqh* is all that is required for a religion to be final and capable of solving every problem? What is to become of planning then?[16] What about ethical and philosophical problems? What about a world-view? Is there any reason to believe that the final religion contains the ultimate and the best ideas in philosophy, ethics, science, etc.? Is it even possible to prove such things? Can it possibly be proven (with extra-religious proof) that a particular philosophical verdict appearing in a particular *hadith* (on the philosophy of history, for example) is better and more advanced than all the verdicts that each and every philosopher and thinker will arrive at and propose until the end of time? Are we currently in the possession of every philosophical verdict until the end of time to be able to compare them with religious verdicts and determine their philosophical standing? I remember very clearly how, in the early years of the revolution, a renowned sham devotee of the *wilayat* and despiser of the West wrote in a renowned newspaper that all the novels that are now written in the West bear the Spirit of the West(!) and I wrote in response: does this mean that you have read every novel written in the West? Whence springs this confidence that allows you to pass a blanket judgement on all that has been written and is yet to be written and all that you have read and have yet to read? Now, I am asking the same question again. Are we in the possession of every possible philosophical verdict or qualified to judge between them? These considerations make it clear, first, that it is impossible to prove the perfection of *fiqh*; second, that even if it were possible, it would be of no assistance to us in proving the cessation of prophethood; third, that focusing exclusively on *fiqh* fails to present a broad and healthy image of religion; and, fourth, that neither the finality nor the perfection of religion are essentially amenable to demonstration and proof.

The new world is the world of new theoretical concepts, not new practical problems! The world is perceived differently today in the light of new scientific and philosophical discoveries. The most important achievement of the modern era is not its technology; it is its science and rationality. It is its in-law concepts and conceptions (*i'tebariyat*).[17]

---

[16] I have written extensively about *fiqh*'s inadequacy in the sphere of planning. See for example "Religion's Services and Benefits" in *Modara va Modiriyat* [Tolerance and Administration], 3rd ed. (Tehran: Serat 1375/1996); and "Minimalist and Maximalist Religion" in this volume.

[17] It is meant: norms, conventions, values, hypothetical statements, commands, prohibitions, figurative statements, etc.

In the light of this science and rationality, phenomena are interpreted and understood differently, because phenomena are intertwined with theories and theory-laden. Human relationships, too, have now come under the new concepts and norms and, consequently, taken on new meanings. These are the elements that make up the modern world's structure and principles, not things like using aircraft instead of mules and camels or artificial insemination or travelling to the moon. And if there is a need for *ijtihad* it is in the realm of harmonising religion's first principles with the first principles of the modern world, not harmonising religion's secondary regulations with the derivative regulations and by products of the modern world.

It is amazing that a scholar of Motahhari's stature is so preoccupied and obsessed with *fiqh* that, in tackling the finality of prophethood, he focuses on this aspect of religion to the exclusion of almost everything else. He believes that solving the puzzle of the finality hangs on solving the puzzle of *fiqh*, and does his utmost to show that, since *fiqh* can be eternally dynamic, so, too, can religion claim to be everlasting and dynamic, and that there is, consequently, no need for another Prophet and Legislator. It is not for nothing that some have said: if Greek civilisation was the civilisation of philosophy, Islamic civilisation is the civilisation of *fiqh*.[18] There is a good measure of truth in this observation. More than breeding philosophers, Islamic civilisation has bred *faqihs*. We can now see that even when a thinker of Motahhari's calibre looks at religion, he looks at it through the eyes of *fiqh* and, when he looks at the Prophet, he sees him in his capacity as a Legislator. He seems unaware of the fact that, even when it comes to solving modern legal problems, *fiqh* alone will not suffice.

New legal problems have come about not just because of the development of new human capabilities and new technological tools, but much more so because of the emergence of new assumptions about and approaches to ethics, humanity, history, rationality, knowledge, rights, society and God, and the discovery of new sciences. And solving the new legal problems hinges on solving the new fundamental theoretical and philosophical problems. And increasing the powers of the Islamic ruler or applying the principles of "no hardship and no harm" will not answer or serve any purpose here. A *faqih* who is unfamiliar

---

[18] Found for instance in the writings of Mohammed 'Abed al-Jabri, the contemporary Moroccan thinker.

with the assumptions people make today about the above-mentioned topics will not be able to understand and solve the concomitant legal problems either. Take the question of elections, on which the jury still seems to be out as far as *fiqh* is concerned. This is because it is not a strictly legal problem. It is laden with potent and hefty theological and anthropological assumptions. And this is a point that Motahhari himself discovered and admitted about the capitalist system—after much soul-searching and consideration in his now neglected book *The Islamic Economy*.[19]

To this day, it continues to puzzle me as to why a theologian like Motahhari systematically turned to *fiqh* in his efforts to prove the finality of Muhammad's prophethood and religion's eternal validity, and never bothered, for example, to tackle such problems as the conflict between science and religion and philosophy and religion. Is it not necessary, in explaining the cessation of prophethood, to show that, whenever a conflict arises between science and religion, religion always emerges victorious in so far as it contains a dynamism that resolves and quells all conflicts? If this point is not spelt out—and it is only one of many essential points within the belief system—of what use to religion is the proof of the eternal dynamism and validity of *fiqh* (assuming it to be provable)?

The determination to prove (with extra-religious arguments) the superiority of Islam's ideas in the fields of philosophy, ethics and *fiqh* over all other existing and conceivable ideas is misguided and inappropriate. The necessity or rationality of the finality cannot be proven in this way. These are ideas that are intra-religious and matters of conviction. The message of the finality is not that we should resolve to achieve impossible tasks and to marshal futile and imperfect arguments. The message of the finality is that we should understand religion (that is to say, *fiqh*, theology, ethics and religious experience) and the purpose of religion in such a way as to leave the door open to its dynamism and vitality. And the very minimum that we can do to make religion dynamic is to see it as minimal.[20]

---

[19] *The Islamic Economy* was originally lectures delivered by Motahhari to a small circle of his friends and scholars before the 1979 Revolution. These lectures were collected and published by his friends immediately after the Revolution. Because of the content of the book that had some socialist tendencies, the clerical establishment resented it and prohibited its circulation.

[20] See "Minimalist and Maximalist Religion" in this volume.

The message of the finality of prophethood is that we should not consider any understanding of religion as the final conception, thereby permitting this sea to feed and be fed by other seas, permitting the prophetic experience to expand and grow, and not permitting any understanding of religion to become official and associated with power.

Servitude bears a message: that none of us is God. The finality, too, bears a message: that none of us is a prophet. More than being theoretical and provable, the message of the finality is practical and practicable. It is an *ought*, not an *is*. It teaches us, not to prove that religion *is* final and dynamic, but to *make* religion final and dynamic. Our understanding of it must be such as to make any other religion unnecessary. And it falls on us to publicise this conception and to teach it.

Of what use can it possibly be to imagine in our own minds that we have proven the finality while, in practice, we present a backward religion that is incapable of solving the simplest theoretical and germane problems; a religion that leaves its disciples begging at other people's doors. We must recognise with certainty that this religion has the required resources to fulfil the needs it claims to and is duty-bound to fulfil. The duty that falls on the religion's disciples is—with reliance on this certainty and with the recognition of the state of the universe and the fact that it cannot beget other prophets—to make the finality of religion radiantly clear; in other words, to leave no room for anyone to feel the need for any other religion. And this will only be possible if we do not overburden it with inappropriate demands and do not turn it into an impediment and barrier to the advancement of the human mind. The smallest task that can be undertaken to this end—by way of a model—is to illuminate the way for the resolution of the conflict between science and religion (and philosophy and religion, and so on). This entails effort [*ijtihad*] in the realm of theory and not just effort [*ijtihad*] in the realm of *fiqh*. This illumination will remove any remaining impediment to religious faith.

CHAPTER FOUR

ESSENTIALS AND ACCIDENTALS IN RELIGION

In this article, the terms "accidental" and "essential" are first presented and defined. Then religion's traits and teachings are divided into essential and accidental traits and teachings. The accidentals are those that could have been other than they are, unlike the essentials. The difference between our categorization of the accidental and the essential and other classifications, such as shell and kernel, law and path, and the like that have some history of their own, is subsequently explored. A number of important questions are raised at the same time to allow the reader to gain a deeper understanding of accidentals and their delicate relationship to essence. The discussion of religion's accidental traits and teachings then begins in earnest: Islam's first accidental trait is the Arabic language, which could have been replaced by another language. The second accidental is the Arabs' culture. The third accidental consists of the terms, concepts, theories and propositions used by the Prophet. The fourth accidental consists of the historical events that entered into the Qur'an and the Sunna. The questions posed by believers and opponents and the answers to them form the fifth accidental. The sixth embraces the precepts of fiqh and Islamic law. The seventh accidental consists of the fabrications, inventions and distortions introduced into religion by its opponents. The eighth accidental consists of the abilities and understanding of the people addressed by religion. Finally, conclusions are drawn and it is suggested in brief that Islam (and any other religion for that matter) is a religion by virtue of its essentials, not its accidentals. And being a Muslim demands belief and commitment to the essentials.

Relationship Between the Essential and the Accidental

First. Consider the three proverbs below, current in Persian, English and Arabic usage:

a. Taking cumin to Kerman.
b. Taking coal to Newcastle.
c. Taking dates to Basra.

The underlying purport or spirit (or essence) of the three proverbs is one and the same. But this single spirit has donned three different outer garments. The garments have the cut and colour of the cultures, geographies and languages of the peoples who tailored them. But the spirit is universal and belongs to no particular land. We take this spirit to be the proverb's essential core, and that garment, its accidental outer layer.

The simple, yet important rules governing the essential and the accidental and the relationship between the two can be enumerated as follows:

1. The above proverb's force and identity lies in its unchanging core and underlying message, not in its varied outer layer and initial sense.

2. Accidental outer layers are subject to a multitude of factors and conditions and appear in countless shapes and sizes; there are no logical boundaries or limits to the way in which they may manifest themselves.

3. There is no such thing as a naked essence or spirit; essences invariably present themselves in some outer garment or form.

4. The defining characteristic of an accidental is that "it could have been other than it is".

5. Although essences never occur without accidentals, confusing the rules that govern them leads to a host of fallacies; therefore, their theoretical distinction from accidentals is an absolute rational imperative.

6. When we want to transfer an essence from one culture to another, we have to engage in something akin to translation. That is to say, we must dress the essence in the garment of the new culture, otherwise it will lead to misunderstandings and a distortion of the essence. A mere mechanical transfer would be futile and unwise. "Taking coal to Newcastle" would not convey anything to Persian speakers, unless it was rendered as "taking cumin to Kerman" or unless the Persian speakers became so acquainted with the culture and geography of the people who speak of taking coal to Newcastle as to be able to extract the essence from the accidental themselves and grasp its cultural sense.

7. Accidentals have local and temporal—not universal and historical—authenticity.

Second. Conceptualising and presenting religion and religiosity in the forms of *shari'ah* (the law), *tariqah* (the path) and *haqiqah* (the truth); or *baten* (the exterior) and *zaher* (the interior); or *qeshr* (the shell) and *lubb* (the kernel) should not be confused with the classification of the contents of religion into essentials and accidentals, although they are seemingly similar.

The shari'ah or Islamic law used to be understood to refer specifically to *fiqh* or religious precepts. But, in the above categorisation it was taken to mean religious knowledge, as opposed to the path, which consisted of religious action. The truth, for its part, did not convey a sense of the inner meaning and secrets of religious teachings, but the attainment of the ultimate goal and the coming to fruition of religion within the individual, the tasting of the rapture of faith and a transformation of the believer's personality and being. This is expressed very clearly in the phrase attributed to the Prophet that says: "The law is my words, the path is my actions and the truth is my [existential] state."

The explanations and analogies presented by Rumi in the preface to Book Five of the *Mathnawi* further confirms this view:

> Hence, the law is comparable to the learning of alchemy from a master or a book. The path is the performance of alchemy and the rubbing of the copper against the philosopher's stone. And the truth is when the copper turns into gold. Alchemists are glad of their knowledge of alchemy, declaring, we are most learned in the field. The doers are glad to be performing their alchemy. Those who have arrived at the truth are glad, declaring, we have turned into gold and have no further need of the knowledge or practice of alchemy...Or the law is like the studying of medicine. The path is abstentions required by the science of the medicine and taking the appropriate medicines. And the truth is the attainment of eternal health and the transcendence of the need for either of the former two. When mortal beings depart from this world, the law and the path fall away from him and the truth remains...The law is knowledge. The path is action. And the truth is union with God.[1]

It was in this sense and for this reason that mystics saw the emergence of truths as the discarding of laws and likened arrival at truths to stepping onto the rooftop of union, whereupon the ladders of knowledge and action could be dispensed with. Rumi says:

---

[1] See *Mathnawi Ma'nawi*, ed. by Abdulkarim Soroush, (Tehran: Intesharat-e 'ilmi va Farhangi, 1996).

Since you have reached the object of your search, O elegant one, the
search for knowledge has now become evil.
Since you have mounted to the roofs of Heaven, it would be futile to
seek a ladder.
After (having attained to) felicity, the way (that leads) to felicity is worthless except for the sake of helping and teaching others.[2]

References to the shell and the kernel were intended in this same way.
Kernel did not mean the pith or core of religious knowledge and teachings, as opposed to its shell and exterior; it meant the state of being
and the exalted rank achieved by the individual, for the attainment and
protection of which all knowledge and action, and dos and don'ts, and
fiqh and ethics were but instruments and shells. In this sense Shabestari
states that: "Law is shell, truth is the kernel; between which lies the
path."[3] It was on this basis, too, that those who had arrived at the truth
and had attained peace considered observation of the law obligatory
for all and in public. Despite "the audacities of solitude", they believed
that the abandonment of religious laws, stripping religiosity of all its
superficies and opposing religious traditions and practices would be
detrimental to the health of the religious community and inimical to
public morality.

The words of Abd al-Quddus of Gangoh, the Indian mystic, quoted
by Muhammad Iqbal, must also be understood in this context when
he said: "Muhammad of Arabia" ascended the highest Heaven and
returned. I swear by God that if I had reached that point, I should never
have returned."[4] As if the law and the path were the religiosity of the
public (in the ritualistic sense), whereas the truth was the religiosity
of the individual.

Seyyed Heidar Amoli's classification of Islam, faith and certainty
into the Islam, faith and certainty of novices, intermediates and cul-
minants[5] is likewise unrelated to our discussion of religion's essentials
and accidentals; similarly unrelated is the division of religiosity into

---

[2] *Mathnawi*, 3: 1399–1401.
[3] Shaykh Mahmoud Shabestari, *Golshan-e Raz* (Tehran: Tahuri, *1368/1989*).
[4] Iqbal, *The Reconstruction of Religious Thought*, p. 125. Iqbal adds: "In the whole
range of Sufi literature, it will be probably difficult to find words which, in a single
sentence, disclose such an acute perception of the psychological difference between the
prophetic and the mystic types of consciousness."
[5] Seyyed Heidar Amoli, *Jame' al-Asrar va Manba' al-Anwar* (Tehran: Intesharat-e
'ilmi va Farhangi, 1368/1989).

three different types, "pragmatic/instrumental", "Discursive/reflective" and "Experiential", which I have proposed elsewhere.[6]

The essential and the accidental in religion do not correspond to any of the above-mentioned classifications. First, here we are talking about religion itself, not about religious knowledge or believers' states of being. Secondly, it is an assumption about nominal religion (religion in itself) that can serve as a presupposition for the comprehension of phenomenal religion (religion in relation to us). Thirdly, as we said, accidental means something that could have been other than it is and appeared in some other form, although religion must always appear in one form or another of accidentals. The essential in religion is, consequently, that which is not accidental; anything without which religion would cease to be religion and the alteration of which would be a negation of religion itself. The essential in Islam is anything without which Islam would not be Islam and the transformation of which would lead to the emergence of another religion.

Third. The historical existence of religions is indisputable, but the existence of a common essence or spirit among all of them is more open to dispute; in fact, it is virtually impossible to prove. Religions are not individual instances of a universal known as "religion" and, rather than having a common quiddity, they simply bear a family resemblance (as Wittgenstein put it), like the members of a family whose eyes, eyebrows, mouths, cheekbones and figures are more or less alike, but have no common core.

Formulating a single definition of religion has presented religious theorists with such hefty problems that they have all thrown their hands up in the air, having gone no further than offering broad and general descriptions. This is why Cantwell Smith, the renowned Canadian religious theorists, says that we must speak of "religions" not religion.

The realists (those who believe in universals) are in the weakest position of all in this respect and have nothing to offer since religion is not, unlike animals or plants, a quiddity among quiddities with specific essential constituents that lends itself to *a priori* definition. Even if they produced such a definition, because, according to logicians, definitions are not subject to demonstrations,[7] a substantial definition

---

[6] See, Chapter Eight, "Types of Religiosity", in this book.
[7] According to traditional logic, logical definitions and demonstrations have elements in common therefore demonstrating a definition would entail circularity.

of religion would continue to remain a matter of taste and undemonstrable, in much the same way as the philosophical definition of any other thing.

The phenomenologists, too, who have stepped into this field only recently, have said things which, instead of being satiating, leave one more hungry than before. The sum total of their work amounts to assumptions that belong to the context of discovery and still need to move into the context of justification, where they can be confirmed or undermined by experience.

All that is left then is an experimental-nominalist- *a posteriori* definition of religion. And even this ultimately leads to Wittgenstein's verdict, which posits the existence of religions—not religion—that have no one thing in common, much like the games of football, chess, horse racing, wrestling, etc., which, according to Wittgenstein's analysis, stubbornly remain games, rather than being different manifestations of a common core known as "game" which is present in all of them.

It is therefore futile to adopt an *a priori* approach to the essentials and accidentals of religion. It is still unclear whether religion must per force contain the concept of God or not. What about an un-interpreted experience of God? What about a personal God? What about the question of resurrection? What about ethics? What about rites and rituals of worship? What about politics and contractual transactions? What about science and philosophy? Whichever religion we set as our model, we find that other religions either fall short of it or contravene it.

Take the inclusion of politics, for example, which is a source of pride to Muslims. For Christians, it is seen as the sullying of religion with worldly concerns and, therefore, a move away from the ideal purity. Buddhism does not have a deity (or an un-interpreted experience of a deity). Hinduism has a number of deities. But Islam and Judaism have a single deity. Judaism has religious laws and precepts. So does Islam. But Buddhism and Christianity do not. Hindus and Buddhists believe in reincarnation, whereas Muslims, Jews and Christians believe in some notions of resurrection in the hereafter.

The deity is also different in different religions. The religion of the Jews is more severe and their God more uncompromising than Christians' religiosity and God, where the emphasis is on gentleness and fatherly compassion. The Prophet of Islam has been quoted as saying, "I have two eyes"; that is to say, my teachings contain aspects of the religions of both Moses and Jesus.

It is clear then that the assumption of the existence of a single pearl in the heart of all these incongruities and incompatibilities is too unfalsifiable to be worth contemplating. It is true, of course, that some sociologists and religious theorists have defined religious phenomena as sacred phenomena and religion as a system of sacred symbols, objects and individuals (sacred people, scriptures, sacred moments and occasions, sacred sites and buildings, sacred stones and waters and directions and words and phrases and images and icons and legacies, etc.). They have also considered the classification of all affairs and events into the sacred and the profane, the lofty and the base, as an essential component of any religion. Although this approach gives a clear sense of the move away from the sacred and towards secularisation in the modern world, nonetheless, it falls on the very first step of providing a precise definition of the sacred.[8] Secondly, it is so minimalist, general, undemanding and modest that it even allows magic and divination to wrap themselves in the cloak of religiosity. Thirdly, it whittles down the kernel so severely and renders it so wafer thin as to leave nothing but a thick shell behind in practice. And, fourthly, even if we accept it and take it on board, it poses no obstacle to the classification of religious teachings into essentials and accidentals.

Suffice it to say that searching for accidentals is a much more fruitful task than seeking to unearth essentials and embarking on a search for the accidentals of one particular religion is more fruitful than trying to uncover the accidentals of religion, in the general sense of the word.

Distinguishing the Essential from the Accidental

Fourth. Now we find ourselves equipped with the required footwear and eye-wear to step into the arena of religion and gaze upon its pages. Bearing in mind the gradual and historical genesis of religion and religious texts; the deconstruction of its ossified structure; the employment of various "contrary to facts condition"; using inductive methods to discern the causes and the goals of the shariʿah (religious laws); discovering the tools and instruments that were in use during religion's genesis and

---

[8] See Mircea Eliade, *A Hisotry of Religious Ideas* (Chicago: Chicago University Press, 1978).

the events that played a role in it; the refinement and definition of our expectations of religion; and the testing of the different components of religion to see whether they are replaceable or irreplaceable are all the principal methods at our disposal for distinguishing the essentials and accidentals of religion.

Arabic Language and Arabic Culture

a. We can say without further ado that, in relation to Islam, the Arabic language is accidental. It would have been enough for the Prophet of Islam to have been born an Iranian, an Indian or a Roman for his language to become Persian, Sanskrit or Latin. As it is, the Arabic language imposed its boundaries and spaces, its brightness and dullness, and its own particular features on the Muhammadan revelation. It became a flute in the hands of the flute player which imposes its own limitations on the tune.

Some of these characteristics belong to language as a whole; others are unique to Arabic. Clarity and ambiguity, literal and figurative meanings, absolutely non-equivocal, less equivocal and more equivocal meanings, etc. exist in every language and there is no escaping them in the realm of speech. The phrasing, structure, etymology, pool of words and literary wealth of Arabic are unique to this language and have exercised a firm grip on Islamic discourse.

b. Not just the language of Islam, but also its culture is Arabic. Hence, not just its language, but also its culture is accidental; in the sense that (theoretically, not in practice) it could have been otherwise. The most minor and most evident aspect of this Arabism is the Arabic language, but its depth and breadth extend much further than this; they extend as far as the use of concepts and conceptions that are the offspring of the Arab world-view and culture, as well as embracing Arab customs, habits, perceptions and traditions. The fact that the Qur'an speaks of the presence in heaven of dark-eyed *houris* (not blue-eyed women) and portrays them as sheltered in their tents (55: 72); that it calls on people to consider how the camel was created (88: 17); that it refers to warm-weather fruits with which the Arabs were acquainted: the banana (56: 29), the date and the pomegranate (55: 68), grapes (80: 28), the olive (80: 29), and the fig (95: 1); that it uses the lunar calendar (the month of Ramadan for fasting, Dhu al-Hajjah for the *hajj*, the "*haram*" sacred months for refraining from war and so on); that it speaks of the Quraysh tribe and "their composing for the winter and summer caravan" (106: 1–2); that it refers to Abu-Lahab and his wife who has "upon her neck a rope of palm-fibre" (111: 5); that it describes the presence in heaven of "uplifted couches and goblets set forth and cushions arrayed and carpets outspread" (88: 14–16); that one of the phrases it uses to convey the coming to an end of all things on Judgement Day is "the pregnant camels shall be neglected" (82: 4); that it mentions the Arab tradition of burying girls alive: ("the buried infant shall be asked for what sin she was slain", (82: 8–9); that it likens the flames of hell to bright yellow camels and speaks of "sparks like to golden herds" (77: 32–33); that it refers to animals that were well-known to the Arabs, such as horses, mules, camels, donkeys, lions, elephants, pigs, snakes, etc. and mentions such things as wool, cotton, camphor, ginger and 70-cubit chains, all objects of daily use for the Arabs; as well as many other similar examples, which can be found through a diligent exploration of the Qur'an and the noble *Sunna* of the Prophet, all reveal how the hue and scent of Arabs' interests, sensibilities, tribal life, violence, hospitality, customs, habits, surroundings and livelihoods have enveloped the central kernel of Islamic thought like a hefty shell.

There can be no doubt that, had the beloved and great Prophet of Islam received his mission in a different environment, the book of revelation and his cannon law would have taken on an altogether different hue. And, without detracting in the slightest from the brilliance and gravity of the message, this would have made it unnecessary for him to speak of mules, *houris*, burying girls alive, the Quraysh tribe, Abu-Lahab and so on. This is not to say that in that case he would present an oyster-less pearl or a naked kernel, but that it would have been wrapped in different accidentals and the words and the message would have been clothed in a different garment and adorned with different ornaments.

The same can be said of the many non-Arabic words (Hebrew, Geez, Persian, Greek, Syriac, etc.) that appear in the Qur'an and number more than two hundred. These were words originating from the learned and colloquial languages and dialects of the religious and non-religious tribes and communities of the time in Arabia which were then used by the founder of the *shariʿah*. They include non-Arabic words for: *marjan* (coral), *yaqut* (ruby), *iblis* (devil), *sondos* (brocade), *istabraq* (shot silk), *qistas* (a balance), *saradeq* (the curtain in front of the door of a house or a tent), *sarbal* (breeches), *zarabbi* (back rest), *namareq* (saddle pad), *seraj* (lantern), *junah* (fin), *jahanam* (inferno), *ferdous* (paradise), *ibriq* (watering pot), *kanz* (storing or accumulating treasure), *asatir* (fables), *ababil* (bustard), *qantar* (a measure for gold), and *maqalid* (keys).[9] The Arabs' trade, contacts, political and religious ties, and wars with other peoples were the main cause of the entry of these words into Arabic and, thereafter, into the language of revelation. There can be no doubt that, if it had been a question of another people, another region and other political-historical-religious ties, the nature, incidence and frequency of these words within the Islamic tradition would also have been different. It is much the same with the tale of the revelation of the Qur'an in the Quraysh dialect or in the seven dialects (*sab'at ahruf*) which was entirely accidental, mutable and a product of the environment in which the revelation occurred.

c. More than creating new concepts, religion brings new propositions and laws, and establishes new relationships between existing concepts. For instance, it changes "there are gods" into the new proposition: "there is One God". It replaces sacrificial offerings to idols to sacrificial offerings to God, it rejects the idea that angels are women, it forbids the worshipping of idols, it declares that human beings are dependent and the Creator is Independent, and so on.

In other words, any religion (and, here, Islam) introduces and uses a particular system of words/concepts which arises from the existing people's language and culture; establishing new relationships between its elements, and, through the repositioning of these elements creating new central and peripheral relationships within them. It is exactly the same in science and philosophy.

The most pivotal concept in the Islamic word system is "Allah" or God. And it is with reference to this pivot that all the other words find their place in the conceptual scheme of the religion; words such as *shukr* (thanksgiving), *sabr* (patience), *ne'mah* (blessings), *mun'em* (beneficent), *tavakol* (trust), *tawbah* (repentance), *ma'siyah* (sin), *du'a* (prayer), *'ebadat* (worship), *taqva* (piety), *kufr* (disbelief and rejection of God), *islam* (submission to God), *iman* (faith), *irtedad* (apostasy), *wilayah* (guardianship), *tasbih* (glorification of God), *jihad* (struggle),

---

[9] For information about the non-Arabic roots and forms of these types of words and the possible ways in which they may have entered the Arabic language and the Qur'an, see the book by Arthur Jeffrey, *The Foreign Vocabulary of the Qur'an* (Baroda, India: Oriental Institute, 1938).

zuhd (asceticism), *resalah* (mission), *da'wah* (call), *besharah* (good tidings), *ayat* (signs), *maghferah* (forgiveness), *rahmah* (mercy), *haqq* (truth), *batel* (falsehood), *dhikr* (invocation), *taher* (clean), *najes* (unclean), *nasr* (succour), *sakinah* (tranquillity), *indhar* (warning), *tazkiyah* (purification), *khashyah* (fear), *hawa* (desire), *'adhab* (chastisement), *fesq* (debauchery), *'aql* (reason), *jahl* (ignorance), *hedayah* (guidance), *dalalah* (perdition), *ikhlas* (sincerity), *rebh* (profit), *khusran* (loss), *shaytan* (Satan), *malak* (angel), *jenn* (jinni), *akhlaq* (ethics), *serat* (path), etc. All these words and their meanings belonged to the Arabs and were products of their culture and world-view. Nonetheless, within Islam and with reference to the new source of authority, they took on a new spirit and hue. In other words, the Prophet of Islam used the bricks at his disposal within Arab culture to construct a new structure, which is related to that culture but also surpasses it.

These Islamized concepts were half-transparent, according to Toshihiko Izutsu, the great contemporary Japanese scholar of religion, because, on the one hand, they belonged to the culture of the Arabs and had an Arab pedigree, and, on the other, they had donned the new Islamic robe and stepped into a new residence.[10] It is this half-transparency that shows very transparently how the culture of a particular people is carried on the shoulders of Islam.

For example, consider two peripheral word sub-systems (or two small conceptual schemes) which are both firmly related to the manner of life and cultural traits of the Arabs in particular and to the ancient life-style in general. The Arabs were both people of commerce and people of the desert. Living and travelling in parched, uncharted deserts; losing one's way; falling prey to monsters, robbers, foes, brigands and ambushes; drifting about; straying from the path; trying to steer by the stars at night; dying in the desert and failing to reach the destination; falling behind from the convoy; being tired and thirsty; looking for signs; following long and winding trails; and constant and severe hardship and insecurity in general were regular features of their lives and travels. The Qur'an, too, has made extensive use of this familiar terminology

---

[10] Strictly speaking, of course, he uses this expression in reference to the key words used in Islamic philosophy. He believes that Islamic philosophy is a system that is composed of half-transparent words. See: Toshihiko Izutsu, *God and Man in the Qur'an: Semantics of Qur'anic Weltanshauung* (Tokyo: The Keio Institute of Cultural and Linguistic Studies, 1964).

related to the concepts of travelling and path/way (*sirat* or *sabil*) and
its symbolism to convey the intended ideas. As Izutsu puts it: "Even
a casual reader will notice that the Qur'an is filled from start to finish
with this imagery."[11] Look for instance at the semantic field or word
system used in the Qur'an in this relation: *mustaqim, sawiiy* (straight
way, path); *'iwaj* (crooked way); *huda, rashad* (being guided to, the right
way); *dalal, ghayyah, taih* (swerving from the right path); *zad* (provi-
sions), and even Satan as a force that hides the right path. It does not
seem that the Arabs had used these concepts for religious purposes or
in a religious context, nor had they tried to create a spiritual conceptual
scheme with them. It was within the Muhammadan revelation that, with
the pivotal place given to the term "Allah", the concepts were pointed
in a new direction and produced a new vista. The Arabs were familiar
with these bricks, but Muhammad was a divine architect who gave new
actualities to the existing potentials. The use of these concepts, made
the Prophet's school of thought and religious teachings so clear and
tangible for the Arabs, and he spoke to them in such a familiar way as
to endorse without hesitation or doubt the Qur'anic statement, "And
We have made the Qur'an easy to understand and remember. Then is
there any that will receive admonition?" (54: 32)

Of course, the legendary insecurity and hardship of the journeys of
the past have disappeared, and contemporary travellers no longer face
these dangers and fears. They face altogether different problems now.
(Passports, visas, national frontiers, residence permits, work permits and
the like which, as it happens, have no place in the Islamic vocabulary,
because they were not part of the language and culture of the Arabs
of the time.)

The Arabs were not interested in writing and books. As the Qur'an
puts it, they were common folk, mostly illiterate (*ummi*). Hence,
although Islam is a religion with a Book, the word system relating to
penning- unlike the word system of paths and tracks and so on—is not
much used in the Qur'an; words such as, accuracy, mistake, legible,
illegible, deleting, proof-reading, editing, erasing, script, author, reader,
binding, transcribing, literacy, illiteracy, pen, ink, paper, markings,
annotation, misquotation, plagiarism, etc. These words could easily
have been used to create a word system or a semantic field for con-

---

[11] Ibid., pp. 32–33.

ceptualising and conveying religious ideas. Nonetheless, as we know, although the words pen, book, ink, etc. do appear in the Qur'an, this symbolism is never used and no such semantic field is created, because it is a symbolism that flows from the culture of and is appropriate to a people who live with books and are fond of them; the Arabs of the age of the Prophet were not people of this kind.

Consider also the word system in the Qur'an associated with commerce: *khusr* (loss), *rebh* (profit), *tejarah* (trade), *qard* (loan), *reba* (usury), *bay'* (sale), *shera'* (purchase), *ajr* (wage), etc. and examples such as "God has bought from the believers their selves and their possessions against the gift of Paradise...so rejoice in the bargain you have made with Him" (9: 111); "those are they who have bought error at the price of guidance and their commerce has not profited them" (2: 16); "who is he that will lend God a good loan and He will multiply it for him manifold?" (2: 245), in other words, asking people for interest is forbidden, but it is permitted with God; "surely man is in the way of loss, save those who believe and do righteous deeds" (103: 1–2); and many other verses that include these same terms and concepts.

It is evident that the Qur'an is filled with the discourse of commerce and the desert, and the concepts and terms belonging to these two spheres have provided the material for the Prophet to shape, formulate and convey the intended ideas. It is possible to imagine other conceptual schemes and semantic frameworks which could easily have replaced these two, but for various historical, environmental, geographical and cultural reasons they were not used by the Prophet and remained neglected. Hence, here, too, we are faced with categories of accidentals which, while being accidental and external, have exercised a profound influence on the central kernel and played a fundamental role in shaping the contents. Nonetheless, there can be no doubt that they are accidental and could have been otherwise—in another environment and culture—with Islam still remaining Islam. It is one thing to ask what pure Islam is and, another, to say that the teachings of Islam (or any other religion) were never presented in pure and naked form. In order to answer the former, we need to tear away the veils assumed in the latter. And then the important question is: how can we be certain that all the veils have been removed and that the chipping away has come to an end for ever more?

Conceptual Limitations

d. But a more lofty point is still to come. We said that, more than bringing new concepts, religion brought new formulations, judgements and word systems. Now we will add to this by saying that judgements (propositions, phrases) are trapped in the clutches of concepts (expressions, terms). Hence, opting for and using specific and limited concepts also restricts the judgements and the field of action, just as bricks and raw material impose conditions and restrictions on the structure and rob the designer and architect of freedom. What this means is that, at times, the garment of the people's culture (from language to tastes and likely occupations, to strengths and weaknesses of thought and imagination, to customs and habits, to theoretical observations, to the richness of the vocabulary and terminology, etc.) sits tightly and awkwardly on the beliefs and ideas, inflicts its own merits and demerits on them, and imposes its own nature on the clay of which they are made.

Mystics' lament against the impediment of language is an ancient tale. Rumi surely spoke for all of them when he said, "would that Being could speak". And this does not just apply to mystics, but to the religious experiences of all the prophets. Not only did they leave unsaid the unsayable, they were also unable to say what they wanted to say in the way they wanted. In other words, what could be said and what could not be said was more often determined not by them but by the culture of the age and the language of the people. And so it was that centuries later Rumi spoke [in a metaphorical language] sweetly and plaintively of the torment of trying to hurl one's spears in an enclosed space: "To dart the lance in these narrow lanes brings to disgrace those who dart the lance."[12]

What logical and empirical, *a priori* or *a posteriori* reason is there to indicate that, for example, the Arabic language possesses the most fertile vocabulary and the most telling imagery and terminology for conveying the loftiest concepts and the most subtle experiences; or that the habits and conventions of the Arabs provide the basis for the best analogies, symbols and sayings for the depiction of the most delicate ideas; or that their experiences, both material and mental (perception, rationality, imagination), have uncovered the most extensive range of facts and arrayed them in the best conceptual and verbal containers;

---

[12] *Mathnawi*, 4: 1486.

or that their language has developed and flourished equally in every field of expression (poetry, science, philosophy, etc.)? Is it not the case that the uneven development of Arabic, its saturation with the material concerns of the Arabs and their ideas, its limited vocabulary and terminology, and the brightness and dullness of its different elements impose inescapable and eternal boundaries and spaces, brightness and dullness on the concepts and judgements of religion? Does the fertility and aridity, and the expansion and contraction of the judgements not become subject to and imbued with the fertility and aridity, and the expansion and contraction of the concepts? Does the expansion of later generations' material, mental and linguistic experiences not subsequently provide a more obedient mount for religion's rider and assist the evolution of the Prophet's religious experiences? Had a different language and culture been available to the Prophet, would his religion and course not have taken on a different form and hue? Can it be proved that the Arabs' world and world-view was better suited to the physiognomy of religion than the world and world-view of the Greeks, Romans or Indians?

There can be no doubt that, had Islam come into existence in Greece or India, instead of in Hijaz, the accidentals of a Greek or Indian Islam—accidentals which penetrate so deep as to touch the kernel—would have been very different from those of an Arab Islam. The powerful ideas of Greek philosophy, for example, would have provided the Prophet of Islam with different linguistic and conceptual tools and a different word system that would have altered his discourse; in much the same way as we can see that, today, after centuries of travels and travails, Iranian, Indian, Arab and Indonesian Islam are very different on the testimony of their religious literature (as well as having many similarities), and not just in appearance but to the very depth of their religious understanding and culture. This is a tale that goes much further than Rumi's story of the three men who did not realise they were all speaking about grapes, because one of them was referring to it by the Arabic word, the second, by the Persian word and the third, by the Greek. The task of the modern-day religious scholars and students of Islam is to compare and contrast various hypothetical religious discourses, belonging to different cultural-historical environments, with the aim of identifying a whole range of accidentals that penetrated to the very core of the essence of Islam and imposed their own nature and physiognomy on it.

We are not talking here about the contraction and expansion that religious knowledge inevitably undergoes by virtue of the questions and new developments in other fields of human knowledge. Rather this is a question of the contraction and expansion imposed on the very core and substance of religion by virtue of the incidentals and accidentals of the age. The more subtle these accidentals and the more intricate their association with the essence, the more sacred and the more desacralizing the religious scholar's work will be. Accidentals always play a dual role as portholes and drapes; they reveal as much they hide, and their existence is as vital as their non-existence. In fact, we have no option but to flee from one accident to another.

Scientific Knowledge of the Age

e. The entry of the scientific theories of the age (medicine, astronomy, etc.) into scripture and religious tradition is also an incidental. Whether we view these theories as correct and true or believe that the founder of religion chose to overlook their truth or falsehood, their being accidental remains clear, since religion was neither intended for teaching us science nor do we have such an expectation of it; nor yet is there any need for exploiting these particular theories.

The Ptolemaic theory of the seven heavens (an understanding that all Muslim commentators had of the relevant Qur'anic verses until the end of the nineteenth century) is neither essential to Islam, nor the only way of depicting God's beneficence and power. The theory could have been replaced by more modern theories of astronomy and yielded the same results and benefits. We may ask whether or not a true religion can use false theories to convey the intended ideas. But the answer to this question has no bearing on accidentality (non-essentiality) of these theories with regard to religion making use of them in the scripture.[13]

---

[13] Yes, if someone is of the view that religious experience was not and is not possible other than within the Ptolemaic world and within the framework of the myths and arcane rationality of ancient times, or that religious thought can only be defended on the basis of ancient, outmoded sciences, they will certainly have thereby not only decreed the end of the prophetic mission but the end of prophetic experience. And they will not only have rendered the existence of religion tenuous in this age, but will have undermined the very possibility of religion today. This is a verdict and an illusion that is neither endorsed by the facts, nor bears any resemblance to the position of this author.

A quick glance at a voluminous work such as the *Behar al-Anwar*[14] reveals that nearly one-tenth of it (10 out of 110 volumes) concerns "the heavens and the universe", that is to say, cosmology and the natural sciences, as well as jinn and angels; magic and the evil eye; the attributes of minerals and precious stones; constellations and heavenly bodies; eclipses of the moon and the sun; the different strata of air, rainbows, winds, clouds and rain; the stillness and movement of the earth; the seven climates; the causes of earthquakes; the description of the human body; the development of the human being in the womb; the nature of dreams; the treatment of illnesses such as fever, hepatitis, madness, epilepsy, intestinal worms, aching joints, bladder stones, piles, phlegm, dropsy and leprosy; the properties of plants and fruits such as senna, pansy, jujube, Chebulic myrobalan and Belleric myrobalan; and *The Prophet's Medicine* and *Rida's Medicine*,[15] with sayings from the Prophet and the Shi'ite Imams quoting revered religious figures being presented on most of these issues.

Let there be no doubt, however, that even if all these sayings were corroborated by a multitude of sources and were definitely authentic and well-founded, we would still not be able to view them as religious narratives, quite apart from the fact that most of these accounts are generally weak and unreliable. The reason for this is that believers do not expect to learn medicine, astronomy, the natural sciences and cosmology from religion. If the noble Prophet of Islam or Imam Rida had not produced *The Prophet's Medicine* and *Rida's Medicine*, it would not in any way have detracted them from their prophethood and religious leadership (witness the fact that the other Imams produced no such works). Now that these works have been attributed to them (and a very dubious attribution it is), they must still not be seen as part and parcel of their religious duties and divine mission. This is what accidental means. And it is a small step from the natural sciences to

---

[14] Muhammad Baqir Majlesi, *Behar al-Anwar* (Beirut: Mu'asesah al-Wafa, 1983). This is mainly a Shi'ite collection of *ahadith* and *revayat* (Prophetic traditions and sayings of the Shi'ite Imams). It also includes some historical subjects and commentaries on Qur'anic verses produced by the Shi'ite traditionist, Muhammad Baqir Majlesi (1616–1686) [Ed.].

[15] The Reference is to books such as: Ali Ibn Musa al-Rida, al-*Resalah al-Dhahabiyyah; al-Ma'rouf be Tibb al-Imam Rida* [Imam Rida's Medicine], ed., by Muhammad Mehdi Najaf (Qum: Maktabat al-Imam, 1982) which is said to have been written by Imam Rida for Ma'mun, the Abbasid caliph. And, to Abdullah Ibn Bastam al-Nishabouri, *Tibb al-A'imah* [Imams' Medicine] (Qum: Ansariyan, 1991–7). [Ed.]

the human sciences. Is the entry into religion of some segments of the human sciences (politics, economics and so on) not as accidental as the entry of the natural sciences? To answer this question, we would have to return to our discussion of "our expectations of religion", as well as to distinguish the prescriptive aspects of these disciplines from the descriptive.[16]

Let us end this section with Ibn Khaldun's testimony on the accidental nature of religious medicine and his verdict on what can rightly be expected from religion:

> ...Civilized Bedouins have a kind of medicine which is mainly based upon individual experience. They inherit its use from the *shaykhs* [old men] and old women of the tribe...Much of this sort of medicine existed among the Arabs. The medicine mentioned in religious tradition is of the Bedouin type. It is in no way part of the divine revelation. (Such medical matters) were merely part of Arab custom and happened to be mentioned in connection with the circumstances of the Prophet, like other things that were customary in his generation. They were not mentioned in order to imply that that particular way of practising medicine is stipulated by the religious law. Muhammad was sent to teach us the religious law. He was not sent to teach us medicine or any other ordinary matter.[17]

f. Also accidental to religion are the many questions, stories and events that have been mentioned in the Qur'an and the *Sunna*, such as wars, protests, enmities, declarations of faith, hypocrisies, insults, taunts and objections; questions about crescent moons, the two-horned [Alexander], death and resurrection, spirit, warfare during the sacred months, menstruation, war spoils; and references to people such as Abu-Lahab and his wife, and Zayd. It is evident that all of this could have been otherwise. Had Abu Lahab never existed or had he existed but been a believer, there would have been no Al-Masad Sura. If the Battle of Badr and the war of the confederate tribes (al-ahzab) had turned out differently, their stories would also have been different in the Qur'an.[18]

Neither the occurrence of these wars, nor the details of their progress, nor yet their accounts in the Qur'an are essential to Islam. Equally accidental are allegations made by the ill-wishers against Aisha (Ch. 24), Abu Lahab and his wife's vindictiveness towards the Prophet

---

[16] The expansion of this idea will have to be left to some other occasion. The author is of the view that the entering of human sciences into religion like that of natural sciences is completely accidental.

[17] Ibn Khaldun, *The Muqaddimah*, p. 387.

[18] See Chapters (111, Al-masad); (3, Al-'imran); and (33, Al-ahzab) respectively.

(Ch. 111), questions about the tale of the two-horned (Ch. 18), the Prophet's marriage to Zayd's wife (Ch. 33), the commotion made by rumour mongers in Medina (33: 60) and the reactions of the Jews and the Christians (Ch. 2). These events could easily have not appeared in the Qur'an and never even have occurred in history without any loss to Islam's main message and central kernel. Now that they do figure in the Qur'an, they should be viewed as no more than accidental, things that could have not been or could have been otherwise. In other words, the Qur'an could have been shorter or longer than it is and still have been the Qur'an, because it is the Qur'an by virtue of its essentials, not its accidentals.

Of course, accounts such as these of questions and events are not confined to the Qur'an. There are countless examples of accidentals of this kind in the *Sunna* and the sayings of the Prophet and other revered religious figures. Questions relating to the issues of loan and inheritance, and the sixth Imam's reply—which is cited by Shi'ite jurists as the main foundation of the theory of *wilayat-e faqih*—falls into this same category. The entry of these accidentals into religion reveal its dynamic, interlocutory nature. They demonstrate the way in which this religion moved in step with the events of the time and the Prophet's actual experiences; how it developed alongside them, affected them and was affected by them; and how its leanness and corpulence (in terms of an aggregate of essentials and accidentals) was linked to the brevity and length of the Prophet's life and the paucity and abundance of his experiences and reactions (which are all accidentals).[19]

Furthermore, the tale of religious questions and answers has other aspects and ramifications that require serious theoretical investigation. Verses 101–102 of Al-Ma'idah contain important cautionary points:

> O believers, question not concerning things which, if they were revealed to you, would vex you; yet if you question concerning them [precepts and the concomitant onerous duties] when the Qur'an is being sent down, they will be revealed to you. God has effaced those things; for God is All-forgiving, All-clement. A people before you questioned concerning them, then disbelieved in them. (5: 101–102)

The author of the *Tafsir al-Mizan*, Tabataba'i, is of the view that the prohibitions in these verses concerns precepts and issues relating to

---

[19] I have already explained at length about the interlocutory nature of religion in "The Expansion of Prophetic Experience", Chapter One, in this volume.

fiqh and practical, not questions about the hour of death and other unknowns, the answers to which would be expected to be worrisome. And the traditions that has been cited in the book after the said verses endorses this interpretation:

> One day, the Prophet was speaking about the obligations of the *hajj*, when someone by the name of Akashah asked his holiness, is it obligatory to perform the *hajj* every year? The Prophet replied, [do not ask for if you do and] I say yes, then the *hajj* will become a yearly obligation for you, and, if it becomes an obligation, and you neglect it, you will go astray. Do not ask me what I have not said to you. The perdition of peoples before you was brought about by the fact that they would ask their prophets [for precepts] and then disobey. It was after this dialogue that the said verses were revealed.[20]

This story has been recounted in *Majma' al-Bayan* and other Shi'i books. In *Tafsir al-Safi*, Feiz Kashani also quotes Imam Ali as saying:

> God made certain obligations incumbent on you. Do not neglect them. And He set limits for you. Do not transgress them. And He forbade you certain things. Do not impinge on them. And He remained silent on certain things. It was not a forgetful silence. Do not occupy yourselves with them.

In his important book, *Hujjat Allah al-Baligha*, in the section on the causes of the revelation of religious laws, Shah Wali Allah of Delhi refers to these same verses and then cites the following words attributed to the Prophet:

> Among Muslims, the one who harms other Muslims most is the onw who asks about something and, by asking, causes it to be forbidden.[21]

The above verses and narratives cast astounding light on the extent to which some religious precepts are accidental and make it clear that a question could itself cause an action to be forbidden or a duty to be made more onerous, rather than merely giving rise to the pronouncement of a precept. In other words, it is as if the question has not so much uncovered a duty but created it. And, although God does not

---

[20] Mohammad Hossein Tabataba'i, *al-Mizan*, Vol. 6, pp. 160–166.
[21] Shah Wali Allah al-Dehlawi, *Hujjat Allah al-Baligha* (Cairo: Al-Turath, 1976), vol. 1, p. 91. Translation of quotations from *Hujjat al-Baligha* throughout this volume are ours, though partially benefited from the *Conclusive Argument from God: Shah Wali Allah of Delhi's Hujjat Allah al-Baligha* translated by Marcia K. Hermansen, (Brill, 1996). [Ed.]

wish to establish certain onerous precepts and harsh duties, if people wish it and ask about it, the duties will be established and become part of religion, and disregarding them will lead to perdition and disbelief in future generations.

This makes it clear what accidents and accidentals the gradual corpulence of religion and the variety of its elements owe their existence to, as well as what might have been included in religion but was not, and what might not have been included but is now. The Qur'an explicitly states that earlier peoples had asked questions of this kind and received answers but, since they had then not acquiesced to them, they had fallen into disbelief.

It also becomes clear by association that certain elements of corpulence—if not to say certain disagreeable and inflations- have come about within *fiqh* (as a this-worldly and human discipline) which are products of forbidden and unwanted questions that have in turn produced much bitterness and many constraints, none of which was desired by the Prophet.

Fiqh: *Essential or Accidental?*

g. We have thus commenced the discussion on the accidental nature of *fiqh*.[22] Some of the precepts of *fiqh* and some of the laws of some religions (including Islam) are accidental in the mentioned sense; that is to say, they are the products of the emergence of accidental (and at times undesirable) questions, which might not have emerged and not have led to the emergence of these precepts and laws. And the holy Qur'an includes some questions and answers of this kind, and rejects and forbids others.

Be that as it may, the accidental nature of *fiqh* is not confined to this characteristic. *Fiqh* is condemned to being accidental in at least two other senses. The first can be extrapolated from Abu-Hamid Al-Ghazali's words.[23] He said that Islamic jurists, *fuqaha*, were this-worldly experts and their science, a this-worldly discipline. He did not consider *fiqh* to be a religious science and believed that the heart remained outside the guardianship of the jurist [*wilayat-e faqih*]. This is because, first,

---

[22] The word *fiqh* is used interchangeably with *shari'ah* (religious precepts) here and in many other places in this book. [Ed.]

[23] Abu Hamed Al-Ghazali, *Ihya al-'Ulum al-Din* (Cairo: Mustafa al-Babi al-Halabi, 1951), the First Quarter, (kitab al-'ilm), on the divisions of knowledge.

the science of *fiqh* is concerned with the formal validity or invalidity of external actions; not with its underlying motive and intention. It even believes that embracing Islam by force is still Islam (although an Islam of this kind is not worth anything in the hereafter). It views a prayer said without sincerity and intermingled with a hundred dishonest thoughts and a fast sullied with lies and ill-will as acceptable prayer and fast, which will suffice and will not have to be compensated for. Secondly, it gives way to a variety of religious tricks for neglecting duties and even teaches tricks of this kind. And, thirdly, (apart from the section on special acts of worship such as the *hajj*, fasting, etc.) *fiqh* is a code for settling disputes and establishing order in society. If people really behave honestly and fairly and do not commit any offences or transgressions, there will be no need for *fiqh*. And, as far as Al-Ghazali was concerned, settling disputes, alleviating disorder and establishing justice in this world is not an intrinsic desideratum for religion; if it had no other-worldly benefits, it would be disregarded by the Legislator. What virtue is there in an orderly animal life after all? In other words, if life in this world was not followed by life in the hereafter, there would be no need for religion or religious jurisprudence [*fiqh*].

The Legislator's intrinsic desire and motive is to ensure other-worldly felicity; however, since for the attainment of other-worldly felicity and preparation for the beatific sight of God, believers need this-worldly calm so that they can perform their duties and acts of worship, the Prophet has, incidentally, cast a glance at this world and established minimalist laws for disciplining people, the settlement of disputes, the thwarting of transgressions and the preservation of the sanctity of religion, reason, life, the species and property.[24] It was on the basis of these views expounded by Al-Ghazali that Rumi wrote his verses:

> If the Law had not exercised a gracious spell (over them), every one would have torn the body of his rival to pieces.

[24] The preservation of *din* (religion), *'aql* (reason), *nafs* (life), *nasl* (progeny) and *mal* (property) are the five aims of Islamic law and the five focal points of *fiqh*, and all of Islam's social laws have been enacted to provide and safeguard them. Al-Ghazali has spoken about them in brief in *Ihya al-'Ulum*, Vol. 3, and more extensively in his books: *Shifa al-Ghalil* and *Al-Mustasfa*. Later, Shatebi, the great Sunni jurist spoke about them at length in his book, *Al-Muwafaqat*.

Know for sure that the Law is like the measure and scales by means of which the litigants are saved from wrangling and enmity.[25]

In the words of Al-Ghazali himself in *The Revival of the Religious Sciences*:

> If this-worldly *fiqh* has a virtue, it is to cleanse the heart of alien and distracting elements so that it can devote itself to religious *fiqh*, and it is thanks to this other *fiqh* that this-worldly *fiqh* can join the ranks of the religious sciences[26]

Al-Ghazali's views are the exact opposite of some contemporary commentators who manipulate the idea of the hereafter for this-worldly purposes. They suggest in their teachings that the thought of the hereafter prevents people from violating and transgressing the rights of others in this world; whereas, according to Al-Ghazali, a world without transgressions paves the way for felicity and bliss in the hereafter.

Fiqh's accidental nature in the second sense can be extrapolated from the words of Shah Wali Allah, the Indian mystic, innovator and theologian of the eighteenth century who produced the important work *Hujjat Allah al-Baligha*.[27] After lengthy introductory remarks therein about divine traditions, felicity, the truth of prophethood, etc. he asks why particular religious laws are ordained for a particular age and people. He writes in reply:

> The crucial point lies in the following verse from the Qur'an: "All food was lawful to the Children of Israel save what Israel had forbidden to himself before the Torah was sent down. Say: 'Bring you the Torah now, and recite it, if you are truthful.'" (3: 93) The interpretation of this is that Jacob, peace be upon him, fell ill and prayed that he would regain his health,

---

[25] *Mathnawi*, 5: 1210, 1214.

[26] Al-Ghazali, *Ihya al-ʿUlum*, Fourth Quarter, (kitab al-muraqibah wa al-muhasibah). This author has written at length on this subject in two places see: "Jameh Tahdhib bar Tan-e *Ihya*", in *Qeseh-ye Arbab-e Maʿrefat* [The Tale of the Lords of Sagacity], (Tehran: Serat, 1375/1996); and "Ihya al-ulum al-din" [Revival of Religious Sciences] in *Daʾerat al-Maʿaref-e Bozorg-e Islami* [The Greater Encyclopaedia of Islam], Vol. 7 (Tehran, 1376/1997).

[27] This book is about the rationale, underlying meaning and characteristics of Islamic practices and laws and the reason for their enactment. According to Shah Wali Allah, the book was the result of a kind of inspiration and illumination. He saw the Prophet of Islam, peace be upon him, in a vision and, in a dream, Imams Hasan and Hossein came to him and presented him with a pen, which they said belonged to their grandfather, the Prophet. And Shah Wali Allah, who had been thinking about the expediencies of Islamic laws for quite some time, became determined to organise and present his ideas in the form of a book after these incidents. (See the preface of *Hujjat al-Baligha*.)

pledging to forbid to himself upon recovery all that he most dearly loved to eat and drink. Upon recovery, he forbid the eating of camel meat and the drinking of camel milk to himself thereafter; and his children followed him in this. Several centuries passed in this way and his offspring grew convinced that eating camel meat was a sign of disrespect to prophets. It was then that the Torah ordained that the eating of camel meat was forbidden. And, when the Prophet of Islam, peace be upon him, declared that he was from the nation of Abraham, the Jews objected, saying: "how can he eat camel meat and drink camel milk if he is from the nation of Abraham." Then, God, may He be Exalted, replied that the eating of all food had been permitted at first and that camel meat was forbidden by virtue of an accidental affair that affected the Jews... Know that the differences between the laws of the prophets, peace be upon them, results from differences in the causes and in what is best for different peoples. For divine laws are laws for preparing human beings and the degree and extent of the duty is appropriate to the characteristics and habits of the people who must perform them. For example, since the people of Noah, peace be upon him, were of a very extreme temperaments- as God Himself has said—uninterrupted fastings were ordained to be a duty for them so that their savage instincts would be broken. And, since this nation is of a weak disposition, they were forbidden uninterrupted fasts. The same applies to war booty, which was not permissible to earlier peoples but which God permitted us in view of our weakness... And anyone who understands the principle of religion and the causes of the differences between prohibitions, will see that there has not been any alteration or transformation in them. And this is why laws are ordained for specific peoples... For example, when an Arab wishes to embark on a task or a journey, if he hears a felicitous phrase, he will take it as a good omen, unlike non-Arabs, and the reports of the Prophet contain some examples of this type of things. Similarly, in the divine laws are expressed branches of knowledge accumulated among the people and beliefs internalised by them, and customs which literally flow in their veins. In this same way, the knowledge, beliefs and habits of a people are taken into account in the ordination of religious laws... And, of course, there is much knowledge and many habits that are alike among Arabs and non-Arabs and the residents of moderate climes... Hence, this knowledge and these habits are considered next by prophets.[28]

So far, Shah Wali Allah has spoken of two important accidentals of religious laws: first, the characteristics of prophets and, second, the characteristics of the peoples being brought under the laws (their customs and habits, as well as their disposition and endurance), such that, if either changes, the laws also change. He counsels in particular

---

[28] *Hujjat Allah al-Baligha*, Vol. 1, pp. 88–90.

that good and bad, and righteousness and wickedness are related to the people's beliefs. He says that, just as, in the minds of Arabs, knowledge is formulated into Arabic words and expressions, good and bad is also made to correspond to their habits and conventions. By way of an example, he says that Muslims came to be forbidden from marrying their sisters' daughters, but not Jews, because, for Jews, a sister's daughter was an alien, belonging to her father's tribe and they did not have any contacts with her, unlike the Arabs.[29]

On the whole, he considers peoples' customs and traditions as having a bearing on their religious laws and says that prophets did not claim to change their peoples' customs, eating and drinking habits, clothing, housing, adornments, marriage, commercial transactions, justice, retribution and punishment, as long as they did not clash with the overall religious interests (acts of worship, moderate living and taking the middle way between hermit-like isolation and kingly extravagance).

> And the learned will know that Islamic law did not bring anything that the Arabs were not familiar with or would have had difficulty accepting on matrimony, divorce, transactions, adornments, clothing, justice, punishment and the division of booty. It was more a question of righting wrongs, such as usury, which had become widespread and was subsequently forbidden... The blood money for murder during the time of Abd al-Muttalib was ten camels. He saw that ten camels did not prevent people from killing each other, so he raised it to a hundred camels. And the Prophet (PBUH) kept this and did not change it. Abu Talib organised the first division of spoils. After any spoliation, one-quarter would go to the head of the tribe. The Prophet (PBUH) made it one-fifth. Qobad and his son Anushiravan used to collect taxes and tithes; Islamic law ordained something similar. The Children of Israel used to stone adulterers, cut off thieves' hands and take a life for a life; the Qur'an ordained the same. And there are many other examples which will not remain hidden to astute researchers. In fact, if you are clever and aware of the circumstances of the time, you will know that the prophets, peace be upon them, also did not bring anything in terms of customs and rituals of worship which had not already existed in the same or similar form among their peoples. Yet, they repudiated the distortions of the Age of Ignorance, and firmly established the times and principles which had become previously confused and they publicised things that had become obscure.[30]

---

[29] Ibid., p. 90.
[30] Ibid., p. 105.

Shah Wali Allah finally issues his verdict on a religion that can supersede all others. He says that the precondition for the success of such a
religion is not for its founder to leave all peoples to their own devices
and to endorse and approve all their different customs and laws. Instead,
he must

> Call on a particular people to follow the correct tradition. He must purify
> them and reform their conditions, and then see them as his own limbs,
> struggling against everyone else with their assistance and scattering them
> to every corner...For the founder himself cannot fight single-handedly
> against countless nations and, since this is the way it is, his divine law
> must, in the first instance, be like a natural religion suited to the residents
> of all the appropriate climes and, next, in keeping with the knowledge
> and manner of life of his own people. And, in his religion, he must take
> into consideration the characteristics of his people more than anyone else
> and then induce everyone else to follow this divine law, because it is not
> possible to leave the matter to the people or to the leaders of every age,
> otherwise divine laws would cease to have any point...Hence, there is no
> easier and better way than to respect—in his religion's laws, prohibitions
> and penalties—the customs of the people he has come to lead, and to be
> more lenient towards the peoples who subsequently follow...[31]

A detailed assessment of Shah Wali Allah's views must be left to another
occasion. For the time being, the point that can clearly be noted in his
views is that the precepts of shari'ah, religious customs, the form and
appearance of rites of worship and other rites, and the regulations
pertaining to individual and social behaviour—not aims and intentions
and the expediencies of laws, which are among religion's essentials
are originally ordained on the basis of the lives and characteristics
and the spiritual, social, geographical and historical circumstances of
a particular people, such that, had these circumstances been different, the customs, precepts and regulations would also have taken on
a different form and shape. It is not as if the ordination of precepts
was based on good and bad per se, without any consideration for the
historical circumstances.

In other words, in the opinion of Shah Wali Allah of Delhi, if the
Prophet had appeared in the midst of some other people, who had had
different customs, rites and conventions, while the aims of his faith (that
is, the preservation of religion, reason, life, the progeny and property)
would have remained the same, the physiognomy of many of his pre-

---

[31] Ibid., p. 118.

cepts would have changed. And, for example, the precepts on talion, blood money, matrimony, cleanliness, uncleanliness, men and women's clothing, and, more generally, the rights of men and women, slaves, non-slaves, Muslims, non-Muslims, etc. would all have taken on a different form, while Islam would still have remained the same Islam.

The question of what kind of *fiqh* would emerge from such a philosophy of *fiqh* need not detain us now. But there can be no doubt that the underlying contention is that most of the precepts of *fiqh* and even its basic tenets are accidentals. Even prayers and fasting have been made proportionate to what people can endure on average. If their endurance was much greater, the obligations may well have been more severe.

Ijtihad: *Cultural Translation of the Accidentals*

On the basis of this view, *ijtihad* too, would no longer be confined to the application of principles of innocence/ or no obligation (*bara'at*), assumption of continuity and the like but would be synonymous with "cultural translation". It would then apply to all accidentals and translate an Arabic "taking dates to Basra" to a Persian "taking cumin to Kerman"; preserving the spirit and transforming the body, in other words. This would amount to taking the conventions, customs and characteristics of different cultures into account and conveying religion's intentions not in form, but in spirit and meaning. The simplest and least controversial consequence of this would be that the phrases used to seal a marriage or divorce would no longer have to be recited in Arabic, but—since they are accidentals—could equally be expressed in Persian or French (and of course this has both proponents and opponents among Islamic jurists). And the idea that the payment of blood money and the sanctity of the sacred months originated from the Arabs' tribal relations and their particular conventions would also mark them as clear instances of accidentals. And the suggestion that slavery was also an accidental imposed on Islam is being increasingly accepted. But the implications are much more profound than this. Transcending accidentals—or translating them into the accidentals of another culture—would have many other rousing, revolutionary and liberating consequences, the discovery and expounding of which would herald a new order and a new paradigm in the discipline of *fiqh*.

h. The events that have taken place in the history of Islam, whether in the age of our main religious leaders or thereafter, are all accidentals and might not have occurred. This being so, they cannot be included in the articles of faith. On the whole, the role played by personalities in religion (apart from the Prophet, whose personality is one of religion's essentials) is entirely accidental and closely related to the accidents of history.

The selection of Abu-Bakr and Uthman as caliphs; the fact that Imam Ali did govern; the fact that the other Shiʻi Imams did not govern; the fact that the Qur'an was collected after the Prophet; the fact that the ummah divided into Sunnis and Shiʻis; and so on and so forth are all accidentals. They must, therefore, be viewed as no more than possible historical events. They were all equally necessary or accidental and, consequently, are all components of historical Islam, not components of Islam as a belief system. And faith pertains to Islam as a belief system, not to historical Islam.

The believers who died during the Prophet's lifetime and did not live to see the events that occurred after his demise were just as much believers as those who followed.

We must take the same view of the tale of fabrications and inventions, and the entry of inauthentic hadiths and inappropriate questions into the body of historical Islam, which are both accidental and undesirable. As can be seen, historical Islam or the history of Islam (with all its actors, events, wisdom, ignorance, and good and bad aspects) is like a body over the spirit of Islam or like an evolution of the Prophet's intentions; an evolution that includes auspicious and inauspicious elements.

Conclusion

Religion does not have an Aristotelian essence or nature; it is the Prophet who has certain goals. These goals *are* religion's essentials. In order to express and attain these intentions and to have them understood, the Prophet seeks the assistance of (1) a particular language, (2) particular concepts and (3) particular methods (*fiqh* and ethics). All of this occurs in a particular (4) time and (5) place (geographical and cultural) and for (6) a particular people with particular physical and mental capacities. The purveyor of religion is faced with specific (7) reactions and (8) questions and, in response to them, gives (9) specific answers. The flow of religion over the course of time in turn gives rise to events, moving some people to (10) acquiesce and others to (11) repudiate. Believers and unbelievers fall into (12) particular relationships with each other and religion; they fight battles or create civilisations, (13) engage in comprehending and expanding religious ideas and experiences or (14) wrecking and undermining them.

These fourteen points, which are all products of the fact that religion has a historical, human, evolutionary, interlocutory and dynamic identity, are the corpulent accidentals that hide within them the precious essence of religiosity. In order to uncover this gem, we have no choice but to peel away those superficies. In order to identify and peel away the accidentals and incidentals we need to deconstruct religion's historical body: in the light of our refined theory of what we expect from religion, first, religious teachings are distinguished from non-religious teachings (medicine, alchemy, etc. are set aside, for example), then, through an exhaustive study and examination of the doctrine's inner components (similar to what Juwayni, Al-Ghazali and Shatebi did with *fiqh*), and by considering theoretical and hypothetical assumptions and historical events that were possible but never occurred (counter-factual: if it had been another people, if they had reacted differently and asked different questions, had had other mental and physical abilities and capacities, had had a different language and culture, had had other habits and customs, if the Prophet had had a shorter or longer life, if he had come in the twentieth century, if Arabia had been industrial, if everyone had become Muslims, if no one had become a Muslim, if Islam had not come to Iran, had not gone to Egypt, if etc. and if etc. in what ways would religion have been different?), the accidental coat and dust can be scraped away until the ultimate discovery of the essence or rather a theory about the essence of religion and the intentions of the Prophet; a theory which is constantly transformed with the discovery of new accidentals and in the light of new counter-factuals.

These investigations will make one thing clear: that no accidental will ever lead us to any essential. Islam as a belief system is the essentials and historical Islam is the accidentals. And being a Muslim entails believing in and acting upon the essentials and thinking about religion in the sense of trying to distinguish the essentials from the accidentals; and *ijtihad* in *fiqh* entails a cultural translation of the accidentals.

CHAPTER FIVE

MAXIMALIST RELIGION, MINIMALIST RELIGION

Maximal View of Religion

In discussing the question of minimalist and maximalist religion, it may be best for me to begin by explaining the considerations and incidents that led me to address this issue. Several events alerted me to the importance of the subject.

The first event goes back to years before the Iranian Revolution (1979). A friend of mine told me about the time in 1969 when there was a cholera epidemic in Mecca. He said that pilgrims were being advised to pay particular attention to matters of hygiene and, for example, to wash their hands with disinfectant after using the toilet. But, he said, the cleric in our convoy was not very supportive of these preventative measures. His argument was that, had it been necessary, it would have been decreed in Islamic law; since there was no precept to this effect in the shariʿah and since it had not been deemed to be a religious duty, it was clear that the measure was unnecessary (he did not say that it was religiously forbidden). He therefore insisted that it was enough to observe the recognised ceremonial ablutions and rinse one's hands with water.

I found the argument very thought provoking. My friend had told me the story as an amusing anecdote, but I kept asking myself whether the cleric's logic did not rest on some underlying philosophy. What was wrong with the suggestion that the shariʿah had said all that needed to be said on matters of hygiene, rendering unnecessary any additional measures? It is the case that, whether in the Legislator's eye the washing of hands constituted the *necessary minimum* in terms of hygiene or the *maximum possible*? Should we take what we find in the shariʿah on this and other matters to be minimalist or maximalist instructions? Should we see them as the necessary minimum or the commendable maximum possible?

There is a view that suggests that all the necessary and sufficient measures, instructions and rules for economics, governance, commerce, law, ethics, knowledge of God and so on for any kind of mentality or life, whether simple or complex, have been included in Islamic law. According to this view the believers require no source (for felicity in this world and the next) other than religion. I call this to be "the maximalist understanding of religion" or "the maximalist expectation of religion". As against this, we have "the minimalist viewpoint" or "the minimalist expectation" that holds that, Islamic law has taught us no more than the necessary minimum in such instances, i.e. on matters that fall within its purview.

I should add here that anything that goes beyond "minimalism" is "maximalism"; in other words, there is no "median" and anything that is not minimalist is maximalist. I should also say that our expectations of religion are being taken as read here. That is to say, we are not concerning ourselves with the question of whether expecting religion to set out rules about governance, commerce, hygiene and medicine is appropriate or not. We are saying, assuming this expectation to be appropriate and assuming that religion fulfils it, does it do so in a minimalist or maximalist way? Let me also add this important point: the precepts of the shariʿah of which we are speaking are not of the nature of unanimously accepted ones; they can certainly be challenged and debated within the framework of the shariʿah itself. Nonetheless, we are not looking at them from jurists' perspective and we will, for the sake of argument, assume that they are valid and uncontroversial.

At any rate, my ruminations made it clear to me that many religious people, be they learned or common people, subscribe to the maximalist viewpoint and expectation; in other words, they wish to find everything that they require in religion and they see this as an indicator of its perfection and all-inclusiveness.

After the Revolution, when religion became an active player in society and set out to tackle social and economic affairs, when it raised expectations, became engaged in resolving problems and moved from the realm of theory to the realm of practice, the events to which I referred began to multiply.

On the second event, I will quote one of the senior officials of the Islamic Republic. In the years immediately after the Revolution, he would say to me: we have spoken to the members of the Association of Qum Seminary Lecturers about the country's economic problems. The gentlemen confidently told us that we should simply apply the precepts of Islamic law, and collect and spend the designated religious taxes and alms according to the shariʿah; all our economic problems would then be resolved. They said that economic problems revealed that the people were not being sufficiently religious and that they were not carrying out the precepts of Islamic law as well and as obediently as they should. Otherwise, all that was required in terms of guidelines and policies for solving economic and social problems had been set out in religion. Later, one of these same clerics explicitly wrote that the shariʿah was perfect in every way, both in terms of precepts and planning, thereby setting his unreserved seal of approval on the maximalist viewpoint.

The third event concerns the question of the penal laws. As we know, according to Islamic law and given the relevant conditions set out in *fiqh*, a thief's punishment is to have his hand cut off. This has been seen by many common and learned people as the best and most effective solution to the problem of theft. Some of our clerics, especially before the Revolution, would write in their books, that there were no thieves in Saudi Arabia and there was complete security during the *hajj* because they observed Islamic law on theft there. These clerics maintained that the problem in a society such as ours was that we did not apply these precepts. In order to solve the problem of theft and to prevent it, the only necessary, appropriate and effective method was to punish thieves in accordance with Islamic law and the precepts of *fiqh*.

The fourth event concerned hoarding. One major problem after the revolution was the incidence of hoarding. The ruling in Islamic law on hoarding is that the hoarded goods (and not just any goods, but just a few specifically named items) had to be taken away from the hoarder and sold at a fair price. This was meant to ensure both that the people obtained the goods they needed and the hoarder did not make exorbitant profits. At the time, a member of the Guardian Council said plainly in an interview that this was the maximum that could and should be done with respect to hoarding, and that this was exactly what they were doing.

Examples such as these abounded. And in each case, the speakers were apparently unaware of the theory they were advocating or its philosophical basis.

As I said, considerations such as these brought me to the conclusion that most of the people in our society—taking their cue from their clerical leaders, of course—believe that religion is a maximal source and reservoir. Later on, when I began my work at the Council for Cultural Revolution and grappled with the dilemma and riddle of the human sciences, I came to understand even better the sheer scale of the pandemonium. One senior cleric was fond of saying that everything that had been said in the human sciences existed in virtual and even actual form in Islamic philosophy. And he justified this position by citing Ibn Sina's statement that men and women are two types, not two kinds! I gradually realised that the hajj convoy cleric was by no means a lone rider, but that he was part of a vast convoy of like-minded people. I understood then that the problem was much too pervasive and deep-rooted to be encapsulated in an amusing anecdote. Expecting maximal results from minimal precepts, demanding solutions for complex lives and minds from precepts appropriate to a much more simple lifestyle, turning *ijtihad* into the extraction of maximums from minimums have led to and become the root cause of serious theoretical and practical problems in our society.

Fiqh: *Minimum "Necessary" or Maximum "Sufficient"?*

It may be useful at this point to linger briefly on the purport of the above stories. In my opinion, there can be no doubt, for example, that cutting off thieves hands in accordance with the precepts of *fiqh* is by no means sufficient to prevent theft in society. It may at times be necessary to implement this precept (as I said, we will not enter into the question of the correctness of these rulings and we will assume that they could be implemented in the appropriate circumstances), but there is a difference between *"necessary"* and *"sufficient"*. In principle, the implementation of penal regulations are effective and beneficial in any given society where natural and normal conditions prevail. But if the conditions are defective and deficient through and through and society is in an abnormal state, then the imposition of these penalties will not solve anything. People must be well brought up, parents must ensure that their children behave properly, people must on the whole be of sound mental and physical health, and a satisfactory livelihood should be guaranteed for all. These are all necessary conditions for controlling theft in society and, in the absence of these conditions, punishment alone would not solve anything; in fact, punishment would be altogether inappropriate. Hence, if we believe that a thief should be punished (and we do), we should see punishment as the minimum requirement for the prevention of theft—and only in a healthy and normal society—for, it is most certainly not the maximum.

Islamic jurists [*faqihs*] have made this same point in connection with the penalty for apostasy. They have said that, if doubts are prevalent in society during a certain period, if people happen to be living through confused and anxious times, nobody can be put to death for apostasy. Setting aside the issue of capital punishment as a penalty, the spirit of the proviso described here is perfectly clear. Penal sanctions belong to normal times. Hence, the duty of believers in the first instance is to bring about normal conditions in society; not to put the cart before the horse and begin Islamising society by implementing punishments regardless of the circumstances. And establishing normal conditions largely depends on providing for people's basic needs, which is the duty of all states, religious or otherwise.

The same can be said of "hoarding". Many things need to be done to prevent hoarding, and not in terms of sanctions and penalties but in terms of economic and political planning. Certainly, after doing all that can reasonably be done and as a final measure, if someone persists and refuses to make do with their entitlement, they must be stopped and their misdeeds halted.

The same applies to hygiene. The minimum that a person can do is to rinse their hands once or twice with water. But, if someone takes this Islamic precept on hygiene as the maximum that they should do under any circumstances, they would be mistaken. In fact, it would indicate the most profound misunderstanding of the logic of religion and *fiqh*. The precepts of Islamic law in this connection are the minimal steps that can be taken in terms of hygiene under the most basic conditions and in the most primitive societies. In other words, even in the most basic living conditions, these minimal precepts can and must be carried out. However, this is not to say that they are sufficient, maximal precepts for more complex circumstances.

Exactly the same can be said about all the precepts of *fiqh* and law; even in the realm of acts of worship per se. For example, the daily required amount of prayer has been stipulated in Islamic law. But this does not mean that this is the maximum amount of prayer allowed. It means that it should be no less than this. Or, take the duty of fasting during the month of Ramadan. The purport of this requirement is that anything less than a month of fasting does not necessarily provide the minimum preparedness for spiritual perfection. Nonetheless, there is nothing to stop one from going much further than this. The payment of religious alms and the tax consisting of one-fifth of one's income is also a minimal financial requirement; paying over and above this would certainly be laudable and even necessary for the good of society. (Let me repeat that I have no intention of going into the disputes that exist within the discipline of *fiqh* on these precepts, for there are Shi'i jurists who do not recognise the payment of the one-fifth tax *khoms* as a duty and no Sunni jurist recognises it at all, other than on war booty.)

Here, we find ourselves at a fateful and delicate crossroads: the bifurcation of religion into this-worldly orientation and other-worldly orientation. This-worldly oriented religion sees the precepts of the shariʿah and ethics as *necessary* and *sufficient* for running society and solving social problems. It sees felicity in the hereafter as following from felicity in this world and being subject to it. As against this, otherworldly-oriented religion sees them as duties, the main aim of which is the provision of felicity in the hereafter. It considers this world as existing for that end only and as a preface to it, and concerns itself with it to that extent and to that extent only. In other words, it sees all precepts as being of the nature of acts of worship per se.

Now, if we consider religion to be otherworldly, there can be no doubt that we have to take it upon ourselves to observe good practice in terms of hygiene and respect other individual and social obligations such as mortgages, rent, contracts and so on; we must perform our religious duties and the precepts of Islamic law in order to benefit from their small this-worldly benefits (which consist of the creation of a peaceful environment and the resolution of conflict) and their great otherworldly rewards. For example, we must see the payment of *zakat* and *khoms* (religious taxes) as a duty aimed at ridding ourselves of the love of material wealth, which incidentally also happens to help the needy (as Al-Ghazali put it), and not in the main as a call to provide funds for an Islamic state (as people think today). We must perform these duties aside from their social consequences. In this reading, the cutting off of hands would not be viewed as a prime method for the prevention of theft. Hence, we would not only have to perform this duty (that is, cut off a thief's hand) but also strive to find solutions for the social problem of theft in its own right. To subscribe to this position is decisively to reduce to a minimum the role of *fiqh* in the resolution of social problems.

However, if we believe that these precepts are intended for dealing with social problems and for solving them—if, in other words, we make *fiqh* this worldly—then, we can no longer assume that the precepts of Islamic law are the bearers of secret and hidden rationale. We must, instead, concentrate entirely on their this-worldly success in resolving problems and, wherever the precepts of *fiqh* do not yield the desired results in today's complex, industrial societies (on issues such as commerce, matrimony, banking, rent, theft, talion, governance, politics and so on), we must change them. In other words, *fiqh* will become an earthly and pragmatic legal science, which is constantly added to or subtracted from in the light of pragmatic considerations. And this would be the clearest testimony to its minimalist nature.

I know that some people like to say, we will set this-worldly and otherworldly interests on a par and hit two birds with one stone. But, alas, this road leads to nowhere. Success in resolving this-worldly problems hinges on the absence of any unseen, hidden interests, such that a law can be judged on its immediate—and not ultimate—consequences. The fanatical formalism of Islamic jurists arises precisely from the fact that they have an eye on the otherworldly consequences of actions and precepts; otherwise, why would they get so obsessed with the payment of alms on the fourfold grains or the hoarding of special items. They keep thinking to themselves, maybe there is some rationale behind the requirement of alms on particular goods which we are not aware of and do not understand; a rationale that will become clear on Judgement Day. It is precisely considerations of this kind that ties *fiqh*'s hands in solving this-worldly problems. *Fiqh* either has to be completely this worldly, such that the hereafter is subject to it, or it must be completely otherworldly, such that this world is subject to it. There is no third alternative.[1]

And even a this-worldly *fiqh* is minimalist, since legal questions encompass only a small part of human life. It is in keeping with early, primitive societies and essentially deals with the resolution of conflicts. This is what Al-Ghazali meant when he said that the Islamic jurist's mandate (*wilayat*) is not over hearts, but over bodies, and, secondly,

---

[1] In 1996 I presented an article at Harvard University entitled "Is Fiqh Possible?". Based on the views of Al-Ghazali, I argued that a *fiqh* that takes both this-worldly and otherworldly considerations into account and places them on a par is impossible. *Fiqh* can either be entirely this worldly, with otherworldly considerations taking second place and being subject to this world, or it can be entirely otherworldly, with this-worldly considerations taking second place and being subject to the hereafter. But placing both on a par and attaching equal value to them, and trying to respect this-worldly considerations while also fulfilling otherworldly ones is impossible and will lead to the negation of both. Also, Fakhr al-din al-Razi's observation about this world being subject to the hereafter and worthy of attention only where necessary (that is, minimally) is interesting in this context: "A prophet's mission is to call people to the Truth and the Hereafter. But because people live in this world and are dependent on it, there is a need to pay heed to this world where necessary." Fakhr al-Din al-Razi, *Al-Matalib al-Aliyah*, ed. by Ahmad Hijazi, Vol. 8, p. 115 (Beirut: Dar al-Kitab al-Arabi, 1987).

that, if the people behaved justly and there were no more conflicts, the jurists would be out of a job.[2]

At any rate, be it this worldly or otherworldly, *fiqh* is confined to "*precepts*"; in other words, it is summed up in a series of shoulds and should nots and dos and don'ts. This is a different matter altogether from drawing up plans and programmes for life and living. Planning is a scientific task, based on a range of skills and know-how, which is completely beyond the scope of *fiqh/the shari'ah*. It is entirely in vain that anyone expects such a thing from *fiqh/the shari'ah*. Drawing up plans for preserving forests and green spaces is in no way a task for lawyers and jurists. Hence, the above-mentioned cleric's claim that *fiqh* is perfect in terms of planning is unacceptable. *Fiqh* is perfect in terms of precepts, not planning, and it is a minimalist, not a maximalist, perfectness, at that.

It may be useful to repeat here that "minimalist" means that, if *fiqh* is this worldly, it has precepts suited to minimal social conditions and fulfils simple and basic legal requirements on issues that may arise anywhere and at any time. It does not deal with the larger requirements of a complex lifestyle. And, if it is otherworldly, it means that it renders possible a minimum of otherworldly felicity and ascension to the lowest reaches of spiritual existence.

It may be said that *fiqh* also has secondary precepts and deems it unconditionally necessary to preserve lives, maintain social order, etc. And, in cases of conflict between two duties, it rules in favour of the greater duty. And, in cases of undue hardship, it annuls certain duties. And it does not consider a harmful precept to be a precept at all, and so on and so forth. Hence, if disinfecting one's hands is necessary for the preservation of life and the avoidance of harm, then it will also become an Islamic duty. And, if it becomes necessary to take further measures to prevent hoarding, then those measures will also become Islamic duties. And, if it becomes necessary to impose other taxes to provide funds for the Islamic state, they, too, will become duties, etc. Yes, this is true. Nonetheless, it has to be borne in mind that, despite all this, *fiqh* will, first, still remain "a science of precepts" that is not capable of planning. Secondly, a *fiqh* of this nature will effectively turn into a rational, human and secular pragmatism, no different from any

---

[2] Al-Ghazali, *Ihya*, "kitab al-'ilm".

non-religious or secular legal system. In other words, in becoming maximalist, it would have ceased to be religious and Islamic.

People think about solving social problems and finding rational solutions to them in every corner of the world. There is no need to call this Islamic jurisprudence. And, if we are to proceed on this basis, then there is no need for us to perform the Islamic ablutions either; it will suffice if we act according to the dictates of the science of hygiene. In brief, this solution, intended to turn the minimalist into the maximalist, would completely wipe the issue out and reduce the role of *fiqh* to zero. Of course this is the natural consequence of the secularisation of religion in the modern age. But then it is no longer appropriate for them to tell us that we have a duty to perform divine precepts. They should say, we have a duty to do that which is rational and to solve individual and social problems using pragmatic and secular methods.[3]

As to our earlier assertion that *fiqh* is perfect in terms of precepts, not planning, we meant true *fiqh* as it should be in principle. Otherwise, actually existing *fiqh* is far from replete even in terms of precepts and, in many instances, it generates conjectural (and incorrect) rulings. Such an aggregate of correct and incorrect things (which cannot be purged of its mistakes) cannot be described as rich and complete. No body of knowledge is definitive and complete. The existing discipline of *fiqh*, too, like any other human discipline, is incomplete and in the process of development. In fact, the suggestion that *fiqh* is rich, complete and maximalist is not very meaningful. Would this pertain to today's *fiqh*, yesterday's *fiqh* or the *fiqh* of twenty centuries hence? Unless we say that the discipline of *fiqh* is potentially, not actually, complete, or that the discovered and undiscovered bases and sources of *fiqh* put together are rich and complete; in which case, this can be said of any discipline. After all, any discipline is potentially complete. As long as all the mistakes are purged and as long as all the correct propositions are discovered, it will no doubt be complete!

All the above examples concerned *fiqh*. The only conclusion we can draw so far, then, is that "*fiqh*" is minimalist, not "religion". If we are to establish that "religion" is minimalist, we must press further in our discussion.

---

[3] I have spoken at length about *fiqh*, governing with the aid of *fiqh*, solving political, administrative and social problems using *fiqh*, and the theoretical and practical implications and consequences of all this in *Reason, Freedom, and Democracy in Islam*, see Chapters Eight and Nine.

Science and Religion

The next point is the relationship between science and religion. The way
in which the conflict between science and religion is resolved is itself an
important issue. But, apart from the way it is resolved, most believers
throughout the world have come to the conclusion that religion was
not intended for the teaching of the natural sciences. Generally speaking, all Muslims, at least, are agreed on this. But fifty years ago, things
were not so clear. I discovered that an Islamic scholar had written in his
book that the science of physics can be extracted from Qur'anic verses
talking about light. Not so long ago, a well-known cleric in Qum said,
given that a discipline as rich as the primary principles of the logic of
Islamic law can be derived from a few Prophetic traditions such as "Do
not undermine certainty with doubt" and the like, why should it not be
possible to extract the science of agriculture from a few *hadith*s. Let us
go and find those *hadith*s. The same cleric has written that the science
of ship building can be learned from the story of Noah. These types of
claims are not confined to the world of us Muslims. It was the same in
Christian and Jewish communities. Similar religious experiences occur
in all religious communities.

At any rate, very few people subscribe to such peculiar notions today.
Most of us have accepted, in other words, that religion is not intended
for the teaching of the natural-experimental sciences. None of us, truly
and in all fairness, expect the Prophet to teach us physics, chemistry,
astronomy, medicine, geometry or algebra and analysis. Even if there
are references to some of these things in our religious narratives, they
are completely incidental; that is to say, they are not a part of religion's
core and central thread. It was not the Prophet's primary mission—nor
the mission of any prophet—to teach these types of subjects. References to these things are entirely *incidental* and marginal; teaching
them always fell outside the purview of the mission assigned to God's
prophets and saints (*awliya*).

Arriving at this conclusion has many happy consequences. For
example, it does away with the problem of the conflict between religion
and science. In other words, it makes us realise that we do not need
to dwell on or quibble over the scientific points that are raised within
religion. This realisation moves us closer to the realisation that, even if
religion has a role to play in the context of explicating scientific issues,
the relevant material is minimalist and peripheral, not maximalist and
central. No one can claim that what religion says about medicine is

maximalist; that is to say, that it has taught us everything we need to know or it is possible to know on medical matters.

But science is not just confined to the natural-experimental sciences. We also have the human sciences. We have economics, political science and sociology. What are we to say about these? The debate on these disciplines remains inconclusive and we have yet to close the chapter on this. We have still not arrived at a consensus on the human sciences similar to the one obtained on the natural-experimental sciences after a lengthy, historical process. But it will be amply clear to anyone who has worked in this field and is familiar with the history of these disciplines that the verdict in this instance is much the same as in the previous one. The verdict on the human sciences, such as economics, psychology and sociology, is the same as that on physics and the natural sciences. Religions, including Islam, were neither intended for teaching us the natural-experimental sciences, nor the human sciences. In other words, on the human sciences, too, we have to see religion as minimalist. We have to say, even if religion has said anything in this respect, it is minimal. Even people who believe that some of the theories proffered by these sciences can be extracted from religious texts have never claimed that religion teaches us the maximum possible on, for example, economics or sociology. It would be patently inappropriate to make such a claim. A fully-fledged science of sociology can never be derived from religion; ditto with economics, psychology and so on. Recent years' experiences in this area in our society have shown very clearly how pointless these endeavours are.[4] The fact that these sciences' criteria and methodology are defined so independently of religion is the best indicator of their being substantively different from religion.

If religions had been intended for the teaching of these disciplines, why did no economist, sociologist or psychologist ever emerge from a background in religious studies? And why did the founders of these sciences not extract their fundamental principles from religious teachings? The fact that some of the contents of these disciplines are in conflict

---

[4] At the Baqir al-Ulum School in Qum, under the direction of Muhammad Taqi Mesbah Yazdi. The efforts of a large number of seminarians and university lecturers ultimately led to the publication of five volumes on Islamic Sociology, Islamic Psychology, etc. The main body of all these volumes is made up of the modern sciences, with the addition of Islamic footnotes! or elementary and simplistic points of criticism. They give no indication of an independent approach to these sciences or any independent definitions or premises.

with religious teachings is additional proof that they are distinct and not derivative.

Ethical All-inclusiveness?

After *fiqh* and science, we come to ethics. It would seem that ethics is the last refuge. We may have been prepared to accept that *fiqh* is minimalist and does not, for example, contain everything that needs to be said about hygiene. Or that religion does not underwrite the theories of the natural and human sciences and that sociology, economics and the like cannot be entirely extracted from religion. But what about ethics?

One of our main expectations of religion is that it should teach us ethics and ethical values; that it should teach us "good" and "bad", and "virtue" and "vice", and the paths to "felicity" and "wretchedness". Is what religion has to offer not maximalist in this respect? In fact, people who believe in a maximalist religion seem to let ethics serve as their model and then extend their notion, inappropriately and without any justification, to the other areas of religion. In other words, they take the view that religion has taught us everything there is to know about ethics and values and felicity and wretchedness; and that, if it has not, it is defective. Then, they extend this ethical all-inclusiveness to every other area of religion.

But what is religion's verdict in the realm of ethics? In order to discover this verdict, it may be useful to divide ethical values into two broad categories: master values and servant values. We define these qualities in terms of their relationship to life. That is to say, we have one category of ethical values that life is for and another category of ethical values that are for life. We call those ethical values that life is for "master values"; in other words, we serve them. And the values that are for life or at the service of life, we call "servant values".

The fact of the matter is that a large part and the main body of ethics is made up of servant values. Ninety nine per cent of values are servants and one per cent (if that) masters. In other words, ethics is for life. It teaches us how to live. It serves and is subject to life. It is intricately related to the way in which we live. Ethicists have told us: "Every context has its own etiquette." That is to say, ethics in any context consists of the etiquette appropriate to that context. Sometimes we are at war and sometimes we are at peace. War has its own etiquette and ethics, and peace, its own particular conventions. As religious scholars put it: "War is deceit." In times of war, you may lie. Lying to and deceiving the enemy is permissible. This is etiquette in the context of war. But you may not deceive and lie in the context of peace and friendship.

Another example: when you are alone, you are permitted to be naked, but you are not permitted to appear naked in public. This is etiquette in a public context. That is etiquette in a private context.

Imam Ali's letter to his son, Imam Hasan, contains much advice on ethical matters. In the main, the advice concerns the values that are at the service of life. For example, Imam Ali told his son: "Hold your tongue. Be silent more often than you speak. Honour your tribe. Do not befriend weak-willed people. Respond gently when a friend is unkind. Waste not, want not." And so on. Or, in Imams' traditions, we find it said: "Keep three things hidden from the public: your associations, your money and your opinions."

Now, is silence really a virtue? Is holding one's tongue intrinsically a virtue and speaking at length, intrinsically reprehensible? This is not the case. Keeping quiet was the etiquette of life under the despotic regimes of the past. In fact, it was how people managed to stay alive.

In a community where expressing an opinion can put one's material and moral standing in danger, people have no choice but to hide their opinions and belongings. The individual has to behave in this way in order to live in comfort and security; otherwise, they would be challenged and harmed. This is what servant values means.

Take lying and telling the truth. They are universally considered to fall within the rubric of ethics. But they are still servant, not master, values. We do not live to tell the truth, we tell the truth to live. We have to be honest in order to live in a secure environment in which we can trust people and have healthy relationships. If we lie, life becomes impossible.

Bribery is bad. Why? Because if things do not proceed on the basis of rules and regulations and bribery becomes the only way you can achieve anything, social life itself will come unstuck. A society can only remain healthy if these vices are kept to a minimum.

It should be said that, when we say these values are at the service of life, we do not mean to detract from their value. We are merely describing their purpose. Telling the truth is not intrinsically good and lying is not intrinsically bad. Their goodness and badness arise from their effects and consequences in life. The consequence of honesty is the establishment of healthy and trustworthy relationships in society. Lying has the opposite effect. Most of the ethical vices and virtues which also appear in religious texts are of this nature.

As against the virtues, the vices create internal and external conflicts for the individual and disrupt personal and social life. In order to protect themselves from personal and social conflicts, individuals must therefore try to ensure that the vices do not gain prominence.

But the tale of the master values is a different one altogether. These are the values that life is for. In the absence of these values, life is not worth living. They are few in number and basically consist of the things that human beings hold most dear, such as "God" or "humanity" or "life itself". The essential point is that religion has been very thorough as far as the master values are concerned, but not so with the servant values, since these values (which are the majority) are entirely linked to the way in which people live and are, in effect, etiquettes, not virtues.

When they say that people's values have changed in the modern world, they mean the servant values, not the master ones. In the debate about development and modernity, the transformation of values relates to the servant values. Ethics means the etiquette of the context: the etiquette of war, the etiquette of privacy, the etiquette of the classroom, the etiquette of the individual, the etiquette of the masses, etiquette towards God and so on. Hence, if the context changes, so, too, will the etiquette. This is not relativism; it is respect for the dictates of context, like a child who grows up and dons a different garment. Ethical exceptions are testimony to this fact. All ethicists have said that lying is permissible in certain circumstances. Why? Because when the context changes, so, too, does the etiquette. This is not by any means tantamount to ethical relativism. Ethical relativism is when you extend this notion to the master values; whereas servant values are the conventions of the context.

Hence, whenever there is a transformation in people's lives, this is inevitably reflected in the sphere of ethics (that is, in the values that are at the service of life). This is one aspect of the matter. The other aspect is that major transformations of this kind have a direct impact on our understanding of life and human beings. This is an extremely important point. People's lives correspond to the depth and breadth of their knowledge. If modern life is complex, it is because people today have a complex conception of the world. The simplicity of people's lives in the past was a corollary of their simplistic understanding of nature, society and human beings.

Industrial farming and non-industrial farming are the products of two different conceptions of land, crops, livestock and the forces of nature. So it is with human political life.[5] On the whole, the modern human sciences are both a mirror of the modern lifestyle and its begetter. And, since religion is minimalist on issues relating to the human sciences, its observations on people's lives and conventions (and ethics) are also minimalist. A simple way of establishing this is as follows: modern human life has not in any way emerged out of religion. No *faqih*, in his capacity as an Islamic jurist, ever put forward a plan for technology and a technical lifestyle. The modern lifestyle emerged by itself and not by anyone's design. No jurist in the world of Islam ever presented projects for the abolishment of slavery or feudalism as systems. *Fiqh* has always followed, not led, social developments, issuing its rulings within the framework of the existing system. This is because *fiqh* is a minimalist system. It is conservative and does not set out to change anything. It is not meant to create a lifestyle, but to rule on the actually existing one. Ethics is identical to *fiqh* and law in this respect. Life is shaped by people's knowledge of the world. As people's knowledge undergoes transformations, so, too, will their lives (as will their religious lives and their religious understanding); it is not the other way around.

Minimal on Theological Issues

We have so far clarified the role of religion and its relationship to *fiqh* and the natural and human sciences. Now, what are we to say about people's world-views and beliefs? Is religion also minimalist on the question of God, the hereafter, the Day of Judgement, resurrection and otherworldly felicity and wretchedness? I wish to suggest that, on these subjects, too, religion has spoken in minimalist terms. No one can prove that religion has said all that there is to say about God's qualities and attributes; in fact, the minimalist reading seems much more plausible. For example, we believe that nothing is hidden from God: "...not so much as the weight of an ant in earth or heaven escapes from thy Lord..." (10: 61) Vigorous theological controversies on matters such as

---

[5] For a more detailed explaination see the athour's articles: "Razdani va Row-shanfekri" in his *Razdani va Rowshanfekri va Dindari* [Knowledge, Intellectualism and Religiosity] (Tehran: Serat, 1370/1990) and "Knowledge and Justice" in his *Modara va Modiriyat* [*Tolerance and Governance*] (Tehran: Serat, 1373/1994).

God's knowledge of the world, clearly demonstrates that not all questions in this respect have been addressed in religion. So much so that a great scholar like al-Ghazali lays charge of apostasy on great Muslim philosophers like Ibn Sina for their view about God's knowledge. One possible reading of Ibn Sina's theory is that God's knowledge does not cover the transitory details of temporal events which on the face of it contradicts the Qur'anic verse cited above. Therefore, Sadr al-din Shirazi took it to account all relevant Kornaic verses and Shi'i hadiths in Kulayni's *Usul al-Kafi* and cited seven theories provided by philosophers and eventually came up with a new theory about God's knowledge.[6] Nonetheless, we have no reason to believe that he has said the last word on the subject. If religion was to have said the absolute maximum on this subject, it would have had to say a great deal more on a number of different aspects of the issue. Since it has not—and the differences of opinion between religious scholars testify to this fact—it is clear that much speculation has been left to theologians and philosophers.

The same applies to God's other attributes. One of the important theological problems in Islamic thought is the way in which God speaks. All Muslims believe that God has spoken to his prophets, but the question is: how does God speak? The exact same problems have arisen and continue to arise in Christianity. And the relevant disputes have never been successfully resolved. Why have there been so many disputes and disagreements? Is it not because the religious texts do not answer all the questions posed by religious scholars and theologians?

Another example, We read in the *Nahj al-Balaghah* that Imam Ali was asked thrice about what "*qadar*" (predestination) meant. Thrice he replied: it is a dark path, do not tread onto it; it is a deep ocean, do not drown yourself in it; it is God's secret, do not trouble yourselves with it. These meaningful non-answers make it clear that cryptic brevity was the order of the day here- even if we think he did not see lengthy expansions and explanations as being in the interest of the people.

---

[6] See: Sadr al-din Shirazi, *al-Hikma al-Muta'aliya fi al-Asfar al-'aqliyya al-Arba'a* (Beirut: Dar al-Turath, 1984).

What Does the Expandability of Religious Knowledge Tell Us?

The history of religious knowledge is testimony to the fact that religious knowledge constantly increases. Not all these increases are derived from the Book and the *Sunna*; they are in part based on the discoveries and experiences of believers themselves. Take the concept of "love", for example. There are explicit references to divine love in the Qur'an: "He loves them and they love Him".[7] It also appears in Islamic hadiths. But these references are by no means as extensive as the references to this concept that we find in our mystical literature. Mystics expanded on this idea and added their own experiences to it. The concept now available to us is, therefore, much sturdier and broader than it was in its original religious form and content. This shows that religion has spoken in minimalist terms on subjects as profound and important as love. As to why, in instances such as these, brevity is the order of the day, it may be that the leader, by virtue of so being, does not say just anything or do just anything. Discovering, speaking about and doing many things have been left to believers themselves. It has been left to them to seize the initiative and be their own trailblazers in these areas.

Shams-e Tabrizi made an interesting observation about a number of his contemporaries: He would say: This or that person "did not submit", i.e. submission to the Prophet.[8] "Did not submit" occurs a number of times in Shams's accounts. He used it, for example, in connection with Muhyi al-Din Arabi and Bayazid Bastami. What Shams was suggesting was that someone like Bayazid Bastami, who was intoxicated by love, was neither a leader, nor a follower, since both leadership and submission demand presence of mind. In the context of submission, this is a prerequisite. Of course, the drunkenness of love is precious. It is a world all its own. But the religious leader cannot be drunk. And it may well be that he refrains from commanding others to be drunk. Nonetheless, his disciples may discover the world of love and attain this rank for themselves.

Religious and non-religious leaders are bound by certain social, historical and human constraints, of which language is the simplest

---

[7] See for instance, Qur'an, 5: 54.

[8] See *Maqalat-e Shams-e Tabrizi* [Shams-e Tabrizi's Essays], ed. by Muhammad Ali Movahhed (Tehran: Intesharat-e Daneshgah-e San'ati, 1356/1978) and M. A. Movahhed, *Shams-e Tabrizi* (Tehran: Tarh-e Nou, 1375/1997).

and most evident. A prophet cannot communicate without using any language, nor can he use a language other than the ones that already exist. Hence, the Prophet of Islam used Arabic and Zoroaster, the Avestan language. Prophets, furthermore, have to speak in keeping with people's mental capacities. These constraints are unavoidable.

It should also be said, for example, that the Prophet of Islam, in view of his standing as a prophet, never produced or recited any poetry. There is even a tale which speaks of him deliberately reciting a poem badly so that no one would listen. The Qur'an, too, refers to this point: "We have not taught him poetry; it is not seemly for him." (36: 69) This does not mean that poetry is a bad thing or that the Prophet's followers should not produce poetry. It simply means that, because of his position, the Prophet was not to mingle his words with poetry. He was not to behave in a way as to make his followers believe that he was in the grip of his imagination; especially so because some Arabs believed that poets were possessed by spirits. But the same restriction does not apply to a prophet's followers and they may even use poetry to propagate religion and have poetic experiences. Unlike the Prophet, Imam Ali did produce poetry or, at least, used poetry in his speeches. There are examples in the *Nahj al-Balaghah* of Imam Ali citing poetry to illustrate some points and there is a collection of poems attributed to him.

At any rate, a religious leader operates under constraints that do not apply to his followers. A Prophet cannot behave intoxicatedly or in a lovelorn fashion. But this does not mean that his followers are forbidden from having these experiences.

Take *malamatigari* (antinomianism) as another example. This, too, was introduced by mystics and Sufis. When a religious community becomes tainted by a variety of ills, such that hypocrisy, pretentiousness, sycophancy, duplicity and the like become rife, sympathetic people who wish to put things right may resort to self-debasement as a cure. "Self-debasement" means appearing to engage in acts of immorality and giving the impression of indulging in unseemly behaviour. It means acting in a way that will belittle the person in the eyes of the pious. Even a cautious *faqih* and *mufti* like Al-Ghazali has recounted that, in order to purge themselves of pride and egoism and demean themselves in the eyes of the public, some accomplished mystics would drink water out of a wine goblet to make the people think they were immoral and impious. Al-Ghazali later explained that this kind of behaviour was not without problems in terms of *fiqh*, but that accomplished mystics were capable of making good this error.[9] You can see in his book, *The Revival of the Religious Sciences*, that he did not issue any *fatwa* in this connection and did not imply irreligiosity. He was so conscious of the dangers of arrogance, pride and conceit that he was prepared to see them crushed by any means. It is interesting to note that the Shi'i *faqih*, Feiz-Kashani, endorsed Al-Ghazali's position on this.[10]

The point I am trying to make here is that the founder of a religion clearly cannot command believers to feign immorality and to engage in antinomianism. Nonetheless, believers themselves may, at certain points in time, resort to this kind of therapy in order to cure emergent religious ills, without incurring any blame on themselves. Innovations and ideas such as these do not arise on a whim. Their discoverers and proponents are genuinely concerned about religion and opt for these ways in order to safeguard religion at its very core.

Minimalist Religion and Everlasting Continuity

In order to be eternal and final, a religion must per force present a central thread and core that is appropriate to every human being in every age and era, and forego certain secondary principles, peripheral issues and unique stances for unique occasions; otherwise, it would be like a garment designed for a particular society, in a particular region, at a particular time, and nothing more. Different eras and societies, with their vast and incredible variations, can only be addressed if one concerns oneself with their minimal shared characteristics and plans for and rules on these. How else would it be possible to design laws that apply not only to pastoral and agricultural societies, but also to industrial and post-industrial ones; laws that can prove useful to all of them and resolve problems that may be encountered by anyone. A cloth that serves as a garment for children and youths, as well as for grown men and women, can afford little more than the barest covering and this is exactly what is meant by minimalist.

---

[9] Al-Ghazali, *Ihya*, (kitab dham al-Jah).
[10] Feiz Kashani, Mullah Mohsen, *Al-Mahajjat al-Bayda fi Tahdib al-Ihya* (Tehran: Maktabat al-Sudouq, 1340/1960). See also the author's article "Jameh-e Tahdib bar tan-e *Ihya*".

Minimalist, not Maximalist Guidance

The history of all religions is testimony to the fact that no religion has been spared the misfortune of being tampered with and distorted. Muslims believe that the sacred books of the Jews and the Christians have been subjected to alterations. Muslims further believe that some of their own religious narratives have been adulterated. Many were hadiths that were no doubt recounted but never handed down to us. Many are the useful points that were never recounted but could have been of great assistance to us. Many are the false, altered and distorted hadiths that have been handed down to us but that we do not recognise as such. Let alone the fact that even some Shi'is—the Akhbaris, in particular—hold that the Qur'an itself has suffered a similar fate.

Serious errors have, in other words, crept into religious texts, such that we cannot claim to be seeing them in their integral form. The accidentals of the Qur'an, too, might have been other than what they are today; if the Prophet had lived longer, the Qur'an might have been much more voluminous, offering much more extensive guidance and settling many ambiguities.[11] Religious knowledge and understanding, too, undergoes growth and development, and contraction and expansion, such that future generations may have a much more refined and accurate understanding of religion than us.

Now, in order to believe that God's intention in the sending of the Prophet and the revelation of the Book has been fulfilled, we have no choice but to say that the minimum guidance necessary has survived all these additions and subtractions, distortions and inventions, essentials and accidentals, and contractions and expansions, and reached us intact; we can say nothing more than this. If it were otherwise and if religion had reached us in a healthier and fuller state, the guidance at our disposal would clearly have been far more complete and our disputes far fewer. Hence, the guidance offered by religion is minimalist guidance (in keeping with its history) and not maximalist (for such a religion would have had to have a different history).

---

[11] See "Essentials and Accidentals in Religion", Chapter Four in this volume.

On the Perfection of Religion

It might be a good idea to say a few words here about religion's perfection and completeness. We all believe, as we read in the Qur'an, that religion is complete: "Today I have perfected your religion for you, and I have completed My blessing upon you, and I have approved Islam for your religion." (5: 3) In other words, God has said that, one day, religion was completed. However, some people have taken "religion's completeness" to mean "religion's all-inclusiveness", or taken it to mean the perfection of religious knowledge, or failed to distinguish between minimalist perfection and maximalist perfection; all three of which are errors. There is a difference between "being complete" and being "all-inclusive". "All-inclusive" means including everything, as if religion is a supermarket in which you can find anything. But "being complete" means that religion falls nothing short of its self-defined aim or its definition of itself or its own particular function in its own chosen field of action and concern. Religious commentators seem to have reached consensus on the point that the verse: "Not a grain in the earth's shadows, not a thing, fresh or withered, but it is in a Book Manifest" (6: 59), does not refer to the Qur'an, but that the Book Manifest refers to what God knows.

Let us imagine that you draw a triangle. In terms of it being a triangle and fitting the definition of a triangle, your triangle is complete and has nothing lacking. But, it is certainly not a rectangle or a pentagon. And no one can say that, because this triangle does not have four sides or a hundred sides, it is incomplete. By analogy, we have to see the perfection of religion in terms of God's aim, the definition of religion and its particular function. Religion is complete in relation to the purpose it was designed for (which is to offer minimal guidance, as we said). But it cannot be complete in relation to our every possible and imaginable expectation.

Hence, if we accept that religion offers the necessary minimum to perfection, its "being complete" lies in the provision of this necessary minimum. There is no contradiction between assuming minimalism and assuming perfection. If it is religion's aim and mission to provide these minimums (whether in the realm of precepts, in the realm of ethics, in terms of a world-view and religious knowledge, and in terms of guidance in general), then a religion that has provided these minimums has performed completely and is in no way lacking.

Of course, if we open wide our greedy, all-embracing eyes and expect religion to do everything that we ask of it no matter how inappropriate, if we want to extract every possible and necessary desideratum from it, if we absolutely insist that our religion must be maximalist, we will soon come to realise that religion, in this sense, is incomplete and can by no means fulfil everything that we expect of it.

Hence, religion (not religious knowledge) is perfect, but not all-inclusive. And its perfection is minimalist and in itself, not maximalist and for us. In other words, even that minimalist perfection lies within religion itself, not in religious knowledge which has undergone and will continue to undergo a whole variety of upheavals and transformations.

On Ijtihad

Let us also add a word about *ijtihad* to our discussion. *Ijtihad* does not only occur in *fiqh*, it occurs in every theoretical field and discipline. A philosopher or ethicist also engages in *ijtihad*. *Ijtihad* is the expenditure of serious thought and consideration within a designated rubric, leading to the discovery of new horizons and the solving of new problems, whether within religion or outside religion. *Ijtihad*, in this sense, cannot lead to a substantive change. In other words, you cannot transform the discipline of *fiqh* into, for example, the discipline of ethics through *ijtihad*. *Ijtihad* results in the expansion of a discipline, within the framework of that discipline, and that is all.

Hence, engaging in *ijtihad* within *fiqh* or ethics does not transform their precepts and teachings from minimalist to maximalist. If we decide that religious ethics, religious precepts and religious teachings have been conveyed to us in minimalist terms, then, no matter how much *ijtihad* we subject these precepts and teachings to, no matter how much we expand on them, the precepts and teachings will never cease to be minimalist. In other words, religion will always remain minimalist and it will not be purged of this quality through *ijtihad*, unless some people set out to make substantive changes in religion, in the name of *ijtihad*; and from them may Beneficent God preserve us.

Excessive Expectations of Religion

As to the final point: what is a religious intellectual to do in the midst of all this? The task of a man of religious learning is clear. A man of religious learning is either a *faqih* and learned in the precepts of God, or a religious ethicist, or a theologian and religious commentator. It is clear what each of these individuals has to do. And, while their field may expand and grow, it will remain well defined. But what of "the religious intellectual", who looks at religion from without, speaks about religion, does not earn a living from religion, thinks about rejuvenating and reforming religion, is sensitive to the rupture between tradition and modernity, is capable of and sincerely devoted to religious thought, wants both submission and rationality, loves both heaven and earth, locates religion within the geography of modern and contemporary knowledge, and is, of course, anxious to safeguard the sanctity of religious thoughts and deeds. What must the religious intellectual base his actions on? What must his thinking focus upon? From what perspective must he view religion?

If we accept that religion is minimalist, we must then also acknowledge that we cannot expect too much from it. One of the duties of people who look at religion from without is, therefore, to drive home the point that a maximalist religion undermines religion itself. Anyone who encourages people to expect too much of religion (in the fields of ethics, practical behaviour, economics, hygiene, planning, governance, etc.) and places this excessive burden on religion, gradually robs religion of its standing and legitimacy.

Some thinkers and historians of ideas in the West are of the view that the coming into existence of "a maximalist god" in the Middle Ages, gradually forced this god off life's stage altogether. What was "a maximalist god"? He was a god who did not feel bound in the slightest by ethical, rational and philosophical norms and granted himself absolute freedom. It was even said that God could perform logical and rational impossibilities, never mind about indulging in ethical misdeeds. People who made these claims did so out of a sense of religiosity and in order to increase God's power and glory. But this maximalist god opened the way for God Himself to be rejected. In other words, this was a defence of God that did Him no favour. The same can be said of maximalist religion. In this case, too, if religion is burdened with exaggerated expectations, the danger is that it will be rejected altogether.

Individuals and intellectuals, who care about religion and who want
to ensure that God's enchanting message is preserved and respected,
must, therefore, try first and foremost to signpost religion's terrain
and jurisdiction, so that no one can disseminate superstition in the
name of religion, or oppress people in the name of religion, or make
exaggerated claims in the name of religion, or indulge in hypocrisy in
the name of religion, or bring about ruin and devastation in the name
of religion. It is to do religion no service if we say that we will meet
your every need with religion and we will extract everything necessary
for governance, politics and economics from it (whether in the form
of precepts or planning).

Indulging in petty tyrannies in the name of religion; imposing
constraints on people on the basis of conjectural precepts; behaving
harshly, unyieldingly and violently; expecting people to abide absolutely
by Islamic law instead of being satisfied with the avoidance of absolute
opposition to it; robbing religion of its role as arbiter in order to turn
into the provider of everything are all offences that can be perpetrated
in the name of religion. It is the religious intellectual's duty to identify
them and to alert others to them. Foremost among the burdens that
must not be placed on religion is the burden of a completely religious
governance. If religion has spoken about governance, if at all, it has
been in minimalist, not maximalist, terms.[12] And this minimum is on
the subject of legitimacy, not administration; and legitimacy itself is
intricately linked to the process of administration.[13] Governance is the
offspring of society and is totally and absolutely in keeping with it. A
complex society has a complex administration and a simple society,
a simple one, and it requires a great deal more than ethical and legal
regulations (such as knowledge of economics, sociology, psychology
and the science of administration). I am confident that no one will
deny that, even if religion has spoken about these subjects, it has been
in minimalist terms. And so, given a minimalist *fiqh* and a minimalist
science, how can religion be expected to carry the burden of governance
completely and successfully? Even this minimalist *fiqh* and minimalist science are such in principle and not in practice. In the context of
practice, they are even more diluted than this.

---

[12] See: Soroush, "Dindari va A'yin Shahriyari" in his book *A'yin Shahriyari va Dindari*
[Religiosity and Etiquettes of Governance] (Tehran: Serat, 1379/2000), pp. 126–146.
[13] See references in footnote 3 above.

It falls upon religious intellectuals to teach believers to expect no more than a minimum of certainities from a minimalist religion; not to tie their religious faith to the rope of theological disputes; to base their actions on that which is *muhkamat*, definite and consensual and to leave knowledge of the rest to God, ranking them among *mutashabehat*; and if a precept causes great controversy, let them know that there is no definite verdict on it, for, had God wished it, religion could undoubtedly have contained much more than it does today, rescuing us from a whirlpool of ambiguities, likelihoods and conjectures.[14]

In the words of Imam Ali: "If there is anything that Satan demands that you know that you do not find in the Book, the *Sunna* and the words of the trustees of God, leave knowledge of it to God, for that is all that God expects of you."[15]

If we approach religion in this way, it will never serve as an instrument of injustice and tyranny, a meal ticket, or a source of superstition and conflict.

---

[14] For more on *muhkamat* and *mutashabehat* see, Soroush, "Evolution and Devolution of Religious Knowledge," in Charles Kurzman, (ed.) *Liberal Islam: A Sourcebook* (Oxford: Oxford University Press, 1999), pp. 244–254.

[15] *Nahj al-Balaghah*, Sermon # 90.

CHAPTER SIX

STRAIGHT PATHS—1
AN ESSAY ON RELIGIOUS PLURALISM;
POSITIVE AND NEGATIVE

Pluralism in its current form (giving official recognition to plurality and diversity; considering different cultures, languages and experiences to be irreducible and incommensurable; and seeing the world as a garden filled with flowers with a host of colours and scents) belongs to the modern age and is associated with two major spheres: one is the sphere of religion and culture, and, the other, the sphere of society. We have a pluralistic religiosity and theory of religion and we have pluralistic societies; and the two are clearly linked. In other words, people who believe in cultural and religious pluralism cannot dismiss social pluralism. One can speak about pluralism both from the perspective of causes and from the perspective of reasons. That is to say, one can explain why some societies have opted for pluralism and have arranged the administration and running of their affairs on this basis, and one can also explain how and why this choice is justified or otherwise. Before turning to social pluralism, it may be appropriate for me to make a few points about cultural and religious pluralism and then to adapt this to the social sphere. Although pluralism would appear to be a modern term, its roots go back deep into history, and not just in the history of our thinking as Muslims, but in the history of all human thought. Of course, its Muslim aspects are more appealing to us which is why I focus on them and why I prefer to highlight and speak about religion in particular.

Today, religious pluralism is generally built on two pillars: one is the diversity of our understanding of religious texts and the second is the diversity of our interpretation of religious experiences. (But, as I will go on to explain, it has many other pillars.) Both in their understanding of scripture and in their experience of transcendence, human beings have to engage in interpretation; they must unveil the silent text or the raw experience and make it speak. This unveiling or revelation does not occur in a uniform way or using a single method; it is unceremoniously

diverse and pluralistic. Herein lies the key to the inception and legitimacy of intra-religious and extra-religious pluralism.

Positive Pluralism: Irreducible Plurality

Diversity of Understandings of Religious Texts

In my theory of "the contraction and expansion of religious knowledge",[1] I have tried to explain the key to the plurality of our understanding of religion and the mechanism through which it occurs. Briefly, the
idea put forward there is that our understanding of religious texts is
per force pluralistic and diverse, and this diversity and plurality is not
reducible to a single conception; and that, in addition to being diverse
and pluralistic, our understanding of religion is fluid. This is because
a text is silent and, when it comes to understanding religious texts and
interpreting them—whether we are looking at jurisprudence [*fiqh*], the
sayings of the Prophet or Qur'anic exegesis—we invariably draw on
our own expectations, questions and assumptions. Since no interpretation is possible without drawing on some expectation, question or
assumption, and, since these expectations, questions and assumptions
always originate outside religion, and, since extra-religious matters are
changeable and fluid and human knowledge, philosophy and science
are constantly growing, accumulating, changing and evolving, the
interpretations arrived at in the light of these expectations, questions
and assumptions will per force be diverse, changeable and evolving.
This, in a nutshell, is the view set out in my theory of "Contraction
and Expansion of Religious knowledge."

Now, whether you find this mechanism convincing or not, you cannot deny the basic point that Scripture and the words of the Prophet
lend themselves to a multitude of interpretations and that, according
to *hadiths*, divine discourse is multi-layered, such that if you peel away
the first layer of meaning, another layer of meaning is revealed to you
underneath it. One reason for this is that reality is multi-layered and
since words reveal things about reality, they too become multi-layered.

---

[1] Abdulkarim Soroush, *Qabz va Bast-e Te'orik-e Shari'at* [Contraction and Expansion
of Religious Knowledge], 3rd ed. (Tehran: Serat, 1375/1996).

This is not confined to the word of God; when we look at the words of such luminaries of Persian literature as Rumi or Hafez, or the contributions of the great masters in any other language, we find exactly this same labyrinthine and multi-layered quality in their works as well. It is this same quality that keeps words and discourse fresh and everlasting. The asset of religions is their penetrating, moving, profound and eternal words, which always have something to say to everyone everywhere; otherwise, they would rapidly age and die. There are numerous *hadiths* that tell us that the Qur'an has seven or seventy layers. There are other *hadiths* that have it that some verses in the Qur'an are intended for very insightful people who will come at the end of time. The history of exegesis, whether in the realm of Islam or in other religions, makes it clear that there have been many different interpretations of God's words. There are *hadiths* that include the phrase "some people tell others things that those others know better"; many are the bearers of *fiqh* or the bearers of religious teachings who do not realise themselves what a precious jewel they are carrying. They are in the possession of a phrase or a Tradition and they pass it on to someone else who actually understands it better than they do.

What all this means is that a single account can be understood to different extents and its multitudinous layers uncovered and explored. Hence, in the realm of interpretation we have always been pluralists and acted pluralistically; in other words, we have accepted plurality and have never accepted anyone as the final interpreter or the final commentator. This has formed the essence of our religious life and our learned understanding of *religion*. The point that needs to be added to all this—and it has been stated in the theory of Contraction and Expansion—is that we have no such thing as uninterpreted religion. Islam means the history of a series of interpretations of Islam and Christianity means the history of a series of interpretations of Christianity, and so on and so forth. These interpretations have always been multitudinous and, whenever someone has not liked one interpretation, they have opted for another interpretation—not seized quintessential religion itself—and religious knowledge is nothing other than these interpretations, faulty and sound. We are immersed in an ocean of interpretations and conceptions, and this follows, on the one hand, from the nature of texts and, on the other, from the nature of ourselves as human beings and the way we understand things. Sunni Islam is one understanding or conception of Islam and Shi'i Islam is another. Both of them, along with their components and implications, are natural and official. No religion in history has been devoid of this plurality. The history of theology is testimony to this fact. What has been lacking is that this plurality has not been theorised or justified, because no one has taken it seriously (except in rare instances). Every sect has always considered itself as being in the right and everyone else as being in the wrong. It is as if, in assuming that every other sect is wrong, each sect has also assumed that every other sect is doomed to non-existence. No one has considered the possibility that this unavoidable plurality of interpretations, conceptions and sects, to which no religion is immune, might have some other meaning and significance (and that it is not enough to say, we are fortunate enough to be correct, so we are following the path of rightful guidance and are heading for paradise, whereas others have the misfortune of being wrong and going astray and, not having understood religion correctly, their practices are unacceptable and they are headed for hell). Maybe it means that this plurality is itself desirable. Maybe rightful guidance is broader than we had imagined. Maybe salvation and felicity hinge on something else, something beyond these antagonistic and divisive dogmas and particular conceptions. And maybe understanding religion is also a collective affair, just like life and civilisation.

Every sect thinks to themselves that the others are probably not to blame for their misunderstanding of religion and that they are little more than unfortunate victims, but we have been fortunate enough to understand things correctly and thus become God's chosen people. But the moment one brushes aside this delusion, the moment a person is prepared to accept that they are not chosen or fortunate or different from the rest or God's special favourite, and see themselves instead as a member of the human race sitting at the same table as everyone else, then they will start taking pluralism seriously. They will reflect anew on the meaning of rightful guidance and salvation and felicity and truth and falsehood and understanding and misunderstanding. Pluralism in the modern world is the product and outcome of this kind of reflection. I know that some people will immediately cry out, but what is the point of all this? Are you saying that we should abandon what we consider to be the truth? Or that we should consider people who have gone astray to be on the path of truth? Or that we should equate truth and falsehood? No, this is not the point at all. The point is that we should not ask these questions in the first place and we should look at the plurality of people's views and beliefs from a different perspective and that we should see and read a different meaning and spirit into them. We should bear in mind that the arena of religious understanding is a playing field in which there are numerous contestants and that there is no such thing as a single-player contest and we should see the game as being contingent on this plurality.

It goes without saying that pluralism in the understanding of texts has a clear upshot, which is that there is no unique, official interpretation of religion and that there is therefore no official interpreter or authority. In religious knowledge, as in any other field of human knowledge, no one's word is compulsorily binding on anyone else. And no particular conception is sacred and beyond questioning, and this is equally true in *fiqh* and exegesis as it is in chemistry, for example. Everyone carries their own burden of responsibility and appears before God singly. We have political rulers, but we have no such thing as theoretical or religious rulers.

Diversity of Interpretations of Religious Experience

This brings us to the second type of pluralism which results from diverse and multiple interpretations of religious experiences; a diversity and multiplicity that is irreducible to one. Just as we have no such thing as un-interpreted religion, we have no such thing as an un-interpreted experience, whether in the natural world or in the world of the soul. Religious experience consists of "transcendence". This transcendence can take different forms. It may occur as a dream, as the sensing of a scent or a bellow, the seeing of a figure or a colour, a feeling of connectedness to a boundless vastness, a sense of contraction and gloom, a sense of expansion and luminescence, a love for an unseen beloved, the sensing of a spiritual presence, a oneness with a person or an object, a detachment from the self and suspension in nothingness, the comprehension of a mystery or the discovery of a secret, a tiring of earthly attachments and flight towards the eternal, being drawn to some gravitational force, a thirst, a vacuum, a flash, a sense of awe, a sense of ecstasy and so on. Different as they are, they can all go under the name of religious experience, an experience that is unconventional and at times strikes with such overpowering force and brings such certainty and ecstasy and luminosity that the person can do nothing other than to surrender and bow down before it. Our Sufis explained these experiences in the following terms: "When the seeker embarks on his journey and begins his travails, asceticism and self-purification, he crosses the temporal and the eternal and experiences episodes appropriate to his differing states, at times in the form of true dreams and, at others, in the form of esoteric visions."[2]

This very suggestion that spiritual experiences involve crossing the temporal and the eternal is itself one way of interpreting experiences of this kind. Jacob Boehme, one of the German masters of mysticism, was no more than a cobbler when, one day, in a sudden, incredible vision he found everything glowing and illuminated and saw into the very essence of things, and it was thereafter that he began to speak of a variety of mystical ideas, notions and concepts. 'Ala al-Dawleh Semnani, the great Iranian mystic, was for his part a soldier in the Mongol army of Arghun Khan. One day he was astride his horse fighting alongside the other soldiers when suddenly, in an instant, it was as if the veil was removed from his eyes and, in an eerie light, he saw the supernatural world of life after death. The fighting had come to an end but he still sat there astride his horse and he remained stunned and confused for two days. Thereafter, he abandoned his profession, turned away from the world and took up the Sufi order. Rumi, too, who speaks in surrealistic terms of taking a broom from the hands of a beloved and sweeping the seabed is in fact recounting a similar experience.[3] And the most forceful and formidable of all was the experience of Ascension, which was a prophetic experience.[4]

At any rate, resolving to know what that bellow was which I heard and who it was harking from, and what the illumination or vision or movement of the heart that I experienced indicated and whence it came,

---

[2] Najm al-Din Razi, *Mirsad al-'Ibad*, ed. Mohammad Amin-Riyahi, p. 289 (Tehran: Bongah-e Tarjumeh va Nashr-e Ketab, 1352/1974).

[3] For more detailed descriptions of these kinds of visions, illuminations, exaltations and experiences and their qualities and attributes see: Najm al-Din Razi: *Mirsad al-'Ibad*; A. Semnani, *Musannafat-e Farsi 'Ala al-dawleh Semnani*, ed. Najib Mayel Heravi (Tehran: Mawla Publications, 1369/1989); Muhammad Iqbal: *The Reconstruction of Religious Thought in Islam*, and Walter Stace: *Mysticism and Philosophy* (London: McMillan, 1960).

[4] The simplest form of religious experiences are the dreams. As it is attributed to the Prophet saying that: "true dreams form one of the 46 elements of prophethood." The number 46 seems rather unconventional here and some mystics have interpreted it in the following way: The noble Lord of Islam was a prophet for 23 years. During the first six months of his prophethood, he received the revelation in the form of true dreams. True dreams are thus one of the 46 elements of prophethood." See, *Mirsad al-'Ibad*, p. 290.

and expressing all this through language and in the form of (occasionally contradictory and paradoxical) concepts is to step into the arena of interpretation. In fact, putting the experiences into words and describing them using concepts is itself an interpretation, and these interpretations vary enormously and are multiple indeed. For example, the non-numerical unity of being was something that was first experienced by mystics. It was then given a philosophical rendering, which gave rise to endless discussions, debates, dismissals and critiques. All religions have been informed by hidden, celestial and revelatory experiences and episodes on the part of their prophets. The prophets of God were not scholars or priests or magicians or self-deluded or mad; they were, in the words of Muhammad Iqbal, contemplatives (*mard-e bateni*). Not just they themselves, but their foremost pious disciples and wayfarers, too, had revelatory and contemplative experiences. As Rumi says:

> Since (the words) *God hath inspired the bee* have come (in the Qur'an), the dwelling-place of its (the bee's) inspiration has been filled with sweets.
> Through the light of the inspiration of God the Almighty and Glorious, it filled the world with wax and honey.
> This one who is (the object of) *We have honoured (the sons of Adam)* and is ever going upward—how should his inspiration be inferior to (that of) the bee?"[5]

Rumi's words allude to the verse in the Qur'an that: "And thy Lord revealed unto bees, saying: 'Make your homes in the mountains and in the trees.' "(16: 68). In the words of Rumi, the effect of this revelation was that bees became producers of honey and wax, "filling their revelatory homes with sweetness". So much for bees. When it comes to humans, who have been so honoured by God and about whom God has stated:

> We have honoured the Children of Adam and carried them on land and sea, and provided them with good things, and preferred them greatly over many of those We created. (17: 70)

Was their revelation any less than that of bees? God reveals things to believers and, while such experiences are effectively revelations, in order to distinguish them from prophetic revelation and not to arouse the suspicion and anger of the public, the Sufis have called them "rev-

---

[5] *Mathnawi*, 5: 1228–1231.

elations of the heart". Be that as it may, they are still revelations. But revelation admits of degree. There are lower degrees and higher degrees; at times it is conjoined to holiness and, at times, it is not. Hence, we have everything from revelation to bees to revelation to humans, ranging from mystics to prophets to poets. These are all religious experiences and, as we said, these contemplative experiences all need to be interpreted. In fact, we have no such thing as raw experience. Stace, the British philosopher, is of the view that even when it comes to Buddhists, who appear not to have a God and to be idol worshippers, the story is in fact more complicated. Buddhists do not have a theory of God, although they do have the experience of God,[6] and this is a very important point. We have to be mindful of this point in the realm of religious experience. There may be many instances in which a person may have discovered something but not be aware of what they have discovered. Feiz Kashani expressed the idea well in the verse:

"Will I experience the joy of embracing you one day?", I cried;
"Look closely, you may already be there", came the reply.

It is exactly the same in the history of science and in the world of natural experience. One of the difficult debates in the history of science revolves around the question of how and when someone may be said to have discovered something. Who discovered oxygen, for example? Who discovered the law of gases?, and the like. Thomas Kuhn, who is renowned in this field, is of the view that a person may be considered the discoverer of something when they are aware of the theory pertaining to their discovery; in other words, when they are aware of what they have discovered. Otherwise, every single person since the dawn of history may be said to have discovered oxygen; after all, everyone was always breathing oxygen and taking it into their lungs. The same can be said of this or that celestial body which many people may have seen without knowing whether it was a star or a planet or to which constellation it belonged. So, it is not enough for you to have something in your clasp or in your mind, you must also have a theory and an interpretation to go with it. This is why we need prophets, which is another point conveyed by Rumi's tale of Moses and the shepherd. One of the main tasks of prophets was to teach us how to interpret our contemplative

---

[6] Stace, *Mysticism and Philosophy*.

experiences. For, although experiences of this kind lend themselves to a variety of interpretations, they are not all necessarily correct.

Hence, another channel through which multiplicity and diversity enter religious thought is multiple interpretations of a single experience. Thus, whether we take religious experience to be a single entity, which has been interpreted in countless different ways, or whether we consider religious experience itself to be diverse and manifold, either way, we find ourselves before a diversity that is by no means reducible to unity; we must take this fact on board and not disregard it. We must, furthermore, have a theory for this diversity.

Rumi must be given the last word here. I emphasise Rumi's works on this subject, first, because I consider him to be the Seal of the Mystics (*khatam al-ʿurafa*) and, secondly, because I find his manner of expression the sweetest and most telling. Rumi uses the term "*manzar*" repeatedly in the *Mathnawi*. "*Manzar*" is what we now refer to as perspective or point of view. "*Manzar*" has a long history of usage both in the fields of astronomy and mysticism. Rumi speaks of *manzar* or point of view on numerous occasions to convey the exact proposition and notion that we are in the process of analysing here. At one point, he says clearly and boldly that the difference between the Muslim, the Zoroastrian and the Jew is a matter of perspective: "From the place of view, O (thou who art the) kernel of Existence, there arises the difference between the true believer and the Zoroastrian and the Jew."[7] He says that the difference between these three does not lie in any disagreement over truth and falsehood, but, precisely, in the difference between their perspectives; and not in the perspectives of the believers at that, but in the perspectives of their prophets. There was only one multidimensional truth and the prophets viewed it from three different angles. Or it manifested itself to them in three different ways and through three different apertures. Hence, they presented three different religions. The existence of different religions is not, therefore, just a matter of changing social conditions or of one religion being distorted and then being replaced by another. In fact, just as the different worldly manifestations of God have imbued the natural world with diversity, so they have lent diversity to religions. The diversity of viewpoints will lead to a diversity of views. And these viewpoints are in fact nothing but the individuals themselves. In this instance, the view, the viewer

---

[7] *Mathnawi*, 3: 1256.

and the viewpoint are all one and the same, and this is the exact heart and core of the contention that is being made here. In the words of the contemporary poet, "We, nothing/we, a glance".[8]

The allegory that Rumi recounts about a group of people trying to form an impression of an elephant in a dark space, which has appeared in numerous variations in numerous other contexts, including Al-Ghazali's *The Revival of the Religious Sciences*, is an extremely eloquent story. At the end of the tale, Rumi draws the conclusion that the normal eye is as limited a sensor as the hands of the people making contact with the elephant's body in the dark. Empirical, sensory vision operates at the level of perceiving an elephant in the dark; it is not capable of grasping the full picture. Not just visual perception, but mental perception as such is likewise limited. And as long as human beings are condemned to being human beings this sentence will apply. What Rumi is telling us is that we are all groping in the dark and that we will, therefore, never grasp reality in its entirety. Everyone sees it and understands it to some extent and from a particular angle, and they describe it to exactly that extent. As Rumi himself puts it in his beautiful analogy, "The breath which the flute-player puts into the flute- does it belong to the flute? No, it belongs to the man (the flute-player)".[9] We are all flutes held against the lips of truth and truth breathes its tale into us. And even if we were flutes with mouthpieces "as wide as the universe", we would still be too narrow for the truth to tell its full tale.

It is much the same in the parable of Moses and the shepherd,[10] which effectively shows the reaction of a man of God to an ordinary person

---

[8] Reference is to Sohrab Sepehri. [Ed.]

[9] *Mathnawi*, 2: 1783.

[10] The story is in *the Mathnawi*, 1: 1720–1815. A selection of it is as follows:

Moses saw a shepherd on the way, who was saying, "O God who choosest (whom Thou willt), Where art Thou, that I may become Thy servant and sew Thy shoes and comb Thy head?

That I may wash Thy clothes and kill Thy lice and bring milk to Thee, O worshipful One;

That I may kiss Thy little hand and rub Thy little foot, (and when) bedtime comes I may sweep Thy little room,...

The shepherd was speaking foolish words in this wise. Moses said, "Man, to whom is this (addressed)?"

He answered, "To that One who created us; by whom this earth and sky were brought to sight."

"Hark!" said Moses, "you have become very backsliding (depraved); indeed you have not become a moslem, you have become an infidel.

What babble is this? What blasphemy and raving? Stuff some cotton into your mouth!

with raw, uninterpreted religious experiences. The shepherd's prayers were based on analogies and anthropomorphism. In his experience the shepherd was likening God to a human being or an infant or the like. He imagined that God would have similar needs and wishes as him and, hence, conceived of Him in such terms. Moses, here, appeared in the position of a discursive theologian seeking the greatest possible

---

The stench of your blasphemy has made the (whole) world stinking: your blasphemy has turned the silk robe of religion into rags.

Shoes and socks are fitting for you, (but) how are such things right for (One who is) a Sun?

If you do not stop your throat from (uttering) these words, a fire will come and burn up the people....

He (the shepherd) said, "O Moses, thou hast closed my mouth and thou hast burned my soul with repentance." He rent his garment and heaved a sigh, and hastily turned his head towards the desert and went (his way).

A revelation came to Moses from God—"Thou hast parted My servant from Me.

Didst thou come (as a prophet) to unite, or didst thou come to sever?

So far as thou canst, do not set foot in separation: of (all) things the most hateful to Me is divorce.

I have bestowed on every one a (special) way of acting: I have given to every one a (peculiar) form of expression.

In regard to him it is (worthy of) praise, and in regard to thee it is (worthy of) blame: in regard to him honey, and in regard to thee poison.

I am independent of all purity and impurity, of all slothfulness and alacrity (in worshipping Me).

I did not ordain (Divine worship) that I might make any profit; nay, but that I might do a kindness to (My) servants.

In the Hindoos the idiom of Hind (India) is praiseworthy; in the Sindians the idiom of Sind is praiseworthy.

I am not sanctified by their glorification (of Me); 'tis they that become sanctified and pearl-scattering (pure and radiant).

I look not at the tongue and the speech; I look at the inward (spirit) and the state (of feeling).

I gaze into the heart (to see) whether it be lowly, though the words uttered be not lowly,

Because the heart is the substance, speech (only) the accident; so the accident is subservient, the substance is the (real) object.

How much (more) of these phrases and conceptions and metaphors? I want burning, burning: become friendly with that burning!

Light up a fire of love in thy soul, burn thought and expression entirely (away)!

O Moses, they that know the conventions are of one sort, they whose souls and spirits burn are of another sort."....

When Moses heard these reproaches from God, he ran into the desert in quest of the shepherd....

At last he (Moses) overtook and beheld him; the giver of glad news said, "Permission has come (from God).

Do not seek any rules or method (of worship); say whatsoever your distressful heart desires.

Your blasphemy is (the true) religion, and your religion is the light of the spirit: you are saved, and through you a (whole) world is in salvation...

transcendental attributes for God. So he shouts at the shepherd and scolds him, saying, do not speak about God in such a ridiculous way! And God then acts as the arbiter between the lowly shepherd and the de-anthropomorphising theologian. Finally, Rumi explains that we are all—no matter how advancedly de-anthropomorphised might be our notion of God—caught up in analogies and anthropomorphism, because we use images that are familiar to us in our descriptions of God and we look at God in a way that is inextricably bound to our own existence. No one can escape this anthropomorphism altogether and conceive of and understand God just as He is in His purest essence, totally detached from any mental preconceptions. Of course, this anthropomorphism may be more coarse or more refined. In the case of the shepherd, it is clearly quite coarse, but Rumi warns us that we are all guilty of this offence to some extent. He says that God accepts our prayers not because they do Him justice, but because He is compassionate; in the end, our understanding of Him is always approximate and tarnished by our own limited preconceptions. We have been allowed to worship anthropomorphically because we are clearly incapable of freeing ourselves from this completely. Nonetheless, no matter how fine a refinement we achieve, we will never be free of some degree of anthropomorphic approximation. And this approximation is precisely the outcome of people's viewpoints and perspectives. And, for every shepherd, there is a Moses. And everyone is to some extent both shepherd and Moses. As far as the mystics and Sufis are concerned, this holds true even of the greatest prophets of God; and so very much the more so for human beings who have not attained the holiness of prophets and have not perceived the whole truth and the whole of reality. Each prophet has shared with his people that portion of the truth that he has been privy to and these portions have been different because prophets' personalities have been different: "And those Messengers, some We have preferred above others." (2: 253) If we wanted to express this in more familiar terms, we could say that God has appeared to each person in a particular light and each person has interpreted this appearance in a different way, and as it is said: "in love, temple and tavern are all the same".

The first sower of the seeds of pluralism in the world was God himself who sent us different Messengers. He appeared to each of them in a particular way and sent each of them to a particular society and instilled in each of them a particular interpretation. And so the furnace of pluralism heated up. Of course, prophets represent the highest peaks of experience and interpretation, but we have had lower peaks as well. "The Glory of God has never ceased, moment upon moment. And throughout time, God has come to all believers in their minds and spoken to their reason...."[11]

The multifaceted nature of interpretation in fact harks back to the multifaceted nature of reality (or, in more familiar Islamic terms, to God having a thousand and one attributes). Reality does not have a single layer or a single facet. And it is not just this multifacetedness of reality but also the multiple viewpoints of the viewers of that reality that give rise to the diversity of interpretations. Rumi says of the human being: "Thou art not a single "thou," O good comrade; nay, thou art the sky and the deep sea."[12] And so it is with language and, above it all, there is God, the most intricate and labyrinthine of all.

John Hick and Noumena/Phenomena Distinction

John Hick, the contemporary Christian philosopher and religious theorist, who is himself an advocate of pluralism, makes this same point using the Kantian noumena/phenomena distinction. In his very readable article, "Jews, Christians, Muslims: Do we all worship the same God?",[13] he first speaks of the apparently uniform image of God in these religions but goes on to suggest that this similarity is the result of looking at things from a distance. As soon as we move closer, the differences become increasingly noticeable and eclipse the uniformity. Of course, in all three religions, God is the creator of the universe and human beings, rewards and punishes people, and displays love and wrath towards them. Nonetheless, in Christianity, the "triune Being" was the One incarnated in this world in the person of His son, Jesus Christ. This God is very different from the Muslim and Jewish God. Allah and Jahweh are not identical either. In Hick's view, the God of the Jews is especially devoted to the Israelites, standing in a unique relation to his "chosen people." According to the Hebrew Bible, He tells them: "You only have I known of all the families of the earth." It is this same God who tells the Israelites to slaughter the original residents of Canaan and to seize their land for themselves. In Hick's opinion, although the

---

[11] Ali Ibn Abi Talib, *Nahj al-Balaghah*, Sermon 213.
[12] *Mathnawi*, 3: 1300.
[13] John Hick, *Disputed Questions in Theology and the Philosophy of Religion* (New Haven: Yale University Press, 1993), pp. 146–163.

God of the Muslims is closer to the God of the Jews than the God of
the Christians, nonetheless, He is totally preoccupied with Muslims, as
if He only recognises them. In wars, He only assists Muslims and He
seems much more concerned about the Arabian peninsula than Pales-
tine. The followers of each of these three religions consider themselves
particularly dear to and favoured by God.

Now, if each of these religions were to deem itself the absolute truth,
not allowing any share of truth, salvation and felicity to anyone else,
what kind of hellish world would we end up with? It is in the light of
this unpleasant possibility that Hick opts for an *a posteriori*—rather
than an *a priori*—approach to religions and examines their histories. He
asks himself, are my Muslim and Jewish friends really any less subject
to God's compassion than I am? Does God really like them any less
than me, the Christian? What have I done that they haven't done? Have
most Christians been more devout, sincere and kind than most Muslims
and Jews? (And is this not a necessary precondition for believing that
Christ is the only saviour?) Have there been fewer saints and righteous
people among Muslims and Jews than among Christians? Have Jews and
Muslims committed more mortal sins? Have these religions produced
more impoverished cultures? In all honesty and fairness, we cannot
say that Christian culture has had a notable spiritual and ethical edge
over other religious cultures. And the truth of the matter is that the
incommensurability and complexity of cultures, beliefs and histories
makes it impossible for us to rank them and to consider any one of
these religions higher or lower than the others. Yes, each of them has
had pluses and minuses. In the sacred texts of all three religions, one
can find a phrase to the effect that, "do not do unto others what you
would not have others do unto you."[14] Judaism has the plus that it
represents the birth of monotheism in the West and has contributed
outstanding figures to Western culture. But it is also marked with the
stain of mistreating the Palestinians now that it has power. Christianity
has the plus that it civilised the pagan people of Europe and it played a
part in the birth of modern science. But it is guilty of having fostered
anti-Semitism and colonising the Third World. Islam, for its part, has
had the plus of acting as a positive and constructive influence on the

---

[14] Ibid., p. 156. See: The Gospel of (Luke 6: 31); (*Babylonian Talmud*, Shabbath 31a);
(*Sahih Muslim*, chapter on iman, 71–72); (*Sunan Ibn Majah*, Introduction, 9); (*Sunan
Darami*, chapter on riqaq); (*Musnad Ibn Hanbal*, vol. 3).

lives of millions of people, and contributing to the cultural enrichment of considerable parts of the world. But it can also be taken to task for the fact that, in some Islamic countries, offenders are punished in cruel and inhuman ways.[15]

The uniformity of the three religions' civilisational roots, the implausibility of the idea that God's compassion is withheld from the disciples of any of the three, and epistemological and anthropological research into cognition and the contribution of mental and environmental proclivities to conceptualisation inclines John Hick to the view expressed by an Arab poet saying: "Although Your Beauty is Singular and we are all speaking of the One Beauty, our interpretations of it are different and diverse." Or in the words of the Persian poet, Foroughi Bastami: "You appeared with a hundred thousand splendours/that I may admire You with a hundred thousand eyes".

Hick uses the Kantian distinction of noumena/phenomena or something as is in itself/something as humanly perceived to distinguish between God as He is beyond any manifestation or attribute and as He stands in relationship to us.[16] And he considers the manifestation of God in different ways and forms to be both the key to the differences between religions and the reason for the validity of all of them. He thus arrives at an authentic plurality in the realm of religions. He says that these religions may be the manifestations, forms, faces and expressions of that One God.[17] They may represent the different ways in which God displays Himself to human beings from different perspectives and in different contexts and situations. He goes so far as to say that "Jahweh, Allah and the Christian heavenly deity, each of whom is a divine, historical personality, are in fact the joint product of God's universal manifestation and the intervention of the human imagination in specific historical circumstances." He believes that God's masculinity in monotheistic religions was not unrelated to the patriarchal character of ancient tribes and he contrasts this with the femininity of the gods of pre-Aryan India which corresponded to different socio-economic conditions. Or, as Rumi would put it, "The jug's drunkenness is from us, not our drunkenness from it; the form is formed by us, not us by it."[18]

---

[15] Hick, *Disputed Questions*, p. 156.
[16] Ibid., p. 158.
[17] Ibid., p. 158.
[18] *Mathnawi*, 1: 1815.

This kind of reasoning, which may appear inappropriate and overly positivistic to us, does not detract in any way from the strength and soundness of Hick's pluralistic position. The idea he is ultimately advancing through his contentions and arguments is that there will be no peace among the peoples until there is peace among religions and there will be no peace among religions until we accept the idea that different religions are different but equally valid responses to the ultimate divine Reality that we know as God.[19] It is interesting to note that, in the introduction to his article, Hick draws on the following subtle and eloquent verse from Rumi to support his case: "The lamps are different, but the Light is the same: it comes from Beyond."[20]

An Alternative Explanation: Formless within Forms

Hick supported his case with this verse from Rumi about the lamp's uniform radiance. Had I been in his place, I would have opted instead for the bold and daring verses of Rumi speaking of the quarrels that develop among followers of even the same prophet when "the colourless becomes a captive to colour". He says that if spiritual refinement reaches such a level as to transcend colour and comprehend that colourless truth, all the quarrels would cease and "even Moses and the Pharaoh would be friends".

> Since colourlessness (pure Unity) became the captive of colour (manifestation in the phenomenal world),
> a Moses came into conflict with a Moses.
> When you attain unto the colourlessness which you (originally) possessed,
> Moses and Pharaoh are at peace (with each other).[21]

The said verses not only lend credence to the idea of the manifestation of the absolute within the limited, the indeterminate within the determinate, the formless within the forms and the colourless within colour, they also unravel a further secret which can itself serve as another pillar supplied by mysticism in support of authentic pluralism. This pillar, which represents a third approach to comprehending and digesting the plurality of religions (alongside plurality in the contexts of understanding texts and interpreting religious experiences), sees the battle between

---

[19] Hick, *Disputed Questions*, p. 162.
[20] *Mathnawi*, 3: 1253 (translation is by Hick).
[21] *Mathnawi*, 1: 24646–2467.

Moses and the Pharaoh as a real battle, in one way; but it suggests that, in another way, it is in fact much ado about nothing or a red herring. It only throws the shallow people off the scent and distracting them from the real awesome wonder and leaving the way open for more perceptive and insightful people to look for the real treasure in a neglected ruin. The insightful can see that, while the treasure actually lies elsewhere, each of the quarrelling parties, deluding themselves that they are sitting on the treasure, imagines himself rich and mighty and the rival poor and weak. And, in this way, God jealously guards the treasure from the fools. "That which you imagine to be the treasure—through that vain imagination you are losing the treasure."[22]

Of course, this approach takes the differences between sects and religions seriously, but it sees the real purpose and meaning of it all as lying outside the disputes themselves and not in the victory of one of the sects over the others. It invites us to learn a different lesson from these divisions, and the lesson is to recognise that, wherever there is some rivalry or contest, it is in fact serving as a cover for a secret and a treasure; it is up to the wise and insightful not to be distracted by this and to seek to unearth the treasure, unravel its secrets and steal the jewel while the others are busy feuding. "Pleasure is (concealed) in pains: the track has been lost, the Water of Life has been taken away into the (Land of) Darkness."[23]

Immersion of Truth within Truth

Elsewhere in the *Mathnawi*, Rumi develops this idea further unveiling another secret and points to a fourth pillar underpinning plurality. Here, he presents the heart and kernel of his stance on the plurality of religions and speaks of the immersion of truth within truth. "Nay, the truth is absorbed in the truth; hence seventy, nay, hundred sects have arisen."[24] In other words, he says that the key to the subdivision of religions into sects and the multiplicity and plurality of religions themselves does not lie in distortions, conspiracies, the ill doings of ill-wishers, the falsifications of falsifiers or the infidelity of infidels (although no creed is free from any of these things). The division and subdivision of religions is

---

[22] *Mathnawi*, 1: 2475.
[23] *Mathnawi*, 6: 1687.
[24] *Mathnawi*, 6: 1636.

not a question of the accumulation of deviation upon deviation, Rumi
maintains, but the product of the labyrinthine nature of the truth and
the immersion of truths within truths. He teaches us that it is the
accumulation of truths and their intricate interconnectedness and the
difficulty of choosing between these truths that leads to authentic and
unavoidable diversity. It is imperative to take this point to heart, to alter
one's view and aspect, and, instead of seeing the world as consisting of
one straight line plus hundreds of crooked and broken lines, to see it
as consisting of an aggregate of straight lines which meet, run parallel
and overlap: truths immersed within truths. And does the fact that the
Qur'an describes prophets as following a right path—in other words,
moving along *one* of the straight paths and not *the* straight path—not
substantiate this?[25]

The problem, as far as Rumi is concerned, is not that some groups
have failed to find the truth and been left empty handed and misguided;
it is that the discovered truths are many, and it is the bewilderment
caused by the multitude of truths and the attraction to and enchant-
ment by some bits and segments of them that brings about the plurality.
The point has been made in a different form in my discussion on the
"Contraction and Expansion" that being objective is something more
than being true. If someone knows that their friend has ten thousand
dollars but does not realise that it is a loan, the person both knows
something that is true and has a picture of the friend's wealth that is
not objective or realistic. In order for the geography of knowledge to
be true to reality it must encompass all the relevant truths, otherwise
it will be a traitor to reality. That is to say, if the structure of reality
was simple, if there was only one or a small number of truths, if there
was no subterranean or overarching layers and no surface and depth to
the real world, if the world of being was not intricate and labyrinthine,
if every truth and secret was easily expressible and decipherable and
comprehensible, and if language was dexterous and invincible in the
revelation of secrets and the exposition of truths, then guidance and
misguidance and truth and falsehood would be easily distinguishable
and the birth of countless sects would seem inappropriate and un-

---

[25] For instance see the following verses addressing Abraham and Muhammad.
"...He rendered thanks for His favours, so that He chose him and guided him to a
straight path." (16: 121); "by the Wise Qur'an that you are sent upon a straight path."
(36: 3–4); "....that He may guide you to a straight path..." (48: 2).

acceptable. But the plurality of truths and their intricate relationship have inevitably flung open the gates to sectarian divisions. Now the only way to dismiss the plurality is to indulge in the simplification of reality, which would only amount to naivety.

We can describe the pluralism we have been speaking about so far as authentic or positive pluralism, because it is based on strength: we have become pluralists because we are rich. Since religious texts and experiences naturally admit of a multitude of interpretations, since reality is intricate and multifaceted, since divine providence and protectiveness dictate multiplicity and rivalry, we have consented to plurality and accepted it, and we have no other alternative. And we see others not as being excusably empty handed but as being blessedly rich. Of course, we also allow a role for reason and we do not forego intelligent criticism, for this, too, is dictated by divine providence and protectiveness.

Positive pluralism also has another sense and source. It is that the existing alternatives and rivals are unique in kind and irreducible. None of them can be swallowed up or dissolved by any of the others, and each of them has incommensurable particularities; like multiple, correct, irreducible answers to a single question. Experiences, like kinds or species, are truly plural and essentially distinct. Likewise, the interpretation of texts and so on. But we also have negative pluralism. In this pluralism, which is also acceptable and legitimate, something is always lacking; either certitude or truth or compatibility, etc. It is in fact an inauthentic pluralism, although important and unavoidable for all that.

Negative Pluralism: Diversity Explained via Negativa

One Destination, Different Paths

Here, too, we will turn to Jalal al-Din Rumi for help, confident that he can guide us thanks to his boundless Sufi riches. Rumi advises Hesam al-Din to seek a master and warns him against embarking alone on the spiritual journey's fearsome trail. He considers it impossible to travel this road without the assistance and effort of masters, and adds that, even people, who seem to have had no master and have nonetheless managed, in rare instances, to get somewhere, have secretly benefited

from the solicitude of an unseen master and have supped at the table
of an invisible but hospitable guide.

> If any one, by rare exception, traverse this Way alone (without a Pir),
> he arrived (at this goal) through the help of the spiritual influence of
> the Pirs.
> The hand of the Pir is not withdrawn from the absent (those who are not
> under his authority): his hand is naught but the grasp of God.
> Inasmuch as they give such a robe of honour to the absent, (what must
> they give their disciples?): undoubtedly the present are better than the
> absent.[26]

It is true that guidance is impossible without a guide, nevertheless,
this guide may operate visibly or invisibly. He may be near or far. Be
that as it may, his business is assistance. We must keep our eyes fixed
on the ultimate destination (viz. salvation), for the starting point and
the journey do not matter much here and do not have their own laws.
Elsewhere in the *Mathnawi*, Rumi conveys this idea in the form of a
charming metaphor: you have lost your camel and you run this way and
that in search of it. You ask everyone whose path you cross if they have
seen it. At times, a clue raises your hopes. At other times, a reply makes
you despair. Another person, copying your actions without having lost
any camel, runs everywhere that you run and falsely asks everyone about
his camel. That earnest quest and this fake one continue until at last
you find your camel. Next to your camel, there stands another camel,
which, as it happens, belongs to the copy-cat seeker. The moment he
sees it, he remembers his long-lost camel. And, thereafter, he comes
to his senses and takes his own path and course.

> When a liar sets out (to journey) with a truthful man, his falsehood turns
> to truth of a sudden....
> The sincere one said, "You have left me, (although) till now you were
> paying regard to me."
> He replied, "Hitherto I have been an idle scoffer and, from cupidity, have
> been (engaged) in flattering (thee)...
> I was stealing the camel's description from thee; (but when) my spirit
> saw its own camel, it had its eye filled (with seeing)...
> My evil deeds have become pious acts entirely-thanks (to God)! Jest is
> vanished and earnest is realised-thanks (to God)!

---

[26] *Mathnawi*, 1: 2972–2975.

Since my evil deeds have become the means of (my) attaining unto God, do not, then, throw any blame on my evil deeds. [27]

The end of the journey makes it clear that you were both on the path of rightful guidance and salvation; one, as a thoughtful seeker, the other, as an imitator or even a mocker. And the unseen guiding hand led you both to the auspicious destination. If we view it all from the perspective of the ultimate purpose, we can see that the sins of the mocking imitator were in fact acts of worship.

Like a burglar who sets out to burgle a house but is so guided by unseen forces that he ends up in his own land and home. Or a person who plants something, pretending that it is a seed, and then finds to his amazement that it has burst into a thousand flowers.

It is thus that sincere seekers on the spiritual path are assisted and guided to the destination no matter what label, banner or affiliation they are travelling under and no matter what religion or sect they belong to. And not just the true seekers—for they may seem deserving—but even the false but diligent imitators are not abandoned without some morsels of guidance. "The disagreement of man kind is caused by names: peace ensues when they advance to the reality (denoted by the name)."[28]

Here, instead of insistence on the absolute correctness of a religion's teachings, the emphasis is on the sincerity of the seeker and his ultimate salvation, and instead of insistence on a visible, religious guide, there is talk of an unseen and hidden guide (or guides). It is as if all seekers and believers are following a single path and are all being assisted from a single source, even though they give themselves and their paths a host of different names, make a host of different claims and start quarrelling over all these imaginary differences.

This accommodating and benevolent pluralism both makes it possible to digest and accept plurality and reassures sects about the justness of their claims that: truth, salvation and superiority essentially and truly belong to us; that others are unknowingly following the same path as us; that they are benefiting from our protection and guidance, albeit unbeknownst to them; and that they will ultimately reach the same point that we have arrived at. Muslims see all travellers on the path of God as ultimately Muslims (on the basis of the verse "the true religion

---

[27] *Mathnawi*, 2: 2980, 2986–87, 2989, 2991–2992.
[28] *Mathnawi*, 2: 3680.

in God's sight is Islam").[29] And Christians such as Karl Rahner see all God-seekers as covert Christians or Christian in all but name. John Hick describes this position as inclusivism (believing in apparent plurality) and contrasts it with pluralism (believing in true plurality), which is his own position. Needless to say, he notes that there is a third widely-subscribed to position known as exclusivism (rejecting plurality). He also quotes Pope John Paul II as stating in his first Encyclical, *Redemptor Hominis*, (in 1979), that: "'man—every man without exception—has been redeemed by Christ' and with 'each man without any exception whatever Christ is in a way united, even when man is unaware of it' (para. 14)."[30]

Exclusivity of God's Guidance?

We can also arrive at this same point on the basis of God's attribute, *hadi*, (the Guide). The question can be raised—if it really is the case today that, from the ranks of all the believers belonging to all the different sects (setting aside non-believers) who number in the billions, only the minority of Twelver Shiʿis have benefited from rightful guidance and all the rest have gone astray or are infidels (according to Shiʿis), or if only the twelve million minority of Jews have been rightly guided and everyone else rejected and damned (according to Jews)—then where has God's guidance been actualised and who has it benefited and in what way have people been subject to God's grace (which is used by theologians to explain prophethood)? And where has God's attribute of "the Guide" manifested itself? How can we believe, as Shiʿites, that the moment the Prophet of Islam, peace be upon him, passed away, a handful of rebels and rogues succeeded in hijacking his religion, thus depriving the bulk of Muslims of the blessing of rightful guidance and reducing to nothing the Prophet's years-long endeavours? Even assuming that a limited number of people acted on the basis of contempt and ambition, what have millions upon millions of Muslims (until the end of time) done to deserve having their acts of worship rejected and their struggles unrewarded, irredeemably doomed to damnation? Does this not amount to saying that God's plans have been thwarted and the Prophet of God defeated? Was the coming of Jesus Christ,

---

[29] The Qurʾan, 3: 19.
[30] Hick, *Disputed Questions*, p. 143.

peace be upon him, the spirit of God, the messenger of God and the word of God (according to the Qur'an), only intended to leave a large number of people deluded into believing in a trinity and going astray? To have his book and his words immediately distorted? Was he in the business of misguidance or guidance? Was he an envoy of Satan or of Merciful and Compassionate God? And if we were to follow this logic, it would mean that large parts of the world are always under the sway and reign of the devil and only a tiny, tremulous part under the protection of God. And the people who have gone astray both quantitatively and qualitatively surpass the rightly guided. And good people are the absolute minority. And the religions that God sent to guide the masses have been easily disfigured by the followers of Satan. Now, most of the people in the world believe in distorted religions or are completely deprived of guidance and goodness, and will reap no benefit in the hereafter from God's compassion.

The above observations are enough to make us pitch the scope of guidance and felicity and to acknowledge that others, too, have a share in salvation, felicity and truth. And this is no more and no less than the spirit of pluralism.[31] In fact, much of the confusion arises from the terms "infidelity" and "fidelity", which are this-worldly, legalistic [fiqhi] expressions (echoed in all the other religions and sects); for they distract us from the innermost workings and layers of this subject. The way to resolve this problem and to digest and accept the plurality is to brush aside these outer layers in our capacity as diligent researchers; to survey the world from the perspective of God's attribute of the Guide; to see guidance and salvation as fundamentally resting on the sincerity of the quest and the determination to worship God, not on devotion to this or that person or the practising of this or that ritual or attachment to this or that historical incident; to separate the superficies from the substance; to distinguish religion's essentials from its accidentals; to rank religion and truth in their merited positions; and to recognise that Satan lurks on the fringes of religion, not at its centre ("And thou art not to suppose that they who disbelieve have outstripped Me; they cannot frustrate My Will").[32] If we look at things from this perspective,

---

[31] I have explained the notion that most of the people of the world are saved, based on the ideas of such great thinkers as Ibn Sina (Avicenna), Sadr al-Din Shirazi and Mulla Hadi Sabzevari, in an article entitled "Karnameh Kamyab-e Anbiya" [The Triumph of Prophets] now published in *Modara va Modiriyat*.

[32] The Qur'an, 8: 59.

pluralism means nothing more than acknowledging God's boundless compassion, the triumph of prophets, the feebleness of Satan's treachery, and the extension of God's kindly hands over the heads of all the world's people.

This is not to say that the followers of all sects and religions should needlessly abandon their own practices, rituals and beliefs, and turn into a uniform mass. All that is required is for them to look at the plurality and diversity of rituals and beliefs from a different perspective; not to imagine that the essential core of rightful guidance is confined to the teachings of theology and *fiqh*; and not to operate on the basis of the assumption that anyone who has a few specific articles of faith engraved on their minds (Shi'is, Sunnis, Protestants, Catholics, etc.) is rightly guided and saved, whereas everyone else is misguided and doomed. Let them also take into account people's deeds, longing and diligence. Let them not imagine that Satan has the upper hand over God. Let them also study the hidden ways in which God chooses to guide people. And let them, most of all, value moral virtues higher than mental habits and shari'ah practices.

This pluralism is negative because (taking its cue from the story of Moses and the shepherd) it does not concern itself with the correctness and truth of theological teachings but with the salvation and felicity of sincere seekers and the hidden assistance provided by invisible guides. And it accepts plurality not in the light of its plurality but in the light of it all merging into one.

Inextricable Mix of Truth and Falsehood

To this can be added the fact that there is no phenomenon free from impurities. It is a matter of some significance that nothing is to be found in the world in pure form. This idea appears in the Qur'an itself where it is said: "He sends down out of heaven water, and the rivers flow each in its measure, and the torrent carries a swelling scum;..." (13: 17)

Mud and dirt inevitably mix in with the water that falls from the sky and appear as foam on the surface of rivers. Truth and falsehood are thus inextricably intertwined. Imam Ali, too, said that if pure truth and pure falsehood existed, no one would hesitate for an instant in opting for truth and rejecting falsehood. But the fact is that "a handful is taken from this and a handful is taken from that, and they are mixed together";[33] the two are presented to us as a mixture.

We are not talking here about the "true" divine religions themselves which are nothing but truth. We are talking about people's understanding of them and the different religious sects which are always a mixture of truth and falsehood. And it has to be said that if one of these sects was the pure truth and all the others absolute falsehood, no intelligent person would fail to distinguish the true from the false and to opt for the truth. But the fact that these quarrels over beliefs (whether intra-religious or extra-religious) have persisted for so long and reached a point where no one is prepared to budge—such that it rarely occurs that a person subscribing to one belief consents to cross over to some other belief—is because everyone sees so much that is beautiful, sound, true and just in their own belief mixture as to be prepared to overlook its shortcomings, and they see enough that is incorrect and questionable in the rival belief as to overshadow its beauty and excellence.

We have no pure race in the world, no pure language and no pure religion. And, as experts in the natural sciences are very willing to admit, no aspect of the natural world is pure either. It is because of this congestion and the intense overlaps and clashes between the various arenas of nature that experience has yet to yield a single scientific law that is not approximate and is one hundred per cent accurate.

Neither Shi'ism nor Sunnism is pure Islam and absolutely right (although the followers of each of these paths maintain this view about themselves). Neither the Ash'arites nor the Mu'tazilites are absolutely right. Neither the *fiqh* of the Malekis nor that of the Ja'faris. Neither the interpretation of Fakhr al-din Razi nor that of Tabataba'i. Neither the Zaydis nor the Wahhabis. It can neither be said that Muslims' understanding and worship of God is free of idolatry, nor that all Christians are following an idolatrous creed. The world is filled with impure identities. It is not as if on the one side we have pure truth and, on the other, pure falsehood. As soon as we recognise this, it becomes easier and more palatable for us to digest plurality.

The followers of any path are entitled to persist in and pursue their own way. The object is not to dissuade them from their chosen path; the object is to understand one's own path better and to digest the idea that plurality and diversity are natural, human, this-worldly and inevi-

---

[33] *Nahj al-Balaghah*, Sermon 50.

table. The object is not to suggest the relativity of truth and falsehood either. We are not saying that truth and falsehood lack meaning and independence, and that whatever belief any sect holds is true. We are saying that the world is a world of impurities; be it the natural world or the world of religion. Be it the individual or the community. And the reason for this impurity is the humanisation of religion. When the rain of pure religion falls from the heavens of revelation unto the mud of human understanding, it becomes tainted by mental processes. And the moment minds embark on understanding this pure religion, they dilute and pollute it with their pre-existing data. Hence religion and religiosity will flow like a muddy river amongst the people until Judgement Day and it is only then that God will adjudicate on the differences between his creatures ("Thy Lord will decide between them on the Day of Resurrection, touching their differences") (16: 124). Or as Rumi put it: "Vein by vein is this sweet water and bitter water, flowing in (God's) creatures until the blast of the trumpet (at the Resurrection)."[34]

There are not only distortions at the level of understanding religion, but at the level of religion itself, too, many fabrications and inventions have been perpetrated in the name of the Prophet and the revered religious figures, making it difficult for religious scholars to distinguish the correct from the incorrect. What we now find ourselves in the possession of (in the form of the Qur'an and the *Sunna*) is neither all that it might have been nor devoid of everything that it should have been (in other words, it is impure). There were probably many *hadith*s which did not survive to our day and there is probably many a *hadith* that has survived but was a fabrication from the start. Many are the questions that could have been asked from our revered religious figures to shed light on things but were either never asked or were never answered out of this-worldly prudence or because of higher considerations.[35]

---

[34] *Mathnawi*, 1: 746.

[35] Is it not amazing and significant that, to prove the theory of the absolute guardianship of an Islamic jurist [*wilayat-e motlaqeh-e faqih*] and to justify their position on the important and immense question of a religious state, Shi'i *faqih*s base everything on a *hadith* recounted by Umar Ibn Handhalah (the veracity of which is disputed by some), with the subject of the Narrative being a question about minor disagreements over inheritance and what was owed to whom. Moreover, it is not entirely clear whether it refers to "an arbiter" [*hakam*] or "a ruler" [*hakem*], which leaves it open to a multitude of interpretations. In fact, it is not even clear or a matter of total consensus that the *hadith* actually supports the position it is used to support. And can it really be that, if a dispute had not arisen between two people over water and land and inheritance and if no such question had been put to an Imam, the immense question of religious

Does the very fact that a number of Shi'i scholars (such as Ali Ibn Ibrahim Qumi[36], Siqat al-Islam Kulayni[37] and Muhaddis Nuri)[38] have held the opinion that the Qur'an itself was tampered with and maintained that it contained errors and alterations not demonstrate (from an epistemological and second order perspective) that the scope of human intrusion in religion is very extensive (at least according to Muslim chroniclers) and that the possession and reading of a Qur'an that has been tampered with is not incompatible with being a Muslim? Does the triumph of tyrants in constricting the Shi'i Imams and preventing them from freely disseminating their views not constitute a vast lacuna in religion for Shi'is (and, in the opinion of Shi'is, for all of Islam)? Had the Prophet lived longer or had other important historical events occurred during his blessed lifetime, would the Qur'an not have been a far lengthier tome? Would it not have clarified many more issues for the edification of Muslims? All this to highlight the extent to which religion becomes human and historical when it enters history; how it is subjected to people's theoretical and practical intrusions; how it is dulled and dimmed by the passage of time and the veils that impede understanding; and how much is gradually taken away from it and added on to it. What remains is the necessary minimum of spirituality and guidance granted and bequeathed to humanity. This is exactly what the reference in the Qur'an to "the descent of revelation" means. And this is the destiny of any religion and creed. In fact, it is the destiny of absolutely anything that enters the hovel of history and nature and dons the garment of humanity and materiality. The imposition on religion of the language of the tribe (Arabic, Hebrew, Greek) is the first and most obvious imposition and descent. And then there follows wave

---

government would have been left unanswered and undefined? Could something so essential to religion have been blocked by such an accident of history? Be that as it may (assuming that we include the question of governance and the state in the aggregate of things that we expect from religion and consider it essential to religion), there were many other hadiths of which no trace now remains, and this is what has caused all the doubt and confusion among religious scholars.

[36] In Ali Ibn Ibrahim's commentary on the Qur'an which is well-known under his own name.

[37] In his *Usul al-Kafi*, Kulayni has included *hadiths* that refer to such tamperings and he has not disputed them. Moreover, in the book's preface, he explicitly states that he believes in the authenticity of all the *hadiths* presented in the book.

[38] See: Hossein Taqi al-Nuri Tabarsi [known as Muhaddis Nuri], *Fasl al-Khitab fi Ithbat-e Tahrif-e Kitab Rabb al-arbab* (Tehran: S.n., 1881). Also, Ahmad Ibn Talib Tabarsi expresses the same view in the book *Ihtijaj*. And Feiz Kashani was not uninclined towards this view (see the sixth preface to his *Tafsir Safi*).

after wave of trouble and turmoil that engulf it and make it clear how "at first religion appeared easy, then came the difficulties".

A religion like this cannot be weighed down with heavy loads, nor can a multitude of promises be made on its behalf or a multitude of tasks undertaken in its name. It is this modesty and unpretentiousness that makes for such pleasant companionship and opens the way to human and religious pluralism. Arrogant egotists, replete with self-adoration and bloated on their boasts and pretensions, are incapable of and unfit to keep the company of others and, abandoned to their baffled solitude, they live with the tedium of dejection.

Compatibility of All Truths

But the story does not end here. Negative pluralism has many more things to say for itself. The eighth basis is the relatedness of all truths. No truth is incompatible and ill-assorted with any other. All truths reside under the same roof and are stars in the same constellation. This self-evident logical point, first, rescues truth from being tainted with being eastern or western or reactionary or progressive. And it makes it clear that the seekers of truth are not banned from facing in any direction and following any course. Secondly, it invites all truth lovers to strive ceaselessly to ensure that their truth is compatible with the truths of others. The upshot of this idea is the following principle: a notion is true if it is compatible with other true notions. Hence, it is the permanent responsibility of every truth-seeking researcher to try to resolve any inconsistencies in the truth table and to adjust the geometry of cognition; not to be eternally satisfied with their own (dubious) truths, keeping a haughty distance from and ignoring everyone else.

The contention being made here is that everyone participates in building the wondrous castle of truth; or, even more, that everyone should be invited to participate and that the castle should be carried on the collective's shoulders. Preventing others from expressing their views and foolishly imagining oneself unneedy of others, is not the hallmark of wisdom or the etiquette of the seekers of truth. The truth seeker is always travelling and always building. If we wish to see an elegant geometry of truth, we must place our brick next to the bricks of others. And if we are satisfied with and grateful for an incomplete segment of truth, we must also respect the incomplete segments of others. One way or another, we have no other option but to accept plurality.

Pluralism of Values and Causes

But if truths are so related and compatible, in the opinion of some contemporaries this is by no means the case when it comes to values, virtues and rites, for there are irreconcilable differences between them (ninth basis). The plurality here is real and deep-seated. No argument has been presented that proves, for example, that social justice and freedom are entirely compatible; in fact, all of human experience suggests that they clash. Hence, individuals and communities ultimately make a choice and opt for one over the other. This choice is caused, not reasoned and, as long as the causes and the clash persist, so, too, will the choice. Isaiah Berlin is apparently of the view that some questions have several irreconcilable answers.[39] It is up to you to decide which answer you want to choose. And, in the words of Aziz al-Din Nasafi, it is difficult to say whether it is better to endeavour to please, to acquiesce and to observe or to retreat, to be content and to vanish from view, "and I have yet to ascertain which must be valued higher than the other and which I must prefer. And, as I write today, I have still not been able to choose and I cannot choose."[40]

It is not at all clear whether it is better to be generous or to be brave or to be combative or to be chaste or to be grateful and patient or to be content and ascetic or to be wise. It is also not clear that anyone can at one and the same time possess every single one of these virtues (except in the rarest cases). It is impossible to have everything. None of the great figures in history have shone in every arena. History's sky is full of stars and this is what makes it beautiful. The same can be said of any single individual being devoid of all the vices; it has likewise not been proved that this is possible. In fact, if we consider the individual's vices to be the collective's virtues,[41] the story of morality and humanity will appear in an altogether different light. More notable still, there is by no means a single method or key to solving specific moral dilemmas; it is

---

[39] Isaiah Berlin,. *Four Essays on Liberty.* Oxford: Oxford University Press, 1969.

[40] Aziz al-Din Nasafi, *Al-Insan al-Kamil.* (Ed.) Marijan Mole (Tehran: Anjuman-e Iranshenashi Faranceh dar Tehran,1359/1980), p. 10.

[41] As expressed by Bernard Mandeville in his book *The Fable of the Bees: Private Vices, Public Benefits.*

a case of real, conflicting plurality: would it be appropriate for a poor person whose children are close to death to steal from another poor person whose children are also close to death and who has managed to scrape together a little food for them? Why should the second person's children enjoy precedence over the first's? Here, we would either have to commend both options (theft and self-restraint) or condemn both. Or we could value one option more highly than the other without reason (and with cause). Daily life is full of such dilemmas. And on the whole the preponderance is with these kinds of bewildering tragic cases, where the individual can taste real choice and doubt. Instances of ethical problems that have simple uncontroversial solutions are very few (or are non-existent). The plurality in judging these practical cases is inevitable and the eventual choice is not a matter of ethical preferences, but the product of a range of possible causes (pressure, poverty, upbringing, boldness, etc.) and the intrinsic irreconcilability of the values.

This pluralism of values and causes, which rises from the silence of reason and the intrinsic irreconcilability of values and multiplicity of choices, is the very stuff of life and people actually live in the heart of it. Every individual is a world composed of individual principles and yardsticks and an individual ideal. And this independence and plurality of worlds displays itself in particular in the realm of values and cultures. This is what cultural incommensurability means and cultural pluralism is built upon it. And it is a small step from cultural and moral pluralism to religious pluralism. We must pay serious heed to pluralism in this sense, for, although it is negative in as much as it rests on the absence of reasons, in so far as it rests on the essential distinctness, clash and equality of values (if this is accepted), it constitutes a positive and authentic pluralism, the gist of which is that it is fundamentally possible to have several different types of life based on several different models (after discarding the improper and objectionable ones), which are on a par and cannot be reduced to a single type; exactly like the pluralism that we find in the realm of the interpretation of spiritual and natural experiences, where (after discarding the false theories) we always face a number of rival theories, which cannot be reduced to one.

Philosophers have also suggested that every individual is a kind unto themselves and that excellence for one is never identical to excellence for any other. Hence, no individual can serve as the exhaustive model for any other and there is more than one Perfect Man (contrary to the common understanding of the Sufi theory of "the Perfect Man"). Therefore, individuals cannot be expected to become exactly alike, to possess uniform virtues and to follow a single path. Here, too, pluralism is authentic, real and based on essential differences. The same can be said of everyone's mental, personal and "existential" states, which are unique to them and do not resemble those of anyone else. People's doubts, anxieties, loves and beliefs are intrinsically different and distinct. Everyone is therefore in a real sense alone, appearing before God singly. Everyone is born alone, lives alone, dies alone and is resurrected alone: "Now you have come to Us one by one, as We created you upon the first time." (6: 94) The discovery of this aloneness and this individuality marks the start of the discovery of a new freedom, freedom from dissolving into the general and the universal, the rediscovery of one's own self, one's own world, one's own religion, one's own morality, one's own existential problems and one's own path to resolving them. Finding oneself, at each moment, at the centre and meeting point of endless possibilities and choices. This is real freedom, based on real pluralism.

Religiosity is Caused not Reasoned

Causal pluralism carries other contentions in its rucksack: the religiosity of most believers is caused not reasoned. It is not as if all Christians, for example, become Christians only after assessing every possible religion and rite and convincing themselves of the justness of Christianity on the basis of incontrovertible arguments. By and large their belief is inherited and emulative. And this holds equally true of Zoroastrians, Muslims, Jews and so on. If the Christian had been born in a Muslim society, he would have become a Muslim, and vice versa. The words on the lips of most believers (if not to say most of the people of the world) is: "This was the faith our fathers practised. We are merely walking in their footsteps." (43: 22) This can be said not only of the general public, but of most clerics as well. The clerics in any religion are generally following, serving, being taught and teaching the same religion that their environment and birthplace approves of and means by theology. They are in truth emulators. Rare indeed are the truly free thinkers who remain unmoved by the pressures, pleasures, approbations and admonitions that surround religion, turn their back on the spiritual and practical rites and customs of their land and people, and refuse to believe in anything except by force of thought and reason. These whales of the ocean of contemplation and reflection are incapable of fitting into the small brooks of run of the mill religions; they are each a creed unto themselves. They are the fortunate few who can say, "God speaks to me in my heart". And only God is privy to their secrets. If anyone possesses certitude and tranquillity, it is them. Everywhere else there is only dogma, prejudice, severity, naivety and intolerance.

Suffice it to say that the average person is a slave to cause, not reason. And the world is filled with average people. They are generally governed by tradition, emulation, background, environment, material needs, rage and the baser instincts rather than by reason, evidence, argument and proof. And on the whole they operate under the sway of determinism, not free will. They are to be excused, not to be held to account. They are in the grip of dogma, not certitude. Prone to feuds, not tolerance. And how can such average, restricted, emulative captives and prisoners (viz. us) put on airs and graces before one another and curse one other? It would be far more seemly for us to be brimming with humility, fellow-feeling and compassion rather than arrogance, enmity and rage. How can a captive behave like a lord? There can hardly be any feud more deluded and senseless than a feud between captives who take themselves for lords. Which brings us again to humble companionship and sensible tolerance, to unknitting our brows and embracing the dictates of destiny, to seeing the wisdom of God behind the workings of the world and bowing down before it.

We are nearing the end of our journey, but I must not neglect to mention one important point: despite the fact that the discipline of theology occasionally stokes the furnace of futile debates, it nonetheless keeps alight the brilliant flame of rationality and rationality is a good worth purchasing on any pretext and at any price. Of course, rational and theological religion is not the pinnacle of religiosity; the experiential, revelational, spiritual variety is undoubtedly superior. But this latter only falls to the fortunate few. By lighting the flame of reason, theologians rescue believers from the chilling aridity of mindless dogmas and contribute to the warmth of wisdom. Theological religion is a hundred times better and sweeter than common, emulative religiosity, and it nurtures within it a plurality of which there is neither sight nor sound in the parched desert of common religiosity. This is a plurality that is built on doubt, not certitude, and it is a pluralism that is negative, not positive. It is quite the reverse with the plurality of religious beliefs, experiences and discoveries which is interwoven with tranquillity, certitude and self-assurance (and is positive). Rationality breeds doubt and rationalism leads to a healthy and beneficial scepticism. Judging by the history of theology, philosophy and other rational disciplines, rather than producing certitude, tranquillity and peace, the project of reason has generated doubts, disputes and arguments. Although this may seem a paltry achievement to lovers and mystics, it is precious indeed to the rational.

Again, judging by history, wherever the flame of theology has been doused by the might of the custodians of canonic religion or the temptations of love and mysticism, ruinous and wicked prejudices have reared their ugly heads and surreptitiously got the better of religiosity. Theological dialogue and the fact that it prevents religious beliefs from "congealing" and is always fluid and amenable to counter-arguments is a blessing that we cannot afford to discard. With canonic religion, it is impossible to speak of ecumenicalism; every sect of emulators has to perform exactly the rites that their religious leader prescribes. No *faqih* has ever raised the cry of pluralism. This is the cry of reflective believers. And reflective believers are dedicated either to reason or to love. Either to industry or to discovery. Hence, theological religion and revelatory religion open the gates to two types of pluralism: a pluralism that is founded on doubt and a pluralism that is founded on certitude. Despite all its muscle flexing, the discipline of theology leads to nothing but conjecture. The strongest testimony to this is the reaction displayed by our own philosophers, who have always viewed theologians with condescension and described their premises as rhetorical, polemical and indemonstrable rather than categorical, essential and necessary. And of course theologians have had the same opinion of philosophers.

On the whole, to reason is to invite the listener to criticise and to be convinced. In this context, recognising and respecting the opponent is the accepted etiquette and airing opposing views, a basic tenet. The diversity of the methods of argumentation, the diversity of the doubts and the diversity of the theological schools is the very stuff and outcome of practising theology. This diversity and plurality and the proliferation of disputes and quarrels does not produce a restful mind or a confident heart. And limping along on the "wooden leg of syllogism" does not lead you to the conquest of any mountain peaks or fortresses. But it does bring diversity into its own, it does honour rational doubt and its does deflate the haughtiness of narrow-minded, bloated, self-righteous bigots. Since we do not know for certain whose propositions are right, we respect all of them and do not drive any of them off the field (epistemological pluralism).

The reason why Iranian society finds it difficult to accept the idea of pluralism today is because, for quite some time now, the tradition of philosophical and, especially, theological ratiocination has been eclipsed and fallen silent. It therefore sees the airing of theological debates as detrimental to the beliefs of the masses. It does not seem to realise that the masses did not acquire their beliefs on the basis of such debates for them to lose it on this basis. On this issue, the responsibility rests solely with religious scholars and leaders, not the masses and emulators; it is up to them to acknowledge and submit to the existence of right paths in religion and politics and to leave the way open for the health and longevity of all seekers of truth. Those who are certain without ever having doubted and those who have chosen unity without ever having known plurality are the most intolerant creatures on the face of the earth.

Pluralistic Society versus Ideological Society

Pluralistic society is a non-ideological society; it has no official interpreters or commentators. It is constructed on plurality-loving reason rather than on unity-loving emotion. It is forbearing and tolerant. Information flows freely within it. It is competitive and harbours a multitude of players. And it resembles nothing so much as nature; in other words, it has springs and autumns, sunshine and rain. It comes into being when the rulers and the ruled all confess that the natural and social world is fundamentally a world of plurality, not unity, a world of differences, not similarities. And that wishing to establish a unified model for everyone's life and religion and language and culture and morality and customs and habits is to wish the impossible and to shoulder an onerous and oppressive burden. Purging the world of its plurality is neither possible nor desirable. If there are ten arguments for the acceptability and desirability of religious pluralism, there are a hundred arguments for the acceptability and desirability of cultural and political pluralism. We hardly need look any further than the Soviet Union, which failed so miserably and hauntingly in imposing a uniform culture and politics on its people. The experience of industrial capitalism, too, is very telling, for although, in Marx's words, "it built the world in its own image", it never succeeded in homogenising cultures but served instead to make the inheritors and possessors of ethnic, local and historical cultures more sensitive and vigilant. Never has the cry of history been more audible: pluralities are with you; make room for them or they will press your back up against a wall.

The Creator of the universe has dexterously and tenderly fashioned a complex and labyrinthine world and peoples. He has painted a rainbow of languages and worlds and human beings, with a palette-full of causes and reasons. He has laid hundreds of mountain passes and valleys along the path of the rational mind. He has roused countless prophets and filled people's eyes and ears with a symphony of sights and sounds. He has divided the human race into a multitude of branches and tribes, not for them to display arrogance and enmity, but for them to be respectful and humble. And let those who wish to flatten and homogenise this beautiful and varied terrain beware, lest they have crawled into the ravine of Satan.

CHAPTER SEVEN

STRAIGHT PATHS—2
A CONVERSATION ON RELIGIOUS PLURALISM[1]

Critical Rationalism or Relativism

Q. What's the epistemological basis of the religious pluralism you have in mind? Specifically, is it rationality and critical realism or relativism? In other words, based on a simplified classification, if we divide episte-mological positions into naïve realism, critical realism and relativism, it seems that your main aim in *Contraction and Expansion of Religious Knowledge* was to move from naïve realism to critical realism. But some of the points that have been raised in the debate on religious pluralism have created the impression that you have moved on even further and are, in effect, advancing a relativist epistemology. In fact, it seems that we can have two types of pluralism. That is to say, we can arrive at the plurality of truth on the basis of two readings: one is based on critical realism, whereby we recognize that we have certain limitations in discovering the truth and that we, therefore, discern the truth in different manifestations; the other is based on a relativist posi-tion, whereby we consider everything to be on a par. In other words, pluralism and a belief in plurality can be constructed both on the basis of critical realism and on the basis of relativism. What's the basis of your position on pluralism?

A. Let us not lose sight of the fact that we are talking about religious pluralism and not pluralism in the absolute sense of the word, which would also embrace philosophy, science and so on.

---

[1] This is an abridged version of "Truth, Reason, Salvation", a chapter in Soroush's book: *Serat-haye Mustaqim* (Straight Paths), Tehran: Serat Publications, 1998. While this chapter includes some new points, it sheds more light on some of the things presented in the previous chapter. The original format of the article, i.e. an interview, is maintained here because some of the questions help the reader to put Soroush's discussion of religious pluralism in the broader context of his ideas about religion and its interpretation and reflect some of the criticisms that his ideas on pluralism have met. [Ed.]

We are discussing religious pluralism and, in terms of meaning, religious pluralism has differences with the pluralism you will find in philosophy. This is a point we have to be careful about, otherwise, it can lead to fallacious arguments.

In philosophy and science, relativism is a dangerous pitfall. Although it is difficult to speak about specific instances in this area, it can be said in general and absolute terms that relativism is not an acceptable position. It is the type of fallacious conclusion that points to some kind of problem or fallacy earlier on in the premises.

Since truth in religion is different from truth in philosophy and science, one has to be careful about terminology. As you suggested, naïve realism is appropriate to a world that is assumed to be simple; sophisticated realism, to a world that is assumed to be complicated. The history of rationality in human societies, the insights human beings have gained into rationality, its twists and turns throughout the course of history, the errors it has fallen into, the impasses it has faced, the antinomies it has generated, the irresolvable disputes that have arisen over the years, and the discoveries that have been made concerning cause and reason have, all in all, rendered people more aware of the truth of rationality, its historicity and its capabilities. Perhaps there was a time when people expected more from rationality, but now science, reason and philosophy have become more modest and this modesty is the outcome of the growth of reason. This rational modesty will also undoubtedly extend its verdict to our understanding of religion.

Hence, my position, in fact, is the sophisticated rationalism or critical rationalism that you mentioned. That is to say, the actually existing world, be it religion, philosophy or nature, is much too complicated to be dealt with by judgements based on naïve rationalism or to sanction dogmatic commitment to one single option. And collective criticism and openness to criticism are among the most important tools that will allow our theories to become more complicated and advanced and possibly allow us to move closer to truth. One of the clear consequences of critical rationalism is to show that most of people's certainties are little more than conjectures. This is not to say that people can never arrive at truth but that arriving at truth has no specific signpost. The signposts mentioned in traditional philosophy, such as observation, certitude, etc., are all fallible. Hence, one cannot easily say, this is true and that is not true. This is why, although, in critical rationality, the definition of "true" (which, of course, has rivals) as the correspondence with facts is accepted, nonetheless, this rationality recognizes that identifying actual tokens of the fulfilment of this definition and finding the propositions that correspond to reality are fraught with difficulty. Critical rationalism is, therefore, much more modest in its claims and it takes human fallibility very seriously.

Q. If there are no signposts indicating that we have arrived at truth, are there also no signposts indicating that we have moved closer to it?

A. No, there are not. We have no clear indication of that either. We must investigate anew ceaselessly. In other words, in critical rationalism, thinking about, interpreting and understanding reality is an interminable process. And it is a collective and a fluid affair. This in itself gives us cause to be very modest and releases us from the urge to make exaggerated and extreme claims.

This critical rationalism applies in every field of human endeavour, including the realm of understanding of religion and accepting of religion. In other words, religiosity and the comprehension of religion is also a collective, ceaseless, interminable and undogmatic process that is open to criticism and refinement. You cannot by any means derive relativism from all this. Whatever the reality may be (in itself), we are faced with complications and difficulties in terms of its verification (for us).

This critical rationalism or complicated rationality or taking human fallibility seriously is an "all or nothing" project; either it applies everywhere or it doesn't apply anywhere. We cannot remove part of reality, such as religion, from its jurisdiction. I think that, if we enter the arena of rationality on this basis, we'll see that at least one type of pluralism, that is, negative pluralism, is absolutely unavoidable. That is to say, it is the natural offspring of this type of rationalism. In other words, what Kant was saying, what we see daily, in the interpretation of religious experiences or experiences, in *fiqh* or in the speculative sciences, will seem very natural to us. It is in the nature of reason to come up against walls on occasion, in the sense that, on a single issue, collective reason can arrive at several different verdicts and none of these verdicts can drive the others out of the field. We have seen many examples of this impasse in philosophy, in the natural sciences, in theology, in *fiqh*, in ethics and so on. It was on the basis of these products of rationality that we came to understand reason better and to arrive at critical rationalism. It is naïve realism that refuses to acknowledge that reason can come up against walls and fails to distinguish between the "in itself"

and the "for us". And it is critical rationalism that forms the basis of
the debate about pluralism. If a person believes that their mind is a
tabula rasa passively recording the truth, and that facts are easily and
non-problematically reflected onto it, they will clearly see no point in
epistemological pluralism. But, then, this person has to answer questions such as, why do we arrive at antinomic propositions? Why have
different schools of philosophical thought survived over the course of
history? Why do we have many instances of irreconcilable verdicts
in the fields of ethics, *fiqh* and law? and so on. We are faced with a
choice here and I believe that human experience has shown that this
rationality that comes up against walls is superior to that rationality
that recognizes no walls.

Cause versus Reason

Q. In the relevant debates and critiques, your view on pluralism has,
on the whole, been presented in such a way as to suggest that your
epistemological position, that is, critical rationalism, ultimately amounts
to relativism. What, in your own opinion, distinguishes critical rationalism from relativism?

A. I believe that what led to the emergence of "relativity" in modern
epistemology was that interest in the *causes* of the emergence of ideas
gained the upper hand and the position of *reasons* was weakened; or,
to put it more figuratively, reason was sacrificed at the altar of cause.
Relativism has often been defined as the suggestion that everything is
relatively true. But it would be better if we defined it in another way and
the current trend in epistemology provides us with this new definition.
Relativism, begins by assuming that the role played by reasons in the
realm of knowledge is negligible or occasionally even zero; the genesis
of knowledge, its essence and content are all attributed to things that are
of the nature of factors and causes. Reasons themselves are eventually
reduced to causes, such that reasons are eliminated altogether. This is
the full and ultimate relativist position.

At the opposite end, we have the position of the pre-Kantian philosophers and scholars, and, of course, Islamic thinkers. They see the role
of cause in producing the content of knowledge as amounting to next
to nothing or being of only rare or passing significance; instead, they

believe that reasons play the determining and crucial role. This is why they consider knowledge of reality to be full, proven knowledge.

Hence, it is more useful if we define our categories in these terms and say that relativism or relativist epistemology is an epistemology which believes in caused knowledge; and non-relativist epistemology is an epistemology which believes in reasoned knowledge. These are two ideal types and form the opposite ends of the spectrum. All along the spectrum, you'll find many different permutations and, in these instances, your epistemology will vary in accordance with the relative importance you attach to causes and reasons.

I would, therefore, like to amend your question a bit, in as much as the sharp distinction that you drew probably does not exist in the actual world. I think it would be more appropriate to say that, when you look at one thinker's views, you may find that they are more inclined to favour causes over reasons, whereas the reverse may be the case when you take another thinker. Speaking for myself, I've never dared, in my own mind, to reduce the role of reason to zero and I earnestly believe that reasons definitely play a role in the attainment of knowledge, as well as in affirming or undermining views, and in criticizing and amending them; although I am, at the same time, by no means oblivious to the role of causes. All the discoveries that have been made in the field of epistemology since the 18th century—which have helped tip the scale against reason—have been in the realm of causes, whereby they have discovered new tokens or examples of epistemological causes; that is to say, causes that play a role in the attainment, generation and transformation of knowledge.

Starting from the time when Francis Bacon spoke about the idols and fallacies of tribes and caves, to Marx's statements about ideology, to the views of the post-modernists, everyone has been investigating and elevating causes and denigrating reasons. They have all demonstrated in one way or another how non-rational factors (of the nature of causes) play games with rationality (and reasons), thereby distorting and tarnishing it. The role of culture, geography, emotion, interests, internal and genetic factors, the subconscious, power and the like in distorting and influencing perception and consciousness is undeniable. When you look at Freud, Foucault and Habermas, in effect they all belong to the same camp. They all point to factors that play a part in shaping, altering and amending knowledge. Freud is interested in subconscious factors (egocentric rationalisations). Foucault is particularly interested in social factors and "power" (power-centric rationalisations). And Habermas focuses on human interests (interest-centric rationalisations). But we can categorize all these things under the same heading: causes.

On the other side, the rationalist philosophers, such as Descartes, can be described as philosophers who are, first and foremost, interested in reasons and believe that a verdict or view can be swayed this way or that by reasons.

On this basis, we can say that post-modernism consists of the establishment of a period in the realm of knowledge and culture when reasons have been sacrificed at the altar of causes, and when reasons are denied any share or role.

In the midst of all this, my own epistemological position, put briefly, is that reasons play a role in the attainment of knowledge and the genesis of its contents; however, when reasons have completed their work and arrived at parity, causes then come into play. In other words, after you have rejected a number of views on the basis of reasoning and kept a number of others, you will ultimately be left with a number of views that are equally tenable. This is the point at which cause may intervene (or will per force intervene), favouring one of the views over the others based on causes, not reasons. Hence, both reasons and causes play a part in the realm of knowledge. It may also happen on occasion that the reasons are strong enough from the start to eliminate all the rivals, leaving only a single view in place. But if the reasons are such that they cannot overcome one another, you will undoubtedly arrive at a reasoned pluralism, which is different from a relativist or post-modernist plural-ism, which is causal. This is a crucial and profound difference.

This, in brief, is my epistemological position. Hence, we should have no further need of the term "relativist" and the like, and we can speak on the basis of our own terminology and within our own framework. I believe that pure relativism is based on pure causality, epistemologically-speaking, while reasoned pluralism falls midway along the spectrum and naïve rationalism lies at the opposite end. Hence, pluralism forms the midway mark and it consists of the remaining justified views, on which causal selection may then operate. At one end of the spectrum, you'll find views based on reasons pure and simple. At the opposite extreme, you will have views that are based only on causes. And midway between the two lies reasoned pluralism, which assigns roles to both causes and reasons, as well as making clear the relationship between the two.

Q. If I understand you correctly, what you are saying is that we have at least two types of pluralism: one pluralism arises from the very nature of the reasoning, that is to say, the reasons point to different conclusions; we also have another type of pluralism which occurs with the intervention of causes, once we have reached parity of reasoning. In other words, at times, we seek to understand something and arrive at a plurality of meanings, whereas at other times we arrive at a parity of reasoning and then causes direct us towards a plurality of views.

A. You referred to different meanings. I wanted to leave this for later. That is to say, we also have a hermeneutic pluralism. I call this interpretative pluralism, as opposed to caused pluralism or reasoned pluralism. In other words, when we embark on interpretation and hermeneutics, we encounter a particular type of pluralism, which we must discuss in its own place. For the time being, I am speaking about non-hermeneutic reason. At any rate, we have not only "caused" views and "reasoned" views, we also have interpretative views. They all fall under the rubric of epistemological pluralism. And, as I said earlier, this epistemological pluralism inevitably affects our understanding of religion and religious knowledge. This is the destiny of religion and religious understanding.

Q. If we assume that a believer is of the view that the religious teachings in which he believes tell him that his religion is true and all other religions are false—and that this declaration is one the essential principles of his religion—can this person accept pluralism or not? Do we have to say that the question of pluralism and our stance towards it takes precedence over and has to precede the acceptance of a particular religion?

A. To my mind, your question is analogous to someone asking themselves the following question: if a religion or school of thought contains the principle of fatalism and if the religion's followers encounter this intra-religious principle in a straightforward and non-interpretative way, then, what are these followers to do with their extra-religious views about determinism and free will? What we have to do here is to distinguish between imitative religiosity and reflective religiosity.[2] Pluralism is for reflective believers, not imitative believers. Imitative believers, who are in the majority, become attached to a particular religion without amending or refining the assumptions and foundations that underpin

---

[2] For different types of religiosity see Chapter Eight.

the comprehension of religion. Since their approach is imitative, they are not concerned about extra-religious views. Hence, their initial and their final understanding of religion are one and the same. It is reflective believers who have an eye on extra-religious views. And, if they arrive at a judgement or view outside religion and are persuaded by it, they will undoubtedly take it on board in their intra-religious thinking. This is something that has taken place in the history of theology and philosophy. The question of pluralism, too, is an entirely epistemological debate, which has theological implications. So, reflective believers have to take it into account as an extra-religious view and apply it to their intra-religious understanding. This is the nature of thought and investigation. Do we not expect the same of Buddhists and Jews? We say that there are certain views in Islam that are extra-religious for them. If they find these views convincing and accept them, and if they clash with their intra-religious views, the rational expectation is for them to reassess and reinterpret their religious understanding. (Of course, reinterpretation applies to a small number of things; if it turned out that many things needed reinterpretation, then, one would begin to lose faith in that religion.) This is in the nature of scholarly religiosity and the debate about pluralism is addressed to scholars.

The question of pluralism is related to discursive religiosity, not pragmatic religiosity. And the clash between the external affirmation of pluralism and its intra-religious denial is of the nature of the clash between philosophy and religion, or science and religion. The solution is always the same: constant, historical, collective assessment by the community of scholarly believers.

Faith and Certitude

Q. Possibly one of the most significant criticisms directed at pluralism concerns the relationship between truth and falsehood. Some people are apparently of the view that, when we grant official recognition to the plurality of religions, we are effectively saying that all religions are true or, at least, that they all have a portion of the truth. It seems that, on occasion, your interpretation of pluralism is that we can find a share of portion of truth in different religions.

Also, would it be possible for someone to reach the extra-religious conclusion that no belief can ever be taken to be the absolute truth yet still maintain, at the intra-religious level, that their own religion is the absolute truth? Or, to put it all more simply, what is your position on the truth?

A. There are several questions here that I must answer separately. First, we have to make it clear in our own minds that attaining certitude is a simple matter and all this haggling over certitude is not very productive. We have two kinds of certitude: caused and reasoned. There are many instances of caused certitude and the certitude of most believers—or the average believer—is caused. That is to say, certain causes (education, family, emotional attachments, media exposure, etc.) have put them in a particular mental state that, which we call "dogmatic conviction", and the same causes perpetuate this mental state. Other causes can, in turn, destroy this mental state and supplant it with another. Creating this kind of caused certitude is extremely easy. The communists easily inculcated faith and certitude in their school of thought using pressure and propaganda. The fascists did the same. The power of publicity can truly work wonders in this respect in our day and age. Hence, creating certitudes of this kind is not difficult at all. Most religious certitudes are of this type. This is how Shi'is attain certitude in Shi'ism, Sunnis in Sunnism, Jews in Judaism and so on. These are all caused, inherited, inculcated, simple, low-cost, plentiful certitudes. Let me add here that promoting a climate of inculcation and intimidating people with religious propaganda deprives believers of free will and choice. It renders difficult or impossible a call to religion that is based on free choice. This is a point that preachers and religious scholars ought to bear in mind: not to sacrifice the call to religion at the altar of insistent inculcation or confuse these two things.

However, we have another, superior kind of certitude and that is reasoned certitude. It has to be said that this type of certitude is rare indeed in all areas of human thought and especially in the realm of religion. We can even cite intra-religious sources on this. It has been stated in Islamic literature that certitude is one of the rarest blessings granted to human beings. Hence, haggling endlessly over certitude is, in my opinion, pointless, because in real life true, reasoned certitude is hard to come by in all areas, including that of religion. And caused, unreasoned certitude is plentiful in all areas, including that of religion. Caused certitude may be attained in a minute, whereas reasoned certitude may remain out of reach over a lifetime. (We will set aside for now that in many cases it amounts to nothing more than a deep conjecture anyway, as Ibn Sina put it.)

There is, of course, a third kind of certitude, a revelational, divine, direct certitude which is specific to God's chosen ones, but that need not concern us here; it is, at any rate, even rarer than rare.

Now, even that caused, unreasoned certitude (which is, in fact, no certitude at all) is acceptable to the Legislator and he is prepared to accept it from believers. Otherwise, a believer's duty would become unbearable. The prophets knew that the faith of the bulk of the people could be shaken and destroyed by the slightest disturbance. This is why, they did not allow irreligious causes and factors to circulate easily in a religious society. It was because of their compassion for the masses and their kindness towards believers. They knew that the people's faith was vulnerable and not based on certitude, and they considered it their duty to protect it. They were prepared to accept as faith even this uncertain, tremulous version. For, everything that is human must be viewed and measured on a human scale and be endurable to human beings, including faith, religiosity and certitude.

To those people who suggest that theological debates damage people's faith and certitudes, I have to say: which certitudes? Do they mean those tremulous, caused, unreasoned, inherited, imitative certitudes? But they were not attained through learned debates and reasoning to be destroyed by learned debates and reasoning. They are products of causes and will be destroyed by other causes. And if they mean reasoned certitudes, theological debates are their begetter and creator, and closing the door to theology and free debate because of its possible pitfalls is like crushing a flower for fear of its thorns. On this basis, the religious community must distinguish between opponents who engage in causal work and those who engage in reasoned work. Why should opposing scholars, theologians and thinkers not be free? If there is any room for concern, it has to do with the cause-oriented people, not the reason-oriented ones. This is something that surely even a traditional religious mind can digest with a bit of self-discipline. Of course, if we look at it from the perspective of modern human rights, everyone should enjoy equal rights, be they proponents or opponents, cause-oriented or reason-oriented. At any rate, when we ourselves accept that even those whose faith is caused will be saved and go to heaven and that even they are on the right path, why must we expect the moon and the sun from others and demand the impossible from them? How can we demand that everyone possess reasoned faith?

"Truth" and "Truth for"

Q. What you are saying concerns certainty, which is a subjective thing. But truth and falsehood are objective. Let us imagine that we reach the conclusion, for example, that we cannot definitively verify the correctness of any belief. That is to say, either we cannot arrive at the truth or, if we do arrive at it, we cannot recognize that we've arrived at it. The upshot of this assertion is that there is no such thing as definite, objective truth, including in the realm of religion. If we believe that there is no definite, objective truth, then we are in fact saying that we cannot arrive at reasoned certitude either. And, if this is the case, it holds true everywhere, including the realm of religion.

Also, if we consider a religion to be true, must we not consider all other religions to be false?

A. The tale of religions is not one wherein one is intrinsically true and all the others intrinsically false. There is no such intrinsic opposition between them (as there is between two diametric opposites). Religions themselves do not adopt such a stance. That is to say, Muslims do not say that Christianity is diametrically opposed to Islam or that Judaism is diametrically opposed to Christianity. They say, each of them was true in its own time. In other words, they acknowledge a kind of plurality and they don't consider any one of them to be absolutely and intrinsically false; instead, they see them all as true, with a qualification. Hence, they say, this one is true and that one is true and that other one is true.

This is an important point: we must bear in mind that we are not confronting diametric opposites or logically contradictory positions. We do not have to say one of them is intrinsically true and all the others are absolutely false because they contradict it.

In the opinion of believers themselves, all religions can be viewed as true with certain qualifications. A is true during period A; B, during period B; C, during period C; and so on. If it is possible, with this qualification, to say that A is true and B is also true and C is also true, then why should it not be possible to add other qualifications that would allow us to say that they are all true? This single qualification has put us in a position whereby we can say that "A", for example, was true until the first century on the Christian calendar, "B" was true from the first century until, let us say, 606 on the Christian calendar and "C" from 606 to the present day. Hence, we have three truths that do not contradict each other, as long as we bear in mind the time qualification.

However, is a time qualification the only possible qualification? Why should it not be possible to find other qualifications that would allow all of them to be true at the same time? Here, the only limitation is the scope of your imagination and power of creative thinking.

The fact of the matter is that the truth of religions is very similar to the truth of indexical propositions. The truth and veracity of such propositions depends on who says them and in what context. The proposition "I am 20 years old" is true if it is being said by a 20-year-old person and it is false if it is said by a 40-year-old person. "It is cold today" is true if it is said on a cold day and false if it is said on a warm day. Truth and veracity in the case of statements of this kind, which are known as indexical propositions, hinge on the "for me" or "for him" and are, in this specific sense, relative. Whereas "the earth is spherical" and "metals expand when subjected to heat" are not relatively true and do not hinge on any "for me" or "for him"; it makes no difference who says them.

Now, "for Christians, Christianity was true until the advent of Islam" is true for Muslims. "For Jews, Judaism was true until the advent of Christianity" is true for Christians and Muslims. This kind of truth is by no means the same as scientific or philosophical truths, which are not qualified by "for Harry" or "for Joe". Hence, the question of truth and falsehood for religions is different from the absolute and intrinsic truth and falsehood of whether the atom exists or it doesn't, there is no question here of whether it is today or tomorrow or whether you're in the north or the south. This being the case, you now have to find some other formula or qualification that will allow all religions to be true alongside one another. You may, for example, say, for Christians who are unaware of Islam or who do not recognize Islam as true, Christianity holds true. There is nothing logically or religiously objectionable about this remark. Don't say, Islam is true, therefore everything else is false. This statement arises from the same kind of illusion that holds that the truth of Islam is like the truth of atomic theory or the truth of the earth's spherical shape. The model of truth has to be changed. Here we are dealing with indexical models; that is to say, "truth for...", not absolute truth. And do not imagine that this means that Christians may be excused for being Christians. After all, was it the case that Christians before the advent of Islam were to be excused? No, there is nothing for them to be excused for; they were and are following a true religion of rightful guidance and salvation. This is how it is in the realm of religion. They are all true with certain qualifications and, if we bring these qualifications to bear, there's nothing wrong with having a plurality of truths.

The conclusion I want to draw is this: The people who say that there is something wrong with a plurality of truth are thinking of the contradiction between the intrinsically true and the intrinsically false; whereas here it is not a question of things that are intrinsically diametric opposites, it is a question of the difference between two indexical systems. And the distinguished individuals here who raise the idea of "people who are to be excused" are mistaken. They are well meaning and wish to exonerate God and reassure God's creatures! May God bless them. At any rate, we have to avoid confusing "truth" and "truth for…".

Q. We find ourselves faced with different religious books that want to tell us something, for example, about aspects of the world that are unknown to us. Now, the question is this: are there not any methods, based on historical reasoning, that would allow us to demonstrate that one of these books is more credible than the others, thereby creating a kind of linear or inclusive pluralism? In other words, we could say, for example, that these religions were true, but that the truthful Books that were sent to them by God have, for example, been distorted in some way or have had large parts of them destroyed. But our Book is, let us say, totally complete and undistorted. We also have other evidence and material that assists us in understanding this Book correctly; whereas the more ancient books do not have these advantages.

Is it not possible, in other words, to say, in a conditional way, that, out of all the religious Books that remain, this one has been better preserved and there is a clear history documenting it, whereas this is not the case with the other Books. Hence, while we are not dismissing the other Books as false (although they are incomplete and possibly distorted), nonetheless we are saying that the Book that we are following is, for example, more comprehensive, and we base our claim on objective historical studies, not on our religious faith. Hence, we are not concerning ourselves with proof (in itself); in other words, we are not saying that this religion is true, the other is false. What we are saying is that, at the level of verification (for us), given these religions, scriptures and texts, this religion is the most credible and accurately preserved on the basis of sound historical arguments.

A. If you make your claim conditional, that is fine. But as soon as you start trying to flesh it out, you will run into pluralism. If—and only if—you could establish, based on reasoned arguments, that one religion or one scripture is definitely superior to the others, then no intelligent person would turn to the inferior ones. This is what the whole argument is about. What has happened in practice is that everyone is claiming that their religion is the superior one. It is this multiplicity of superiors that has given rise to pluralism.

Q. Of course, in a way, we can flesh out our argument. In the context of the for us, we can say, for example, that we have a better-documented and more reliable history of a particular prophet. Or we can show in a well-argued way that there are better-preserved sources supporting the newer religion than the older religion, and that the material at our disposal is more voluminous. This can apply to both the scripture and the prophet and other revered figures of a particular religion.

A. Look, pluralism comes into play when we have rejected everything that we can possibly reject on the basis of reasoning and evidence. Ultimately, we have been left with a number of religions of more or less equal standing. This is where we ask ourselves: first, do we really have a plurality of this kind or can we still drive out all but one of them? And, secondly, if we really are faced with this plurality, what approach must we adopt to it, practically and theoretically? This is the why and the wherefore of pluralism. We must also constantly bear in mind that what pluralism is suggesting is not that all possible and existing statements and claims are of equal weight and standing, and everything that anyone says is true. This is patently nonsense. This is certainly not the claim we're making and no intelligent person would believe such a thing.

Nominalism and Pluralism

Q. It might be a good idea to speak at greater length about something that came up during the discussion. It seems that one of the theoretical pillars of religious pluralism is a particular conception of the kernel of religion. Do the numerous religions which are, let us say, more or less based on equally sound arguments, all have a single kernel? Can we, in other words, speak of a family resemblance between them? Of course, you spoke about the kernel of religion on three different levels. But it may still be possible to press you further and ask, what is the kernel of religion and how would you define its relationship to pluralism?

A. Asking about the unified essence of religions only arises if we are realists and if we have decided that religions are all of the same kind. Otherwise, why shouldn't we simply decide that each religion is a kind onto itself, refusing to speak of it as superior or inferior, or just decide to be nominalists? Nominalism gives us pluralism, as does the view that every religion is a kind onto itself.

The third alternative, which is founded on the idea of excellence and degree, arranges religions along a single line and considers them all to be of the same kind. There is no other method for discovering the unified kernel of religion—if we believe in it—than reflection, observation and the like. But discovering their similarities can be carried out by induction, which is the method used by sociologists of religion.

On the face of it, some of our mystics have favoured the third alternative; in other words, they considered the differences between prophets' experiences and revelations to be one of degree, not of kind. On this basis, they use the expression "the perfect Muhammadan revelation". In other words, they believed that the other prophets had also made revelations, but that they were imperfect and that, when it came to the Prophet, he made "a complete revelation". This is also the basis for the expression the Seal of the Prophets; by this they meant that, after the complete revelation, there can be no further or higher revelation.

Now, if we look at prophets' experiences in a pluralistic light and consider them to have been substantially different (either because we are nominalists or because we find that which we have received from the prophets so markedly different), we will find ourselves faced with different trees that bear different fruits. And these fruits have different qualities and effects; one is sweet like the date, another is sour like the currant, one is crisp like the apple, another is soft like the mulberry. Of course, this implies that they have shared qualities as well. If you look at them in an *a posteriori* fashion, you may discover that they all contain a certain amount of fructose or water. Nonetheless, they are different and it is not as if the currant is the advanced form of the date, or the date, the perfected form of the currant. We cannot classify them in this way, but they are all beneficial and effective.

In this way, plurality is the norm in this world. It is very strange for us to be proceeding on the assumption of unity, determined to crush the pluralities. That is to say, if you believe in the principality of quiddity (as many of our philosophers have done) or if you believe in nominalism (and many theologians, especially the Ash'ari theologians, have done) the plurality of essences is the order of the day in the world, with unity representing only a thin veneer over the pluralities. The world is really filled with different things and different species. This is incontestable. There is nothing wrong with acknowledging this same plurality of "species" in the world of religion; especially when it comes to religious experiences and prophetic revelations. Why must we rule out this plurality of species or make it so emaciated as to have it dissolve into unity? Plurality is clearly the norm in the real world: the plurality of natural forces, the plurality of things and species, the plurality of experiences. And, although they have commonalities, their plurality (whether in nominalist terms or because of the principality of their quiddity), is irreducible to unity.

Q. Can we arrive at a well-argued preference for one of these experiences? In other words, can we find a justification for saying that this experience is superior to and more profound than all the others?

A. If we subscribe to the idea of the plurality of kinds, there is little room for this type of argument. Let me give you a simple example. One of the best display cases for the plurality of kinds of experiences is the world of arts and letters. You have the experience of Sa'di's poetry, you have the experience of Hafez's poetry, you have Khaqani, Nezami, Rumi and others to the present day and all the contemporary poets. The works of all these masters are similar in terms of being products of the imagination, creative works and so on (this is the generic similarity or family resemblance). Nonetheless, there can almost be no question of saying that one of them is superior to the others or the perfected form of all the rest. In other words, you are sincerely faced with a true plurality, such that each poem and each poet is a kind unto themselves, despite certain similarities. The whole thing becomes more evident still if you widen your scope and go beyond Persian literature to embrace other languages. I believe that one of the best arenas for seeing and tasting plurality par excellence, as differences in kind, is the world of the arts and letters. This world of inspiration is not that dissimilar from the world of religious experience; creativity flows through both of them and the poet or the prophet is both the mover and the moved, both the receptacle and the creator. This goes back to the nature of these people who are undergoing the experience and the fact that they are different "species", with none of them necessarily being a more excellent version of any other, such that it would be impossible to arrange them in a linear form. This is the way I see it.

Q. So, at any rate, we go as far as we can with our arguments about what is superior or inferior until we reach the point where we are virtually faced with several alternatives of equal standing which defy ordering. Is that right?

A. In fact, our arguments or reasoning guide us until we arrive at kinds. When you arrive at this point, you are faced with "species"; that is to say, an actually existing plurality. Here, various attractive attributes come into play. You may be attracted to and enchanted by the poetry of Hafez. I may feel the same way about Jalal al-Din Rumi, but be unable to prove that Rumi is superior to Hafez or demonstrate why I was enchanted by Rumi, whereas you were enchanted by Hafez. This plurality is the end of the line. You cannot transform this plurality into unity. It is irreducible. Reasons lead us to "species" and species are irreducibly plural.

Truth and Salvation

Q. It might be a good idea now to discuss another one of your assumptions in your treatment of pluralism: the question of "salvation" and "being rightly guided" and its relationship to the truth. Are you of the opinion that "being rightly guided" stands in some kind of necessary relationship to "being in the right" or "correspondence to truth", or is it the case that, if someone is sincere in their actions, this sincerity will necessarily guide them and lead them to salvation?

A. We have already spoken about the question of truth in the realm of religion and we stressed and insisted on the point that the truth and falsehood of religions is conditional and follows the indexical model. It is, therefore, possible to have several religions, all of which may be true, existing alongside one another. They will direct their followers to the truth and, hence, to salvation. The people who criticize or reject this idea seem to find it unbearable to imagine that there could be any truth other than the truth that they like or accept; everything else must therefore be false. And since there is a relationship between being rightly guided and the truth, they do not believe that anyone outside their own religion can be rightly guided. But, on the basis of what we have said, several religions may all be true and their followers may be rightly guided and saved (and not excused).

Secondly, we must see what "being rightly guided" and "being saved" hinge on. Look, we can proceed here on the basis of several assumptions and criteria. One is that, when we speak about "rightful guidance" and "salvation", we are mainly speaking about other-worldly salvation. In other words, we are not just thinking about this world. Now, let us assume that the exclusivists are right and there is only one truth. If an individual has not found this single truth in this world but proceeds on the basis of sincerity (within the limits of their capacities and understanding), what could possibly be wrong with saying that this individual will attain the truth and salvation in the hereafter? Why must we make it a condition of salvation that you arrive at the truth in this world? Why must we imagine that anyone who failed to arrive at the truth (as we understand it) in this world will fail to arrive at the truth—and, therefore, salvation—in the other world too and can only end up in hell?! The holy verse that says "But those who were blind in this world will be blind in the Hereafter, and most astray from the Path" is speaking about the blind, not about those who can see but who've failed to see some truths. These people are not barred from seeing the truth in the hereafter; hence, they too may be seen as taking the path of rightful guidance. In brief, if being rightly guided means following the path to the truth, this path may arrive at the desired end both in this world and in the next; ultimately leading the follower to the truth.

Q. We could say that they will be saved because they do not display hostility towards the truth and, if they were to see the truth, they would accept it. They now think that they have arrived at the truth, but if they realize that the truth lies elsewhere, they will turn to it. And this absence of hostility towards the truth can itself be seen as rightful guidance. In other words, we can take guidance to mean a willingness to accept the truth and an absence of hostility towards it.

A. Yes. It is no mean guidance for a person to be willing to accept the truth and to have no inherent obstinacy against it. We are gradually being guided to the right definition of "rightful guidance". So far we were looking at guidance with our eyes firmly on the destination, whereas guidance is about the road, not the destination. Hence, we shouldn't be saying that only those who have reached the destination (in the sense of definitely true beliefs) are rightly guided, but that anyone who has stepped onto the path of truth has a share of rightful guidance. It is amazing that we all read for ourselves and ask God to guide us to the "right path", yet we still forget that guidance is about the path and not a series of complete ideas lodged in our brains. The Qur'an specifically contrasts one who follows "vain desire" with the rightly guided and says: "Then seest thou such a one as takes as his god his own vain desire? God has, knowing (him as such), left him astray, and sealed his hearing and his heart (and understanding), and put a cover on his sight; who then, will guide him after God (has withdrawn Guidance)?" Hence, we have two roads: the road of vain desire and the baser instincts and the road of guidance, and anyone who does not, in thought and in deed, follow their baser instincts is on the road of guidance. End of story. And this is the very road that will, sooner or later, in this world or in that, lead the follower to salvation. As Rumi puts it: "If the desires are rife, then faith is not/for if faith is the gate, then the desires are the lock".

The prophets, for their part, have shown us ways of combating the desires. Those who have found those ways (or some of them) without the prophets are definitely rightly guided, because the personality of the prophets is not what is relevant here. The relevant point is their teachings. Regardless of how anyone finds their way to these teachings it is a boon. Personalities are accidents in religion. What is essential is the message. Of course, in practice and in the real world, most people need a prophet and cannot find the path to rightful guidance unaided. And even if they do, in the opinion of some mystics, they only manage to skirt around it.

Q. If pluralism holds true, then why do we preach our own religion and invite other people to it? What would be the point of *jihad*, enjoining others to the good, seeking martyrdom and so on?

A. The straightforward answer is that anyone who, by reason and by love, is committed to something, sees beauties in it that they do not see in other people's beliefs and ideas. They are, therefore, eager to present these beauties to others; in other words, the call to religion becomes a kind of "presentation"; that's all. Just like an artist who puts his canvasses on display. If we say that pluralism holds sway in the world of arts and letters (which it does), does that mean that Sa'di and Hafez mustn't present their poetry and put it at the disposal of others? Everyone wishes to adore and be adored. Some people are more disposed to being adored and others, to adoring. Let the world of loving and being loved prosper and thrive. There is much to be gained by many here. The world of religion, too, is a world of adoration and charms. And, in order to charm, a host of beauties, purities and pieties must be presented.

Let me also say again that pluralism does not imply that everything that is said is true. Hence, the call to religion can help expose falsehoods.

Q. It may also be that someone wants to find something better or to convey and teach to others things that he is more familiar with.

A. Yes, that is right. But the prevailing interpretation seems to be that the reason for *jihad* is to wipe all but one religion off the face of the earth and to make all the faithful believe in the same thing. This kind of *jihad* does not fit in with pluralism. If, according to the critics, even those who bear no hostility will be saved and will benefit from a minimum of salvation, why do they have to be eliminated?

Some people have even said that, if we subscribe to religious pluralism, there will be no certitude left that people can fight for. This is bizarre demagoguery. Don't people fight to save their livelihoods? Don't people fight and die for their homelands? Most such wars are instinctive and motivated by love. And, as it happens, their underlying assumption is pluralism. Everyone knows that every nation has its own homeland, that it has the right to defend its homeland, that it has the right to love its homeland more than all other homelands. And, yet, people resist when they are attacked. In other words, despite the assumption that there are different homelands (pluralism), they sacrifice their lives for their homeland. Why should it not be the same in the world of religion? Aggressors have to be thwarted in any case. The answer to peace is peace, and the answer to war is war. We will set aside for the time being the fact that pluralists also do away with the need for a range of pointless quarrels—which is very laudable, but we are not concerned with these consequences at the moment.

As to the point that "the prophets preached their own religion and did not think about religious pluralism", this is certainly true. But we are not prophets. This is an important idea that I feel strongly about: there are many things that the Prophet did that we must not do. The Prophet said, you must hail me. But we have no right to say that people must hail us. The Prophet waged primary *jihad* (to convert non-Muslims to Islam). But, according to most Islamic jurists, we do not have the right to wage primary *jihad*. When we stand outside religions, if we arrive at pluralism, we must act on its implications. The Prophet came to add a religion to other religions. He carried out his task. The unintended consequence of this was that it stoked the furnace of pluralism. We are now faced with this blazing furnace, whether we are prepared to given it official recognition or not. Let us recall that the appearance of the prophets was like the growth of different trees, each of which bears its own fruit, with its own taste and its own benefits. They founded an orchard. A single tree does not an orchard make. That was their task. Now, in the words of Saʿdi, "we are the bystanders gazing upon the orchard".

Plurality of Meaning and Text

Q. We spoke about causal pluralism and reasoned pluralism. It may also be useful to speak about interpretative pluralism or textual pluralism.

A. You will undoubtedly be aware of the quarrel between Kant and Schopenhauer. Kant believed that noumena are beyond our ken and we have no access to them. We must content ourselves with phenomena and call it a day. Schopenhauer, on the other hand, argued that noumena and phenomena are, after all, interrelated and it is not as if they are worlds apart and disjointed (which seems to be a very reasonable thing to say). Schopenhauer was of the view that noumena are very ugly (judging by phenomena); that the real world is very ugly and terrifying, in other words. This was why he believed we had to seek recourse from this ugly world in aesthetics and the arts. This is a very fundamental point. This is how I see the relationship between science and metaphysics. Science deals with phenomena and metaphysics claims that it can deal with noumena. It believes that it can circumvent methods and go hunting directly for quiddities and essences, and discover the rules that govern them.

On this basis, we have to say that there is and must be a relationship between science and metaphysical philosophy. If science consists of formulating the rules that can be obtained using scientific methods and if metaphysics consists of formulating that which is learnt by intuitive experience and phenomenological methods—and conveying the rules that govern reality itself—then it would be impossible for these two techniques to be unrelated. There is a serious link between them. On the whole, there has to be a link between the thing "for us" and the thing "in itself".

The conclusion I want to draw is this: if we decide that some things are antinomic—that is to say, in some instances reason really comes up against a wall and has to contend with two totally contradictory positions, such that it is impossible to come down decisively in favour of one or the other (at the level of the "for us")—then we have to conclude that the underlying fact or the "in itself" is such that it confounds reason. We must not say that, when the mind falls into confusion, it is no reflection on reality and reality itself is straightforward. The facts that have caused the confusion must be different from other, straightforward facts.

Now, when we come to texts, this point is patently clear. Texts are actually and intrinsically ambiguous. They are laden with different meanings. Take for example the Qur'anic verse "They followed what the evil ones gave out (falsely) against the power of Solomon..." (2: 102) The late scholar Tabataba'i has written under this verse that there are one million two hundred and sixty thousand different interpretations of it. Hence, at the level of understanding (the thing for us) we are faced with a multiplicity of meanings. This is where we have to say that there is a relationship between the thing "in itself" and the thing "for us". This incredible range and variety of meanings speaks of an underlying structure that is ambiguous and lends itself to different meanings.

In the world of texts and symbolism, we are really faced with this lack of clarity. That is to say, even if we accept the judgement of philosophers about actual entities (anything that has no well defined boundaries does not exist), this is in all fairness unacceptable in the world of texts and one of the reasons is precisely what we said. The admission of metaphors, analogies and the like into language was not a conscious, wilful decision; speech itself dictated it. It is not as if it was possible to speak without using figurative language and some people just took it into their heads to introduce figurative expressions in order to widen the scope for speakers. The same goes for ambiguity. Precision and care have never obliterated the intrinsic ambiguity of language.

The world of meaning is basically and essentially a plural world. You may exceptionally find an instance where there is only one meaning, but plurality is the rule. You will arrive at a "correct meaning" of a text when you apply well-honed methods for understanding a text within your capacities (methodological capacities, mental capacities, etc.), not when you reach the "true" meaning of the text, because there is no such thing as "the true meaning". There can be a number of correct meanings. Of course, you can speak of an alien meaning, which is a meaning that does not follow from your method; nevertheless, it is not necessarily an "incorrect" meaning.

Yes, a text has structural limitations that do not allow just any meaning. The fact remains, however, that a text does not necessarily have a single meaning. In the realm of texts, there is no such thing as "truth" in the sense of correspondence with the author's intention. When an author uses a phrase to convey a meaning, he has understood one of its meanings and chosen it on that basis. Nonetheless, that phrase can have other meanings. If an author bears it in mind that a text can have meanings independent of the author's intentions, he wouldn't easily accuse others of being misguided. Here, "guided" and "misguided" themselves take on different meanings.

And when we speak about texts here, we are not just speaking about the written variety; we are referring to any system of symbols or signs which is neither of the nature of reasons used to justify a claim, nor of the nature of causes used to provide an explanation; they are of the nature of symbols used in discovery and understanding. You may find this symbolism in religious experiences, in dreams, in the attributes of the Creator, in written texts and so on. The discovery of a fact through symbols brings into play interpretative or hermeneutic rationality. Here, we arrive not at a reasoned or caused understanding, but at an interpretative understanding, which is essentially, intrinsically and inevitably pluralistic.

Q. It may be said that, in view of their limited capacities, human beings cannot succeed in making a text convey only the intended meaning. But God has absolute power and He can ensure that a text conveys only the meaning He wishes to its readers. This would rule out the possibility of any textual ambiguity.

A. First of all, we can see that that is not how it is turned out in practice. If God was meant to have spoken this clearly, we would not have a verse in the Qur'an that has one million two hundred thousand meanings; but we do. And, if it is said that, in these cases, God wanted these verses to have multiple meanings, whereas in other cases, he did not, this claim is unfalsifiable. That is to say, if it is false, we have no way of establishing it.

Secondly, we can reject the claim by saying that there is evil in the world and the philosophers have themselves conceded as much and said that the occurrence of evil in the world is incidental and secondary, and not essential. In their own words, this is a result of the shortcomings of matter and not a sign of any weakness or oversight on the part of the Creator. In other words, God has created something which has certain characteristics and inherent qualities. And these inherent qualities manifest themselves in the form of evil, flaws and imperfections. The same can be said of language. In this instance, God uses a tool that is inherently vague and unavoidably ambiguous, even when used by the Creator.

The conclusion here is not that divine power has manifested some blemish but that, we are faced with a logical or rational impossibility which is irresolvable. And the Creator's power does not extend to impossibilities because they are devoid of quiddity.

Q. Hence, in the case of sacred texts, we have to say that there is a correspondence between the text and the Author or Speaker's intention; in other words, the multiple meanings of the text are all the Creator's intentions.

A. Yes. That is to say, God knew the nature of the implement and substance He was wielding, and He knew that His creatures would arrive at different interpretations. We therefore have to say that they are all the Creator's intentions and, if God made it incumbent on people to discover His "true meaning", it would be asking something of them that is beyond their capacity. Language by its very nature does not allow the discovery of a single meaning. To put it in philosophic terms, text has not been actualized, it is potential. And this potential lends itself to many meanings.

Q. Another inference would be to say that this plurality is a product of the differences between the minds of the readers.

A. This would lead us to the same place. Meaning means understandable meaning. Differences between minds means differences in the accumulated information in those minds. And the accumulated information in people's minds is the prerequisite and premise for the comprehension of meaning. Hence, the differences between the minds ultimately goes back to the different meanings of a text that have entered the different minds. And the very fact that different minds obtain different meanings from a text means that the text allows many meanings and that they are all appropriate to it.

PART TWO

CHAPTER EIGHT

TYPES OF RELIGIOSITY

The disagreement of mankind is caused by names:
Peace ensues when they advance to the reality (denoted by the name).[1]

Errors of judgement often occur when a single term carries multiple meanings or a single meaning goes under different names. Arriving at uniform judgements about these multiple meanings or making multiple judgements about that single meaning is to fall into error and go astray. And disentangling entangled terms is the duty of all seekers of knowledge. Religiosity is one such term. When we ask ourselves: "Was Iranian society more religious under the Qajar Dynasty (1779–1925) or is it more religious today? Are modern Western societies less religious than communities in the Middle Ages?" Or, when discussing the issue of secularity and secularization a bit of thought and reflection brings us to the realization that we will never find the answers to our questions unless we disentangle the different layers and categories of religiosity. It may well be that society is more religious today in one sense and less so in another. Hence, distinguishing the different layers and categories of religiosity is a must for anyone interested in theories of religion and secularization, knowledge and reform.

If we take the volume of mourning ceremonies and fasts and tears and supplications and candles and pilgrimages and bows before the clergy, then the Qajar period will seem to be in the lead. If we take the volume of critical studies and opinions and debates about religion, we are quite likely to judge today's society more religious and more religion-minded. If we probe further and see that every category of religiosity offers different readings of God and the Prophet and sin and obedience and felicity and wretchedness, then we will grasp the gravity and sensitivity of the matter more clearly.

Categorizing religiosity is certainly not a new or innovative idea. When the Holy Qur'an speaks of the people of *yamin* (the ones on the right) and the *sabiqoun* (the vanguards), it is presenting a kind

---

[1] *Mathnawi*, 2: 3667.

of categorization of different types of religiosity.[2] And mystics, who speak of religion of the Law (*shari'at*), religion of the Way (*tariqat*) and religion of Truth (*haqiqat*) or of the religion of novices, the middling and the masters, are pointing to this same truth.

This article, too, will present, in brief, a categorization of different types of religiosity which has differences and similarities with the above-mentioned classifications. We will call our three types of religiosity, respectively: 1. Pragmatic/Instrumental religiosity; 2. Discursive/Reflective religiosity; and 3. Experiential religiosity.

Pragmatic/Instrumental Religiosity

In this type of religiosity, a belief or practice's ultimate purpose, utility and outcome (this-worldly or other-worldly) are of paramount importance to the believer. It is a religion for life rather than life for religion.

In its purely otherworldly forms, it wears the garb of asceticism and Sufism and, in its this-worldly forms, the garb of politics and statesmanship. Its central axis is emotion and practical reason. Among the general masses, the emotions gain the upper hand and, among learned people, practical reason (that is to say, the capacity to match means to ends).

Pragmatic religiosity is mundane, causal (not reasoned), hereditary, deterministic (not arising from choice or free will), emotional, dogmatic, ritualistic, ideological, identity-bound, concerned with outward superficies, collective-communal, legalistic-juristic, mythic, imitative, obedient, traditional and habitual. Here, the volume of deeds is the measure of the intensity or diluteness of conviction: performing the hajj numerous times, visiting shrines, praying frequently and so on. Through these practices, the religious person feels more successful and closer to God. Mass rituals and rites nourish this religiosity more than anything else. The frequency of communal prayers, mourning ceremonies, Qur'anic recitations, retreats, Friday prayers, gatherings and preaching sessions, crowds of believers at shrines and mosques, hordes of fighters in the arenas of jihad amount to the glorification and splendour of this type of religiosity and serve as a source of pride to it. It both stirs up the emotions and draw strength from them.

---

[2] The Qur'an, Chapter 56.

Since this type of religiosity is hereditary and not based on reasoning, since emulation and obedience play the biggest role in perpetuating it, since it devotes itself to deeds rather than thought and reflection, and since it is constructed upon emotion and excitation rather than rational endeavour and inquiry, it gradually becomes tainted by dogmatism and prejudice and loses the capacity to tolerate dissent. It defends set habits and traditions dogmatically and sees people who tend to raise questions and reflect upon things as crooks and heretics. Hence, slowly but surely it goes down the path of casting out and excommunicating people.

This is the religiosity of the clergy, and clerics like to emphasise the importance of submission and emulation, religious passion and possessiveness, and the performance of rites and rituals to believers. In this way, a believer's religion becomes their identity and they defend it in the way they would defend their homeland or property or life, not in the way a scientist would defend a truth. In other words, they want religion so that they can feel like somebody and distinguish themselves from others, not because they want to arrive at some truth. Believers, in this type of religiosity, are the servants and God is the master and the sultan (not the God of wisdom, nor the Alluring Beloved). And the Prophet wears the cloak of a commander, issuing orders about what a believer may and may not do, and speaking of glad tidings and ominous portents (not an illuminated mystic with exalted experiences, nor a wise and brilliant thinker). And sin amounts to disobeying his orders rather than being something that causes a contraction of the heart.[3] And obedience is a transaction aimed at attaining some gain or benefit, not something that causes an expansion of the heart nor yet a participation in a spiritual experience. And following the Prophet means carrying out his commands. Morality is always relegated to second place in this religiosity and is considered to be decorative at best, entailing no religious burdens or duties in itself.

Since imitative believers do not have the courage and strength to look at the Transcendence for themselves or to tackle difficult concepts, they look for mediators and they find what they are seeking in the form of religious figures past and present. In this type of religiosity, religious figures are transformed into myths and lose touch with human history and geography. Our fathers and mothers wept for centuries for

---

[3] Allusion is to al-Ghazali's reference to the Prophetic saying "al-ithm hazzaz al-qlub."

the Imam Hossein who was assisted on Ashura by mysterious spirits and, under every stone they turned over on the day he was martyred, they discovered fresh blood.[4] Not once did they ask about the social or historical significance of his uprising and, centuries after the fall of the Umayyads and Abbasids, their pilgrimage invocations still called for vengeance against the culprits who murdered him.

Dogmatic distinctions drawn between "us" and "them" and believers and infidels, the firm and unyielding categorization of people, the simplification of the world and the refusal to see the complexities, subtleties and variations of human existence, and, subsequently, engaging in unsubtle behaviour inappropriate to the elaborate and mysterious nature of life, creating strict ideological divisions, seeing people as either heavenly or hellish, viewing God as an impatient avenger, imagining God as one's own God and the Protector of one's own sect who is uncaring about everyone else, narrowing the definition of truth and broadening the definition of falsehood, highlighting the differences between sects and seeing one's own sect as the axis and measure of truth and falsehood and the creator of the true human identity, ignoring the common attributes of human beings and emphasizing every small difference in belief, and compartmentalizing humanity into so many different sects are some of the characteristics and defining features of this kind of religiosity.

Now, learned pragmatic religiosity is itself of two types: this-worldly and other-worldly; and, of course, it has important differences with the pragmatic religiosity of the common people. Here, the central axis is practical reason, not emotion. And practical reason engages in planning and measures means against ends. But, whatever it does, it is practical and wants religion for its utility.

Since this-worldly, learned, pragmatic religiosity acts rationally, it has no affinity with myths, it does not blow the horn of emulation, it does not sitr up blind emotion, it does not spare tradition the rod of criticism and it has no particular fondness for the clergy; nonetheless, and most importantly, it seeks "movement" and change rather than truth, which is precisely the main attribute of ideologies. It turns religion into the servant of politics (revolution, democracy, etc.). And, concentrating

---

[4] Similarly in Christianity, it is believed that on the day of Jesus' death certain cataclysmic and extraordinary things happened. See for instance the Gospels of Matthew, 27: 51–53 and Luke, 23: 45.

on the ultimate goal, it tries to pick out what it finds useful in religion and to set aside anything in it that is of no use. The God of this kind of religiosity is an observing, supervising God who expects people to fulfil their responsibilities. His servants are hardworking, shrewd, reward-minded and responsible employees. His Prophet is a prudent politician and a methodical planner. The otherworldly felicity or wretchedness of his followers depends on their this-worldly felicity or wretchedness. Its religious personalities are historical and non-mythical, and as subject to criticism and analysis as anyone else.

There is no trace of wonder or secrets or the inner world in this type of religiosity. Seeing human beings, the world and history in simple, ideological terms remains the order of the day. The collective and demonstrative aspect of religion (apart from its ritualistic dimension) is firmly in place. Political, social, revolutionary or democratic religions are products of this kind of religiosity. Sin is akin to breaking the law and reward is synonymous with achieving the goal or reaching the desired destination. And obedience to the Prophet is like the shrewd obedience of an employee to a superior, not of an apprentice to a master, nor of a lover to the beloved. The element of action is still prominent, but here it is purposeful endeavour directed towards a this-worldly goal. Religious law and *fiqh* are justified in rationalistic terms. Morality, too, takes on a revolutionary or democratic sense and, ultimately, neither morality nor *fiqh* are seen as possessing any mysterious qualities or secret and hidden aims. Most modern religious intellectuals and reformers fall into this category; figures such as Sayyed Jamal al-din Afghani, Muhammad ʿAbduh, Ali Shariʿati and Sayyed Qutb.

The bulk of clerics in all religions throughout history have fallen into the opposite category: otherworldly, learned pragmatic believers. And their only difference with the pragmatic common people is that what the masses obtain second hand, they obtain from the source. Apart from this, their religiosity is no different from that of the common people in terms of its being causal, hereditary, dogmatic, ritualistic, collective, juristic, mythic and obedient. Their God and Prophet and devotion and sinfulness are also of the same variety. In fact, they are the ones who teach the masses their utilitarian religiosity. Their morality is a religious (not rational) morality. And, in terms of knowledge, they are single-sourced. And their world is a mystified world filled with hidden powers and mysterious acts of assistance and invisible hands. Among these believers, the performance of duty gains the upper hand over the pursuit of purposeful designs and shrewd policies.

Secularity, vis a vis, pragmatic/instrumental religiosity amounts to abandoning outward religious practices and sentiments, and secular is one whose actions are not motivated by a sense of religious duty.

Discursive/Reflective Religiosity

Describing the difference between the lover's approach to God as opposed to the scholar's, Mansour Hallaj used to say: "The Beloved is laden with allures, not secrets". And with his unerring grace, Rumi attributed both these qualities to the Benevolent Creator and said:

> When the tongue tells of His mystery and coquetry, Heaven chants (the prayer):
> "O Thou that art goodly in covering!"
> What covering (can there be)? The fire is in the wool and cotton: whilst thou art covering it up, it is (all the) more manifest.[5]

In discursive religiosity, there is no talk of the allures of God and his saints; that is the business of the experiential believer. Here, it is all a question of His Secrets; not secrets in the sense of myths, but secrets as rational problems and puzzles that one must grapple with like a mental wrestler. And, here, the rationality is a theoretical rationality, which is sensitive to the appropriateness of a premises to a conclusion, not just a practical rationality that is concerned about the appropriateness of a means to an end.

If we identify pragmatic religiosity by its dogmatism, discursive religiosity can be identified by a lack of dogma or by a sense of rational wonder, and experiential religiosity, by certitude. Hence, on entering the realm of discursive religiosity, dogma is exchanged for doubt and wonder, and, as dogmatism is left behind, it becomes easier to head down the road to certitude. Rationality always brings along two hefty companions: one is the tireless raising of whys and wherefores and maybe sos and maybe nots, and the other is a relentless individuality. No rational thinker ever stops posing questions, destroying and rebuilding ceaselessly, and no two rational thinkers are ever identical. It is emotion that drowns people en masse and indistinguishably in a sea of excitation. This is not how rationality operates. Rationality both

---

[5] *Mathnawi*, 3: 4730–4731.

allows its followers independence and individuality and endorses these qualities; it deems these attributes to belong to rational thinkers by right. In the pragmatic religiosity of the common people, all believers practise their religiosity in the same manner and their beliefs and actions are very similar. But, on stepping into the realm of discursive religiosity, individual religiosity and religious individualism enter in. Every rational thinker has their own conception of religion, that is to say, their own understanding of God, the Prophet, revelation, felicity, wretchedness, sin and obedience; an understanding that belongs to that believer alone, results from their own reflections and is subjected to constant questioning and revision.

This is why discursive religiosity is unstable and in a state of flux. The religiosity of the masses has the stability of paralysis. The same kind of constancy and uniformity cannot be expected from discursive religiosity. Rational storms will inevitably stir and rouse the ocean of religious belief and knowledge; swimming in these tempestuous waters represents the skill and excellence of and even life itself to the discursive believer. For the discursive believer, worshipping is precisely all this examining, re-examining, rediscovering, doubting and pondering, while sin would amount to submitting uncritically to beliefs, succumbing to popular vulgarities, following superstitions and famous personalities, and refusing to engage in doubt and reflection. And the believer's felicity lies in the excellence of his theoretical skills. Theologians and exegetes are two of the prominent representatives of this category. This religiosity is reason-based (as opposed to causal-based), investigative, reflective, based on choice and free will, wondrous, theological, non-mythical, non-clerical, individualistic, critical, fluctuating and non-imitative.

Here God appears in the form of a great rational secret and, awed by His Splendour, His servants seek to unravel the secret. And the Prophet is like a great teacher and philosopher who has conveyed his lessons in the most intense form, while believers are like his students and novices who strive for a rational understanding of his words, and non-believers are like ungrateful pupils or like untutored people who are incapable of even recognizing their own ignorance. Thus the Prophet's target is also perceived differently. Here, his target is believers' intellects, not their emotions. And believers become followers of his school to the extent that they can find rational fulfilment. The Prophet's task is to teach and to pledge their betterment, not to demand and compel, and the believer's task is rational—not physical and emotional—acceptance and surrender.

There is no role for the clergy in this religiosity, since it is not founded on myths and rituals, and it has no place for emulation. It is on good terms with religious pluralism, because individual religiosity and religious individualism are synonymous with a plurality of conceptions and interpretations. It cannot be turned into an ideology because it has no time for dogmatism and official interpretations, or for simplistic views of the world, human beings and history. It is basically inclined towards the truth, not towards movement or an identity. Its particular form of worship is thinking and one can enter into dialogue with its religious figures without having to praise and revere them unquestioningly.

It conceives of moral virtues as things that help the individual arrive at a better and more advanced understanding of error. It considers the worst forms of villainy to be dishonesty and duplicity and deception and pride and arrogance and mischievous cunning and pretentiousness and irrationality.

Discursive believers are per force multi-sourced and their religious understanding recedes and advances in keeping with the contractions and expansions of their minds.

This type of religiosity has been scorned by both pragmatic and experiential believers. When Shari'ati spoke of "philosophers as history's fatheads", he revealed the nature of his own religiosity. Rumi, for his part, likened the cunning displayed by theologians and discursive believers to a diver's derring-do under the sea that proves more dangerous than beneficial:

> Intelligence is (like) swimming in the seas: he (the swimmer) is not saved:
> he is drowned at the end of the business.
> Love is as a ship for the elect: seldom is calamity (the result);
> for the most part it is deliverance.[6]

Al-Ghazali, too, scorned the science of theology and said that it led to (1) pride; (2) prevented people from struggling against their baser instincts; (3) created the illusion of certainty while engendering doubt; and (4) represented a contrived development that had not existed during the time of the Prophet.[7] The first two moral points must be resolved rigorously and diligently. The third point must be conceded and accepted, but it must not be seen as an ill or a vice because the oar of logic and reasoning cannot steer the mind to the shore of peace.

---

[6] *Mathnawi*, 4: 1403, 1406.
[7] See: *Ihya al-'Ulum al-Din*, "kitab al-'ilm".

There, waves and turbulence are the rule and calm the exception. As to the fourth point, it calls for an explanation: the science of theology belongs to the age of consolidation, not to the time when religion was being founded and the age of the Prophet when the furnace of revelation was ablaze and when the presence of the Prophet's glowing personality meant that there was no need for any theological mind to try to shed light on things or to grapple with problems. The age of the Prophet cannot be compared to other ages, nor can uniform rulings be made about the two. Theologians came on the scene in order to study the words of the Prophet with reverence for knowledge (not as blind followers). They laid the foundations for exploring his teachings from a great distance and in his absence. Compelled by the separation in time and the urgencies of their own age, they proceeded on the basis of the reasoning and culture of their own time. They thus succeeded in nurturing the science of theology like an embryo in the womb and then entrusted it to future generations as the legitimate child of religious history. This has been the historical destiny of and the course taken by every religion; it is not the brainchild of heretics and deviationist. Fakhr al-din Razi (thirteen-century commentator-philosopher) and Muhammad Hossein Tabatabai (twentieth-century commentator-philosopher) can be identified as two distinguished examples of Muslim discursive believers.

In discursive religiosity, the more robust is the rope of criticism, the more narrow is the thread of blind reverence, and it is this very robustness and narrowness that provokes the sneers of the scornful. The main characteristic of this type of religiosity is that the personality of the guide is in abeyance and it is his teaching instead of his person that serves as the candle lighting the way for believers. Since the emphasis is on approaching that teaching through rationality and logic, the independence of the words from the speaker and the teaching from the teacher becomes clearer and more prominent. Here, reason assists the guide rather than the guide assisting reason. This is precisely something that neither pragmatic nor experiential believers like or tolerate, since they both lay rationality, humanity's greatest blessing, like a sacrificial offering at the feet of the master and beloved.

Discursive religiosity, which is like a rational form of existence to the believer who has no motive or aim in discovering other than discovery, opens the way for the mind to discover independent, non-religious concepts. In this type of religiosity, secularism is synonymous to holding non-religious explanations of natural and human phenomena. Thus, although this type of investigative, probing, critical, learned, theological, non-sanctified, anti-mythical, pensive, argumentative, non-emulative, discursive religiosity is not in keeping with the unwavering faith of the masses and the loving certitude of the few, it can, nonetheless, be seen as a respectable and independent kind of creed in its own right, for none of the three types of religiosity is a measure of the truth or falsity of the others. This religiosity is a sapling that grows in a tremor-prone land of reason. Those who are born in this terrain choose to make their homes here while others choose other ways, in keeping with their own dispositions.

Experiential Religiosity

When we come to experiential religiosity, we step from the domain of separation into the domain of union. The previous types of religiosity can be described as religiosities of distance, for the first was physical and practical and the second mental and reflective. The first was based on instrumental rationality and the second on theoretical rationality. One was after utility and the other after knowledge. But experiential religiosity is neither physical nor mental, neither instrumental nor theoretical; it seeks the evident and the manifest, and if discursive religiosity is concerned with hearing, the experiential believer is concerned with seeing:

> I've heard the inebriating melody of faith
> What I long for now is to see its face.

Experiential religiosity is passionate, revelatory, certain, individualistic, deterministic, quintessential, reconciliatory, ecstatic, intimate, visual, saintly, mystical and mysterious. Here, God is a graceful and alluring beloved. The Prophet is an ideal (*murad*), a contemplative man (*mard-e bateni*) and a model of successful religious experience. To follow him is to share his passions, to extend and repeat his experiences, and to be drawn into the magnetic force field of his personality.

Sin is that which muddies, weakens or destroys the devotional link, the power of discovery and the state of union. And worship is that which tinder-like feeds the flames of ecstasy. Heaven is the experience of union and hell the bitterness of separation.

> When the preacher spoke of the fear felt on Judgement Day
> He was depicting the terror of separation.

Here, secularity means experiencing the being as deaf and blind void of divinity; a kind of atheistic existentialism. The certainty that is unattainable in discursive religiosity is picked like a fruit from the tree of experience here and the free will that was seen as a virtue there now gives way to the passionate compulsion of love:

> The word "compulsion" (*jabr*) made me impatient (uncontrollable) for love's sake, while it confined in (the prison of) compulsion him who is not a lover.[8]

And the teacher who was eclipsed by his teaching there, re-enters the scene here, casting light like a glowing moon. In this religiosity, the plurality of experience and positive religious pluralism are matters of principle. Experiencing the encounter with the Transcendence is the norm and religious individualism unavoidable. Here, instead of being the cause of the believer's religious experience and excellence, rites and rituals are the effect of that excellence, that is, they follow and flow from the believer's passionate devotion to God, instead of being an instrument for achieving it. Hence, ritualism and dedication to religious practices are not the central axis of this religiosity.

Here, everything is personal: my religion, my experience, my Beloved, my morality. The link with the spiritual guardian is what makes the religion. Whoever inflames the believer and fills him with light is his spiritual guardian (*wali*) and prophet. And the guardian addresses the believer's heart, not his mind or emotions. The experiential believer's morality, too, is the morality of love; it can, therefore, give way to disregard for good manners and correct behaviour, for the behaviour of love is the behaviour of the ill-mannered. This abandonment of good manners can go as far the abandonment of all formality and end up in "the audacities of the recluse", and some times the intoxication of love alters all senses of the "permitted" and the "prohibited":

> The intoxication that arises from the scent of the unique King-
> a hundred vats of wine never wrought *that* (intoxication) in head and brain.
> To him (the God-intoxicated man), then, how should the obligation (to keep the Law) be applicable? The horse is fallen (out of account) and has become unable to move.[9]

---

[8] *Mathnawi*, 1: 1463.
[9] *Mathnawi*, 3: 673–674.

The awesome mystery of the Truth enters the very being of the experiential believer like a mighty guest and renders him so stunned and silent that even his intonations and prayers take on a different form and content. And, although he gives the appearance of mingling with people, inside, he is enthralled by his own experiences, and, although he seems to use the same words as others do, he fills these vessels with different meanings. The fruit of love is union and ecstasy, and the etiquette of love is secrecy, for God understands every language.

> In this place of presence (all) minds are lost beyond control;
> When the pen reaches this point, it breaks.[10]

---

[10] *Mathnawi*, 3: 4661.

CHAPTER NINE

THE PROPHET PRESENT

Prelude

Once reason had stepped into the realm of religion it was to stir up many storms. Believers were brave indeed to invite such a corpulent guest as reason into their homes. The entry of reason into the realm of religions was a colossal, historic and ancient event, and the aftershocks produced more or less similar effects and consequences throughout the realm. Among Muslims, too, the debate over reason and its relationship to religion created an enormous rift within Islamic theology; viz. the well-known and oft-encountered rift between the Ashʿarites and the Muʿtazilites, the likes of which is to be found in most other religions.

The advent of reason opened the way to "secularism" and "secularisation". The occurrence of these two phenomena, that is to say, the coming into existence of "secularism" in the mind and subsequently "secularisation" in the external world, had a much broader ambit than the traditional references to the separation of religion and politics or the separation of church and state would have us believe. The independence of a host of human concepts and social institutions from religion lies at the root and heart of secularism/secularisation. If we wanted to summarise secularism in three phrases, they would be as follows:

a. acting on the basis of non-religious motives;
b. explaining the world, life and human beings on the basis of non-religious concepts and constructs;
c. discovering the independence of such constructs as science and politics and so on from religion.

When secularism in this sense came into being, that is to say, when these motives, approaches and explanations surfaced, religion per force lost its hegemony over many aspects of human life and became, at most, a rival among rivals. And it was inevitable that politics and the state would also be affected by this development and declared to be independent from religion.

In fact, it may be more appropriate to speak of "the independence of politics from religion" rather than "the separation of politics from religion". Nonetheless, it must be recognised that it was not just politics that was found to be essentially independent from religion, but that philosophy, the arts and sciences, and many other social institutions and aspects of human life became likewise independent. Hence, separation should be understood in the sense of independence and people's secularity seen as arising from their awareness of this sense. In other words, people gradually realised that these constructs had always been essentially independent from religion but that, over the course of history, they had accidentally and incidentally become associated with religion.

At the heart of secularism lies the view that politics, science, art, etc. have an essence and substance that is independent from religion and that religiousness is not a part of their definition. Of course, they are free to don a religious garb and accidentally mingle with religion; for example, when they are recommended by a prophet or a religious leader or included by them in a religious system as part of a greater aggregate, but this does not mean that they have become religious in essence. Concomitance does not always mean necessary connection, nor does the association of two things necessarily entail similitude or identity of essence; it can at most suggest fellowship between them. Many different plants coexist in a garden without dissolving into a unified essence or losing their independence and without it leading to any logical or essential interdependence. This idea can be expressed more simply by saying that religious knowledge is a subjectless knowledge or that the only axis that can bring together and unify the different elements of a religion is the religion's founder or the religion's end. There is in fact no common subject. This is why the language of religion is more like a conventional language than a technical-specialist language. The philosophical views in religion pertain to the discipline of philosophy (with its own particular subject, end, principles, problems and definitions). And its legal views pertain to the discipline of law (with its own particular subject, definitions, etc.). And it goes without saying that an aggregate comprised of the discipline of law, the discipline of philosophy and other disciplines cannot have a common subject; it can only be lent a contingent unity through a common motive and end.

The thinkers who have tried to prove some segments of religious teachings rationally and philosophically have in effect injected an independent life into the relevant teachings. When you want to prove something mathematically, you must first give it a quantitative and mathematical demeanour and then entrust its proof to the discipline of mathematics. By the same token, when you want to prove something rationally, you must first turn it into something on which the blade of reason and proof can prove incisive; in other words, you must first give it an independent rational identity and bring it under rational and philosophical constructs so that you can then subject it independently to philosophical proof. The same can be said of the work of Islamic jurists and the practitioners of other disciplines and skills. From the moment when thinkers, religious scholars and theologians arrived on the scene, sliced religion into different segments, took a segment each and, wishing to be of service to religion, resolutely set their minds on proving it rationally, they placed the stamp of independence onto these religious segments' foreheads. Part of religion became philosophical and fell under philosophy, part of it became legal and fell under law, part of it became empirical, and so on and so forth. In other words, each part returned to its source. Resolving to prove religious constructs by the force of reason was like cutting open the body of religion and revealing the non-religious nature of the constructs within it. This occurred in all religions.

The Essence of Religiousness

These observations raise an important question: what, in view of all this, is the essence of religiousness? What does religiousness of a human institution, a feature of human existence and/or a concept arise from and what is its ambit? Is there any concept or theory that has no identity other than being religious? If it is stated in a religion that "the earth is spherical", we say that religion has said it but that it actually belongs to the science of physics or astronomy. If it is stated in religion that camel meat is objectionable, we say that religion has said it but that it actually belongs to the science of nutrition and medicine. If it is stated that a human being is made up of a soul and a body, we say that this belongs to the discipline of philosophy and so on. What is it, then, that belongs to no other discipline and is fully and essentially religious? Does religiousness have its own field of knowledge—as do mathematics, philosophy or psychology—with its own particular theorems and concepts? Do religious propositions have their own particular and distinctive properties? It would seem not. Religion has no distinctive epistemological terrain to distinguish it and fence it off from other fields of knowledge; it is a composite of propositions, each of which belongs to a different discipline. It is even difficult to classify motives as religious. For example, when people fight for justice, can we say that their motives are purely religious? You may ask, is justice not religious? To which most philosophers of ethics respond very clearly, no, justice is not religious. Prophets have advocated justice. They have encouraged and urged people to observe justice, but the meaning and essence of justice is not religious; that is to say, even if prophets had not spoken about justice, the concept would have existed and would have been of great interest. Moreover, religions must underline justice in order to be appealing to people, not to present it as if it is their own contrivance and invention. Religion is just, but justice is not religious; this can be said of most important ethical values.

Hence, we cannot even claim that justice-seeking activities and struggles are motivated by religion. Even if we maintain that seeking justice and being just are laudable by virtue of the fact that they have been commanded by God—as it is the Ashʿarite's position—we can still go on to ask if God is a religious concept. Must everything associated with God be considered religious? Are theologies not at least partly philosophical? Are the activities and attributes of the Creator not debated by metaphysicians? Did God not exist before religions and is it not possible to discover God independently from established religions?

Now, if we rule, on this basis, that all or most concepts are independent from religion and that none of them is essentially religious, then we will naturally and logically find ourselves asking, what then constitutes "being religious" and wherein does it lie? What is that property that we know as "religiousness", which exists in some things and not in others? This is where the matter becomes particularly serious and delicate and this is where philosophers of religion can prove enormously helpful. For if, in truth, there is no concept or construct that is essentially religious—if, in other words, everything that we see and know is a guest of religion—then how can we place any hope in religion's existence and survival? If every good in the shop is on loan, would it not be foolish to contemplate investment? And, if they are all guests and likely to return to their homes at some point, then who is the host and where is his home? In sum, if part of religion belongs to philosophy, part of it to hygiene, part of it to law, part of it to ethics, which is the part that belongs solely to religion?

Some people have linked religiousness to the personality and authority of the founder of religion (prophets and/or sages). They believe that the essence of religiousness lies not in religion's teachings, but in the attribution of the teachings to the founder. The teachings themselves are composed of a variety of elements, each of which belongs to a particular discipline and is in essence independent. But when a prophet arrives on the scene and speaks to the people about these elements, the teachings take on a religious hue. Hence, the religiousness of the teachings lies in the fact that they all issue from one source (e.g. prophetic revelation). The corollary of this idea is that, in the case of theistic religions, if someone who is not a prophet—that is, a person not in the possession of religious experience and not on a mission from God—imparted to us the same recommendations and teachings, we would not consider his words religious. "Religiosness" is a characteristic of something that must have a special provenance. Of course, this religiosness is, as we said, not essential, but accidental or incidental. In other words, it is not like blood flowing through the teachings, but like a garment worn over them that can be taken off and removed. If a prophet speaks of "pollination", pollination does not turn into a religious phenomenon; it continues to belong to biology.[1] It would be the same if he spoke of matters mathematical, philosophical, legal, etc. None of these things would become religious other than contingently. Hence, here, everything goes back to the personality of the prophet. This is an extremely important point. Prophets' personalities are pivotal in religions. It is not for nothing that, in the opinion of believers, if someone believes everything that a prophet has said and considers it sound on the basis of reason and experience, and even acts upon the prophet's commands, but does not accept his prophetic mission, that person is not a believer. A person, who accepts Islamic teachings but is unconcerned about where the teachings came from and who delivered them, is not "a Muslim" in the opinion of Muslim theologians and jurists.

Religion cannot be viewed in such a way as to marginalise the personality of the prophet or to render it unnecessary altogether. Anyone who denies the historical relationship of a particular religion's claims and teachings with the pivotal personality of the prophet or does not

---

[1] As for instance in the Qur'anic verse: "And We loose the winds fertilising, and We send down out of heaven water..." (15: 22)

take this relationship into account is not considered a believer (a Muslim, a Christian, etc.) by the followers of that religion.

If someone makes this the criteria for religiousness, they would appear to be presenting an estimable and valid measure, but let them be aware that they have opened the door wide to secularism and secularisation. A reasonable person may ask, if there is just us and the teachings that the prophet delivered, what difference does it make whether we recognise the prophet or not. What role does this historical relationship play in the nature of the teachings and in what way does it transform them? What does it amount to other than an emotional attachment between the prophet and his disciples? What difference does it make whether or not we know the name of a religion's founder? It is exactly as if an exquisite book had been written centuries ago by an unknown author. Why do we need to know the author's name to benefit from the book and why should we embark on investigations and research to identify the writer? There is just us, the book and its contents, irrespective of whether we attribute it to a particular person or not.

Hence, although we can say that religiousness hinges on the historical and causal relationship between a religion's teachings and its prophet, this degree of religiousness does not impede secularism. A religion of this kind could very easily disintegrate and break into pieces—in view of the essential independence of its teachings from its historical fountainhead—with each piece returning to whence it came, such that people could debate and criticise, and accept or reject the teachings without taking the fountainhead into account. In other words, things could lead to exactly where they have led.

Thus, if we define religion as "that which was brought by the prophet" and make "religiousness" a function of attributing the teachings to God's envoy, the name of religion, its social and authorial aspects, its civilisational structure and its historical survival would be safeguarded in a way, but the way would also be opened to secularism and the dismemberment of religion. On the basis of this idea, religion is composed of elements, none of which are religious; there was only one religious person and he has now departed.

To reiterate: if the prophet teaches mathematics, mathematics does not become religious. And it is exactly the same if he teaches psychology, philosophy, biology or art. The contents of these things will not change in any way, nor will their definitions. They will remain exactly as they were meant to be. In this sense, religious teachings are intrinsically secular (non-religious) and assume religiousness only by virtue of their attribution to a historical person (the prophet). And this person played no role other than to present and deliver the teachings, and did not alter their nature. So, when he departs and his historical presence is eliminated, religion is orphaned and its elements gradually return to whence they came, regaining their original nature and revealing their independence from religion. We can see the significance of this if we bear in mind that, when something that is not essentially religious becomes a guest of religion, instead of religion being imposed on it, it imposes its imperatives on religion. When religion uses mathematical, legal and philosophical concepts, it is dragged in their wake. Law, for example, has certain imperatives and it establishes certain relationships with history and societies which are unavoidable. Hence it is impossible to construct a trans-historical law, and so on and so forth.

Another response to the above-mentioned question has been based on the concept of religious experience. It has been said that it is, in fact, religious experience that is essentially religious. And this religious experience is exactly that which, in the case of prophets, is known as "reception of revelation". It is difficult to define "religious experience" and much ink has been spilled over it. It is not my intention here to give an exact account of what constitutes religious experience. Suffice it to say that believers hold that the Prophet had a gift for it and was its recipient, agent and bearer. The important point in this context is that, if we only take the Prophet's religious experience into account, this second response will ultimately lead us to exactly the same place as the first.

The Prophet's historical personality hinges on his spiritual personality and his spiritual personality, in turn, hinges on his religious experience or his revelational experience. If the Prophet did not have such an experience, he would not have been a prophet but an ordinary person like anybody else. With the Prophet's demise, prophetic experience is also ceased and religion is orphaned once again. We must find a mechanism that perpetuates the Prophet's presence and experience, otherwise the disintegration and secularisation of religion will be certain. And concentrating on the social aspects of religion, regardless of religious experience, will turn religion into a totally non-religious and secular doctrine. But the Prophet's religious experience is not enough. We have no such religious precept as "the Prophet's experience will suffice". The perpetuation of religion demands the perpetuation of this prophetic experience. Hence, we must seek a religious experience that is defined in more general terms.

It is religious experience itself that is essentially religious and anyone who is a bearer of it is a "prophet" to a certain extent and a bearer of religion to that extent. The Prophet, peace be upon him, was referring to exactly these kinds of experiences when he said:

> At times, I am with God throughout the night. He gives me food and drink.

It is clear that these words are meant allegorically, as Rumi puts it:

> When (the Prophet's saying), "I pass the night with my Lord," was uttered, (the words) "He gives (me) food" and "He gives (me) drink" referred metaphorically to (spiritual) food and (drink).[2]

This "companionship" and "soiree" is the very "experience" that is essentially religious, the only truly and quintessentially religious phenomenon that lit prophets' souls like a divine spark for a short or long while and opened their eyes to the inner verities of the world. And wherever the way is opened to experiences of this kind, there, the truth of religion is to be found.

We can see that religion has two countenances: one is the external countenance that manifests itself in the form of social systems and civilisational institutions. This aspect is more clearly manifested in Islam than in any other religion. The other is the inner countenance. If we view the historical personality of the Prophet merely as a deliverer of religious teachings and the architect of a social system, if we see him as the builder of a doctrine and consider his structure viable in the absence of its builder, we will be left with a religion that is very prone to secularisation. But if we take into consideration the Prophet's inner personality and his profound religious experience, if we see religiousness as arising from that experience and believe that religion is only viable in conjunction with that experience, we will not see the preservation of social systems and civilisational institutions in the absence of religious experiences as the preservation of religion; they will appear to us like soulless bodies and lifeless figures.

---

[2] *Mathnawi*, 1: 3738.

From this perspective, prophethood takes on a different sense and meaning. Here, the Prophet is not just an employee or an emissary who arrived one day to perform a duty and is now gone and out of reach. This is how the Wahhabis view the Prophet. According to them, the Prophet was merely an emissary who came to deliver a message and then left. Now, there is only us and the message. This seemingly sounds true but sometimes it is misdirected to invalid consequences. Yes, it is true that we should not attach excessive importance to the Prophet as a historical person to the detriment of his teachings. The Qur'an tells us:

> Muhammad is naught but a Messenger; Messengers have passed away before him. Why, if he should die or is slain, will you turn about on your heels? If any man should turn about on his heels, he will not harm God in any way; and God will recompense the thankful. (3: 144)

In other words, stand on your own feet. Do not rely childishly on the Prophet. When the Prophet departs from the world, do not allow things to go back to where they were. The Prophet has come to present a system of teachings to the people and to build a nation independent of himself. He does not have eternal life and must eventually depart from this world. Look upon his lasting teachings, not his mortal self. The Prophet has carried out his task and can now serve as a model. You can henceforth benefit from his teachings and his mode of behaviour and continue his way. This is all true. But following the Prophet must be interpreted in a more profound sense. The Prophet was not a Marx or a Confucius or a Gandhi to found a doctrine and then leave. Prophethood was an experience. As long as the flame of that experience continues to burn, prophethood will be alive and well. To follow the Prophet is to follow his experiences. And following is not passive imitation and repetition, it is active participation in the experiences of the guide. This is true in every field. The best followers of a thinker are not mere imitators; they are investigators and thinkers who actively share in the master's thoughts and reflections. It is exactly the same when it comes to following the masters of religious and mystical experiences.

Christians say that salvation and felicity are only possible through Jesus. Muslims say that salvation and felicity are only possible through adopting Muhammad's way. These exclusivist claims can be understood in the following way. Jesus and Muhammad were not and are not by any means simply historical personalities. These noble men were not mere employees who completed their task and left, never to return

again. To say that one can reach God through Jesus means that, by
being close to him and achieving a spiritual connectedness with him, it
is possible to re-experience his experiences today, to share in his ardour
and raptures, and to step into the world that he had entered, thanks
to his succour, grace and assistance. This is an important realisation.
This is what it means to say that a religion lives. No one can say this
about Marx. Marx, too, founded a very influential school of thought.
But no one claims that it is possible to achieve this-worldly felicity by
establishing a spiritual connectedness with Marx. His existence was
historical only and that historical being is now dead and gone. Now,
Marx exists only in his books. His presence flows through his students,
but only in a metaphorical sense. But the followers of religions do not
view their prophets in this light; nor should they. Relying on and being
aware of the Prophet's "inward guardianship" (*wilayat-e bateni*) is the
precondition for the endurance and vitality of religion. Inward guardianship means the presence of the Prophet's personality, the possibility
of connectedness with him and, most important of all, the possibility of
re-experiencing his experiences. This is precisely what "the expansion
of prophetic experience" means. If the prophetic experience does not
evolve and expand among believers and if prophetic experiences are
not relived, believers are not in the presence of religion at all. At most,
they are in the possession of a soulless social system, a shell without
substance, a worldly ideology like Marx's or any other ideology. And
what else are we to call this but a secular religion?

Religious Experience: the Quintessence of Religion

We are now in a position to say that "religiousness" hinges on something
of the nature of religious experience. The Prophet was like a volcano,
with every word he spoke, molten lava. In other words, everything
was merged together and appeared uniform. But with the passage of
time, each segment of the molten material solidified at its own particular point of solidification and broke away from the rest. The unity
changed to plurality and it cannot be unified again other than by the
grace of religious experience. Ordinary imitators are content with
the plurality but mystical and experiential believers can—in the light
of their unifying experiences—rediscover the original unity that the
Founder saw.

> Blessings on Universal Love, the (supreme) Master, (which) gave oneness
> to hundreds of thousands of motes!
> (They were) as dust scattered on the thoroughfare: the hand of the Potter
> made them one jug.[3]

All the emphasis placed nowadays on the political, social and civilisational aspects of religion is in fact emphasis on something that is not
essentially religious but only contingently; and as such it, consequently,
has many this-worldly rivals. Unless the roots are in water, there is no
hope that these branches can bear fruit.

If we consider religiousness and religiosity and their continued
endurance to hinge on religious experiences, and if we see the Prophet
as these experiences' recipient, agent and guide, we will consider the
evolution and endurance of religion to hinge on the endurance of these
"prophetic" experiences. We will, therefore, view religious practices
(from prayer and fasting to fighting injustice) as religious to the extent
that they contribute to the realisation of these experiences, evoke them
and keep them alive at the individual and social levels. Otherwise, they
are either leaves and branches and superficial protuberances. Or else
they constitute this-worldly beliefs that, laudable though they may be,
lack any religiosity. And no one will attain these religious experiences,
inward realisations and spiritual flights other than with the assistance
of a divine guardian (*wali-ullah*).

> If any one, by rare exception, traversed this Way alone (without a Pir),
> He arrived (at his goal) through the help of the spiritual influence of
> the Pirs.[4]

It is only with the aid of a guardian and by partaking in his experiences that one can attain spiritual excellence and step onto the path of
eternal felicity. To this end, everyone must find their own guardian. In
pragmatic, collective, this-worldly religiosity, the guardian is the Legislator whose dos and don'ts must be obeyed and whose guardianship
is external. Everyone is addressed equally by the Legislator and everyone thinks of their own this-worldly and otherworldly interests. But
in experiential religiosity, where everything revolves around religious
experience, the individual must find and choose their own guardian

---

[3] *Mathnawi*, 2: 3714–3715.
[4] *Mathnawi*, 1: 2974.

(that is, the person who inspires religious experiences in them); or, in fact, the guardian must choose them.

> When the Pir has accepted thee, take head, surrender thyself (to him):
> go, Like Moses, under the authority of Khizr.[5]

Mind that it does not say "when you choose the *pir* (guardian)." The difference between "being chosen" and "choosing" is the difference between determinism and free will and love and reason. The connectedness and proximity between the guardian and the disciples' spirits and hearts become an unending source of inspiration, linking the two individuals together.

In experiential religiosity, individuals are addressed personally and inwardly by their guardian. Ostensibly, what prophets said was addressed to everyone and the jurists have also maintained that these precepts are general and for the public. Hence, if they said "pray" or "fast", they meant that everyone should pray and fast. This is true, but only at the level of religion as a collective ritual. In the realm of experiential religion, where it is a question of partaking in the experiences of a powerful soul, the addressee is fundamentally different. Here, everyone must discover personally and inwardly who is addressing them, who moves them spiritually and who sets the strings of their being vibrating; who, in other words, exercises guardianship over them. And, to find this guardianship, the individual must travel long and hard and undergo a multitude of experiences.

In discursive/reflective religiosity the experiential presence of the Prophet's personality falls to almost zero. The same can be said of imitative, pragmatic/instrumental religiosity. And religious teachings fill the place of the Prophet's personality. This is why, in these two types of religiosity, the door is opened to the disintegration and dismemberment of religion. But in experiential religiosity or guardianship-oriented religiosity, the Prophet's personality is pivotal and irreplaceable. And to follow the Prophet is to follow his experiences. In this context, the addressee is also different. Here, the utterances are no longer absolute, public and collective; they are entirely personal. One can only wait and see whose ear is attuned to the guardian's voice and who finds themselves addressed by him. It is exactly as if someone were to speak Chinese in a crowd made up of Iranians, Chinese, Indians, Turks and

---

[5] *Mathnawi*, 1: 2967.

Arabs. It is evident that the speaker would only be addressing the Chinese, because, if everyone was to understand what he was saying, then he would not be addressing them in Chinese only. Addressing people demands that certain conditions should pertain and, in the realm of religious utterance, these conditions are extremely subtle. Everyone must ask themselves in seclusion: are these words addressed to me? Am I the one being spoken to? Even in ritualistic, collective, legalistic religion, the question arises. There, too, it must be seen whether every community in every historical era was being addressed by the Prophet's every word or not. The assumption made by some Islamic jurists which leads them to extend the precepts of *fiqh* to the moon and to Mars is only an assumption; there are rival assumptions.

At any rate, guardianship-oriented, experiential religiosity is extremely personal in nature, not in the sense of isolation and detachment, but in the sense of falling into a personal relationship with God and the *wali*, the saint/divine guardian. It is on this basis that the experiential believer moves away from the religion of the common people and towards true religion. He steps into the radiance of God's guardianship and approaches Him singly.

Rituals

Religious rituals are effectively aimed at evoking religious experiences and, the more they do so, the more religious they are. This is why individuals do not all stand in the same relationship to these rituals. One person may find the *hajj* very evocative, another, giving money to the poor or serving the masses, yet another, late night vigils and prayers. The telling measure is the extent to which the relevant ritual expedites and facilitates inner experiences and engenders a new personality in the believer. If we take away these experiences, there will be nothing left of religion but an aggregate of social norms and principles and collective rituals. Even if a religion of this kind succeeds in making the world flourish, it will have done nothing more than non-religious doctrines. Communities the world over have, more or less, managed to meet their collective needs with a measure of wisdom and foresight. If this is the only reason we need a prophet, then, in Ibn Khaldun words, we have no further need of the Prophet.

It would seem that there are two ways of looking at religion: from one perspective, the Prophet is thought to be addressing the collective or society at large, and the individual thereby, and, from the other perspective, he is addressing the individual, and society thereby. If it is the collective that is being addressed, then religion becomes a social system, with the inscribed teachings replacing the Prophet and with religion's politics, economics, theology and ethics gradually taking their own independent course and returning to their sources. Thus, the organism that is religion will have been objectively dismembered and what will remain of the original molten, uniform material that emerged from the furnace of revelation will be solidified, disjointed pieces floating in the stream of history. This will occur even with the establishment of a religious state and no unity from within will lend unity to external appearances. In fact, it was when the inward aspects of religion and religious experience began to be neglected that emphasis on external appearances and politics and the state gained ascendancy and began to dominate. This was also when the disputes over *fiqh* and theology began to proliferate and escalate. This, too, was when experiential religiosity found itself pressed into a corner, with discursive and pragmatic religiosity having the field to themselves. The periphery replaced the centre and preamble became confused with conclusion. And the Prophet was no longer at hand and others took his place. And there was nothing left of religion but a secular shell with countless hangers-on and claimants.

But if the individual considers himself addressed by the Prophet, he will commence religion from the heights of ascension and, having flown to the heavens, he will then share his achievements with people on earth. In other words, he will make religious experience the central axis and religion's this-worldly features, the periphery. And he will concern himself with and attend to these features to the extent that they contribute to that experience. And he will not lend affairs that are independent from it a religious demeanour and purpose. He will love this world for the sake of religion, not religion, for the sake of bringing about a flourishing world. He will push aside this-worldly tyrants to be nearer to God; instead of bringing God into the fray, the better to fight tyrants in His name.

The incongruity between our position and the Prophet's position in relation to the pearl of religion must be understood and made understood again. The Prophet first discovered a pearl within his own religious experience (a sense of awe, adoration, inspiration, humility and submission towards an exalted presence, wonderment at its beauty and majesty, the discovery of the hidden secrets of the world and the purpose of life), then he wisely and protectively wrapped the pearl in the oyster of the law (*shari'ah*), both to prevent it from falling into the hands of unbefitting people and to indicate where it lay for the benefit of the fitting. His disciples began with the oyster and, generally mistaking it for the pearl, started peddling oysters. The Prophet's cry rang out like thunder with awe at the beauty of the lightning he saw. The disciples heard the thunder but did not see the lightning at all; so they fell in awe of the thunder.

Today, we must seek the pearl, which lies outside the oyster of time and place. We must look again for the lightning, which seems so hidden from public eye. The rediscovered pearl will fill the oyster with spirit, meaning and value.

We must revive experiential religiosity. The modern world has politicians, economists, etc. aplenty. It is the Prophet who is not longer at hand and it is him we must bring back. We must start from the pearl of religion and place the oysters of the age at its service. In a word, we, too, must take the path that the Prophet took.

CHAPTER TEN

PROPHETS UNHEARD

In order to perform his mission, the noble Prophet of Islam both turned into a different personality himself and called on the people he was addressing to become different people so that they could hear and understand his words. This was the way of all prophets. On the one hand, they wanted their words to be heard and their call to be taken seriously and, on the other, they knew that people, as they were, were not receptive to their words. Hence, they invited people to transform themselves and to be other than they were so that they could be a good audience for their call. Here lies the paradox of messengers' mission.

It was as if the people that the prophets found themselves addressing were not the proper audience, but that the true audience first had to be created by the prophets themselves and substituted for the original listeners, so that the then transformed audience could lend an ear to and hear what they were saying. If people had asked prophets, what do you want from us? prophets would have replied: "We want you not to be who you are and who you have been thus far, because, as long as you remain who you are, you will not understand and accept what we are saying." "We call upon you to change, but in order to realise that change is desirable you have to change in the first place." Their task was like trying to awaken sleeping people who believe themselves awake but who must in fact first be awakened before they can acknowledge that wakefulness is a good thing and that they had never been awake before. This was a major problem encountered by all prophets as they faced their peoples and it is a difficulty that anyone who has a divine mission to reform people thoroughly and substantively will experience in their dealings with other people and in the way other people behave towards them. In brief, he must first awaken people with *causes* so that they can then value wakefulness on the basis of *reasons*. Their cry of "waken" first awakens the sleeping person like a cause and, having awakened, the person can then understand the cry.

Here, I will try to elucidate the substance of this problem and the key to understanding the significance of what prophets did and the broad chest that God had granted to them.

In the Al-Inshirah Sura, which is one of the Meccan suras, we find the account of the Prophet's fortitude and God's benefaction towards him told as follows:

> Did We not broaden thy chest for thee and lift from thee thy burden, the burden that weighed down your back? Did we not exalt thy fame? (94: 1–4)

Moses, peace be upon him, asks that God may grant him this same fortitude:

> Lord, broaden my chest and do Thou ease for me my task. Unloose the knot upon my tongue, that they may understand my words. (20: 25–28)

The Prophet had a broad chest in all these senses and anyone who performs prophetic work must possess this broadened chest to a greater or lesser extent in relation to receiving and interpreting secrets and inspirations; in relation to the injustices people perpetrate against them; and in relation to the special problems that their call and mission are certain to generate.

On the question of the Prophet's broad chest and fortitude, historians and his biographers have left us with an amazing allegorical story. In Ibn Hisham's (d. 834) account of the life of the Prophet, which has been used as a source by most other chroniclers, the story relates to when he was a little more than two years old. In other historical books and compilations of the traditions of the Prophet, it is said to have occurred when he was ten or twenty.

In Ibn Hisham's *al-Sirah al-Nabawiyyah*, the story is told in the words of Halimah, his nursemaid:

> One day, Muhammad (PBUH), was playing with my son. Suddenly my son came running to me and said, Mother, something bad has happened to Muhammad. It seemed as if some people had attacked him. I went to him and he said to me, "Two people, wearing white garments and carrying a golden tub approached me. They laid me down. They opened up my chest and took out my heart. They took a black piece of meat out of my heart and threw it away. Then, they washed my heart with the snow they were carrying in their golden tub. They then put it back in my chest, let me go and left."

If we do not assume that the different accounts of this tale are simply multiple renditions of a single story, on the testimony of historians this incident occurred five times over the course of the Prophet's life, and some Qur'anic commentators have cited it under the verse "Did We not broaden thy chest for thee". Some specialists on the life of the Prophet have cast doubt on the veracity of the story and said that spiritual refinement and cleansing have nothing to do with a person's physical heart; these must have been the imaginings of Arab story tellers and superstitious people who thought that purity of heart and spirit amounted to the cleanliness of the meaty heart that lay in a person's chest. But more learned views have also been expressed on this subject; for example, by S. M. H. Tabataba'i, the author of the *Tafsir al-Mizan*, who well understood the incident and explained that it was no more than an allegory and a kind of vision, and that it was not be taken in a literal sense. The incident occurred deep in the Prophet's subconscious. It was as if he saw a transcendental event unfolding in symbolic form before his eyes, just as a person may dream of pearls being thrown before swine and understand it to mean that they are trying to impart knowledge to people who are unworthy of it.

Ibn Hisham also cites the Prophet himself telling the following story: One day I was playing stones with my playmates in the street. To move our stones from one place to another, we had taken off all our clothes and we were carrying the stones in them. I suddenly felt an unseen person punching me and saying: "Muhammad, you put your clothes back on." In other words, you should be covered. You should not follow other people's bad habits and customs. You are different from others. And I put my clothes back on.

These incidents, narrated in authoritative historical accounts, reveal that Muhammad was being prepared for undertaking a great task and that he was being inculcated with goodness and purity, in anticipation of the grave responsibilities he would later have to shoulder. The Prophet grew up, flourished and became a prophet under this kind of moral and spiritual supervision and care and under the auspices of exalted forces that command the universe from end to end.

The Paradoxical Nature of Prophetic Mission

The prophet's mission can be summarised in a single phrase: "He had come to change people." The phrase is easy to express but extremely difficult to accomplish. There are two kinds of changing: a changing of accidentals and changing of essentials. In other words, a changing of derivatives or a changing of fundamentals. For example, a person can easily change their house or their clothes or their friends or their home country. (Of course, once a person becomes attached to their affairs and establishes extensive existential links with them, even changing these things can be difficult.) These are changes in people's external attachments and traits. But there is another type of change that relates to a person's essence and identity. There, the task is difficult not only in practice, but also at the level of theory and comprehension. A person is bound to wonder what is going to be done to him and what the outcome of the change will be. When you change a garment and don another, you know exactly what you are doing. You know what you are setting aside and what you are taking up, and what your criteria and wishes are in the process. Most important of all, you yourself remain unchanged. After donning the new garment, you are still the person you were. You want the new garment for the same "self" that you were before and still continue to remain. But, if the person himself is to change, then who do they want the new identity for? For the "self" that will no longer exist or for the person who is yet to be and they know nothing about? On the basis of what criteria are they to assess the change and to decide in favour of it? As for the present criteria, they will be subsequently rejected and as for new criteria, namely the criteria that are to emerge after personality changes, they are not yet at hand and are yet to be acquired. If the possibility of going back is also foreclosed, the problem is redoubled.

It is very difficult to say to person, change your very existence so that after—and only after—changing, you can confirm that what we did to you was not a bad thing and that the change was an auspicious occurrence in your life; like a child who first has to study before he can understand and confirm that studying is a good thing. (And a child who considers himself grown up and knowledgeable at that.) In other words, in these circumstances, the criteria for assessment come about after the event and as a result of undergoing it. This is the fundamental difficulty that prophets face in making their call and carrying out their work. How can anyone be asked to do something that they are not currently in a position to evaluate and will only be able to evaluate after the fact?

If a surgeon were to say to you that they would be prepared to take out your brain and to put the brain of someone else, who you do not know, in your skull instead, with which brain and according to what criteria would you respond to the offer? With the current brain or the future one? If the criteria used by your current brain are valid, why change them and, if they are not valid, how can you act on them? And the future brain is not yet available and its criteria are unknown. And, even if you are not prepared to change your brain, the question could still be asked as to why you are so attached to it. Maybe the second brain will be better than the first. The offer made by prophets was very similar to this and, by understanding it, we will be in a better position to understand what we do to ourselves when we believe in and entrust ourselves to a prophet's call; what it is within ourselves that we hand over to the caller. What a blaze God's callers light in the very foundations of the human personality; and, if their call takes root and spreads the world over, what a world will replace the existing one.

In fact, the call of prophets never takes hold completely the world over and the faith and transformation that they call for is only fully realised in a few rare individuals, with others benefiting from the transformation only relatively and incompletely.

The problem that prophets faced was not that the patients did not take the medicine that they were being offered, but that the patients did not consider themselves ill at all and did not see prophets as the presenter of any cure. In other words, the first prerequisite of agreement was lacking. When you describe as ill someone who considers themselves well, you not only fail to win their friendship, you light the flame of hostility in them as well. And how difficult it is to be friends with someone who sees their friend as an enemy.

The above examples may seem somewhat fanciful, artificial and exaggerated, but they are not exaggerated in the slightest. Take the following example: when you speak to an arrogant or prejudiced person and call on them to abandon their arrogance and prejudice, what is the problem you will encounter? You talk to them, you counsel them, you reason with them, you paint a picture of the bright and joyous future that awaits them, you point out everything that is wrong and ugly about arrogance and prejudice, but the essential problem remains that the arrogant person will only be prepared to listen to you once they have abandoned their arrogance. The prejudiced person will only accept what you tell them once they have set aside their prejudice. But the person who has abandoned their arrogance and prejudice and is prepared to listen to you is not in need of your counsel, and the person who has not abandoned these defects *is* in need of your counsel but will not listen to you. You are faced with a paradox, then. The person first has to change themselves before they can be receptive to your words. Therein lies the problem. The existing person cannot hear you and the person who will hear you is yet to be born.

Prophets, too, put their fingers on the very point in people's beings that was the main impediment to their call being heard; viz. that selfsame arrogance and prejudice. They spoke with infinite patience to people who were not in a condition to hear them. Their audience had to turn into different beings in order to be receptive to prophets. Changing was the precondition for believing and, yet, believing was the only way to change.

A phrase has been attributed to a number of experiential mystics and theologians of the Middle Ages, which has always been treated with derision and rebuke, by reason-oriented and discursive/reflective believers. I want to give the phrase its due here and to show that the people who uttered it were not speaking out of ignorance or on a whim, and that they were in fact conveying vast meaning with a few little words. The phrase, which has apparently been traced to Augustine and thereafter is: "I believe that I may understand".[1] The objection of the objectors seemed to be that the opposite is true and that it should be said instead: I understand and reason that I may believe. This is a criticism that falls within the framework of logical considerations and reasoning. It poses the question: why do you believe in something that you do not know or understand? First you have to exercise your reason and, after you have mastered something rationally, then you can believe in it. What sense is there in believing blindly in something you do not understand?

Certainly, on a superficial and simplistic level, the phrase is invalid. However, "I believe that I may understand" operates on a much deeper level than this. It means that I am laying down my fractiousness and prejudice to prepare myself for understanding. I change myself, I acquire a new mind, I tear away the veils so that I can understand and see. Tearing away the veils demands a kind of belief, a belief that is of the nature of commitment and trust. As Hafez, the thirteen century Persian poet, put it, sometimes a person is their own veil; in other words, the person's being the way they are prevents their understanding and advancement. Hence, they must first believe—that is to say, they must first change

---

[1] *Credo ut intelligam.*

themselves—to then be able to move and advance. As Rumi says: "The explanation (of the mystery) thereof is not (give) by the intellect: do service (to god), in order that it may become clear to you.[2] And this is the purport of the wise phrase that says: "Faith gives a person a new existence, not a new mind, new logic and new thoughts."

We used the example of awakening people who are asleep. The Qur'an gives the example of bringing to life people who are dead:

> O believers, respond to God and the Messenger when He calls you unto that which will give you life. (8: 24)

Do you see the paradox? A dead man is incapable of doing anything, including responding to a call. Yet, although dead, he is being called upon to behave as the living would do so that, by so doing, he will come to life! Hence, all of the Prophet's efforts are aimed in the first instance at making people who are asleep realise that they are asleep, at making people who are ill realise that they are ill, because this very realisation and acceptance is a key to felicity and an opening to faith. To this end, shaking and disturbing people and creating turmoil and turbulence in their beings is the principal method he uses.

Being a reviver was, thus, the Prophet's main attribute. Alongside it, the Prophet, peace be upon him, had other attributes as well, such as being a resolver of conflicts and a reconciler of hearts:

> And He brought your hearts together, so that by His blessing you became brothers. (3: 103)

Everyone who embraces a new faith and, in all sincerity, adopts a new way and a new rite, experiences this revival and "*coming to life*". Repentance, too, is a basic and rudimentary form of "*revival*". In repentance, the person rebels against themselves, rises up against their own being and, if successful, attains a new "*self*". "Repentance" is not just "regret", it is a "*return*". It is a turning of the page of the book of one's being. It is to turn oneself back to front. And this is the selfsame difficult task that requires assistance and grace.

Prophets, too, began their call with "repent" or "flee to"; that is to say, turn away from who you are, transform yourselves, flee to God, completely shift your vantage point. Without this "facing to the front", no further step is possible. Alas, but as long as people have their backs

---

[2] *Mathnawi*, 3: 2526.

turned to the Prophet, they will not hear him. And, in order to hear him, they must repent.

The first thing that prophets proposed to people was humility and submission. The story of Adam and Satan is the story of us all. By leading Adam astray, Satan, who is arrogance and defiance personified, tainted every human being with the brand of defiance and arrogance. Now, prophets appear on the scene to call on people to repent and return to their unsullied former state. According to religions' teachings, people are now fractious, arrogant and defiant creatures, who, because of this arrogance, refuse to be humble and submit. In other words, they have fallen into the paradoxical state that we spoke about earlier. It is interesting to note that our religious narratives have it that a human being is closest to God when he prostrates himself before Him. This is to say that throwing oneself to the ground and forfeiting one's arrogance is the best state in which a person can find himself in relation to God. Prophets told people to relinquish their fractiousness and become servants of God, but they knew that, as long as people did not relinquish their fractiousness, they would not hear this call.

Here, we need a leap of faith, a sort of existential leap. We must just leap and undergo this change. This is the fundamental transformation that one experiences on acquiring faith. Hence, the expression "I believed", which entails human will, is not an entirely apt description of this stage. It would be more appropriate to say: "belief befell me." In other words, a passive verb should be substituted for an active one. Like "I doubted"; instead of which we should say "doubt befell me", since "doubting" is not something that is willed, but something that we become afflicted with. The same can be said of the expressions "I laughed", "I cried", "I understood", "I willed", which should in fact be "laughter befell [upon] me"/happened to me and so on.

Of course, believing has different stations and, at some of these stations, it is appropriate to use the expression "I believed". But, at that station of belief where a person's existence undergoes a fundamental change and his personality turned inside out, the expression "belief befell me" is most appropriate. Not everyone is actually blessed with this phase; this is the meaning and significance of God's words when He tells the Prophet:

> Thou guidest not whom thou likest, but God guides whom He will. (28: 56)

It is as if this kind of faith is a special blessing that is only bestowed on some. It is an experience that suddenly strikes and sweeps through one's entire being. It is a transformation of such magnitude that it can truly (not metaphorically) be described as coming to life after being dead. Love, which is made of the same fabric as faith, is a similar experience. It was not for nothing that, after such a transformation, Jalal al-Din Rumi said:

> I was dead, I became alive; I was weeping, I became laughing;
> The power of love came, and I became everlasting power.[3]

The problem that prophets faced was that they were asking something of people that was very difficult and, since they knew this to be the case, they were undemanding and patient, and did not harbour high expectations. They knew that they would have a small circle of companions and trustworthy disciples, who would understand their message and internalise it in the depths of their minds. Then, there would be other, bigger circles, further removed, the members of which would reap less benefit from the shining rays of their beings.

Prophets did not expect very much of people, because, if true faith is a kind of revolution in one's being, a complete and utter upheaval of one's entire existence, then it is bound to be a rare occurrence. God had taught the Prophet in the Qur'an that, had He wanted to, He would have guided everyone:

> Did not the believers know that, if God had willed, He would have guided men altogether. (13: 31)

Following the Prophet Is More than Following His Commandments

Of course, religiosity has three levels or three types: imitative and pragmatic; reflective and discursive; and mystical and experiential. In the light of these three types of religiosity, three ways of following the Prophet are conceivable:

Following the Prophet at an imitative and pragmatic level is to obey his dos and don'ts, such as, praying, fasting, not drinking wine and so on and so forth. Undoubtedly, this is not the highest form that being

---

[3] *Divan-e Kabir*, Ghazal # 1393 (trs. Arbery).

a disciple of the Prophet can take. It is dictated by the nature of ritu-alistic, imitative religiosity.

The second way is to be a disciple of the Prophet's world-view and wisdom, benefiting from him in a theoretical and cognitive way. For example, the Prophet's principal definition of people was that they were servants of God and contained no element of divinity. This was his conception of human nature. Nature, the supernatural, angels, Satan, life after death, all had a place in his world-view. The life of a Muslim who believes in these things should, in principle, be different from the life of someone who does not believe in them. Scientific discoveries, too, have unmistakable impacts on our lives. For example, today, we know that our world contains parasites and bacterias, but our fellow human beings in the past were unaware of these things. They therefore lived in a way that did not take microbes into account. But, today, since the existence of microbes has become a part of our cognition and world-view, we take them into account in our daily lives. Evidence of this can be found in our medicine, nutrition, hygiene, etc. The same can be said of religious life. Our religious world-view affects our ethical and material life and distinguishes the path of a believer, who considers himself a servant of God, from that of a non-believer, who does not. Of course, all believers have a basic notion of the teachings of religion; but most ordinary believers do not have a thorough-going, scholarly conception of them, or a well-structured, rational, cognitive system. This second way of following the Prophet is to be found at the level of discursive religiosity.

This brings us to the third way of following the Prophet, namely, partaking in prophetic experiences. Here, it is not a question of either purely practical imitation or a purely theoretical venture. It is to experi-ence ardour in the light of the Prophet's ardour and to partake of his rapture and illuminations. The Prophet's most important experience was the transformation of his personality. Of course, being a recipi-ent of revelation and being privy to the inner secrets of the world are aspects of prophetic experience, but the person who became a vessel for revelation and had access to the inner world was someone who had been transformed through and through. In other words, he had first acquired a prophetic existence/personality so that he could then have prophetic experiences.

Ibn Hisham's *Sirah* cites the Prophet as saying: The first time Gabriel appeared to me, he ordered me to read. And, since I replied that I could not read, he took my hand and pressed it very hard and repeated,

"Read!" "I cannot," I said. He pressed my hand very hard again and said: "Read!" After the third time, I was so afraid and trembling so much that I read.

This pressing and trembling was not just on the surface; it reverberated throughout the Prophet's being and wrought a complete transformation. Afterwards, his speech, his hearing, his sight and every other aspect of his being were completely other than they had been before. Once he had acquired Prophetic sight, everything that he saw was prophetic. Once he had acquired a prophetic personality, every word that he uttered was prophetic. Thereafter, everything that he did was true and right. Following the Prophet at this level is to embrace his every truth and right. The Prophet's prayers, truth-telling and tireless struggles were not aimed at achieving excellence. It was because he had achieved excellence that he did these things. They were not the causes of his excellence, but its effects. For imitative believers, behaving ethically and complying with the precepts of the shari'ah are causes of excellence. But, in moving closer to the source of excellence, experiential believers become sources of goodness and values themselves, and, like overfilled treasure chests bursting at the seams, they scatter their gems throughout this world and the next.

> Since the light of that (spiritual) substance has shone forth,
> He has gained independence of these hypocrisies.
> Therefore do not demand of him the testimony of act and speech,
> For through him both the worlds have blossomed like a rose.[4]

Prophetic experience is not summed up in a person having true visions. (True visions are believed to be one of the forty-six components of prophethood.) Certainly, visions are a kind of prophetic experience. But, first and foremost, the experience entails a revolution within the self. And the presence of the Prophet's personality is pivotal to this revolution.

In pragmatic and discursive religiosities, there is no need of the Prophet's presence. The Prophet lived in the world for 63 years at a certain point in history and then died. We are now in the possession of his Book and his Tradition. Anyone who wants to obey the Prophet's dos and don'ts at the level of pragmatic religiosity, or anyone who wants to take scholarly advantage of his teachings, is in no need of the

---

[4] *Mathnawi*, 5: 244–245.

Prophet's presence. The Book and the Tradition, available in writing or in oral accounts, contain all that they need. But the highest form of religiosity, which is mystical, experiential religiosity, requires his direct presence. The mystical wayfarer must receive his spurs from the Prophet. This is the religiosity of love and love is impossible without a beloved. You can study the teachings of a dead philosopher but love can not be directed to a non-living beloved. We have no need of Ibn Sina, Mulla Sadra, Descartes and Spinoza's actual presence today to study their teachings. They are all present enough in their works. Lessons can be learned entirely in the masters' absence, using books and tapes. But this is impossible when it comes to pious love and mystical faith. Here, presence is the crux of the matter.

> An unrespectful person present is better than one absent:
> though the ring be crooked, is it not on the door?[5]

> If any one, by rare exception, traversed this Way alone (without a Pir), he arrived (at his goal) through the help of the spiritual influence of the Pirs.
> The hand of the Pir is not withdrawn from the absent (those who are not under his authority): his hand is naught but the grasp of God.
> Inasmuch as they give such a robe of honour to the absent, (what must they give their disciples?): undoubtedly the present are better than the absent.[6]

An invisible and deceased beloved is out of reach. Spiritual guardianship is pivotal in experiential religiosity. The existential transformation we spoke of earlier is only possible when a person moves into the magnetic force field of a spiritual guardian, someone who is steeped in inward experiences. It rarely ever happens that a person undergoes such a revolution singly and unaided. It is not for nothing that we find it said in the Qur'an:

> Those to the fore, they who are brought nigh to the Throne; a throng of the ancients and how few of the later generations. (56: 10–14)

It is as if, as we move further and further away from the Prophet, as his objective presence dims within us, and as the oversights and veils of history multiply and abound, that quality of being to the fore of faith

---

[5] *Mathnawi*, 2: 1360.
[6] *Mathnawi*, 1: 2974–2976.

and the concomitant existential transformation also become increasingly difficult to attain.

Every people and clan is blessed with its own portion in life. Those who were contemporaries of the Prophet and God's great saints (*awliya'*) had a greater chance to be more blessed in the realm of faith than subsequent peoples. As our religious narratives put it, today, we find ourselves before black ink on white sheets—or words on paper—and intermingled with hundreds of fabrications and distortions and errors, and burdened with dozens of different readings at that. This is how we come to embrace faith. How can we compare our circumstances with a time when the furnace of revelation was still aglow and when Muslims could experience, by the week and by the month, the actual descent of revelation upon the Prophet, the improvement of their lives, the coming and going of angels, and the presence of a heavenly being beside them?

Today, we must think much harder about what we want from the Prophet and what are main expectations of him is. The expectation of the majority is for the Prophet to leave their personalities and their livelihoods alone, not to disturb their enjoyment, not to expect too much of them and to content himself with proposing a few, superficial changes, such as steering clear of certain things in their lives such as pig meat, wine, blood, urine, etc., giving alms and going on the *hajj*. But this is mere obedience and emulation, not faith. And there is a great distance between obedience and faith. There can be no doubt that these acts of obedience are highly laudable and a cause of felicity, but they only alter a few of our affairs. We will only truly benefit from the Prophet's guardianship, ascension and call when we open the page of our hearts to his words, open up our entire existence to him and prepare ourselves for a complete transformation. This is faith. Doing what is permissible and not doing what is impermissible is laudable, but it is not faith. This is "submission" [islam] which is, of course, a station of faith:

> The Bedouins say, 'We believe.' Say: 'You do not believe; rather say, "We surrender", for faith has not yet entered your hearts.' (49: 14)

Yes, you have surrendered and you have altered certain incidentals, but you have not laid down any of the things in your heads. You obey the Prophet's commands but you are still the people you have always been. Where is the person who has changed his entire being?

> I am the (devoted) slave of him who will not sell his existence save to
> that bounteous and munificent Sovereign...
> I am the (devoted) slave of that high-aspiring copper which humbles
> itself to naught but the Elixir.[7]

Copper abandons being copper in contact with the philosopher's stone
(elixir). It trades itself in and gives everything it possesses to acquire a
new existence. This is not to say that it engages in a commercial transaction, as if to say, "I am exactly as I was, I'm just striking a new deal."
No, this is commerce. It is submission and obedience (which is fine, of
course). But it does not constitute following the Prophet in a prophetic
way. The Prophet himself spoke like a merchant at times. The Qur'an,
too, uses the language of commerce on occasion, with such words as
trade, loss, usury, debt and profit appearing therein:

> O believers, shall I direct you to a commerce that shall deliver you from
> a painful chastisement? (61: 10)

Or:

> Those are they that have bought error at the price of guidance and their
> commerce has not profited them. (2: 16)

Or on the payment of interest:

> Who is he that will lend God a good loan, and He will multiply it for
> him manifold? (2: 245)

This is because human beings, throughout the course of their history,
have more often than not had a tradesman-like mentality and orientation and the tradesman tends to invest and expect a profit. The Prophet,
peace be upon him, was aware of this and was content to speak to
most of the people he addressed in this language. He would say, give
something, relinquish some of your comforts and desires, and obtain
something in return from God. But it would be mistaken to imagine
that this was the sum total of the Prophet's aspiration and mission. As
Rumi says:

> The prophets, every one, ply this same trade: the people (to whom they are
> sent) are (really) destitute, (yet) they (the prophets) practise beggary,
> Crying, "*Lend to God, lend to God*," and persevering contrariously in (the
> exhortation) "Help God!"[8]

---

[7] *Mathnawi*, 5: 490, 492.
[8] *Mathnawi*, 5: 2700–2701.

It is valuable if a person does not commit certain sins for fear of the torments of hell, or if he carries out certain charitable deeds in the hope of blessings in the hereafter. Nonetheless, this is not the highest order of faith; it is to remain in one's former identity and to effect some changes to one's affairs and contingent traits. This is not to abandon the self. This is not to trade in one's entire being. This is not what copper does when it rubs against the elixir. True faith is a true gamble. It is a forfeiting of the self. It is an upheaval and a revolution. It is to understand that the human being is himself a veil and, to tear this veil, he must tear himself. This is a lover's experience. When lovers abandon themselves to the beloved and experience a complete transformation, they do not do so by choice or as an act of volition. They simply lose themselves in the attractions of the beloved and become someone else altogether. This is religiosity in the third sense, which is the essence and truth of faith. This type of faith is a courageous and loving leap, of which prophets are the greatest instructors. And they speak of it patiently and undemandingly, knowing that it cannot be expected of everyone and that it is not possible for everyone. It is a rich and profound blessing, and anyone who attains it can only be grateful to God. This is why the presence of the great prophets must be seen as a blessing granted by God to humanity. Thanks to the shining rays of prophets' beings, a new horizon opens up before humans, giving them the opportunity to undergo a most fundamental change, a change that will set their former beings ablaze with its auspicious spark and set them on an irreversible journey that leads to heaven and God's paradise. And those who are so blessed, may they be eternally grateful to God.

A question may arise here that if most people have not benefited from the Prophet's call, how can we suggest that most people are rightly-guided, an idea put forward in my treatment of religious pluralism? The answer is that when I say that most people have not benefited from what the Prophet truly wanted of them relates to the kind of passionate faith that brings about a transformation in a person's entire being. Few people have been blessed with this level of faith. But most people have been blessed with rightful guidance in a general sense and they have, by and large, used it in a tradesman-like way. They obey the Prophet's dos and don'ts and reap the benefits. This is guidance too, but it is not the highest form of guidance, which involves partaking in the Prophet's experiences and rapture. Few people have been blessed and will be blessed with this latter form of guidance. Hence, what I am suggesting here is perfectly compatible with religious pluralism. In the debate on pluralism, I am not saying that everyone has benefited from every order of guidance from the very highest to the very lowest, but that people generally benefit from rightful guidance to some degree and that prophets have, therefore, succeeded in their task.

If we examine the records of prophets' achievements, we can see that they were successful and that their call reached the majority of the people. People more or less accepted the values that prophets revered and arrived at a kind of positive satiety, rather than a negative satiety with respect to prophets' teachings. (Positive satiety in the sense of "falling in with" and negative satiety in the sense of "turning one's back on".) But this is not to say that everyone experienced that colossal, extraordinary and rare transformation of the self. This is something for the minority.

CHAPTER ELEVEN

FAITH AND HOPE[1]

In this discussion, I will elaborate on the meaning of religious faith and its relationship to religious experience, religious convictions and religious practices. Then, I will discuss the impact of critical rationalism on faith and how faith manifests in different types of religiousity.

Religious Faith

Religious faith, as I understand it, consists of believing in and becoming attached to someone, as well as trusting them, thinking well of them and loving them. In saying this, I have mainly defined faith in God, because God is the central axis of monotheistic belief systems. Faith cannot be equated with belief per se; not every instance of belief—even dogmatic belief—can be seen as an instance of faith, because in faith you not only have belief, but you also have trust, commitment, devotion, love, humility and submission. We have many beliefs which, while being matters of absolute certainty, are not described as matters of faith. For example, on the basis of our religious teachings, we have total conviction in the existence of Satan. But we certainly do not have faith in Satan, because we do not consider him worthy of our trust and see no virtue in him.

The same can be said of certain things that fall under the rubric of science and philosophy. It would be difficult to say that philosophers have faith in the principality/facticity of existence (*esalat-e wujud*) or in the principle of causality.[2] Or that scientists have faith in atomic theory.

---

[1] This article is from Soroush's book: *Akhlaq-e Khodayan*. Some changes are made here to both its format and content by the author.

[2] Prior to Sadr al-din Shirazi (c. 1571–1640), Muslim philosophers would think that quiddities are matters of fact and their existences are abstractions from their facticity. But according to Sadr al-din Shirazi it is the other way around. Rather than quiddities, existence is the real substrate of things and quiddities are mere abstractions. This is the theory of principality/facticity of existence (*esalat-e wujud*). [Ed.]

The reason for this does not lie in any lack of certitude or conviction in these theories; it is simply that other requirements and conditions must be met, alongside belief, for us to be able to use the word "faith" in any meaningful sense.

When religious faith—in the sense and with the conditions I have set out here—comes about in someone's mind or heart, there is a complete transformation in their entire being. This transformation in one's very being is different from any transformation that may occur merely in one's mind. A believer surrenders their entire being to their faith. And, as some philosophers have put it, faith gives a person a whole new existence and life; it does not just plant a new piece of data in their minds. This devout existence is the very opposite of an a non-devout existence. A non-devout being is essentially bent on rejection, disobedience and denial, whereas a devout being is brimming with humility and surrender. If we turn to religious texts, we find evidence corroborating this interpretation. There is a verse in the Qur'an, for example, that states:

> ...those only are believers who, when God is mentioned, feel a tremor in their hearts, and when His Signs are recited to them, it increases them in faith, and in their Lord they put their trust. (8: 2)

The tremor in the heart is a sign of humility and surrender, and it is an indication of the relationship of love and submission between the faithful and the object of faith. It is also clear that trust is one of the other attributes of the faithful and, without entrusting oneself, faith is incomplete, such that the inclusion of trust in the definition of faith must be seen as an analytic inclusion, not as a necessary or incidental attribute. Or take the following verse:

> Only those believe in Our Signs, who, when they are recited to them, fall down prostrate and proclaim the praise of their Lord, not waxing proud. Their sides shun their beds of sleep as they call on their Lord in fear and hope. (32: 15–16)

Here, too, prostrating oneself, humility, hope and trust have been depicted as signs of faith. Faith, as I have described it, admits of degree, just as love can grow and grow, and just as trust and commitment and devotion may abate or intensify. The discovery of the object of faith's merits and goodness and beauty and majesty is a gradual process and can, therefore, strengthen a person's faith. This is why the believer can grow more corpulent or more lean in terms of faith, just as a disbeliever can be afflicted with corpulence or leanness.

I have deliberately not referred to certitude or unwavering belief, because including certitude in the definition of faith is problematic and suspect. Some Muslim thinkers have defined faith as dogmatic and unwavering belief. And when they've encountered the idea that faith admits of degree (something that is explicitly stated in the Qur'an), they have resorted to contrivances and tried to explain it as relating to the corollaries of faith, not it esessence. Of course, certitude does not admit of degree, but faith does, and this is itself a reason for believing that faith and certitude are not one and the same thing. In faith, there must be a degree of conviction. As long as a person is more convinced about something or someone's existence and goodness—rather than their non-existence—and, as long as, on this basis, the person takes a risk and grows fond of that being and dares to hope and, sensing a certain amount of success, finds their hope, trust and conviction fortified and embarks on even greater hopes, risks and sacrifices, this person can be described as a faithful. Here, the elements of risking, hoping and entrusting oneself gain higher marks than certitude and absolute conviction. We see an example of this in Rumi's response to Shams' call. He took a lover's gamble and relinquished everything he had with magnanimity.

The terms hope, doubt, longing, trust, etc. have been used so often in the Qur'an in connection with faith as to lend credence to the idea that, as far as the Qur'an is concerned, faith is comprised of these components. Hence, certitude ought to be nudged in their direction, not they in the direction of certitude. That is to say, certitude must be defined with reference to them, not they with reference to certitude. Faith, as Rumi describes it, is beating on a door in the hope that a head will emerge, throwing oneself into flames in the hope of finding light, investing in the hope of a gain. This investment involves taking a risk but anyone who refuses to invest for fear of a loss stands to lose even more.

> The merchant of timid disposition and frail spirit neither gains nor loses in his quest; Nay, he suffers loss, for he is deprived (of fortune) and despicable: (only) he that is an eater of flames (ardent in search) will find the light.

> Inasmuch as all affairs depend upon 'maybe', the affair of religion is most Worthy (to inspire hope), for by this means you may win salvation.

Here it is not permitted to knock at the door (with importunity); naught but hope (is permissible): God best knoweth the right course.[3]

Was the Prophet not referring to this same element of risk when he invited people to "a religious trade":

O, ye who believe! Shall I lead you to a bargain/trade that will save you from a grievous penalty? (61–10).

In the history of Christianity, for its part, the role played by certitude in faith is so negative that a great thinker—theologian like Thomas Aquinas saw uncertainty as the very terrain and bedrock of faith. He said that, if there is indisputable evidence demonstrating the veracity of something then certitude will ensue inevitably and passively, and there'll be no room for the "act of faith". It is the paucity of corroborating evidence that creates space for faith and risk and hope. In Protestantism and for Luther, too, trust plays a bigger part in faith than certitude and conviction. Research by Wilfred Cantwell Smith, the contemporary Canadian religious theorist, also shows that, for Christians in the early centuries, faith tended to convey a sense of trust, rather than certitude and absolute conviction.[4] It should be pointed out that the argument here is that faith does not begin with certitude and is not necessarily based on it; it is not being suggested that faith is incompatible with certitude or cannot end up as certitude. In brief, the fact that faith is an act on the part of the faithful (as opposed to the passivity of certitude) and the fact that it admits of degree (as opposed to the static nature of certitude) means that they are two different things.

Religious Experience: Cause or Reason for Faith

As to the religious experience: I believe that religious experience is both the cause of and the reason for faith. If you do not like the word "experience", we can use the word "disclosure". In any religious experience or disclosure, a being, a truth or a secret unveils itself to the person. This secret or truth is on occasion so beautiful, enchanting, glorious

---

[3] *Mathnawi*, 3: 3087–3090.
[4] See: R. Swinburne, *Faith and Reason* (New York: Oxford University Press, 1981); E. Gilson, *Reason and Revelation in the Middle Ages* (New York: C. Scribner's Sons, 1966); W. C. Smith, *The Meaning and End of Religion* (New York: Macmillan, 1963); idem, *Faith and Belief* (Princeton: Princeton University Press, 1979).

and majestic as to engulf the discoverer's entire being and make them fall under its spell. An occurrence of this kind produces most of the characteristics we attributed to faith, such as belief, trust, commitment, devotion, humility and submission, and transforms the person into a faithful. This faith is unwilled and lacks the component of risk; it only exists in the state of trance. When the person comes to and begins to think about the experience, then the element of risk comes into play. Faced with distractions and temptations, they must choose their path and rely on their discovery. It is at this point that faith is born as "an act" and it consists of a mixture of knowledge, will, love and hope.

Religious beliefs, for their part, formulate religious experiences and religious disclosures into theories. In fact, the relationship between religious beliefs and religious experiences is the relationship that philosophers establish between "conceptual knowledge" and "pre-conceptual knowledge". "Pre-conceptual knowledge" consists of naked and unmediated pieces of information which have not yet been covered up with theoretical garments. We may even describe "pre-conceptual knowledge" as knowledge combined with oblivion, that is to say, a kind of unconscious or oblivious knowledge. But when the mind begins to formulate things, the formless knowledge gets formed; in other words, the discoveries are formulated into concepts and propositions that are objective and inter-subjective and can be presented to others. These terms and propositions are also non-personal, cultural and contemporaneous, that is to say, they are entirely in keeping with the subject's culture.

Religious practice, in turn, abates and intensifies along with the abatement and intensification of faith. In other words, religious faith produces the will to action. When faith is stronger, the will to action is correspondingly stronger. A number of contemporary analytical philosophers, and even some past theologians, have considered action to be analytically entailed by belief, such that inaction for them implies lack of belief. The story of "the station between two stations" (*manzelah bayn-e manzelatein*) and the debate over the question whether a sinful person can be properly called a true believer and the hot controversies among the Ash'arites, Mu'tazilites and the Shi'is over these issues are only too well-known.

As a simple example, take Al-Ghazali. Al-Ghazali was someone whose very existence was interwoven with the fear of God. This fear was not just something that he had experienced once; it had come to engulf his whole being. The fear that permeated Al-Ghazali's being also guided his actions. In the first instance, he experienced a terrifying God. Then he placed his faith in Him. And later still, he produced a theory in keeping with this awesome God and presented it in various forms in his writings. His belief in this awesome God also affected his deeds and, when a God of this nature had appeared to him, he abandoned all joyful life. He fled from Baghdad to Damascus and became a recluse there. Even on his return to Khorasan, when Sultan Sanjar, the Seljuq king, and the military commanders invited him to resume his teaching post at the academy, he declined, saying he had made a pact with God and did not wish to break it. This was the nature of Al-Ghazali's religious experience and faith. As to the experience and faith of the Prophet, it is clear for all to see: it all began in the cave of Hira and his experience in that cave became the basis of all his subsequent thoughts and deeds. As Mohammad Iqbal says in his poem: "He [the Prophet] retreated to Hira; then there he produced a people, a religion and a state."

Yes, along with faith, an individual will always also acquire an image and form of the object of faith; there is no escaping this. The two things are interwoven. Nonetheless, they are not one and the same. The substance (matter) of religious beliefs is provided by experience; its form, by the culture of the age and the discoverer's conceptual resources; and, faith, by will, love and hope.

Forming the Formless

Also, there can be no doubt that religious environments are conducive and predisposed to religious experiences and beliefs, and that they give a sense and form to religious discoveries and lend them conceptual formulation. There can also be no doubt that religion and religious theories have tended to be cumulative; that is to say, subsequent experiences are built upon previous experiences, completing one another and growing, in a sense. But to suggest that the first experience must itself have come about in a religious culture, this is much more dubious. Here, cause and effect are so interwoven as to make it difficult to disentangle them. As Walter Stace has shown in his book *Mysticism and Philosophy*,[5] the religious experiences of mystics throughout history and within a variety of cultures have been so similar and have had

---

[5] Walter Terence Stace, *Mysticism and Philosophy*.

so many common features as to make it possible to say that religious experiences occur independently of religious cultures. But when they are recounted and presented to others, they are expressed in terms of the prevailing religious concepts and culture. We must not forget something that Rumi tells us repeatedly: in a religious experience, the person involved has a formless experience and then they put a form on it. Hence, the naked experience is always covered up by some garment and the garment is cut and sewn from the available material. This material varies from age to age. Hence the garments are age-bound. In theological jargons: no transcendence without anthropomorphism. And, as Rumi puts it:

> The form came forth from Formlessness and went back (thither), for *Verily unto Him are we returning*.[6]

Now, we might raise the question as to whether any of these forms are more in keeping with that formless experience? Or do all the forms stand in an equal relationship to it? This is a question that needs to be borne in mind in any discussion about the relationship between religious experience and religious belief: can any one theological systems based on religious experience claim to be closer to that formless core?

Of course, the experienced-based faith is by nature very rare. Therefore, what I have been speaking about is faith as an ideal type or in its purest form; in itself not for us; in principle not in practice. This was all at the level of the in itself, not the for us; in the context of definition, not realization. But as you know, we rarely encounter anything in its purest form in our lives. For example, if we were to define quintessential water it would be one thing; real water, another. Quintessential water is neither hot, nor cold; neither salty, nor muddy; and so on and so forth. But the water that exists in jugs and brooks and oceans tends to have a combination of these qualities.

When we speak about faith in relation to the bulk of the people, we have in mind the attachment, belief and hope that I mentioned, which can result from personal experience, inculcation, habit, education, upbringing or anything else. The fact of the matter is that religions themselves recognise and allow this kind of faith. And we certainly have no wish to disallow it. But if these faint, diluted faiths cannot draw strength from pure, concentrated faiths, they will be unstable and

---

[6] *Mathnawi*, 1: 1141.

transient. Pure religious faith and experience is what prophets have. Their faith has reasons as well as causes. But the faith of the bulk of the people is usually caused not reasoned; passive, not active; determined, not willed; unconscious, not conscious.

The faith of most believers is mediated faith. That is to say, they do not usually have direct experience of the transcendental. But since they trust the Prophet, they find God in this way, through him. And, in the course of their lives, for instance, if some of their prayers are answered, their faith may become more intense; otherwise, not. This is why, in my discussions on prophethood, I have emphasised the point that, in monotheistic religions, the prophet is a key, matchless factor. And most believers first place their faith in their prophet and find God in this way and make Him the object of their faith.

At any rate, whether it is the prophetic experience or an individual's religious experience, this is a necessary condition (not a sufficient condition) of the birth of a phenomenon known as faith in history and in the general culture of humanity. Then, it is necessary to have a will to action and hope, so that the leap of faith is made possible. Today, we tend to say that someone has faith if they display the general qualities and symptoms brought about by a faith-giving experience; qualities such as belief, humility, devotion, submission, surrender, trust and the like. They cannot be said to have logical certitude, but they have faith. And their faith is acceptable to the founders of religions. The fact that you see that sowing doubt is discouraged in religion and that there are even some harsh precepts against apostates and heretics shows that the Legislator knew that believers' convictions are unsteady and can be shaken; they are nonetheless described as believers, because they display trust, humility and devotion towards the object of faith, and these are qualities that follow from faith.

* * *

Doubts and Criticisms

I believe that the most important criticism that can be directed at the formulations of religious experiences has to do with whether a formulation is in keeping with the experience. This kind of criticism is, of course, different from any scientific or philosophical criticism that would concern itself with these formulations in their own right and their relationship to one another. Also, one meaning of the veracity of religious beliefs is harmony and accord between a person's religious beliefs and the views and theories that exist in the other fields of human knowledge and discovery. The truth table approach tells us that, wherever they may be, truths must be in accord. This is one type of criticism. Hence, one of the duties of a pious person or theologian is to establish accord between their religious findings and other human findings.

Another meaning of veracity, which is "correspondence with fact", guides us towards another type of criticism. That is to say, if we believe that religious theories are, in reality, garments thrown over naked experiences, the question that needs to be asked is whether these garments are well-fitting or not? Answering this question is, in my view, extremely difficult, which redoubles the need for investigation and criticism. The person who has had the experience must constantly ask themselves: is this theoretical formulation in keeping with what I experienced or not? Here, the question I raised earlier comes into its own: can it be said that some of the forms that we lend to a formless entity are more appropriate to it than others? Does an utterly formless entity not stand in exactly the same relationship to all forms? If we accept that all physiognomies are equally similar or dissimilar to that formless entity and that all theories are, in a sense, equally valid, then the way will be open to theological pluralism and pluralistic belief.

In any event, I believe that the door is never closed to the criticism of religious beliefs and experiences, and both the person who has had the experience and the people who hear and learn about it must never lay down the banner of criticism. If we accept that, at least at the level of expression and presentation, experiences always draw on the existing reservoir of judgements and concepts, then we must constantly review, elucidate and clarify this reservoir in order to refine those forms and beliefs. Hence, the criticism of religious experiences and beliefs is always oriented towards the removal of the outer garments and layers in order to move closer to the inner layers of religious experience and belief. Of course, this type of criticism robs us of mundane faith. But why should we worry about that? If we come to the conclusion that faith is something that is attained gradually and that it can abate and intensify and be refined and purified, then we will not see any contradiction between the examination of faith and faith itself. There is no conceptual or judgemental incongruity between faith and belief, on the one hand, and change and criticism, on the other. What logic and conceptual coherence rule out is the combination of change and certitude, but certitude, as we saw, is not entailed either by faith or belief.

A person who has a religious experience is a sculptor who is never satisfied with the figure he sculpts. He is constantly chipping away at it, remoulding it and shaping it into a new form.

> Do not be intoxicated with these cups, which are (phenomenal) forms, lest thou become a carver of idols and an idolater.
> Abandon the cups, namely, the (phenomenal) forms; do not tarry!
> There is wine in the cup, but it is not (derived) from the cup.[7]

The question may arise that would not this constant process of doubt and rational criticism may pose serious threats to the very foundation of faith and disturb the believer's mental and psychological serenity and stability?

In my discussion on "Types of Religiosity", I was in fact trying to answer these kinds of questions. The truth of the matter is that we have to distinguish between different types of religiosity. In the faith of the bulk of the people, there's no place for whys and wherefores. This kind of faith will become more fragile if subjected to questions and criticism and will ultimately fall into decline. This is why, in the realm of communal religiosity, religion turns into a half-congealed, half-dogmatic ritual. Throughout the course of history, the general mass of believers have followed this kind of religion and faith. But we have two other types of religiosity as well: discursive religiosity and experiential religiosity. Discursive religiosity has basically come into being through questioning and it thrives on questioning. Pragmatic/instrumental religiosity did not come into being on the basis of questioning, but on the basis of imitation, so it thrives on imitation and its survival depends on imitation. The minute it is confronted with questions and criticism, it melts like snow. But how can discursive religiosity, which in fact begins with questions and criticism, ever conceive of an end to this questioning? No one can claim that there exist only one type of religiosity, that is, the imitative, pragmatic, ritualistic, mythical religiosity of the general masses. We must also accord recognition to discursive religiosity. On the testimony of history and the testimony of the discipline of theology (which has consistently existed among the followers of all religions), as

---

[7] *Mathnawi*, 6: 3707–3708.

well as on the testimony of the human intellect—which is essentially given to rationality and inquiry and cannot be banned from posing questions—discursive religiosity has existed and will continue to exist. Hence, if we accept that there is a type of religiosity that begins with criticism and questions, we cannot construct a barrier halfway down its path and ask the gnostic believer to proceed no further. We therefore have to accept that there is also a probing type of faith as well as an imitative type. This probing faith will find and has found its own way. We have had many examples of theologians, scholars and philosophers who, while persisting in their faith, were engaged in a permanent process of refining their beliefs and looking for possible errors. Also there were times when they experienced serious misgivings and doubts, but since these misgivings arose from faith, we see this as a virtue rather than a vice.

Of course, the individual is terrified by such misgivings because they are afraid of losing their trust, commitment and devotion. Hence these fears and concerns are faith-based. It is like a problem arising between you and your friend. When this happens, you can do one of two things: one, you can use it as an excuse to break off your friendship; two, you can use it as an excuse to ensure that you don't lose them and do your utmost to preserve the friendship. In exactly the same way, as long as the urge to preserve faith, commitment and trust is there, it has to be seen as a misgiving within faith, a misgiving which implies no lack of faith, which is, on the contrary, identical to faith and an example of the risk of faith. As Rumi put it: "I tremble over my faith like a mother over her child." In this light, the weakness and strength that the person experiences along this path are a weakness and strength that is intrinsic to the game of faith. It is like a battle in which you occasionally advance and you occasionally retreat; but all this advancing and retreating amounts to the same thing: fighting and overpowering the enemy. You will also find this in experiential religiosity where mystics have spoken repeatedly and in different terms about the contractions and expansions they have experienced. At times the Beloved was hidden to the mystic and, at times, the Beloved appeared to them. Sometimes their nights were as bright as days; at other times, their days as dark as nights. But, despite all these trials and tribulations, they remained true to their faith and were people of faith.

Of course, if the foundations of faith collapse altogether, faith will become impossible. Faith and trust demand a minimum of conviction.

This is generally and conditionally the case. For every faith, a particular precept applies that must be fulfilled directly and cannot be deduced from that conditional proposition.

I will repeat again: faith is something that admits of weakness and strength, that trembles and even upends. All these conditions are permissible within faith (quintessentially), and so much the more so for the actually existing faiths, which are like muddy waters and afflicted with a variety of ailments. God Himself reveals in the Qur'an the tremors that some believers undergo: "…the believers were tried, and they were shaken most mightily." (33, 11) In any great trial or test, there is always severe tremors and turbulence. Like autumn winds, this turbulence tears some leaves off the tree and leaves some in place. This is in the nature of a leaf: it is clinging to the tree by a thin thread. A storm may on occasion uproot the tree itself; what, then, can you expect of a poor leaf?

Now, in the field of discursive religiosity certain developments in recent centuries such as the emergence of new formulations of the "problem of evil" and specially the mechanical (naturalistic) explanation of the world, etc. have posed a serious threat to the religious faith and apparently have led to the abatement of the will to believe on the part of the believers.

It was not without reason that people like Al-Ghazali, in the past, were so hostile to the field of theology and that Rumi believed that "the leg of the syllogists is made of wood", that they made the path to guidance more onerous and that doubt considered to be in deep association with gnostic-based faith. Again it was not without reason that some people saw the growth of the field of theology as a sign of the weakness of faith. They had condescendingly tell theologians that when a person turns from experience to theory, it shows that the fire of experience has cooled; that it amounts to leaving the orbit of faith and busying oneself with the secondary aspects of faith instead.

At any rate, this is nothing new and we see this phenomenon in every religion's history. All the same, as philosophers have always said, refuting the premised does not necessarily lead to the refutation of the conclusion. In other words, if you disprove the reasons for the existence of something, you cannot conclude that that thing does not exist. Even if we disprove all the reasons for the existence of God, it does not mean that God does not exist. It only means that we have no reasons for His existence. This is why, both for pragmatic and experiential believers, disproving the reasons for the existence of God does not undermine their faith. They did not obtain their faith through reasoning so it isn't shaken if the reasons are disproved.

However, there is no denying that discursive religiosity is somehow different. When someone enters the arena of criticism and theory, then they will be buffeted by strong storms. These storms may at times weaken and undermine their faith and, at times, strengthen it. Here we have a full scale battle scene and, in battle, you cannot afford to fall sleep. Both doubt and certitude spring forth from evidence and reason. Under the bombardment of reasons, doubt and certitude are, therefore, bound to abate and intensify. In the science of probabilities there is a rule that says: all probability is conditional. In other words, an event can become more or less probable depending on the conditions surrounding it. By the same token, rational certitude is likewise always conditional; if the conditions change, so certitude is pulled this way and that.

In view of all this, gnostic believers must not compare their religiosity to the religiosity of pragmatic and utilitarian believers. They must not imagine that the more thoughtless a person is, the more pious they are. This is totally false. In fact, this is one point on which Al-Ghazali is open to reproach. When Al-Ghazali abandoned discursive religiosity, he began to long for a return to the common's type of faith. He says somewhere that the concerns and dilemmas that a theologian experiences in the course of their lifetime may flare up when they are on their deathbed and they may, then, leave the world faithlessly; whereas an old woman who has never known such concerns and dilemmas and whose faith has not been tainted with theology will leave the world piously. This is a surprising judgement coming from Al-Ghazali. If a gnostic believer and theologian—who has stepped onto the terrain of qualms and dilemmas—persists along this path with sincerity and strives to discover and understand the truth, he will be a true player in the field of faith.

I have said a great deal but one important point remains to be said and that is that everything that befalls a human being is humane. Human beings cannot be asked to do something that is beyond their capacities. Faith, doubt, certitude, struggle, etc., are all human affairs and we cannot expect them to be otherwise. Apart from people who are asleep or frozen, everyone experiences qualms and misgivings and highs and lows. The ocean of everyone's existence undergoes fierce storms and turbulence. As Rumi says:

> It has come down in the traditions (of the Prophet) that the heart is like a feather in a desert, the captive of a violent blast.[8]

Or,

> The fierce waves of the seas of the Spirit are a hundred times as many as was (the multitude of waves in) the Flood of Noah.[9]

Human beings are not like mountains; they are like oceans. Hence their faith is ocean-like and turbulent too. It would be strange if they were always placid. "If innocent Adam succumbed to sin / who are we to claim to be free of it?"[10] If Adam suffered from temptations and dilemmas, how can we ordinary mortals be expected not to be sucked into the whirlwind of temptation and not to tremble like willows? Mundane, pragmatic religiosity seems to be the only exception to this rule; but experiential and discursive religiosity are both equally subject to it. We must correct our image of human beings and see placid faith as a weak, diluted and deficient form of the phenomenon, not as a model of true faith.

According to Islamic story of Adam, human beings' descent to earth and their life in this world followed from two "original" sins: one was Satan's sin in not prostrating himself before Adam and, the other, Adam's sin in eating the forbidden fruit, which itself resulted from a frailty of will: "We had already, beforehand, taken the covenant of Adam. But he forgot: and We found in him no constancy." (20: 115) Hence, people who want to return human beings to a blissful paradise and a placid swamp must turn back the clock, go as far back as Adam and dissuade him from the original sin!

Of course, it is common knowledge that new philosophies are, more often than not, non-religious philosophies. They are basically not intended for or geared to proving religious claims; unlike older philosophies and, especially, what is described as Islamic philosophy. In the past, the religious climate of societies made it impossible to draw non-religious or irreligious conclusions from philosophy. Even if such conclusions were drawn, they did not gain prevalence. But in modern secular and liberal societies, some philosophical teachings are completely at odds with past religious teachings. It is on this basis that

---

[8] *Mathnawi*, 3: 1639.
[9] *Mathnawi*, 6: 2084.
[10] Hafez, *Divan*.

I think discursive religiosity today has become heftier, as well as more difficult and more valuable, than discursive religiosity in the past.

Need for Religious Experience

I have already suggested in Chapter Nine that, in the modern world, we must continue the path of the prophets. In other words, we need to bring religious experiences back to life in order to allow the construction of a new theology. In other words, to allow create a garment for those naked experiences woven of the language of the age we leave in. If the passion of religious experiences subsides, no theory in the world will really be able to revive and rekindle religious faith. Rumi use to say: "Sometimes a locksmith makes locks and sometimes he makes keys". Today, lock making seems to be all the rage! The possibility of religious experience has, therefore, declined drastically. Of course, the difficulty of religious experience has made one thing more clear: the chance of any claims to prophethood seems remote and implausible in the modern world. Hence, it can be said with greater certainty that the Prophet of Islam was the Seal of all prophets. That is to say, the historical climate is no longer conducive to prophets. As I said in Chapters Two and Three, the world has been so demystified that it has become much more difficult to attain the intense and rich, prophet-like experiences.

Having said all this, nevertheless I think it may be possible to say that all three types of religiosity are tending to become heftier and stronger. Pragmatic religiosity is continuing to play its role in reassuring believers and it has an elaborate clerical machinery. Discursive religiosity has become much more hefty, in view of the books that have been written and are being written on the subject and in view of the extensive and comprehensive scholarly debates and critiques that are taking place in connection with this type of religiosity. As for experiential religiosity, it has gained more supplicants, who yearn for it, since the other two types of religiosity are not entirely satiating. Today there are many non-religious people who long for a shred of the religious faith possessed by believers. This longing will do its trick one day. At any rate, one thing is certain: in the modern, demystified world, the God discovered by believers and the theories woven around Him may well be different from those of the past.

To be sure, not that all scholarly debates over religion is produced by believers. However, a good number of the scholars involved in discursive religiosity are believers themselves. Discursive religiosity is nourished by criticism and questions. Nonetheless, the concerns of the gnostic are the concerns of the pious; these are not detached and dispassionate mental processes. In other words, it's not as if they approach religious questions in the way a mathematician approaches numerical puzzles. Quite the reverse. They enter this field on the basis of commitment to theology and piety. It also has to be said that discursive religiosity should be seen as a collective endeavour in which there are both victories and defeats. In other words, part of the collective may be suffering from weakness, while another part is enjoying strength. A new discovery or theory, or the resolution of a doubt may intensify some people's faith, just as the emergence of a new doubt may diminish some people's faith. The history of theology is replete with such victories and defeats. Anyone who looks at these endeavours as a whole may decide that, in this battle, the defeats have outnumbered the victories; or they may conclude that there have been more victories than defeats. In truth, I have no reason to believe that the defeats have outnumbered the victories or to draw the conclusion, on this basis, that this process has caused more harm than good. And none of the distinguished people who have spoken about this subject have presented any reason that would corroborate such a position. The important point is that, today, discursive religiosity has become a need like food—and not just as "medicine", to borrow al-Ghazali's analogy.

Furthermore, if we assume the necessity of a clear mind, free of contradictions and open to correct information, for the interpretation of experiences, we can say that the refinement of religious beliefs will help improve and further rectify the interpretation of religious experiences. This, too, may be one of the blessings of theology and discursive religiosity. It is the story of Moses and the shepherd all over again.[11] Shepherds have experiences and people like Moses concern themselves with the interpretation of experiences. Those who are afire with passion need those who are steeped in learning, the gamblers need the enlighteners. Scholars and theologians can fill the knowledge vacuum.

Religion has suffered far more from dogmatism, opportunism and greed than from the doubts raised by scholarly gnosticism. Hence, if we are to build a barrier against something, it should not be against

---

[11] For a summary of the story see "Straight Paths 1" in this volume.

the spread of gnosticism but against demagoguery and opportunism perpetuated in the name of religion. Whatever else we might say about theologians, we have to acknowledge that they keep alight the flame of wisdom and religion-mindedness, and our whole discussion here about faith, hope and certitude falls within the framework of discursive religiosity. We must therefore applaud theologians and value their efforts. We must celebrate their victories and not be alarmed by or resentful of their defeats; for today's defeats can pave the way for tomorrow's victories. Let's not forget that all these debates are about the preservation of faith and are replete with faith. A historian once said about Darwin's theory that Darwin had delivered a blow to the study of God that no atheist had ever been able to do. Atheists kept alive the debate about the existence or non-existence of God, but, with his theory, Darwin rendered the whole debate unnecessary and pointless. Once this occurs, we have stepped into the arena of irreligiosity; but as long as there are discussions about the existence of God, religious experience, the truth of faith, Satan, the existence of the other world and so on, we should be glad, because it keeps the flame of religion alight.

*　*　*

Relation of Legal Precepts to Formless Experience

Another question remains that: can we see Scripture itself, which is the outcome of prophetic experience, as a form over that formless entity or a garment sewn over that core? If so, should we abide by the form or the formless entity? Scripture, especially in Islam, consists of two parts. One part is comprised of mythical forms thrown over the truth. The other part is concerned with life, transactions and laws, where God plays the role of the commander of that which must be done and that which must not be done; or, rather, the commander and the legislator is the Prophet, and God has affirmed his legislation. At any rate, the elements that relate to commands and jurisprudential and legal regulations are not at all of the nature of forming the formless. As to the first part, that is, the propositions that relate to God, resurrection, Satan, creation and so on, these are all of the nature of mythical forms over formless experience. As a matter of fact different religions are like different forms over some formless disclosures. One belongs to the Prophet of Islam, another to Jesus Christ and so on. All the forms

stand in the same relation to that formless absolute. If we wanted to
resort to an analogy, we would have to say that these forms and that
formless entity stand in the same relationship as languages to a thought.
Thought is that formless entity and languages are the external forms
thrown over that thought. All languages stand in the same relationship
to that language-less thought, but the languages are all different from
one another and stand in different relationships to us. A Chinese person
can understand Chinese better than English and the reverse can be said
of an English person. And thoughts in a Chinese person's mind take on
a Chinese demeanour and, in an Indian's mind, an Indian demeanour.
The thoughts themselves may vary in terms of richness and depth, and
this, in turn, is reflected in the languages and their manifestations. The
followers of prophets see their leader's revelation as self-contained and
complete and, on this basis, they distinguish between the prophets. And,
in order to prove these distinctions, they point to the physiognomies
drawn over that formless entity.

As to the question of whether one can forego the existing forms
or not, it has to be said that, rationally, individuals are entitled to do
so and to lend a new form to their formless experience. But, first of
all, most people do not have a formless experience, so the question
of giving it a form does not arise. They must, therefore, rely on the
prophets and be grateful to them. Secondly, people who do have this
experience—in other words, mystics—while being entitled to lend a
new form to their experience, must bear in mind two points: one, from
the social perspective, as long as they are living within a community
of pragmatic believers, they must conform and not speak about their
new forms. The prophets and, especially, the Prophet of Islam, were
saying that they had founded a community and a civilization based
on certain myths and physiognomies pertaining to the truth, and they
would not allow anyone to wreck these. The other point is that, from a
personal perspective, the individual must not forget that these existing
forms have a history and a tradition, and it would be best not to cut
oneself off from all this and ensure that one's brook is attached to the
sea. In other words, they must not be indifferent to their forbearers'
formulations and forms. After all, they treaded this same path and may
well have been much more skilled at it than we are.

Of course, if you take the bulk of Muslims, their entire identity has
been dependent on the text and their reference point has always been
the Qur'an and the *Sunna*. As to those exceptional individuals who
have had their own direct experience, they were never text-bound to

begin with. In fact, that is what was meant by allegorical interpretation (*ta'wil*). These interpreters were seemingly bound by the text, but, in fact, they were setting aside the text. This was a matter of degree, of course. Hence, when one says, we will be less text bound, it is just so. We will brush aside some of the forms that belong to a specific time, region or culture and, as Rumi put it, become less drunk from the jug of forms. This process of breaking through the idols of form and melting away the form of idols is a continuous one, for which no end is imaginable. And let us not forget that all of this belongs to the realm of experiential and discursive religiosity. Pragmatic religiosity lives with its mythical forms and does not alter them. Clerics are the guardians of these mythical formulations and they see the preservation of the collective, ritualistic identity of the community as being dependent on the preservation of those ancient, unchanging forms.

One may ask that if you draw a distinction between the form and the formless, or between the text and the experience expressed in the text, it would seem that a believer can only persist in being committed to a particular "form" if they are convinced that, throughout the course of history, that form has been and will continue to be the best covering for that formless entity or the best explanation for that experience. However, in view of our theory of Contraction and Expansion, it would seem that this assumption is not true. It is quite likely that that formless entity will find better explanations and forms in the future.

It is true, for two reasons: one is based on the arguments I presented in the theory of Contraction and Expansion; the other is that it is conceptually difficult to say that one form is eternally superior to another, because that formless entity stands in exactly the same relationship to all forms. It is exactly the same as speaking about the length and width of an abstract transcendental concept. All widths and lengths are equally appropriate to it or equally inappropriate to it. Hence, all the existing forms are equally explanations, models or manifestations of that formless entity. The difference lies in their relationship to us. In Rumi's words, an individual may become more drunk drinking from one jug than from another. This has to do with us, not with that formless entity. The God who appeared to the Prophet of Islam was a beautiful God. The God we know in Islam is the God of the Prophet of Islam. When the Prophet says: "God is beautiful and He loves beauty; I've seen my God in the most beautiful face possiblee", he is describing his own experience of God. God never appeared to the Prophet of Islam with an ugly face, or, if He did, that great man never told us.

But, theoretically speaking—just as the mystics have said—the ugly things in the world are just as much a manifestation of God as the beautiful things; although, as human beings, we tend to be more drawn towards the beautiful than the ugly: we become more drunk from this jug than from that. And, of course, the height of a pious devotee's endeavours is to see that formless wondering in its pure formlessness.

> Formlessness throws you into absolute bewilderment
> From non-instrumentality a hundred kinds of instruments are born.[12]

---

[12] *Mathnawi*, 6: 3714.

CHAPTER TWELVE

SPIRITUAL GUARDIANSHIP AND
POLITICAL GUARDIANSHIP

The occasion of Ghadir Khumm[1] marked the start of profound and important developments in the world of Islam. It had an acute impact both on the theological theories and the social destiny of Muslims, and it ultimately turned into a factor that forged the greatest and most lasting rift in their ranks. It, moreover, contributed to the development of the seminal concept of "guardianship" (*wilayat*), which can easily be described as the most potent and most problematic idea and concept ever to have occurred in the world of Islam. This is why examining this seminal concept and that important incident is among our theological and social duties, and I will try to raise a few points in this respect here.

Ghadir and Some of Its Consequences

As I said, the Ghadir incident had a lasting impact on the Prophet's people both theologically and politically. The secret to this lay in the fact that Muslims disagreed over their reading of the incident and came up with at least two fundamental and notable interpretations, which have endured to this day, with neither abandoning the field in favour of the other. Reliable historical accounts and *mutawatir hadiths*[2] tell

---

[1] Ghadir Khumm is the name of a location between Mecca and Medina where on his way back from his last Hajj pilgrimage, shortly before his death, Prophet Muhammad stopped to address a large gathering of Muslim pilgrims. There he delivered a sermon whose content along with a Qur'anic verse (5: 67) have been the main source of Shi'i's claim of Ali's right to succeed the Prophet. [Ed.]

[2] *Hadith*s, Prophetic Traditions, are classified in different categories according to the level of their authenticity and the soundness of the chain of their transmitters. The highest value is given to *mutawatir hadith*, which had been transmitted by numerous reliable narrators at different stage that the possibility of its being fabricated is excluded. [Ed.]

us that, on the Day of Ghadir, the noble Prophet of Islam presented
Ali to Muslims and said:

> ...Anyone of whom I am the *mawla*, Ali, too, is his *mawla*. O God, be
> a friend to those who befriend him and an enemy to those who show
> hostility to him, support those who support him and abandon those who
> desert him.

This much of the Prophet's sermon is *mutawatir* and accepted by both
branches of Islam, Shi'is and Sunnis.[3] Some Shi'i historians and chroniclers of the Prophet's life have recounted a very long sermon delivered
by him on the Day of Ghadir which is entirely Shi'i in content and
totally conforms to the beliefs that Shi'is were later to insist upon and
to use to differentiate themselves from other Islamic sects.[4]

At any rate, no significant dispute arose over the event itself nor over
the Prophet's words. The disputes began rather over their interpretations. That is to say, the question arose as to what the Prophet had
meant in saying these words in those circumstances. What exactly does
"*mawla*" mean and what position was Ali being appointed to and in
what way did Muslims become duty-bound towards Ali as a result of
the words spoken by the Prophet? Is it the case, as Shi'is claimed later
on, that, on the Day of Ghadir, the Prophet established and imparted
the notion of the Imamate? Did the Prophet appoint a specific person
by the name of Ali (and his children thereafter) to this position, thereby
establishing a new article of faith for Muslims? We are familiar with
the historical and unresolved disputes between Shi'is and Sunnis in this
respect and there is no need to rehearse them again here.[5] Nonetheless
we are concerned with other aspects of the subject now and are not
seeking to prove or disprove either the Shi'i or Sunni position.

As I said, in view of the Day of Ghadir and the phrase used by the
Prophet on the occasion, the important concept of "guardianship"

---

[3] For Shi'i sources see for instance: Allameh Abdulhossein Amini, *Al-Ghadir*;
Muhammad Baqir Majlesi, *Behar al-Anwar*. This event is recorded several times in
different Sunni Tradition literature as well. See for instance its transmission by Ahmad
Ibn Hanbal, the great Sunni traditionist. Reference to this incident and the Prophet's
statement can also be found in other Islamic literature. Jalal al-Din Rumi, for instance,
who was not a Shi'i, has referred to this incident and elucidated the meaning of "*mawla*"
in the *Mathnawi* (Vol. 6, verses 4538–4542).

[4] See for instance Majelsi's *Behar al-Anwar*.

[5] See for instance: Abdulhossein Amini, *Al-Ghadir* (Tehran: Dar al-Kutub al-Islamiyah, *1952*); or the more thorough book which is the product of a Shi'i and a Sunni
theologians' correspondence: Abdulhossein Sharaf al-Din 'Ameli, *al-Muraje'at*.

(*wilayat*) became a widely debated topic among Muslims. Of course, the issue of "guardianship" had already been clearly set out in the Qur'an, with God Himself described as the Guardian (*wali*) of the faithful:

> God is the Guardian (*wali*) of the believers; He brings them forth from the darkness into the light. (2: 257)

Believers are under God's guardianship and one of the consequences of this guardianship is that God brings believers out of the darkness and grants them light. In addition to God's guardianship, there exist also Satan's guardianship as well as the guardianship of idols. The Qur'an tells us that infidels are robbed of light and plunged into darkness by idols.[6] But Satan exercises no mastery or guardianship over believers who have entrusted themselves to God.[7] Satan's rule and mastery only extends to the people who are under his guardianship; that is, people who have opted for his guardianship and have chosen him as their guardian.[8] Be that as it may, what the Prophet said about Ali raised the possibility in the minds of Muslims of the concept of guardianship being associated with a specific individuals and, subsequently, specific people, such that references to it abounded and became commonplace in Shi'i religious literature, and the idea took on a contentious theological life of its own.

Sense and Essence of Spiritual Guardianship

The concept of *wilayat* (guardianship) is also the most central issue in theoretical mysticism. Mysticism is the theory of the immanence and manifestation of God in the world. "Mysticism" should not be taken to mean an ethical demeanour or journey. Of course, mystics are good and pious men, and cleansed of the vices. But mysticism is not an expression of ethical values and judgements. Rather, it is the interpretation of the world in terms of God's attributes and names. This is where the concept of guardian and guardianship enters into mystical

---

[6] "... And the unbelievers—their guardians are idols, that bring them forth from the light into the shadow." (2: 257)

[7] "When thou recitest the Qur'an, seek refuge in God from the accursed Satan; he has no authority over those who believe and trust in their Lord." (16: 99)

[8] "His [Satan's] authority is over those who take him for their friend and ascribe associates to God." (16: 100)

theories. God has attributes and names, and He has manifested Himself in the world through these attributes and names. This world is the manifestation of God. Let us not confuse the theory of manifestation with the theory of causality. Philosophers concentrate all their efforts on arguing that this world is the effect of God. In other words, they present God as "the ultimate cause" and the world as His "effect". They prove God's existence through the theory of causality. May their efforts be appreciated and rewarded! But this is not enough for mystics, for they do not see the relationship between God and the world as merely one of philosophical cause and effect. They take things much further than this. For them, the relationship between this world and God is the relationship between the manifestation and the manifest. It is as if this world is a window in which God displays himself, such that the manifest is present in the manifestation; nay, even further than this, such that this world is not the manifestation of God, but *is* God manifest. When God displays Himself through the window, He is present in the window but, more than this, the window itself is God manifest. That is to say, He does not manifest Himself through the window, He manifests himself as the window. Consequently, it is not a question of saying, look at the world and infer the existence of a creator thereof. This is to take the long way around. Mystics would say, look at this world and you are looking at God. Seeing this world is the same as to see God. In other words, this world is godly and divine, and to live in it is to live in God. Or as *misterum teremendom* precedes any inference to God's existence.

> Verily, there is no evidence for a sun except the light of the lofty sun. Who (what) is the shadow that it should be an evidence for Him? 'Tis enough for it that it should be abased before Him.
> This majesty (which I have attributed to Him) in (the matter of) evidence declares the truth: all perceptions are behind (Him), He is outstripping (them).
> All perceptions are (mounted) on lame asses; He is mounted on the wind that flies like an arrow.[9]

It has been recounted that the Prophet once said: If you throw a rope into a well and allow it to descend to the depths of the earth, it will land on God. In the same vein and in the *Mathnawi*, Rumi recalls the Prophet saying that his Ascension to heaven was no different from

---

[9] *Mathnawi*, 3: 3716–3719.

Jonah's journey to the depths of the sea and into the belly of the fish. "There, too, he found God. There, too, he saw the majesty of God. I ascended to heaven and there, too, I found God. There, too, I saw the majesty of God. Anywhere you go in the universe, you will find God." Ascension is possible in any direction because God is everywhere and, in the words of the Qur'an we read: "…whithersoever you turn, there is the Face of God." (2: 115). Put this alongside the words attributed to Ali which he spoke in response to one of the Jews: A Jewish man asked Imam Ali, where is the Face of God? Ali lit a fire and asked the Jew: Where is the face of the fire? The man replied, its face is everywhere, a fire has no front or back. Ali said, God has no front or back either; everywhere, it is His Face. The Face of God *is* God, so, every which way we turn, there is the Face of God. Of course, Ali offered an answer in keeping with his interlocutor's sensibilities. Rumi spoke of love in these same terms and said that love had no back; it is all face. All this to say that the theory of the manifest and the manifestation goes well beyond the idea of cause and effect and proposes a deeper conception of the relationship between God and the world. Rumi said:

> (But) when a son of man is born twice, he plants his foot upon the head of (all) causes:
> The First Cause is not his religion; the particular (secondary) cause has no enmity against him (does him no harm).[10]

One meaning of this "treading upon the causes" is that such a person would be freed of philosophical cause and effect and would no longer conceive of God as the ultimate cause. "The Prime Mover" is not his religion; rather this person would see God as the manifest present in every aspect and manifestation of the world. He would not sense any distance whatsoever between this world and God. And, once the world becomes a divine manifestation, this person will themselves have attained a special stature. And this is where the idea of "guardianship" begins to enter in. All of God's attributes and names, gentle or harsh, *teremendom* or *facinance*, display themselves in this world and have discernible manifestations. Some beings are like little mirrors in which God cannot appear in His full grandeur. Some beings are the manifestation of all of God's names and this, according to mystics, is "the Perfect Man". Such a person is thereby recognised as "the manifestation

---

[10] *Mathnawi*, 3: 3574–3575.

of God's every attribute" or "the consummate being", and seen as the highest order of existence. "The Perfect Man" is a big mirror that can reflect the divinity's every ray. This is the person who, according to mystics, keeps the world upright: "From your integrity flows the integrity of the universe", as Hafez puts it. And he is God's true vicegerent and His fullest presence and representative in this world.

Rumi conveys this same idea in a veiled form in the tale of the pious mystic Daquqi in the third volume of the *Mathnawi*. There, he says that the story of Moses pursuing Khizr was symbolic in nature. It meant that the Perfect Man possesses every excellence such that even a person of Moses's stature has to seek him out in his own quest for excellence; just as, if an ocean sees a beaker of water, it wants to embrace it so that it can become fuller still.

> If I am seated in the midst of the Sea, yet have I set my desire on the water in the jug.
> I am like David: I have ninety ewes, and yet desire for my rival's ewe hath arisen in me.
> Ah, there is a very occult mystery here (in the fact) that Moses sets out to go towards a Khizr.[11]

Without ever necessarily giving the particulars of any single person or naming anyone, in their theories, mystics considered the existence of such a being as definite, actual and real. This person would be none other than the divine guardian or God's grand saint (*wali-e a'zam*).

The word "guardianship" conveys a sense of unmediated "proximity" and "kinship". "Proximity" has different forms and types. Two people who are fond of each other are one another's guardians. When someone can take unmediated and direct decisions on someone else's behalf, they are that person's guardian. Among the Arabs, the first spring rain is known as "the vernal" (*wasmi*) and the rainfall that follows immediately and directly thereafter is known as "the guardian" (*wali*). The word "succession" (*tawali*) also comes from the same root. A child's father is his guardian in the sense that there is no mediation between the father and the child and the father can directly supervise and take decisions on the child's behalf. A captain who has direct command over his soldiers is their guardian or guard. In all these instances "guardianship" (*wilayat*) consists of a direct and unmediated relationship between two people or two institutions or two aggregates or two

---

[11] *Mathnawi*, 3: 1951–1952, 1957.

groups; it is, in this way, akin to affection or leadership or succession or submission or assistance and the like.

The divine guardian or God's grand *wali* is someone who has the greatest affinity to God and, in whose being, God is most consummately reflected. He is God's *representation* and God's *representative*. I want to underline these two senses, because the word "guardian" or *wali* has been used in exactly these two ways. And the conflation of these two meanings has had enormous theological-political implications in the history of Muslims. "Representation" is one thing and "representative" is another. "Representative" is someone who is on a mission. "Representation" is someone who reflects another's attributes like a mirror. As to whether someone's best "representation" would also be their best "representative", and whether these two attributes necessarily coexist in an individual is the very colossal question we must grapple with. But before we do, it might be a good idea to explore further the concept of guardianship and the rules that govern it, especially as a way of shedding light on the spiritual journey.

Our mystics have distinguished between two types of proximity to God: "supererogatory proximity" (*qurb-e navafeli*) and "duteous proximity" (*qurb-e fara'ezi*). There is a divine saying (*hadith qudsi*) attributed to the Prophet by both Sunni and Shi'i chroniclers, which has served as a rich source for mystics and Sufis. According to this *hadith*, God has said: "My servant voluntarily moves closer and closer to me through the performance of supererogatory practices and laudable deeds and acts of worship, to the point where I become his eyes, his ears and his hands."[12] Compare this with the words spoken by God to the Prophet in the Qur'an:

> When thou threwest, it was not thyself that threw, but God threw...(8: 17)

---

[12] This account, which may be the best known and most authoritative *hadith qudsi*, appears in *Sahih-e Bukhari*: "In the performance of supererogatory practices, my servant grows so close to Me that I become his friend and, since I become his friend, I become the ears with which he hears and the eyes with which he sees and the hands with which he gives and takes and the legs with which he walks. If he calls on me, I respond and if he seeks My protection, I offer him My protection. And I never hesitate so much in the performance of any task as in taking the life of a pious man, for he does not desire death and I do not desire his unhappiness." This *hadith* has also been recounted with minor differences in Ahmad Ibn Hanbal's *Musnad*, in Al-Ghazali's *Ihya al-'Ulum*, in Abu-Talib al-Makki's *Qout al-Qoulub*, in Abu Nasr Sarraj Tusi's *al-Luma'*, and in Abolqasim al-Qushayri's *al-Risalah* among others. See also: W. A. Graham, *Divine Word and Prophetic Word in Early Islam* (The Hauge: Mouton & Co, 1977).

Or:

> Fight them and God will chastise them at your hands…(9: 14)

In these verses, it is a question of people serving as God's tools and instruments; God performs his task via human beings. When you throw something, it seems as if you have thrown it, but it is in fact God who has thrown it. But in the above narrative, the proximity is of a different nature. The narrative says that, through the performance of voluntary acts of worship, the believer grows so close to God that God becomes his eyes and his ears and his hands; whereas in the verses in the Qur'an, it is humans who become God's hands.

Through these verses and that narrative our mystics have learnt that there are two types of "God's guardianship" (*wilayat-e elahi*) or "proximity to God" (*qurb-e elahi*). And they have called them "super-erogatory proximity" (*qurb-e navafeli*) and "duteous proximity" (*qurb-e fara'ezi*) or "loving proximity" (*qurb-e muhhebi*) and "the proximity of the loved" (*qurb-e mahbubi*). In one, we become God's hand and, in the other, God becomes our hand. In one, we become God's eye and, in the other, God becomes our eye. It is as if, in one, God becomes a human being and, in the other, a human being becomes God.

Suffice it to say that, our religious-mystical literature contains lofty concepts of this nature regarding the relationship between God and his servants, which convey the highest order of proximity and one-ness between God and the servant of God, and are extremely difficult to understand in their full subtlety and intricacy. Mystics' rapturous paradoxical statements as well as the mysteriousness of mysticism all fall within this framework. It was not without reason that Rumi's verse included the words, "Lo, you are the one of whom God said 'By Me he hears and by Me he sees'; you are the mystery, nay, you are the source of mystery".[13] A person's proximity to God does not just mean going to heaven. There is also the matter of God's affection. It is a tale of loving and of being loved. The idea Mulla Sadra puts forward in *Mafatih al-Ghayb* is the outcome and concentrated essence of countless discussions on the subject by mystics and specialists in theoretical mysticism, such as Muhyi al-Din Arabi, Dawoud Qeissari and Sadr al-Din Qunawi, among others. The idea is that a spiritual guardian or *wali* "has annihilated in God and is held fast by Him". This annihilation in and being held fast

---

[13] *Mathnawi*, 1: 1937.

by God embraces both the two types of proximity we spoke of earlier. "Annihilation in God" is not to be understood in the sense of "dying, vanishing, going up in smoke and ceasing to exist"; it means that the individual loses their human attributes and comes to life with divine attributes. The characteristics of God manifest themselves in the individual and he attains a divine and godly existence. But being held fast by God conveys the sense of God appearing in a human form.[14] Mystics believe that God's guardians or *awliya* possess this characteristic and that the world is never without such saints. In the words of Imam Ali in the *Nahj al-Balaghah*:

> God always has servants, at various times, to whom He speaks in their thoughts and in the very depths of their minds.

And in a phrase to his disciple, Kumayl, he said: The earth will never be without overt or covert Proof, (*wali*). Rumi presents the same idea:

> Therefore in every epoch (after Muhammad) a saint [*wali*] arises (to act as his vicegerent):
> the probation (of the people) lasts until the Resurrection.
> He is the *Mahdi* (the God-guided one) and the *Hadi* (the Guide), O seeker of the (right) way: he is both hidden (from you) and seated before your face.
> He is as the Light (of Muhammad), and (Universal) Reason is his Gabriel; the saint that is lesser than he is his lamp (and receives illumination from him).[15]

The concept of "guardianship" in the sense we have set out here is the richest concept in mysticism. You can go so far as to describe mysticism as "the study of guardianship" and you would not be at all off the mark. Muslim mystics believed that the Prophet was God's grand guardian and the Perfect Man. Shi'is believe that guardianship in this sense was transferred by the Prophet to Ali and his descendants. Although Sunni mystics do not adhere to this Shi'i belief, they believe, nonetheless, that grand Sufi masters (*aqtab* and *mashayekh*) possess divine guardianship and are the bearers of it in this world.

As to whether God's guardian (*wali Allah*) can himself know that he is God's guardian or not, is a secondary issue and two different views have been proffered on it. In any case, one of the most important duties

---

[14] Sadr al-din Shirazi (Mulla Sadra), *Mafatih al-Ghayb*. (Ed.) M. Khawjavi (Tehran: Mo'aseseh Motale'at-e Farhangi, 1363/1984), pp. 487–488.
[15] *Mathnawi*, 2: 812, 815–816.

of God's guardians or saints is to be of spiritual and tangible assistance to the wayferers of the path of rightful guidance and to offer them mental, moral and spiritual support.

Rumi is one of the people who has presented the tale of guardianship in the clearest and most lucid terms, without resorting to technical mystical terminology. There are references throughout the *Mathnawi* to masters, guardians (*pir/shaykh, wali*), disciples, wayfarers (*murid, salik*), etc. and the attributes of masters and the duties of disciples towards their masters have been explained at length. The main point in it all is that, on the path and the journey, the individual cannot proceed wilfully and unaided; they must be prepared to bend to the will of a master and to step into the master's shadow.

> Any one who moves without the head (guide) is a (mere) tail (base and contemptible):
> his movement is like the movement of the scorpion.
> Going crookedly, night-blind and ugly and venomous—his trade is the wounding of the pure bodies (of the unworldly).
> Beat the head of him whose inmost spirit is (like) this, and whose permanent nature and disposition is (like) this.[16]

> The shadow (protection) of the (spiritual) Guide is better than praising God (by one's self): a single (feeling of) contentment is better than a hundred viands and trays (of food).[17]

> Do not break with the prophet [spiritual master] of your days: do not rely on your own skill and footsteps.
> Beware! Do not fly but with the wings of the Shaykh, that you may see (receive) the aid of the armies of the Shaykh.[18]

Without this protective and guiding shadow, the disciple cannot arrive at the glowing rays of Truth. Even if, in rare and exceptional cases, certain individuals manage to find their way to felicity and rightful guidance unaided and without following a master, they have to recognise that they must have been guided from afar by a master without realising it.

> If any one, by rare exception, traversed this Way alone (without a Pir), he arrived (at his goal) through the help of the spiritual influence of the Pirs.
> The hand of the Pir is not withdrawn from the absent (those who are not under his authority): his hand is naught but the grasp of God.

---

[16] *Mathnawi*, 4: 1430–1432.
[17] *Mathnawi*, 6: 3784.
[18] *Mathnawi*, 4: 542–544. See also, 4: 1429–1431.

Inasmuch as they give such a robe of honour to the absent, (what must they give their disciples?!): undoubtedly the present are better than the absent.

Since they are bestowing (spiritual) food on the absent, see what bounties they must lay before the guest.[19]

A disciple's duty in the face of such a master, who is a saint of God, is absolute obedience. The disciple is not allowed the slightest criticism or unruliness towards the master. Testing the master and objecting to him are totally unacceptable. "When thou hast chosen thy Pir, be not faint-hearted, be not weak as water and crumbly as earth."[20] When you have chosen your master, you must follow him and obey him unquestioningly, for the master's misjudgement is still better than the disciple's correct judgement. "In the sight of God his backsliding is better than obedience; beside his infidelity all faiths are tattered (worthless)."[21] This is exactly what Al-Ghazali advises in *The Revival of the Religious Sciences*: If the master errs and the disciple follows him, this is far better than for the disciple to protest, even though he may be correct. This is because the disciple has not yet attained excellence. It is not appropriate for him to be unruly and haughty. He must simply obey. "Self-regard and haughtiness are blasphemy in this creed", as Hafez stated. The disciple must be the ear, not the tongue. He must be the listener, not the speaker.

> Be a vassal since you are not a lord: do not steer (the boat) yourself, since you are not the boatman.
> Since you are not (spiritually) perfect, do not take a shop (by yourself) alone. Be plaint to the hand, in order that you may become leavened (like dough).
> Give ear to (the Divine command), "*Keep silence,*" be mute; since you have not become the tongue (mouthpiece) of God, be an ear.[22]
>
> When thou art neither a swimmer nor a seaman, do not cast thyself (into the sea) from a (feeling of) self-conceit.[23]

What is demanded here is not clever objections and pedantic cunning and wit, but respect, obedience and submission.

---

[19] *Mathnawi*, 1: 2973–2976.
[20] *Mathnawi*, 1: 2978.
[21] *Mathnawi*, 1: 1579.
[22] *Mathnawi*, 2: 3441–3143.
[23] *Mathnawi*, 1: 1607.

> When the Pir has accepted thee, take heed, surrender thyself (to him):
> go, like Moses, under the authority of Khizr.
> Bear patiently whatever is done by a Khizr who is without hypocrisy, in
> order that Khizr may not say, "Be gone, *this is (our) parting.*"
> Though he stave in the boat, do not speak a word; though he kill a child,
> do not tear thy hair.[24]
> Inasmuch as His hand binds what is broken, it follows that His breaking
> is assuredly mending.
> He that knows how to sew (together) knows how to tear (asunder); what-
> soever He sells, He buys (something) better (in exchange).[25]

Of course, it has to be said that the master, too, has certain attributes. These are also explained extensively by Rumi. In brief, one of the characteristics of God's saints or guardians is that, when someone is in their presence, they uncontrollably find themselves cleansed and purged of all their former ideas and thoughts. They totally lose themselves. The charisma, insight, control, mastery and awe that the master's personality exercises over the disciple overshadow anything and everything else and make the disciple completely forget their former selves. The disciple may have prepared a thousand things to say and a thousand objections and points to raise but no sooner does he find himself before the master than they all melt away. The guardian's presence fills the disciple with warmth and drunkenness. "For within them there are a hundred immediate (spiritual) resurrections, (of which) the least is this, that their neighbour becomes intoxicated."[26]

Rumi has it that, when the Prophet was asked, when is the Resurrection? He said, I am the Resurrection; I resurrect your entire being.

> They asked him [Muhammad] concerning the Resurrection, saying, "O (thou
> who aret the Resurrection, how long is the way to the Resurrection?"
> And often he would say with mute eloquence, "does an one ask (me who
> am) the Resurrection concerning the Resurrection?"[27]

Rumi says that this is an attribute of all God's saints: they bring about an upheaval and a revolution in the disciple's being, because the guardian's being *is* a resurrection. He is in a state of constant movement and ascension. When another person approaches them and steps into their shadow, he too rises, comes to life and is freed from death.

---

[24] *Mathnawi*, 1: 2967–2969.
[25] *Mathnawi*, 1: 3881, 3884.
[26] *Mathnawi*, 6: 1301.
[27] *Mathnawi*, 6: 752–753.

Hark! For the saints are the Israfil of the (present) time: from them to the dead comes life and freshness.

At their voice the soul of every dad one starts up from the body's grave in their winding-sheets.

He (that is thus awakened) says, "This voice is separate from (all other) voices: to quicken (the dead) is the work of the voice of God.

We (had) died and were entirely decayed: the call of God came: we all arose."[28]

The least benefit that a person draws in communing with the guardians of God is that he will be inebriated and filled with light and warmth by their words, leaving behind the former coldness, weariness, despair, death and darkness. "The work of (holy) men is (as) light and heat; the work of vile men is trickery and shamelessness."[29] Rumi's description here of the effects of guardianship also apply to faith and love. Faith nurtures and revives the individual and instigates a resurrection within their being. Anything that comes in the name of religion or faith but fills one with weariness, sorrow, fatigue and inertia is not faith.

The very important point to take note of here is that everyone must search for and find their own guardian. Do not imagine that anyone who is a guardian of God (wali Allah) is also your guardian. Your guardian is someone who communicates with you and moves you directly and without any mediation. Each person's guardian is that someone whose guardianship, presence and words fills them with warmth, inebriates them, touches them and impels them to move forward, to fly and to change. There is a difference between a guardian per se and a guardian of mine. Just as there is a difference between a professor per se and a professor of mine. In the world of learning, there may be very distinguished experts and professors but I can only learn from one or a few of them, not from all of them. It is exactly the same with guardianship. God has many guardians, but each person has their own specific guardian. And this guardian may be alive or dead. Death is corporeal; the spirit never dies.

At the same time, care must be taken to avoid a possible error or danger. This special guardianship does not mean that the guardian must act according to the disciple's wishes and whims. Moving and jolting the disciple is one thing, pandering to their desires and wishes is another. And Rumi warns us against false guardians whose main charm is to

---

[28] *Mathnawi*, 1: 1929–1932.
[29] *Mathnawi*, 1: 320.

pander to our sense of self-importance and self-love. Such people may
be "your guardian", but they are not "God's guardian", he says.[30]

Another of the guardians of God's attributes is that their presence
is God's presence. If you want to commune with God, commune with
God's guardians. If you want to see God, see God's guardians. God
does not exist in space and time. His presence is the presence of His
Guardians. God's guardians are His absolute agents in this world. They
are His presence. Capture their hearts and you will have captured God's
heart. Displease them and you will have displeased God. If you win the
approval of God's guardians, you will have won the approval of God. If
they withhold their approval from you, He will withhold His approval
from you.[31] Recall the *hadith* that said: "I become his eyes, his ears and
his hands," and this will all be easier to comprehend. It goes without
saying that, in the presence of such a lofty being, one must be humble
and respectful and venerational, for their presence is His presence and
their heart is His Ka'ba.

The Prophet is God's guardian and God's other guardians or *awliya*
are spiritually—and not necessarily physically—related to him. The
awliya may appear anywhere; it makes no difference. They may be in
Baghdad or in Heart or in Tehran. They may be Arab or non-Arab.
"They are all his descendants, regardless," in Rumi's words.[32] There is,
therefore, no need to seek physical, family links with the Prophet. It
is enough for them to be his spiritual descendants. This is all that the
mystics' theory demands. This theory cannot pinpoint specific individuals before the fact.

Wilayat *and Imamate in Shi'ism*

Now let us look at the theories of guardianship (*wilayat*) and the
Imamate in Shi'ism. Shi'is see Ali and his descendants as God's indisputable guardians or saints, in the sense that we have been using the
expression. As we said, the concept of guardianship is taken from the
Qur'an and it is not specifically Sunni or Shi'i in itself. But the mystical theory of guardianship and its association with the Perfect Man,

---

[30] See for instance, *Mathnawi*, 5: 903–904.
[31] See al-Kulayni's *Kitab al-Hujjah* where he ascribes all these to the Shi'i Imams
who are considered to be "*awliya Allah*".
[32] See *Mathnawi*, 6: 176–179.

the manifestation of the names of the Creator and so on is something that Shi'i philosophers and mystics have borrowed from Sunnis and then made it applicable to specific individuals. The greatest Islamic mystics have been Sunnis. First and foremost, there was the great master Muhyi al-Din Ibn Arabi in the thirteenth century. Then there was his student Sadr al-Din Qunawi and his expositor Dawoud Qeissari, as well as Rumi, Jami and Iraqi, who were all Sunnis. We have one great Shi'i master of theoretical mysticism by the name of Seyyed Heidar Amoli who wrote *Jame' al-Asrar va Manba' al-Anwar*, as well as *Asrar al-Shari'ah va Anwar al-Tariqah*. However, even Amoli was wholly influenced by Muhyi al-Din Ibn Arabi's theories. As to Sadr al-Din Shirazi, who is said to have amalgamated theoretical mysticism with philosophy, and his direct and indirect disciples.[33] They were all, without exception, proud to study and expound Ibn Arabi's views. Of course, they had minor differences with him as well, since Muhyi al-Din Arabi considered himself the seal of the Prophet Muhammad's guardianship and Shi'is, obviously, found this impossible to accept. On one occasion, Ibn Arabi even goes so far as to say, God wanted to show me the *Saheb al-Zaman* (the Lord of the Age) but I did not wish to see him and declined.[34] Feiz Kashani who did not accept these words by Ibn Arabi, wrote in one of his books:

> Look how God has left this person in the hands of Satan that he may remain in the land of bewilderment and never say a sound word in religious matters and that he may weave such nonsense as to make even children and women laugh.[35]

Nonetheless, despite the theological disagreements between Shi'i mystics and Muhyi al-Din and Sunni mystics, the roots of their thinking on the subject of guardianship are very, very close.

But the Shi'i theory of the Imamate is a different story altogether. Shi'is believe that the Prophet designated Ali as the Imam. This "appointment" concerns the mundane position of the leadership of

---

[33] Some of his disciples such as Mulla Ali Nuri, Aqa Mohammad Reza Qumshe'i, Mulla Isma'il Khaju'i and Mulla Hadi Sabzevari, were all effectively pupils of Muhyi al-Din Arabi's school.

[34] "Saheb al-Zaman" is one of the titles of the Twelfth Imam of the Shi'is who is believed to be in occultation and will return at the end of the time to bring peace and order to the world. [Ed.]

[35] See Abdulkarim Soroush, "Jameh-e *Tahdib* bar tan-e *Ihya*," in his *Qesseh Arbab-e Ma'refat* [The Tale of the Lords of Sagacity].

the *ummah*. "Appointing to guardianship" is meaningless. After all, guardianship is a spiritual position and, if someone has the necessary attributes, then they qualify and, if they do not, they do not. Spiritual guardianship is like learning. No one can appoint another person to the position of being learned. No one becomes learned by virtue of being appointed and no one loses their learning by being removed from an appointed post. Appointment pertains to political and social posts. If someone wants to be a ruler or a governor or a delegate, they need to be appointed. This is because being a governor or a ruler and the like are conventional and must, therefore, be designated as such.

At any rate, Shi'is believe that the Prophet appointed Ali as the Imam; that is, he appointed him as the head of the *ummah* and all Muslims were duty-bound to accept this leadership. In this way, Ali was appointed to a worldly post. Had it not been for this appointment, Ali would still have been one of God's guardians, they would argue, but he would not have been the nation's Imam. It may well be that, today, too, there are many guardians of God and that they are, in the words of the mystics, veiled by the robes of God, such that they are not recognised by anyone but Him. These saints are in a position of guardianship but they are not in a position of worldly power or Imamate. Shi'is believe that, when the Prophet said, "Anyone who considers me their *mawla* should consider Ali their *mawla*," what he meant was, you, who have accepted me as your political leader in your lives, accept Ali in the same way. Hence, Ali became the Imam (of course, this is if we see the Prophet's words on the Day of Ghadir as an act of appointment, rather than suggestion). As it happened, after the Prophet's demise, some people did not accept this designation and followed their own course. If we were to look at this in a purely sociological way, using Max Weber's terminology, we would say that Shi'is chose to follow the path of the Prophet's charismatic leadership, whereas Sunnis opted for a traditional or rational approach.

According to Shi'i belief, although the Prophet's words on the occasion of Ghadir was not meant to designate Ali to "spiritual guardianship", nonetheless, his personal inner distinctions were involved in his appointment by the Prophet to the leadership position (*imamate*). Be that as it may, when the people pledged allegiance to him, it was not a question of his spiritual guardianship, his infallibility or any theory about the consummate human being. It was a question of discernible guardianship and this-worldly-religious leadership. Anyone who studies Shi'i theological texts on "the *imamate*" will find this to be the case. For example, Nasir al-Din Tusi, in his very important book *Tajrid al-i'tiqad* and Shaykh Tusi in his *Tamhid fi al-Usul* begin the discussion by saying that the appointment of the Imam was an imperative of God's grace. Just as God's act of sending prophets was an imperative of His grace. The two things are of the same fabric.

And what does "grace" (*lutf*) mean? Shi'is borrowed the "principle of grace" from the Mu'tazilites. What is meant by "grace" is that it is incumbent on God to do something that will move people towards faith and worship and away from infidelity and committing sins. Theologians were of the view that grace was incumbent on God; otherwise, human beings would be able to argue against Him. In the absence of prophets, people would not have known what God wanted them to do and what not to do. Prophets teach people these things. Hence it is an imperative of God's grace to send us prophets "so that mankind might have no argument against God" (4: 165). If He did not do this, it would be reprehensible and the All-Wise does not commit reprehensible deeds.

Shi'i theologians would take things further and say that this same principle of grace also makes it imperative on God to make the Imams known to the people. The presence in society of the Imam (in the precise sense of a politico-religious leader) would incline people further towards devotion, make them more aware of and more active in the performance of their duties, and keep them freer of sin and impiety. Hence, it was an imperative of God's grace to appoint a politico-religious leader for society. Then, they would say that this politico-religious leader also had to be infallible and free of sin and error, since people were not infallible themselves. If people knew right from wrong, if they were not drawn into temptation, if they were not inclined to quarrel and transgress, there would be no need for leaders and politics at all. But since people do quarrel and transgress, a political leader must rule over them to prevent iniquity and unruliness. Now, if the leader himself is prone to error and sin, he would, in turn, need a leader to keep him in check. And this would lead to an infinite regress. Now, the infallible leader has to be named via the Prophet, because infallibility is a hidden attribute. It is not as if people can tell be looking at someone whether they are prone to sin or not. Infallibility, "like the path to treasure, is not visible to all". In Rumi's words "one saint becomes known by another".[36]

---

[36] See *Mathnawi*, 2: 2338.

Clearly, the leader also had to be the noblest person in society. It would be reprehensible if a less distinguished, less virtuous and less capable person was set above some other more distinguished, more virtuous and more capable person and made the Imam. This was the political theory of the Shi'i *Imamate*. This politico-theological theory, which deemed the actual presence of an infallible leader and a living, definitive authority to be a constant necessity in society, ran into difficulties with the occultation of the Twelfth Imam. The opponents of Shi'ism and even Shi'is themselves now began to ask how—if the principle of grace was true—society could be left without an Imam and his important duties left undone. There is much evidence to show that, for quite some time, Shi'is awaited the imminent reappearance of the Twelfth Imam and believed this followed from the "principle of grace." But, as the period of occultation and absence persisted, they came to believe that possibly they were responsible for the Hidden Imam's lengthy absence and that the "principle of grace" has not been invalidated. This is exactly the idea put forward by Nasir al-din Tusi—in line with Sharif Mortaza—in *Tajrid al-I'tiqad*, and by others after him.

> The Imam's presence is a grace on the part of God. His leadership is another grace. As for his absence, we are to blame.[37]

People caused his absence and deprived themselves of him. The Imam went into occultation because people had not valued the Imam as much as they should have done or because some people had tried to kill him or because of some other reason.

During the absence of the Hidden Imam, there is no discernible leadership. The theory of the *Imamate* was aimed at proving the need for the existence of a this-worldly-religious authority and a discernible, living, infallible leader. But during the Imam's occultation, the theory no longer holds. The Shi'is must now resort to another theory to explain the need for the existence of the Hidden Imam and the manner in which he guides them.

As we said, after the Imam's occultation, Shi'is were bewildered for quite some time. They were convinced that he would soon reappear and would not abandon the nation for long. Hence, they used to bury their

---

[37] *Kashf al-Murad fi Sharh Tajrid al-I'tiqad*, written by Khajeh Nasir Tusi, commentated by Jamal al-Din Hasan, known as Allameh Helli. Beirut: A'lami Publications, 1979, p. 388.

khums alms[38] or leave it to their heirs so that it could be presented to the Imam upon his return. Using *khums* to fund an Islamic state is a very recent idea. So, for a fairly long time, Shi'is did not have any clear theory about their society's leadership. But, when centuries passed and the Imam did not reappear, the need to produce an alternative theory about the Imamate was increasingly felt. This was when the theory of spiritual guardianship became stronger still. It was decided that the Hidden Imam was not an Imam in the sense of being the ruler in society and that his presence was no longer the imperative of the principle of grace. In fact, he is a guardian of God and this spiritual guardianship has not disappeared. He is still with the *ummah*, providing the people with inward and spiritual guidance—not political leadership—from behind the scenes. He is taking them by the hand and invisibly moving them towards God. He possesses exactly the characteristics that the mystics have attributed to the saints.

At the present time, the Shi'i theory about the Imamate is a theory about spiritual guardianship, not about discernible or external leadership. The presence of a discernible Imam used to be an imperative of Shi'i theology. But, the Imam's occultation effectively changed this theory. Today, in order to prove the necessity and reality of the Hidden Imam's existence, one has to turn to theories about spiritual guardianship. These changes are the outcome of developments in Shi'i history, which resulted in one reading of "the Imamate" gradually giving way to another. For Shi'is today, the concept of the discernible *Imamate* as it appears in the discipline of theology no longer holds; except perhaps at the end of time when the Hidden Imam will reappear. But the concept of spiritual guardianship remains firmly in force.[39]

---

[38] *Khums* is a religious tax that the Shi'is pay in addition to *zakat* which both Sunnis and Shi'is pay. *Kums* is the equivalent of one fifth of one's annual surplus. [Ed.]

[39] The bewilderment felt by Shi'is in the light of the Twelfth Imam's occultation and the subsequent upheaval in the theory of the Imamate were indisputable components of Shi'i history to the point where many religious scholars were forced to take up their pens to resolve the bewilderment and doubts. Ali Ibn Babawayh Qumi wrote a book in the tenth century by the name of *Al-Imama va al-Tabsera min al-Heyra*. He said in the preface that he had written the book because many Shi'is were starting to have doubts about the foundations of Shi'ism in view of the Imam's prolonged absence. The same can be said of Ibn Qibah's *Naqz Kitab al-Ashhad* and other Shi'i scholars.

See, in this connection, Hossein Modarressi Tabataba'i, *Crisis and Consolidation in the Formative Period of Shi'ite Islam* (New Jersey: Darwin Publications, 1993).

Confusing Spiritual Guardianship and Political Guardianship

Now, a few simple but important conclusions can be derived from the above discussions.

First, as said, the theory of spiritual guardianship demands absolute obedience from the disciple. In the spiritual journey, when you are faced with a grand master or a guardian, you have no choice but to submit unquestioningly and to reveal to him absolutely everything that lies within you. There, it is not even a question of the relationship between a student and a teacher. Students are allowed a slight degree of license in the face of their teacher. They can ask questions, raise objections or even spot and expose the teacher's mistakes. But there is absolutely no question of any of this in the relationship between a master and a disciple. There, choice is devoid of all meaning. Mystics' theories tell us that, contrary to popular belief, the disciple does not choose the master, it is the master that chooses the disciple. The choice is made from above. He casts his net and catches his quarry. It is in this kind of guardianship that dissolving and annihilation occur, and are in fact unavoidable.

Secondly, if you try to combine the *Imamate*, in the sense of discernible or external leadership, with the theory of spiritual guardianship (with all its imperatives) you will end up with very strange results. If an Imam is to be taken both as an Imam (in the sense of discernible external leader) as well as a spiritual guardian, then the resulting system of his rule would be extremely terrifying and dangerous. For, it will demand people to submit themselves to the mundane authority exactly in the same way as disciples would do to spiritual guardians. The two domains must be kept completely separate. Confusing and combining these two contexts has been the source of much misunderstanding and many ills. Spiritual guardianship demands that you obey absolutely. Here, giving priority to the views of the underling over those of the superior is utterly inappropriate. Here, the underling must per force dissolve and relinquish the self. But this guardianship is not a guardianship that can be extended over society at large. This guardianship could not be the guardianship that even an Infallible Imam exercised over his nation. The Infallible Imam, assuming that he has been appointed via the Prophet, is an Imam in the sense of exercising discernible, external, political leadership. And what "external, political leadership" means is that the underling may quibble with the ruler, criticise him and even disobey him. The underling may reject the ruler's reasoning. All these things are possible in the context of external leadership.

It has been said that, Rabi' Ibn Khothaym, that same famous Khajeh Rabi' who is buried in Khorasan and whose resting place is a site of pilgrimage, refused to fight alongside Ali in one of his battles.[40] He said: I do not consider this war proper; allow me to perform some other task instead of accompanying you. Imam Ali accepted and sent him elsewhere. This is the nature of external leadership. When Imam Rida (the Eight Imam) accepted Ma'mun's offer to be his vicegerent (cr. 813 CE), many Shi'is—who considered him as their spiritual guardian—questioned his acceptance of the offer and disputed the matter with him. It is also well documented that the Shi'is used to question Imam Baqir and Imam Sadiq (the Fifth and Sixth Imams respectively) that why they did not rebel against the caliphs of the time as their ancestor, Imam Hossein, had done? And they demanded a satisfactory rational explanation. It was not as if the Imams, by virtue of being Imams, were considered immune from being questioned and challenged. As a matter of fact, the Imams did used to explain their actions and enlighten people. And the mere fact that someone answers your questions demonstrates that they consider themselves accountable and believe that they must justify their behaviour.

The situation is completely different when it comes to spiritual guardianship. There, the master himself is the proof and the justification, and he does not consider it necessary to justify his actions. It may be that some of the companions of Imam Ali and the other Imams had a master-disciple relationship with those great men. But that relationship would have had no bearing on the world of politics and would have been purely personal. There were also people who stood in a master-disciple relationship with the Prophet. It has been said that the Prophet's phrase "Salman is of my household" can be taken to mean that there was a special, spiritual relationship between the Prophet and Salman. (Of course, it can be and has been interpreted in a socio-political sense as well, in as much as Salman was not an Arab and was subjected to harassment and mistreatment because of his Persian origin.)

---

[40] Look at Shaykh Abbas Qumi, *Safinah al-Bihar* (under the entry of Rabi' Ibn Khothaym).

At any rate, Abu Dhar, Salman, Miqdad, Kumayl and Meytham had special, spiritual links with the Prophet and Imam Ali which others did not enjoy. From these individuals' life stories it would appear that these noble people were privy to Imam Ali's secrets and possibly stood in some kind of master-disciple relationship with him.[41] But—and a thousand buts—there was no question of any of these things in society at large. Ali was not the society's Imam in the sense of being a spiritual guardian, who expects unquestioning devotion. In his capacity as the leader of the *ummah*, Ali behaved quite differently and communicated his expectations to the people at an entirely different level. The people, too, saw him in a different light. A society's leader or manager bears the responsibility for the management or mismanagement of that society and must be accountable. Hence, in his capacity as the political leader, he was "Ali, the Imam", not "Ali, the *wali* of God". This same Ali used to say to people: "I am not above making mistakes. I may err. Therefore, do not hesitate to give me rightful advice." When Ali uttered these words, he was not indulging in polite formalities; nor did the people take it as such.

It is very clear what ambiguities and fallacies the intermingling of the concepts of spiritual guardianship, on the one hand, and the *Imamate* or external leadership, on the other, have generated in political theories current in contemporary Iran. The ruling Shiʿi clergy in Iran wishes to benefit from the mystical theory of guardianship and the theological theory of the *Imamate* and the rational theory of government based on pragmatism all at once. It wishes to roll all these things into one without paying due attention to the hidden contradictions there in. That is why the anachronistic fallacious contradictory notion of Islamic state proves to be so ineffective and totalitarian in practice.

The orthodox Shiʿite theory of the *Imamate* that was based on the principle of God's grace made it imperative that an infallible person, who was the noblest of beings and was introduced and appointed via the Prophet, should take up society's leadership. But what is to be done now that no such person is available and the theory no longer holds? Is it possible to salvage the situation by clasping onto the theory of spiritual guardianship instead? This theory belongs to the quest for

---

[41] For specific stories revealing such private spiritual relationships of these individuals to Ali see for instance, *Nahj al-Balagha* on Kumayl and Shaykh Abbas Qumi's, *Muntaha al-Amal*, vol. 1, on Meysam Tammar.

spiritual excellence and to a limited circle of disciples. It is a theory about spiritual leadership, not political leadership, and it is inappropriate and even extremely dangerous in the context of running a state. Hence, in these circumstances, Shi'is must, like all other rational beings, think of a rational solution to managing their society. And, today, that rational theory consists of acting in accordance with the people's choice. On the basis of this theory, the elected individual is no longer an infallible and noble being. There is no room either here for the principle of grace or of being presented and appointed via the Prophet. The only consideration is the interest of the society. It may well be that the ruler will not be the noblest being or a saint. No alas.

It may also happen that, at some point in time, a saint from among the guardians of God will take up the reins of power. Nonetheless, in the context of statesmanship, this ruler, too, must submit to the imperatives of political, this-worldly leadership.

The only path open to us now is to accept and fall in with a rational and public interest-oriented theory of statesmanship. No one has forbidden the devout from acting rationally.

Thirdly, the guardianship of the *faqih* does not overlap in any way with mystical and spiritual guardianship. They are two completely separate things. It is only the common terminology that has made some people confuse and combine this guardianship (in the sense of leadership) with that guardianship (which is restricted to the guardians of God and the select few). It would, henceforth, be better use the term "the *rule* of the *faqih*" instead of "the guardianship of the *faqih*" in order to avoid any confusion and fallacies and to make it perfectly clear what lies therein.

Ruling has a completely this-worldly and non-sacred meaning and is in no way ringed by a halo of spirituality. And if it is the continuation of anything, it is the continuation of the Imams' external leadership, not their spiritual guardianship. This is why the unquestioning obedience that belongs to the realm of the Sufis does not extend to this sphere, which is the sphere of politics. Of course, all these would only matter if we accord a degree of credence and legitimacy to the theory of the guardianship of the *faqih* (as do a minority of Shi'i *faqih*s). However, if, as is the case with the majority of *faqih*s, we do not think that guardianship, in the sense of political leadership, is either the duty or the sole prerogative of *faqih*s, then the house crumbles to the ground once and for all and there is no need to worry about its portico.

APPENDICES

THE WORD OF MOHAMMAD[1]
AN INTERVIEW WITH ABDULKARIM SOROUSH

Michel Hoebink[2]

Muhammad is the creator of the Koran. That is what well-known Iranian reformer Abdolkarim Soroush says in his book *The Expansion of Prophetic Experience* that will be published early next year. With this view, Soroush goes further than some of the most radical Muslim reformers. In an interview with Zemzem, he gives a foretaste of his book.

Abdolkarim Soroush is regarded as the intellectual leader of the Iranian reform movement. Initially, he was a supporter of Khomeini. He held several official positions in the young Islamic republic, among which that of Khomeini's adviser on cultural and educational reform. But when the spiritual leader soon turned out to be a tyrant, Soroush withdrew in disappointment. Since the early 90s, he is part of a group of 'republican' intellectuals who started out discussing the concept of an 'Islamic democracy' but gradually moved away from the entire idea of an Islamic state.

Soroush's basic argument is simple: all human understanding of religion is historical and fallible. With this idea he undermines the Iranian theocracy, because if all human understanding of religion is fallible, no-one can claim to apply the shariʿa in God's name, not even the Iranian clergy.

In *The Expansion of Prophetic Experience* Soroush makes clear that his view on the fallibility of religious knowledge to a certain degree also applies to the Koran. With thinkers such as Nasr Hamid Abu Zayd and Mohammed Arkoun, Soroush belongs to a small group of

---

[1] The interview was originally done in English. This is its text as provided by Michel Hoebink and posted on Soroush's webpage. The Dutch version of it was posted on www.ZemZem.org (fall 2007). A Persian translation of it was posted on Radio Zamaneh's webpage. [Ed.]

[2] Michel Hoebink works for the Arabic department of Radio Netherlands World.

radical reformers who advocate a historical approach to the Koran. In his new book, however, he goes one step further than many of his radical colleagues. He claims that the Koran is not only the product of the historical circumstances in which it emerged, but also of the mind of the Prophet Mohammed with all his human limitations. This idea, says Soroush, is not an innovation, as several medieval thinkers already hinted at it.

Q. How can we make sense of something like 'revelation' in our disenchanted modern world?

A. Revelation is 'inspiration'. It is the same experience as that of poets and mystics, although prophets are on a higher level. In our modern age we can understand revelation by using the metaphor of poetry. As one Muslim philosopher has put it: revelation is higher poetry. Poetry is a means of knowledge that works differently from science or philosophy. The poet feels that he is informed by a source external to him; that he receives something. And poetry, just like revelation, is a talent: A poet can open new horizons for people; he can make them view the world in a different way.

Q. The Koran, in your view, should be understood as a product of its time. Does this also imply that the person of the Prophet played an active and even constituent role in the production of the text?

A. According to the traditional account, the Prophet was only an instrument; he merely conveyed a message passed to him by Jibril. In my view, however, the Prophet played a pivotal role in the production of the Koran.

The metaphor of poetry helps me to explain this. Just like a poet, the Prophet feels that he is captured by an external force. But in fact—or better: at the same time—the Prophet himself is everything: the creator and the producer. The question whether the inspiration comes from outside or from inside is really not relevant, because at the level of revelation there is no difference between outside and inside. The inspiration comes from the Self of the Prophet. The Self of every individual is divine, but the Prophet differs from other people in that he has become aware of its divinity. He has actualized its potential. His Self has become one with God. Now don't get me wrong at this point: This spiritual union with God does not mean that the Prophet has become God. It is a union that is limited and tailored to his size. It is human size, not God's size. The mystical poet Jalaluddin Rumi describes this paradox with the words: 'Through the Prophet's union with God, the ocean is poured into a jar.'

But the Prophet is also the creator of the revelation in another way. What he receives from God is the content of the revelation. This content, however, cannot be offered to the people as such, because it is beyond their understanding and even beyond words. It is formless and the activity of the person of the Prophet is to form the formless, so as to make it accessible. Like a poet again, the Prophet transmits the inspiration in the language he knows, the styles he masters and the images and knowledge he possesses.

But his personality also plays an important role in shaping the text. His personal history: his father, his mother, his childhood. And even his moods. If you read the Koran you feel that the Prophet is some-times jubilant and highly eloquent while at other times he is bored and quite ordinary in the way he expresses himself. All those things have left their imprint on the text of the Koran. That is the purely human side of revelation.

Q. So the Koran has a human side. Does this mean that the Koran is fallible?

A. In the traditional view, the revelation is infallible. But nowadays there are more and more interpreters who think that the revelation is infallible only in purely religious matters such as the attributes of God, life after death and the rules for worship. They accept that the revelation may be wrong in matters that relate to the material world and human society. What the Koran says about historical events, other religious traditions and all kinds of practical earthly matters does not necessarily have to be true. Such interpreters often argue that this kind of errors in the Koran do not harm prophethood because the Prophet 'descended' to the level of knowledge of the people of his time and spoke to them in the 'language of the time'. I have a different view. I do not think the Prophet spoke the 'language of his time' while know-ing better himself. He actually believed the things he said. It was his own language and his own knowledge and I don't think that he knew more than the people around him about the earth, the universe and the genetics of human beings. He did not possess the knowledge we have today. And that does not harm his prophethood because he was a prophet and not a scientist or a historian.

Q. You refer to medieval philosophers and mystics such as Rumi. To what extent do your views on the Koran find their origin in the Islamic tradition?

A. Many of my views are rooted in medieval Islamic thought. The idea that prophethood is something very general that can be found in different degrees in all people is common in both Shiʻi Islam and mysticism. The great Shiʻi theologian sheikh al-Mufid does not call the Shiʻi imams prophets, but he attributes to them all the qualities possessed by prophets. Also mystics are generally convinced that their experiences are the same as those of the prophets. And the notion of the Koran as a potentially fallible human product is implicit in the Muʻtazilite doctrine of the created Koran. Medieval thinkers often did not express such ideas in a clear or systematic manner but rather tended to conceal them in casual remarks or allusions. They did not want to create confusion among people who couldn't handle such thoughts. Rumi, for instance, states somewhere that the Koran is the mirror of the states of mind of the Prophet. What Rumi implies is that the Prophet's personality, his changing moods and his stronger and weaker moments, are reflected in the Koran. Rumi's son goes even further. In one of his books he suggests that polygamy is permitted in the Koran because the Prophet liked women. That was the reason he permitted his followers to marry four women!

Q. Does the Shiʻi tradition allow you more freedom to develop your thoughts on the humanness of the Koran?

A. It is well known that in Sunni Islam, the rationalist school of the Muʻtazilites was badly defeated by the Ashʻarites and their doctrine that the Koran was eternal and uncreated. But in Shiʻi Islam, Muʻtazilism somehow continued its life and became the breeding ground for a rich philosophical tradition. The Muʻtazilite doctrine of the created Koran is almost undisputed among Shiʻi theologians. Today you see that Sunni reformers are coming closer to the Shiʻi position and embrace the doctrine of the created Koran. The Iranian clergy, however, are reluctant to use the philosophical resources of the Shiʻi tradition to open new horizons to our religious understanding. They have based their power on a conservative understanding of religion and fear that they might lose everything if they open the discussion on issues such as the nature of prophethood.

Q. What are the consequences of your views for contemporary Muslims and the way they use the Koran as a moral guide?

A. A human view of the Koran makes it possible to distinguish between the essential and the accidental aspects of religion. Some parts of religion are historically and culturally determined and no longer relevant today. That is the case, for instance, with the corporal punishments prescribed in the Koran. If the Prophet had lived in another cultural environment, those punishments would probably not have been part of his message.

The task of Muslims today is to translate the essential message of the Koran over time. It is like translating a proverb from one language into another. You do not translate it literally. You find another proverb which has the same spirit, the same content but perhaps not the same wording. In Arabic you say: He is like someone who carries dates to Basra. If you translate that into English you say: He is carrying coal to Newcastle. A historical, human view of the Koran allows us to do this. If you insist on the idea that the Koran is the uncreated, eternal word of God that must be literally applied, you get yourself into an un-resolvable dilemma.

AYATOLLAH SOBHANI'S FIRST LETTER

At the height of Westerners' anti-Islamism, led by Dutch media earlier and by Danish media now, there are reports that a group of people in the latter country are engaging in anti-Islamism using the figurative arts and trying to portray the Prophet and the Qur'an in an ugly light with sacrilegious cartoons and a film. In these circumstances, I read an interview with Mr Abdulkarim Soroush which was posted on Aftab News website on 3 February 2008, citing the Arabic Service of Radio Netherlands and the Persian translation of it on Radio Zamaneh.

I cannot say, without definite proof, that what I read in this interview is his theory through and through, but I can take his silence in the face of this report to be an unpardonable sin. In circumstances in which the West's atheists are bent on combating Islam and isolating Muslims, an individual who was raised in an Islamic environment and in the midst of ulema and learned people, and whose words were for a while a boon in Iranian media, says things which point to the conclusion that the Qur'an is the product of the Prophet's mind! and that the Prophet played a key role in its creation!

In December 2005, I wrote an open letter to Mr Soroush and I brought to his attention his errors on the question of Imamate and caliphate, and I asked him once again to return to the fold of the Islamic nation and, especially, of the ulema and the seminaries.[1] I told him that this kind of noise and fuss soon passes away and is like a wave in the ocean, which falls silent after a time, and that what remains is right and truth. I imagined that my fatherly letter would prove effective. People who

---

[1] Reference is to a lecture delivered by Soroush in France summer 2005. Its publication in Iran generated a wave of response and public correspondences between Soroush and some of his critics such as Hojatul Islam Saeed Bahman Pour. In that lecture Soroush had questioned the prevalent version of the Shi'i doctrine of Imamate and its interpretation as being incompatible with the doctrine of Finality of Prophethood because it ascribes certain privileges to the Shi'i Imams that put them at par with Prophet Muhammad. He also criticized the widespread superstitious ideas regarding the Hidden Imam, calling this type of Shi'ism, sponsored mostly by the state clergy, unfounded and *Ghali* "extremist." [Ed.]

had read the letter said that it was pleasing. But his interview about the Qur'an increased my disappointment and sorrow. I thought to myself: He is going further astray with every passing day. I asked myself: What factor can it be that is so exploiting this individual with both university and seminary credentials? An individual who, with a luminous face and charming language, used to teach the *Nahj al-Balaghah*. He used to explain the *Hamam*[2] Sermon in a most appealing way. How did it come about that he became so distanced from this group?

Let me move on from this preface and, by writing this letter and assessing his ideas, leave a window open again to the possibility that he will reconsider his ideas. In the hope that, on reading this letter, he will return to the fold of the Islamic nation again.

School of doubt or "sophism"

In the 5th century B.C., in ancient Greece, a group of people turned to the school of doubting everything, even their own existence and the existence of the external world, and they presented strange ideas and beliefs. The growth of sophism gained the upper hand in Greek thought for a while, but it was brought to an end by great philosophers and thinkers, such as Socrates, Plato and Aristotle, because they exposed their fallacies and ended the disease of sophistry. By setting out his logic, Aristotle was able to offer humanity a kind of rigorous and realistic thinking. Although the said thinkers offered valuable services to human thought, nevertheless, before long, another school by the name of "skepticism" was founded by Pyrrho (275–365) and the school of denying realities turned into the school of absolute doubt, but that too did not last long and became history.

Islamic philosophers, such as Ibn Sina (Avicenna) and Mulla Sadra, have said some eloquent things in this respect and anyone who is interested can refer to a book entitled *Perception in Islamic Philosophy*, written by the author of the present letter.

With the West's recent rise, the school of skepticism reappeared in "pseudo-scientific" guises. A group of Western philosophers decided—instead of adding another floor to philosophy's solid edifice—to bring down the whole structure once again. Their skill became that of speaking

---

[2] Ali's famous sermon on piety and characteristics of the pious. [Ed.]

of doubt about everything. In Foroughi's[3] words, "British philosophers' skill was nothing but to bring down philosophy's splendid edifice, as it had been constructed thus far, without adding anything to it."

Of course, doubt can occasionally be a stepping stone to certitude and, without doubting, one will not reach certitude. But a beautiful doubt is one that serves as a bridge to certitude and as a stepping stone, so to speak, not as an abode. But, unfortunately, doubt is an abode to these people; not a road or a stepping stone.

Another disease, which is born of this same school of doubt, is the airing of theories without the slightest reason or proof. And whenever they are asked: What's your reason for saying this, they say, "I think". But why do you think this? For what reason? Asking about their reasons and proof is forbidden!!

Ibn Sina states: Anyone who accepts what someone says without reasons and proof, has ceased to be a human being. But, unfortunately, this disease (airing theories without reasons)—and accompanied by a set of dramatic statements at that—has gradually become widespread, whereas the logic of the Qur'an is this: "Say: Produce your proof."

Dr Soroush, in his previous discussion (on the subject of the Imamate and caliphate), he was unkind to the Shi'i Imams, but, here, he has gone a step further and been unkind to the realm of revelation and the Qur'an.

I ask God to stop him here and not to allow him to take another step, lest his felicity in the next world (which I am sure he seriously wants) is further endangered.

The theory in brief

The fact of the matter is that he says inconsistent and contradictory things in explaining his theory, and it cannot be summarized into a single point. He keeps jumping from pillar to post, so to speak, so that, if an objection is raised on one point, he can escape. I will now set out his remarks in a few main points.

---

[3] A twentieth century Iranian scholar. [Ed.]

An Experience Like Poets' Experiences

Dr Soroush says:

> Revelation is 'inspiration'. It is the same experience as that of poets and mystics, although prophets' are on a higher level. In our modern age, we can understand revelation by using the metaphor of poetry. As one Muslim philosopher has put it: revelation is higher poetry.

Analysis

This theory is not a new theory; it is the same as the one that the unbelievers in Mecca used to use to explain the Qur'an. They would say: Just as, Emra al-Qays [6th century Arabian poet] creates meanings and words in the light of inspiration, Muhammad is the creator of the Qur'an's meanings and words through the same method. Undoubtedly, what they meant by poem was not poetry in the sense of versification, but, rather, human findings and imaginings through thought, whether in the form of poetry or prose. The Qur'an speaks of this theory of theirs and criticizes it.

"Saying: What, shall we forsake our gods for a poet possessed?" (37: 36)

And they would also say:

"He is a poet for whom we await Fate's uncertainty." (52: 30)

And sometimes they would explain away the Qur'an in three ways considering it a creation of the Prophet's thoughts. Sometimes they would say: The ideas are a hotchpotch. Sometimes they would say: He is lying in attributing his words to God. And, finally, they would say: He is a poet who has put his imaginations into these forms:

"Nay, but they say, a hotchpotch of nightmares! Nay, he has forged it; nay, he is a poet!" (21: 5)

The Qur'an criticizes this theory and states:

"It is the speech of a noble Messenger. It is not the speech of a poet (little do you believe)." (69: 42)

And it states in another verse:

"We have not taught him poetry; it is not seemly for him. It is only a Remembrance and a Clear Qur'an." (36: 69)

So, these people had ranked the Prophet among poets and the theory that we are discussing now is no more than this, even if the term "on a higher level" has been added to it. On the whole, the logic is the same.

If he (Soroush) is saying, Poets were their own source of inspiration, but the Prophet received his inspiration from the Almighty, then he is conjoining a disparate with a disparate; hence, it is an unsound and inappropriate analogy.

Setting this point aside, what is the reason for the theory anyway? Do we have any evidence for it? Unfortunately, the interview in question is, from start to finish, a string of propositions and terms, without any justification. If the Qur'an is really a poetic deliberation, then why does it challenge others to produce even one *sura* (chapter) similar to its? Have you ever seen a poet who forecloses what he has done to all others and says: No-one, so long as the world shall last, will ever be able to compose a poem like my poem?

Here, we can also tell the propounder of the theory: This exposition and argument of yours about the Qur'an is nothing but a poetic experience. In other words, your being has cultivated this idea, etched it on the page of your mind and made it flow from the tip of your pen, without there being any reality behind it.

If poetry and poets and such things lack everlasting value, then, what you are saying is lacking in exactly the same way.

The Prophet is the Qur'an's Creator and Producer

Elsewhere, he says:

> The metaphor of poetry helps me to explain this: Just like a poet, the Prophet feels that he is captured by an external force. But in fact—or better: at the same time—the Prophet himself is everything: the creator and the producer. The question whether the inspiration comes from outside or from inside is really not relevant, because, at the level of revelation, there is no difference between outside and inside.

Analysis

These words and phrases tell us that the propounder of this theory considers the Qur'an to be the manifestation of the Prophet's inner being, which is known as "inner revelation". The argument that prophets' revelations were a manifestation of their inner selves was first suggested by a group of proselytisers; that is to say, by priests and Orientalists. And most of all by an Orientalist by the name of Emile Dermenghem, who has stirred up quite a fuss in this respect. With his childish efforts, he wants to present sources for the Qur'an, one of which is the manifestation of the inner being. In *The Life of Mahomet*, he writes the following about his own theory:

> Muhammad's inner mind or, in modern terminology, his inner self had discovered the baselessness of idolatry. In order to attain prophethood, he set out to worship God and he went into reclusion in the Cave of Hira. There, he achieved a high degree of conscientious faith. He gained breadth of thought and redoubled visionary insight. At this stage, he became so powerful as to be worthy of guiding the people. He was always thinking until he knew for certain: he was the Prophet whom God had roused to guide humanity. This knowledge came to him as if it was being sent down from the sky and Almighty God was speaking to him through Gabriel.

The thing that distinguishes what poets feel from what prophets feel is exactly the thing to which Mr Soroush has attached no relevance. Poets believe that the source of inspiration is inside themselves and prophets believe that the source of inspiration is outside themselves. But, unfortunately, this biggest point of difference has seemed very slight to him and he's said: "The question whether the inspiration comes from outside or from inside is really not relevant." Whereas this is precisely the glaring difference between these two inspirations.

People who aren't very skilled at philosophical and mystical matters are unable to distinguish the boundary between these two types of inspiration and these two feelings. So, the unbelievers at the time of the Prophet, too, because they weren't able to understand the difference between these two types of feeling, used to think to themselves: How is it possible for someone to receive an inspiration from outside and be given a mission to guide the people? The Qur'an recounts this idea of theirs as follows: "Was it a wonder to the people that We revealed to a man from among them: "Warn the people and give thou good tidings to the believers that they have a sure footing with their Lord"? The unbelievers say: "This is a manifest sorcerer." (36: 2)

Opponents over the ages have had arguments and ideas for combating "Muhammadan revelation", but the substance of the false arguments and interpretations has always been the same. The thing is that, in the present age, those same arguments, interpretations and accusations, put forward by Abu Jahl and Abu Sufyan,[4] have changed shape and have been presented as new products and as scholarly research.

---

[4] Abu Jahl and Abu Sufyan were the two chief opponents of Muhammad in Mecca. [Ed.]

Meanings from God, Words from the Prophet

In the bits mentioned so far, the theory's propounder has used brief and more detailed points to say that the Qur'an was produced by the Prophet himself. But elsewhere in the same interview, he says:

> The Prophet is also the creator of the revelation in another way. What he receives from God is the content of revelation. This content, however, cannot be offered to the people as such, because it is beyond their understanding and even beyond words. It is formless and the activity of the person of the Prophet is to form the formless, so as to make it accessible.

In this theory, he is saying that the concepts and meanings are from God, but the shape and form were the Prophet's creation. He has, thereby, denied part of the miracle of the Qur'an, which lies in the beauty and sturdiness of its phrasing, and he has suggested that only the meanings are from God. So, the Qur'an is the joint work of God and the Prophet, because the meanings are from God and the form is from the Prophet. It is as if it is a joint stock company, where the capital is from God and the shaping of the forms is by the Prophet.

Now, the question arises: Is this theory feebler than the first theory? There, everything was from the Prophet, except for a weak link with God. But, here, the formless meanings are from God and the form is from the Prophet!

The question also arises: What is your reason for suggesting this partnership? Is a God who is capable of sending down meanings, incapable of shaping the forms?

Moreover, the Qur'an itself attests to the opposite of this theory, because it repeatedly tells the Prophet what to say. For example: "Say: God is One." In other words, both the meanings and the forms are from God.

Conditions of the Prophet's Life Produced the Qur'an

The theory's propounder sometimes considers the Prophet to be the independent producer of the Qur'an and says: He is everything and plays a pivotal role. And sometimes he speaks about a kind of partnership between God and the Prophet. But, sometimes he wants to say that the conditions of the Prophet's life produced these concepts, ideas and meanings. In other words, he sees the times as the producer of this product (the Holy Qur'an) and says:

> But his personality also plays an important role in shaping the text. His personal history: his father, his mother, his childhood. And even his moods. If you read the Qur'an, you feel that the Prophet is sometimes jubilant and highly eloquent, while at other times he is bored and quite ordinary in the way he expresses himself... That is the purely human side of revelation.

Now, the question arises: In this version, he wants to present the Qur'an as an entirely human book and he wants to make it seem like the situation of other writers, whose conditions of life have a full impact on their perspectives and interpretations; in other words, that inclinations and cultures have had a full impact in its formulation. If this is the case, why does Muhammad's God deny all of this and say that only revelation was involved in the creation of the Qur'an: "Your comrade is not astray, neither errs, nor speaks he out of caprice. This is naught but revelation revealed, taught him by one terrible in power." (53: 3–5)

Suggesting that the Qur'an is a human book conflicts with hundreds of Qur'anic verses. Here are some of these verses:

1. "If it had been from other than God surely they would have found in it much inconsistency." (4: 82)
2. "A Book We have sent down to thee that thou mayest bring forth mankind from the shadows to the light." (14: 1)
3. "We have sent it down as an Arabic Qur'an; haply you will understand." (12: 2)
4. "This is a Book We have sent down, blessed." (6: 92)

In view of these clear statements, how can we see it as a human book and consider it to have been produced by a human being, bearing in mind that there is no doubt about the honesty and sincerity of Muhammad, *al-amin*, peace be upon him.

Misperceptions and incorrect information

We have explained his main theory here which is expressed in four different ways; without him giving any reasons for his theory. And this contradiction is itself the clearest testimony to the fact that it is unfounded.

But alongside this theory, there is also a series of wild and unseemly remarks, which we will briefly mention:

1. He says:

> But nowadays, there are more and more interpreters who think that the revelation is infallible only in purely religious matters such as the attributes of God, life after death and the rules of worship. They accept that the revelation may be wrong in matters that relate to the material world and human society. What the Qur'an says about historical events, other religious traditions and all kinds of practical earthly matters does not necessarily have to be accurate. Such interpreters often argue that these kinds of errors in the Qur'an do not harm prophethood because the Prophet 'descended' to the level of knowledge of the people of his time and spoke to them in the 'language of the time'.

Now, we ask: The term "more" and "most" that he uses, accusing Islamic interpreters of the said notion—who are these interpreters who, over the course of fourteen centuries, have acknowledged that the Qur'an may be wrong on issues relating to life? They only consist of Orientalists and their followers, like the head of the Qadianis and the people influenced by them, such as Egyptian writers.

What does it mean to discriminate between errors like this anyway? What does it mean to say that the Prophet is wholly truthful and accurate on the supernatural but wrong on some tangible and objective issues? And even if one interpreter has said this about the verse he has in mind, this does not mean that everyone thinks like this. The Qur'an describes the Prophet's knowledge and learning as the greatest divine wisdom and states: "God has sent down on thee the Book and the Wisdom, and He has taught thee that thou knewest not; God's bounty to thee is ever great." (4: 113)

How can knowledge that is considered great by the Qur'an possibly be wrong on the second category of issues?

2. Then, he goes even further and describes the Prophet's knowledge in the following terms:

> I have a different view...I do not think that he knew more than the people around him about the earth, the universe and the genetics of human beings. He did not possess the knowledge we have today. And that does not harm his prophethood because he was a prophet and not a scientist or a historian.

Now, we ask: What is your reason for saying that he did not know these things and that his knowledge of these things was at the same level as that of the Arabs in the age of ignorance?

We do not want to speak about the Qur'an's scientific miraculousness here, because I have spoken at length about this in my book, *Marzha-e E'jaz* (The Frontiers of Miraculousness). The noble Prophet, peace be upon him, via revelation, and his infallible successors, such as Ali, peace be upon him, in the *Nahj al-Balaghah*, and Ali's son, in the *Sahifeh Sajjadieh*, have revealed a series of scientific facts that the world of their time and the world of yesterday could not have imagined. It is very unfair to deny all the scientific facts in these books and then to make excuses and say: He was a Prophet, not a scientist. In other words, he was a Prophet, not a scholar; he was a Prophet, he did not know the secrets of the world.

Allegations about the Mu'tazilites

Since the theory's propounder has considered the Qur'an to be the product of the Prophet's thinking, he tries to find partners and cohorts for himself. And, to this end, he's found no one easier to pick on that the Mu'tazilites. And he attributes the following idea to them: Belief in the idea that the Qur'an is a human product, which can contain mistakes, is implicit in their doctrine of the created Qur'an.

Of course, although the Mu'tazilites are now extinct and no prominent figure remains from their ranks, some of their books are available to all. Perish the thought that they consider the Qur'an to be a creation in the sense that is was a product of the Prophet's thinking. Basically, the idea in question was put by Christians in the 8th century to the Abbasids: Was the Qur'an eternal/uncreated or temporal/created? Some people came to believe that the Qur'an was eternal and some that it was temporal. Chroniclers considered the Qur'an to be eternal and the Mu'tazilites considered it to be temporal, because eternality is unique to God and everything else is temporal. And one of these creations is the Qur'an which is an action of God and God's action is not disjoint from the temporal. And, if they said that it was created, they meant that it was created by God, not a product of the Prophet's thinking. Hence, in our religious narratives, emphasis has been placed on neither calling the Qur'an "eternal", nor "created", because, if they call it "eternal", it is a kind of polytheism and, if they call it "created", the enemy will exploit this and consider it to mean that it was a creation and invention of the Prophet's thinking. So, the unbelievers of the time of the Prophet, peace be upon him, used this same formulation and said: "We have not heard of this in the last religion; this is surely an invention." (38: 7)

Allegations about Rumi and mystics

Again, in order to find support for his ideas, he brings in Rumi and he says:

> Rumi states that the Qur'an is the mirror of the states of mind of the Prophet. What Rumi implies is that the Prophet's personality, his changing moods and his stronger and weaker moments are reflected in the Qur'an.

Attributing things to people is easy but proving it is hard. Which Rumi verse leads to the conclusion that he is suggesting? Whereas Rumi has hundreds of verses in which he explicitly states the opposite, such as...

> Although the Qur'an came to us from the Prophet's lips,
> anyone who says it wasn't said by God blasphemes.

Setting tasks for Muslims

He ends his remarks by setting tasks for Muslims. He says: "The task of Muslims today is to translate the essential message of the Qur'an over time." The question arises: Since you have said that the Qur'an is a human book that can contain mistakes, what need is there for translating it into the language of the day? Why cover up the mistakes in this way? By presenting the Qur'an as a fallible human book, you have distanced yourself from the Islamic community; there is no further need for your advice. It is those who remain in the group who can offer advice. But when an individual bids farewell to a group, they thereby lose their position as leader, guide and counselor.

Finally, let me say: I wrote this letter with the utmost regret and sorrow, but I hope that the interview is not by him and that the translator or translators have translated it incorrectly; in which case, he has a duty to correct the mistakes in order to undo the damage.

The propounder of the theory is also hereby requested—in relation to "Muhammadan revelation" and the doubts that have been raised about it by Orientalists and their followers—to refer to my review of *Twenty-*

Three Years,[5] written by the author of the present letter. In this book it has been clearly proven that all these arguments and interpretations, with all their razzle-dazzle, are just another version of the judgments of the age of ignorance and, in fact, the content is the same although it has been presented in two different guises. The fact of the matter is that the Arabs of the Prophet's time—because of their naivety—imagined that their view constituted proof, whereas the modern critics present the same ideas in a scientific guise and offer the "mirage" as water.

February 2008

---

[5] *Twenty-Three Years* is a book written in early 1970s by journalist Ali Dashti, an Iranian modernist. In this book, Dashti tried to prove that Muhammad's prophet-hood was a purely natural phenomenon and had nothing to do with supernatural providence and that his success in Arabia was due to his ingenuity and clever talent in administration and military activities. It also asserted that the Qur'an contained a number of contradictions and was fully under the influence of the Arab culture of the time. The book created great controversy and was finally banned, its author accused of blasphemy. [Ed.]

BASHAR AND BASHIR[1]
SOROUSH'S FIRST RESPONSE TO SOBHANI

To the Esteemed Scholar Ayatollah Ja'far Sobhani,

Greetings and salutations. I saw your fatherly, considerate and well-meaning letter on the website of Fars News Agency. I found that it contained good admonitions and a call to the good. I have no doubt that your clerical duties, your zeal as a believer and your commitment as a Muslim led you to write the letter. I will not be so bold as to suggest—as you did—that "there are agents in play here and they are exploiting you", both because I have no proof or evidence to suggest such a thing, and because I believe that phrases like this do not sit well in a learned, well-intentioned, fair-minded debate. Before your letter, four other seminary scholars had taken part in this debate, and they all spoke in the language of analysis and reasoning, without recourse to derision and accusations of heresy, apart from the 'Qur'an expert' who, abandoning the norms of civility, used an injudicious turn of phrase and described me as an enemy of the Qur'an.[2]

Be that as it may, what surprised me was, first, that you said: 'I consider his [Soroush] silence over this report to be an unpardonable sin.' Are you absolutely certain that I have been silent? Did you not read my interview with *Kargozaran* newspaper in this connection? Or, is it the people who keep you informed who have sinned by not telling you everything?

Here, I will reproduce the interview and, then, I will explain some of its points at greater length. And you will realize that the answers to many of the criticisms that you and others have levelled at me are clearly and adequately contained therein. I am confident that if you had seen it earlier, you would have gone to much less trouble and would

---

[1] *Bashar* and *Bashir* are two Qur'anic terms referring to Muhammad as a human (*Bashar*) and to his prophetic role as the bearer of good tidings (*Bashir*). [Ed.]

[2] Reference is to Baha al-din Khoramshahi, a lay author, researcher and translator of the Qur'an. Defending the orthodox view of the Qur'an, Khoramshahi used this expression in an article responding to Soroush's interview. [Ed.]

have spoken much more kindly, and your comments would have taken a different line and form.

* * *

The Text of the Interview[3] [with *Kargozaran*]:

Muhammad's Word, Muhammad's Miracle

Q. Some newspapers and websites have been saying recently that Soroush has officially denied that the Qur'an was revealed by God and has said that it is the earthly word of Muhammad. Is this true?

A. Maybe they are joking or, God forbid, they have political or personal motives.

Q. So, what is your view and your explanation?

A. Hopefully, they are well-intentioned and have simply misunderstood things. Otherwise, anyone who is acquainted with the Divinity's universal dominion (*wilayat-e kuliyyeh illahiyyeh*) and with the closeness of God's apostles to Him—and knows about their experience of union with Him—would not speak in this disbelieving manner. God's apostles are so close to God and they so lose themselves in God that their word is the same as the word of God, and their commands and prohibitions and their likes and dislikes are the same as God's commands and prohibitions and likes and dislikes. The beloved Prophet of Islam was a human being and he acknowledged and was conscious of his humanity, but this human being had, at the same time, acquired such a divine hue and quality—and the intermediaries (even Gabriel) had so fallen away from between him and God—that whatever he said was both earthly and divine; these two things were inseparable.

> Like a stone that's entirely turned into pure ruby
> it's filled with the sun.[4]

God willing, if people reflect on this fine, mystical point, the problem will be solved and the key to what is being said will be discovered.

---

[3] *Kargozaran* (8 February, 2008).
[4] *Mathnawi*, 5: 2025.

Q. So what about Gabriel descending to bring down revelation?

A. Mystics are of the view that Gabriel is not closer to God than Muhammad is; in fact, it is Gabriel who complies with the Prophet. Do we not have it in the story of the Prophet's ascension to heaven that Gabriel was unable to accompany the Prophet to higher levels and was afraid that his wings would burn? What does this story tell us? Did the late Khomeini not say: 'It was the spirituality of God's Prophet that brought down revelation to us...In other words, the Holy Prophet brought truthful Gabriel into this world.'[5] Does this mean that it was not God who sent down Gabriel?

To say that the Qur'an is Muhammad's word is exactly like saying the Qur'an is Muhammad's miracle. Underlining one is not a negation of the other. Anything that happens in the world happens in accordance with God's knowledge, permission and will. A monotheist has no doubt about this. Be that as it may, we say that the cherry is the fruit of the cherry tree. Do we have to say that the cherry is the fruit of God in order to be a monotheist? Let's not wrap the old Ash'arism in the garb of modern sanctity. Let us speak in a righteous way and strive to understand the meaning of delicate and subtle points. The Qur'an was the product of a virtuous tree—the Prophet's persona—which bore fruit by God's permission, and this is identical to revelation being sent down to us and an act of God. "Have you not regarded how Allah has drawn a parable, a good word is like a good tree: its roots are steady and its branches are in the sky? It gives its fruit every season by the leave of its lord." (4: 24–25)

My advice to the fair-minded (I do not know what to say to the ill-minded) is exactly the same as Rumi's advice: They must set aside any suspicion of God's apostles and not view them as separate from God. They must not dislodge and bring down these beloved, revered figures from God's presence, proximity and dominion.

---

[5] *Sahifeh-ye Nur*, Vol. 20, speech dated 14 April 1987.

Q. It seems that you have composed some poems in this respect. Is that right?

A. Yes, in a long ode that I composed about three years ago and dedicated it to the Prophet, the conqueror of the territories of the transcendence, I said:

> O the carriage of vision, O you, the conqueror of the territories of the
> transcendence
> On the night of the Ascension, you ascended from orbit to orbit
> From darkness to the realm of imagination, from there to the new
> moon;
> Moving fast, leaving Gabriel, lamed, behind...
> You were the heavenly bird and you were the flying

My allusions in these verses are to a Prophetic supplication saying: 'Prostrate to you my darkness, my imagination and believes in you my heart.'[6]

* * *

As you can see, the idea that the Qur'an is 'a product of Muhammad'—a Muhammad who was totally human—is entirely reasonable and well-established, and enjoys the endorsement of a large number of Muslim thinkers and mystics over the centuries. It has a profound meaning that is a hundred times more profound than the idea that it is 'a product of Gabriel'. And, of course, there is no conflict between this and the notion that the Qur'an was recounted by Gabriel ('Verily this is the word of a most honorable Messenger'), because, as Ayatollah Khomeini put it—and this is the formulation favoured by all Muslim mystics—'Gabriel, too, was brought down by the Prophet'. In this process and in relation to God, outside and inside are one and the same; as are the past and the future, and above and below. This is why I said that, when it comes to the phenomenon of revelation, 'there is no difference between from within and from without'. The God that true monotheists recognize is inside and outside the Prophet in equal measure. What difference does it make whether we say that God's

---

[6] Commentators have interpreted this Prophetic saying (*sajada laka sawadi wa khiyali wa amana beka fouadi*) as saying that: *sawad* (darkness) alludes to his material bodily existence, *khiyal* refers to his imaginal existence and *fowad* (heart) refers to his purely immaterial existence. [author]

revelation comes to him from inside or from outside, and whether we say Gabriel appears to him from outside or from inside? Is God supposed to be outside the Prophet and is the Prophet supposed to be at some distance from God? I do not know why the notions of God's closeness to His servant and the absorption of the contingent in the Necessary have been forgotten and replaced with the image of a sultan-emissary-peasant. What can Ayatollah Sobhani's explanation be for offering this misleading image?

Secondly, the Tale of the Poetry

What I am saying is that, in order to understand the unfamiliar phenomenon of revelation we can use the more familiar phenomenon of the creation of poetry and artistic creativity in general. This is simply at the level of pure imagery. Did Al-Ghazali not say, 'If you want to know what revelation is, take a look at the satanic temptations that you sometimes feel. By looking at them you can get a slight sense of what revelation is like,' because the Qur'an itself uses the notion of devils' revelations and says: 'The Satans inspire their friends to dispute with you.' (6: 121)

Ayatollah Sobhani, it is important that you bear in mind that, today, what people understand by poetry, in the sense of elevated, artistic creativity, is very different from the conception that Abu Jahl and Abu Lahab had of it, and using the image of art to give an approximate sense of revelation neither detracts anything from the weight of the Qur'an nor adds anything to Abu Lahab's weight! Allameh Tabataba'i used to say that revelation was mysterious intelligence; I believe that mysterious art is a more appropriate expression.

Thirdly, Appealing to Rumi

I am glad to see that you are of one mind with me in thinking that drawing on the verses of Mowlana Jalaleddin Rumi is to draw on the experiences and knowledge of a wise mystic, who holds a secure and elevated position in Islamic mysticism, and that citing his verses as evidence does not mean basing oneself on 'poesy', and that, in the Mathnawi, Rumi is, in fact, a composer (nazem), not a poet (sha'er). My plea to Ayatollah Sobhani is that he should study this noble and inspirational book in earnest and not remain on the surface but dive for the pearl in the ocean of that free-minded mystic's teachings, and not confine himself to a few of Rumi's commonly-known phrases that are often quoted out of context and which can be misleading as the basis of judgment. To sweeten your palate, let me cite the following verses:

> The Gabriel will tell you the rest,
> nay it is you who's whispering in your own ear
> It's neither an I, nor an other, but a you who are I
> Like times when you sink into sleep
> from within yourself you appear before yourself
> When you hear something from yourself, you imagine
> someone else has told you a secret in your sleep
> You're not uni-layered, my good friend
> You're the oceans' deep and the universe.

As you can see, Rumi speaks of Gabriel as one of the gradations of human beings, whom he sees and describes as many-layered creatures, and he views human beings as deep oceans, with multiple layers, such that one layer can whisper secrets into the ears of another layer. He sees this as exactly the same as the whispering of secrets into one's ears by Gabriel. He even views speaking to another in one's sleep as speaking to oneself. In this way, he opens a window to understanding the mechanism by which revelation and inspiration work. It is as if, in the process of revelation, a turbulence and tumult occur in the Prophet's persona, such that the Prophet's higher self speaks to his lower self. It goes without saying that all these things occur with God's permission and by God's doing, "And the Lord beseights them from all around." (85: 20)

When Rumi says: 'a thousand Gabriels are hidden within this human being' and says: 'If Ahmad were to display the illumination within him, Gabriel would faint for all eternity,' he is not engaging in mere niceties and is not suggesting a merely superficial and conventional superiority. Ahmad (Muhammad) is truly superior to Gabriel; that is to say, Gabriel is lost in Muhammad's grandeur.

Fourthly, as for "Humanness" Implying Idle Passions and Desires

It is a mystery to me how Ayatollah Sobhani could have failed to see my many references to 'the divinity of the Prophet's being' and why he imagines that humanness means having idle desires and passions. What can we call this kind of oversight and mistake?

The Muhammad, peace be upon him, who is the agent and recipient of revelation is a blessed (*mu'ayyad*) and pure (*mutahhar*) human being. So, 'what comes out of the pitcher is exactly what's in it' and the fine tree (*shajarah tayyebah*) of his being cannot produce anything but fine fruits.⁷ But let us set the Prophet aside for a moment and look at fallible human beings like you, like Avicenna, Kant, Descartes and Popper. Can we say, since they were not prophets, everything that they said was tainted with idle passions and desires? Even if we assumed that the Prophet's revelation is entirely human and earthly, we would still not be able to conclude that it was based on idle passions—let alone the fact that his revelation was entirely mundane *and* entirely divine. In other words, it is a supernatural thing that has been made to fit the dimensions of nature. An ahistorical thing that has been historicized. An exalted phenomenon that has 'descended to temporality'. A sea in a pitcher. A breath blown into a reed-pipe. And it emanates from a God who is sitting among the people and a person who has been filled with God. In Rumi's words:

> You can seek water in a brook or you can seek it in a jug
> for, the jug, too, would be empty without the brook.

You have to concede that your metaphysics is a metaphysics of absence (*bu'd*) and separation (*feraq*), whereas my metaphysics is one of presence (*qurb*) and union (*wesal*). The impression that you have of God and Muhammad seems to be the imagery of a speaker and a loudspeaker or a tape recorder. The speaker speaks and the loudspeaker reflects it. So, the Prophet, like a loudspeaker, is nothing but a means and a tool. How far indeed is this from the idea that the Qur'an descended onto Muhammad's heart.⁸ It would seem that you think that the Qur'an descended onto Muhammad's tongue, not his heart. But the impression that I have of that relationship, "We are nearer to him than his jugular vein" (50: 16), is the imagery of a soul and a body, or, more simply, a gardener and a tree. The gardener plants the seed and the tree bears fruit. The fruit owes everything—ranging from its colour, scent and shape to the vitamins and sugars it contains—to the tree from which it has emanated; a tree that has been planted in special soil and is nourished by a special light, food and air. And, of course, both the planting and the fact that it bears fruit is with God's permission and monotheists have no doubt about this. And, of course, the tree's

---

⁷ Reference is to the Qur'anic verse (14: 24) [Ed.]
⁸ Reference is to the verse (26: 193–194) [Ed.]

existence is, in effect, God's will and there is no distance between them. It is not like conventional human phenomena where one person issues a command and another implements it. What I do not understand is why, in your eyes, God's administration is like human beings' executive and managerial administrations.

Let me speak more clearly: Although all of nature is godly, everything in nature is natural. And, in a human realm, everything is human. And, in history, everything is historical. Hence, in the process of revelation, the Prophet is an active agent, not a passive means. He is 'a human being' upon whom the Qur'an has 'descended' and from whom it has emanated. Both these notions appear in the text of the Qur'an. The two qualities 'descended' and 'human' are present in the deepest layers of revelation. And, without taking these two important qualities into account, we can arrive at no reason-pleasing interpretation of the Qur'an. Let me put it more simply again: I am not saying: God produces no fruits; I am saying: In order for God to produce fruits, He plants a tree and the tree produces fruits. I am not saying: God does not speak; I am saying: In order for God to speak, a Prophet speaks and his words are considered to be God's words.

On the basis of your imagery, it would appear that the speaker can put any words in the loudspeaker's mouth, ranging from poetry, philosophy and mathematic to Arabic, English, Chinese, etc. But, on the basis of my imagery, not every type of fruit can grow on a particular tree. An apple tree can only produce apples, not cherries. It would be taking Ash'arism to the absolute limit if we were to say that a particular tree may well produce any and every type of fruit.

Even in the imagery of the speaker and the loudspeaker, the loudspeaker does not just sit there; it plays a role, it imposes its own contingencies on the speaker's voice. In Rumi's words: 'The breath that the reed-pipe player blows into his pipe / is in keeping with the pipe, not in keeping with the player'.

This is how it comes about that: the formless meaning is from God and the form is from Muhammad; the breath is from God and the reed-pipe is from Muhammad; the water is from God and the jug is from Muhammad. This is a God who pours the ocean of His being into the small jug of a figure known as Muhammad Ibn Abdullah. And so everything becomes imbued with Muhammad: Muhammad is an Arab, so the Qur'an becomes Arabic. He lives in Hijaz amid tent-dwellers, so paradise, too, occasionally, appears as if it has been designed for Arabs and tent-dwellers, with black-eyed women who are sitting in tents.

The Qur'an's eloquence, too, has highs and lows in keeping with the Prophet's moods. Rain is viewed as one of God's mercies, much more so than the light of the sun. And so on and so forth. And this is what we mean when we say that revelation and Gabriel complied with the Prophet's personality. This, too, is the meaning of the wise claim that was made by Abu-Nasr Farabi and Nasir al-din Tusi, who said that the Prophet's power of imagination plays a role in the process of revelation and, in Rumi's words, puts a form on the formless. Muhammad's human-historical persona is visible everywhere in the Qur'an and this God-nurtured persona is the entire blessing that God has bestowed on Muslims. Hence, the words that this sanctified, mortal apostle speaks are the words of God! And this is what Rumi meant when he said:

> Although the Qur'an came to us from the Prophet's lips,
> anyone who says it wasn't said by God blasphemes.

From the Prophet's lips means emanating from his persona, in which Gabriel too is lost. Can God possibly speak in any other way? If you have another solution for the problem of "God speaking", be so kind as to explain it to us.

Not just mystics but philosophers, too, come to our aid now and challenge Mr Sobhani. Have philosophers—and best of all and most of all Sadr al-din Shirazi—not said that 'any temporal being (hadeth) is preceded by time and material potentiality?' Muhammad's revelation, too, had to occur in particular material and historical conditions, and these conditions were fully involved in shaping it. They played the part of the formal and material cause of revelation. Please note that it is more than a question of words and meaning; it is a question of the form and the formless, and the words are one of the forms. What Muhammad brought into play were his own limitations in existential and historical terms, in terms of his learning and his character, and so on and so forth; limitations that no being can avoid or escape.

Let me ask Mr Sobhani this: Why is the Qur'an in Arabic language? No doubt, he will reply: God in his wisdom willed it so. I do not deny this, but I am saying that the "Arabness of the Prophet" of Islam is the very act of the Divine willing and the same with all the other things.

Fifthly, the Possibility of the Qur'an and the Prophet's Knowledge Containing "Flaws"

What is meant by "flaws" are the things that are viewed as errors by human beings; i.e., are incompatible with the findings of human learning. It is not stated anywhere in the Qur'an that God taught His Prophet everything about every field of learning, nor did the noble Prophet ever make such a claim himself, nor did anyone ever expect the Prophet to know everything, ranging from theology and divinities to medicine, mathematics, music and astronomy. Contrary to Mr Sobhani's view, the Qur'an, too, says, 'taught you *things* that you did not know' (4: 113). It doesn't say, 'taught you *everything* that you did not know'. In logicians' jargon: the proposition without quantifier is equivalent to a proposition with existential quantifier. Moreover, it says to the Prophet, 'Say, God, increase me in knowledge.' (20: 114).

Ibn-Khaldun wrote in *The Muqaddimah* that the things that the Prophet said about medicine were the same as the ideas and beliefs of the desert-dwelling Arabs of the time and he used to go to a doctor himself. And Ibn-Arabi said—in *Fusus al-Hekam*, (in "fas shithi", in the section on how being perfect does not mean being superior in every way to the imperfect) that:

> The noble Prophet used to prohibit the Arabs from interfering in the pollination of palm trees and from transferring pollen from male trees to female trees. Then, when the trees began yielding less fruit, he realized his mistake and said: 'You are better acquainted with this-worldly affairs and I am better acquainted with religious affairs.'

This is the same Ibn-Arabi, the reading of whose *Futuhat Makiyyah* the late Ayatollah Khomeini recommended, as a splendid example of Islamic and mystical teachings, to Gorbachev, in his famous letter to the [then] Soviet leader.

Ibn-Arabi also cites another narrative about the Prophet in which he is said to have found Umar's idea about what to do with the captives of the battle of Badr better than his own idea. The Qur'an, for its part, says about Abraham, that he did not recognize the angels and was frightened by them. Ibn-Arabi has said: Abraham did not know how to interpret dreams and, so, he took his son to the altar by mistake. So, if anyone maintains that the Prophet's knowledge of mathematics, natural philosophy and this-worldly affairs—not his insights and knowledge of divine secrets—was on a par with the knowledge of his times, they will not be far wrong, and, at least, they will not have said something that contravenes religion's basic imperatives.

As for Apparent Incongruities between the Qur'an and Human Findings

Is it not the case that everyone who has embarked on non-literal interpretation has acknowledged that, on the face of it, there seem to be incongruities between the Qur'an and human learning? In fact, non-literal interpretation is nothing more than an attempt to replace one bit of human learning with another. In *Tafsir al-Mizan*, in his commentary on the verses about rebellious devils who try to listen to those on high and are driven away by meteors (37: 1–10), your teacher, the late Allameh Seyyed Mohammad Hossein Tabataba'i, said, with full scholarly forthrightness and sincerity, that the interpretations of all the commentators of the past had been based on ancient astronomy and the literal meaning of the verses. He said that these interpretations were wrong, that their wrongness was now obvious and certain, and that new meanings had to be found for these verses. He then used Greek-o-Islamic philosophy, which is another field of human learning, to suggest strange interpretations which are unlikely to convince many people. In fact, he expresses his own qualms about the interpretations and says:

> Perhaps these are examples of the metaphors that God uses and what is meant by the sky is the kingdom of heaven, which is home to the angels, and what is meant by meteor is celestial light that drives away devils. Or, perhaps it means that devils attack truths in order to upend them and the angels drive them away with the meteors of truth and repel their falsehoods.

It is as if the late Tabataba'i had forgotten that the projectiles were being hurled at the devils from the lower sky, not from the kingdom of heaven. ('We have adorned the lower heaven with the adornment of the stars and to preserve against every rebel Satan.')

These are the kinds of twists and turns and contractions and expansions that occur in exegesis. And a meaning that was self-evident to our predecessors becomes farfetched to us. And the surface appearance of verses, which was compatible with ancient science, is reinterpreted in order to make it compatible with modern science. The commentators are in no way to blame for these contractions and expansions; this is the character and nature of hermeneutical exegesis in general. But the point is that, logically, an incompatibility has to be acknowledged first before an interpretation is undertaken. Then, methods and ploys are devised to resolve the incompatibility. Taleqani[9] went even further than this and, in his *Partou'i az Qur'an*, in his interpretation of Verse 276 of Al-Baqarah ('Those who indulge in usury shall not rise again except as he rises, whom Satan has demented by his touch'), he said quite openly:

> Considering madness to be a result of being touched or possessed by jinni and Satan were beliefs of the age of ignorance among the Arabs and the Qur'an has spoken in the language of the tribe.

And this is a view that has also been expressed by some modern Arab exegetes. So, Taleqani did not attempt to interpret this verse and accepted 'the mistake', but he offered a rationale for the inclusion of the mistake in the Qur'an. And his position is neither strange nor a heretical. Jarallah Zamakhshari, a Mu'tazilite, expressed the exact same view eight centuries before Ayatollah Taleqani and wrote in *Tafsir Kashshaf*: 'It was one of the false beliefs of the Arabs of the age of ignorance that a blow by an ogre causes epilepsy... The Qur'an came down to us in keeping with this belief.' And Al-Alusi said in *Tafsir Ruh al-Ma'ani* that this was the position of all Mu'tazilites.

The point that calls for reflection in all this is that this fluid Islamic exegesis and theology has today become so afflicted with rigidity that even the views of insiders are considered to be the views of outsiders and seen as the inventions of Orientalists. What calls for even greater reflection is that no one in the past excommunicated any Mu'tazilite on these grounds, although some less than polite Ash'arites wrote that those who denied ogres [i.e. the Mu'tazilah] had been touched by ogres themselves and had gone mad. Rumi, too, referred to this Mu'tazilite-Ash'arite dispute when he said: 'No sooner had a philosopher denied ogres; than he would be possessed by an ogre'.

The tale of the seven heavens is even clearer. Without exception, all exegetes in the past used to explain it according to Ptolemy's theories. And why ever not? The literal meanings of the verses very clearly

---

[9] Ayatollah Sayyed Mahmud Taleqani (1910–1979) was a contemporary Iranian Islamic reformer. He published his series of commentaries on some chapters of the Qur'an under the title: *Partou'i az Qur'an*. [Ed.]

pointed to it. It was only in the 19th and 20th centuries that modern exegetes (Arab and non-Arab) decided—in the light of modern science—to reinterpret these verses, and they proposed new, non-literal yet dubious meanings.

In short, there is no denying the fact that, on the face of it, there are incompatibilities—occasionally severe—between the Qur'an and science. The problem can be tackled in various ways: You can either embark on outlandish interpretations (Tabataba'i), or you attribute it to a correspondence with the culture of the Arabs of the time (Mu'tazilites, Taleqani), or you say that there is a distinction between the language of religion and the language of science, and you consider the language of religion to be wholly symbolic and metaphorical (some Christian theologians), or you go down the path of some contemporary thinkers who say that truth and falsehood does not apply to the products of revelation, or you say that the meaning comes from God and the words come from the Prophet (Wali Allah al-Dehlawi).

Whatever the method, I place verses of this kind in the category of accidentals (which I have spoken about at length in *The Expansion of Prophetic Experience*) which are not germane to the Prophet's mission and the fundamental message of religion. So, I pass by them without undue concern. And, if I had to choose, I would opt for the Mu'tazilites' method. But the idea that the Qur'an is historical has a clear meaning. I have spoken about this, too, in that book. Among other things, it means that it contains answers to the questions that were asked by the ordinary people of the time, as well as references to the Prophet's family concerns. These are all things that could have been absent from the Qur'an.

I do not think that, today, you will win anyone over to Islam or prove, for example, that Islam is superior to Buddhism by insisting that there are seven skies, or that epilepsy and madness are caused by ogres, or that meteors are used to drive away nosy devils who try to spy on angels. What people find irresistible in Muhammad's revelation is not figures of speech of this kind but Suras such as Al-Hadid (Chapter 57), which is named after iron but is made of silk. Al-Ghazali said that it was one of the Qur'an's jewels. And it has brought together, firmly and kindly, God, resurrection, faith, alms, fighting, humility, monasticism, and so on. Its cry of 'Is it not time that the hearts of those who believe shall be humbled?' alone suffices to shake one's being and light the flame of faith in one's heart.

As to Ayatollah Sobhani's assertion that

Since you describe the Qur'an as a human book and containing mistakes, what need is there for us to translate it into and interpret it in today's language...By presenting the Qur'an as a human book that can contain mistakes you have moved away from the Islamic community. There is no further need for advice from you. It is only those who remain in the group who can offer advice.

I explained what I meant by human and by "flaws". Now let me say this: First, it has been said in the Qur'an: 'Do not say to the one who greets you, "You are not a Muslim."'

Secondly, note Tabataba'i, Taleqani and Zamakhshari have all said the same thing.

Thirdly, present us with your own unerring and graceful criteria for resolving these problems, thereby opening people's eyes, swaying their hearts and pointing the way out of the impasse of the contradictions between science and the Qur'an. (Incidentally, I have spoken of a cultural translation, not of putting the Qur'an in today's language. The details of what I said are available in the article 'Essentials and Accidentals in Religions' in *The Expansion of Prophetic Experience*.)

Fourthly, do not call on critical believers to turn into uncritical imitators. Do not frighten people, who are following a course thoughtfully and studiously, with threats of a bad end and infelicity. If there is any felicity, it lies in sincere study and research (even if, in your view, it has led to an improper result), not in mundane imitation.

Although I do not doubt your good intentions and value your good guidance and instructions, I will not abandon research and reflection. I will cling to and rely on the noble rope of reason and thought, and I am so intoxicated by the pleasant scent of this reliance that I will never quit the "perfume-sellers stall."

I look at Muhammad, the Prophet of God, who, like an intoxicated lover-artist in the field of spiritual experience, has adopted a receptive pose, opened up his inner eye, and become filled with God. And, thereafter, whatever he sees and whatever he says is godly. He sees human beings and the world (however it may be, with seven skies or seventy skies, with four elements or with 104 elements) as interwoven with Him and moving towards Him. And joyful and brimming with this prophetic discovery, he speaks of his experience to others, enchants them and draws them to himself like a magnet and washes away their blemishes like an ocean.

I feel great affection for this *basher-e bashir* (human herald) and if, for me, this clay bears the scent of God's words it is because it has been imbued with Him. Once, many years ago, when I was speaking to Muhammad, peace be upon him, I wrote:

> Our "law" is in effect a "cure"[10]
> Our Scripture is Muhammad's emanation
>
> Neither an angel, nor aggrieved with clay
> You were our herald, a human and pure

*   *   *

I will stop here for fear that I might go on at too great a length. I will content myself with what I have said and forego some more minor points. Whilst thanking you for your painstaking endeavour and your well-meaning letter, let me say that I welcome any opportunity for discussion and debate, and I hope that the debate will continue. Let me also add that, at present, I am teaching at a university in the United States; that is to say, I am doing a job here that I am not allowed to do at home thanks to the broadmindedness of Iranian officials. When I return to Iran, if possible, I would like to invite you to a safe and calm venue where we can discuss things face to face, so that you can distinguish the wheat from the chaff. Moreover, since I believe that the highest aim of religiosity and the purpose of all this mystical and theological soul-searching is to construct a dynamic, moral and just society, I feel compelled to ask you to speak out not just on theoretical matters but also when you see bad actions and immorality. Do not remain silent in the face of injustice, remain true to scholars' covenant with God, do not fall into step with the unjust and, in this way, serve as a model to others.

> Were it not for some unwelcome ears
> I'd say a word or two from the heart
>
> But since a suspicious world is seeking doubt
> we will let the discussion run beyond the skin (of words).[11]

Abdulkarim Soroush
Washington D.C.
March 2008

---

[10] *Qanoun* (Law) on medicine and *Shefa* (Cure) on philosophy are two major books by Ibn Sina (Avicenna), the great medieval philosopher and physician. [Ed.]
[11] *Mathnawi*, 5: 2141–2142.

AYATOLLAH SOBHANI'S SECOND LETTER

With greetings to the most learned Dr Soroush,

I received your letter and the second interview, which had been published in some newspapers...[1]

We live in an age in which there are many factors, ranging from satellite broadcasts to films, radios and numerous new-fangled ideas and -isms, that lead youngsters astray and each one of them is targeting our young people's faith. In these circumstances, the expectation is that a learned person like yourself... will avoid any ambiguous remarks that harm belief.

For example, when we say that the Qur'an is the book of the Prophet, peace be upon him, what this means is that the Qur'an is God's book that was revealed to the Prophet. But you use this phrase and then follow it with a few sentences that run counter to what everyone means by it, and you say: "The Prophet played a pivotal role in the production of the Qur'an." Or: The Prophet's moods, ranging from joy to sadness, have had an impact on his book. Or: Some of the verses of the Qur'an do not possess a high degree of eloquence and they are related to the moods and to the tree from which the fruit has been picked!!

Do these phrases and these points—regardless of how we explain them—help young people's faith or do they set the haystack of their faith ablaze?...

But let me set aside these sincere admonitions and reminders and turn to the things you said in your second interview and in relation to my criticisms. Let us examine their main points:

---

[1] A few personal remarks and recommendations are omitted here. They are already presented in the Ayatollah's first letter and repeated here and there throughout this letter as well. They are not, however relevant to the core subject of the debate. [Ed.]

The Nature of Revelation in this Interview?

In your interview, the nature of revelation has been expressed in a few sentences. We will cite a few of them:

> The Qur'an was the product of a virtuous tree—the Prophet's persona— which bore fruit by God's permission ("it gives its produce every year by the permission of its Lord." (14: 25). And this is identical to revelation being sent down to us and an act of God.

Elsewhere you say:

> The Muhammad, peace be upon him, who is the agent and recipient of revelation is a blessed and pure human being. So, "what comes out of the pitcher is exactly what is in it" and the fine tree of his being cannot produce anything but fine fruits.

In a third place, you say:

> And this is what we mean when we say that revelation and Gabriel complied with the Prophet's personality…And the Prophet's power of imagination plays a role in the process of revelation…And Muhammad's human-historical persona is visible everywhere in the Qur'an.

Yet elsewhere, you say:

> In the process of revelation, the Prophet is an active agent, not a passive means. He is "a human being" upon whom the Qur'an has "descended" and from whom it has emanated. And both these notions appear in the text of the Qur'an. The two qualities "descended" and "human" are present in the deepest layers of revelation. And, without taking these two important qualities into account, we can arrive at no reason-pleasing interpretation of the Qur'an.

Analysis

We will content ourselves with these parts of your remarks. Then, we will accept "Muhammadan revelation" (the Qur'an) as arbiter so that it can rule on this reason-pleasing!!! interpretation.

The Qur'an resolutely rejects this theory. The Qur'an never considers the Prophet relevant as an agent, nor does it consider the Word of God to be the fruit of the Prophet's being. Instead, "Qur'anic revelation" says that it has made whatever there is flow from his tongue without being tampered with and without being combined with the Prophet's human ideas and thoughts:

We have revealed to thee an Arabic Qur'an. (42: 7)
We have sent it down as an Arabic Qur'an. (12: 2)
This Qur'an has been revealed to me that I may warn you thereby. (6: 19)
And hasten not with the Qur'an ere its revelation is accomplished unto thee. (20: 114)
Say: I follow only what is revealed to me from my Lord. (7: 203)

The Qur'an insists that divine revelation must only be the Word of God and not be intermingled with anything else, even the pure and exalted temperaments of the noble Prophet; whereas you are insisting on the opposite.

Pay close attention to the following verse: "If it had been from other than God surely they would have found in it much inconsistency." (4: 82)

Please think carefully about the phrase "If it had been from other than God". If the Qur'an were the fruit of a good tree, then the tree would definitely have an effect on the fruit, in which case it would no longer be pristine; it would become divine revelation intermingled with humanity.

Perhaps you have read the interview with Cardinal Jean-Louis Tauran, head of the Catholic Church's interfaith council, where he said:

> I am not prepared to hold theological dialogue with Muslims, because they have accepted a notion that we have not accepted; they say that divine revelation was written as dictated by God and that it has come to them in a pristine state.

But your theory, which sees divine revelation as the fruit of the noble tree of the Prophet's being—albeit a tree planted by God—ultimately takes revelation out of its pristine state and gives it a human tint.

Is what you are saying not similar to what the Cardinal is trying to suggest. You have said:

> A clearer analogy is a gardener and a tree. The gardener plants the seed and the tree bears fruit. And the fruit owes everything—ranging from its colour, scent and shape to the vitamins and sugars it contains—to the tree from which it has emanated; a tree that has been planted in special soil and is nourished by a special light, food and air.

If divine revelation is the fruit of the Prophet's being and if his personality is the agent and the recipient, then, why does he underline the following point: "Move not thy tongue with it to hasten it; Ours it is to gather it and recite it. So, when We recite it, follow thou its recitation. Then Ours it is to explain it." (75: 16–19)

If the meanings are from God and the form is from the Prophet, then, why does the Qur'an insist on this "do this" and "don't do that": Don't hasten it and do follow Gabriel's recitation. If the Prophet was moulding revelation into forms, autonomously and consciously, what does reading it hastily mean? And why does the Qur'an say: Follow Gabriel's recitation?

Paying careful attention to these verses shows that revelation descended onto the Prophet's heart and was spoken to him, with these exact meanings and words—which theologians have described as a kind of descent of "the invisible" to "the visible" (*ghayb* to *shuhud*)—and that no human being played an active part in the formulation of the Qur'an. In view of this, is it correct to say that, in the process of revelation, the Prophet is an active agent?

Although these kinds of theories may be presented with good intentions, do they not ultimately help those who detract from revelation's standing so that they can gradually give it a human tone and colour, and, then, place their own ideas alongside revelation's ideas and gradually diminish divine revelation's position?

Mr Soroush! You consider "mystics' religious experiences" as complementary to and an expansion of the Prophet's "religious experience". You thereby remove the boundary between Prophetic revelation and mystical revelation. In your *The Expansion of Prophetic Experience*, you've gone so far as to say:

> Since revelation is a religious experience and since other people also have religious experiences, so, other religious experiences, too, add to the richness of religion. And, with the passage of time, religion expands and is consolidated. Hence, mystics' religious experiences are complementary to and an expansion of the Prophet's religious experience. Hence, God's religion gradually becomes more and more seasoned. This expansion and consolidation occurs in religious knowledge; nay, even in religion itself.[2]

So, the doctrines of Islam, from primary to secondary, have been enriched over the past fourteen centuries and are, consequently, a mixture of Prophetic experience and mystics' experiences. Is this how it really is?

---

[2] In the Ayatollah's letter a reference is given to page 28 of the Persian version of the book (*Bast-e Tajrubeh Nabavi*). However, it should be mentioned that these sentences are not exact quotations; rather they appear to be a paraphrase and rearrangement of several phrases and arguments throughout the chapter. [Ed.]

With utmost respect to mystics and mysticism, we consider the wild outpourings of some mystics to be the very opposite of the Qur'an's monotheism. For example, when a mystic considers the contingent world to be the same as God and says, "Praise be to God who created things and He is one with them," or where Rumi considers the necessary and the contingent to have been one before they became divided.

I do not want to go on at great length about these instances; otherwise, there are many more instances of conflict between Prophetic experience—as you put it—and mystics' experiences; far too many to include in this letter.

Muhammad, Peace Be Upon Him, Is Human

In the interview—and even in the title—the Prophet's humanness has been emphasized, which is surprising. Has anyone denied his humanness? The real Prophet has to be sought in the following verse: "Say: 'I am only a mortal the like of you; it is revealed to me that your God is One God.'" (18: 110) This verse sees the Prophet in two lights:

1. a human being like other human beings
2. the recipient of revelation

The first is the attribute that the Prophet shares with other human beings and it can be dissected and analysed using materialist principles. The second is the aspect of revelation and the supernatural; this is not something that can be measured and dissected and analysed using material means. It falls into the category of the "unseen", so to speak, and is beyond human comprehension. It is a matter of belief as stated in the following verse: "This scripture is infallible; a beacon for the righteous who believe in the unseen." (2: 3)

Basically, the Qur'an speaks about the "seen" and the "unseen", although both are visible and seen in relation to God. But in relation to us limited human beings, some things are seen and some are unseen. In view of this, a set of realities are unseen because our senses cannot grasp them. They are beyond our minds' horizons; for example, the realm of Limbo, resurrection, Prophethood and revelation. We have to grasp these through their signs and traits, not through their species and genus or nature thereof.

Notion of Speaker and Loudspeaker

You have likened the universal Muslim belief in the pristine quality of revelation, which is higher than, superior to and untainted by human temperaments, to a speaker and a loudspeaker. And you have said in this respect:

> The impression that you [Ayatollah Sobhani] have of God and Muhammad seems to be the imagery of a speaker and a loudspeaker or a tape recorder. The speaker speaks and the loudspeaker reflects it. So, the Prophet, like a loudspeaker, is nothing but a means and an instrument.

I am sorry, but we have never considered the Almighty and the Prophet to be a speaker and a loudspeaker. We believe that God is the "message giver" and the Prophet is the "message deliverer". But this delivering is miles away from a loudspeaker. The difference is that the message-deliverer has to reach such a high level of spiritual and mental perfection as to have ears that can—in addition to hearing this-worldly sounds—perceive otherworldly sounds so that he can hear the angel. His eyes have to become so acute as to be able to see the angel. And, in terms of spiritual power, he has to reach a point where, in addition to the material world, he can see the unseen world without trembling or panicking, so that he can receive divine revelation and not tamper with it in the slightest and, then, deliver it to his followers. Is the position of such an individual the position of a loudspeaker?

The Prophet and waiting for revelation

One of the clearest proofs that revelation was not the fruit of the Prophet's being but a crown of glory on his soul and spirit is that the Prophet, peace be upon him, used to sit and wait for revelation. The Jews used to reproach Muslims for praying in the same direction as they did and the Prophet was waiting to hear a definite answer from God in this respect. He constantly waited for revelation and would turn to look at the sky. And his soul and spirit would link up to the world above so that revelation could come to him from God in this connection. And so we read in the Qur'an:

> We have seen thee turning thy face about in the heaven; now We will surely turn thee to a direction that will satisfy thee. Turn thy face towards the Holy Mosque; and wherever you are, turn your faces towards it. (2: 144)

You quote a great mystic[3] as saying that the Prophet himself used to make Gabriel appear. We studied for more than fourteen years with that great mystic and we have published his scholarly views. I do not remember him saying this phrase. And even if he did, the phrase was preceded by something and followed by something that made it clear what he meant. Otherwise, that devoted mystic, who led a great revolution, would not say anything contrary to the Qur'an. Regarding the appearance of angels, the Qur'an states that they appear on God's command, not on the Prophet's: "We come not down, save at the commandment of thy Lord." (19: 64) Perhaps what that great mystic meant was that Gabriel came to the Prophet because of his prayers and entreaties.

In the eighth year into the Prophetic mission, the unbelievers of Quraysh contacted the Jews of Kheybar because they considered them knowledgeable about past religions. They asked them about the prophet-hood of Muhammad, peace be upon him. They said: Ask him three things; if he answers correctly, that is a sign of his prophethood.

Their three questions were about "the two-horned", "the men of the cave", and "spirit." The noble Prophet sat and waited for revelation in order to answer them. It was not as if he answered them immediately by picking the fruit from the tree of his own being. So, divine revelation addressed him in the following way: "They will question thee concerning the two-horned. Say: 'I will recite to you a mention of him.'" (18: 83)

Then, it was stated about the third question: "They will question thee concerning the Spirit. Say: 'The Spirit is of the bidding of my Lord. You have been given of knowledge nothing except a little.'" (17: 85)

I imagine that all these verses, which rightly testify to the theory of most exegetes, are enough to prove my point. Let's go back to another issue.

Prophet, Not Scientist?

In both interviews, you openly and implicitly say the Prophet, peace be upon him, "is a prophet, not a scientist". Of course, this is another one of your ambiguous remarks. The phrase "is a Prophet" indicates veneration for a lofty position. "Is not a scientist" denies that he has

---

[3] Reference is to Ayatollah Khomeini. [Ed.]

knowledge of the human learning. It's as if you don't see his lack of knowledge as much of a fault!! Of course, "not a scientist" is acceptable to all in the sense that learning, unlike the case of other human beings, is not a product of his mind.

Now I will tell you something

The Qur'an states: We taught Adam the names. It's obvious that what is meant by names is not words and phrases, but the truth of things, as is stated: "And He taught Adam the names, all of them; then He presented them unto angels and said: Now tell Me the names of these if you speak truly.'" (2: 31)

Please pay careful attention to the two following words:

1. He presented them
2. tell Me the names of these

These pronouns reveal that He presented the secrets to Adam and that Adam knows about the truths of things and the secrets of creation.

Now would it be correct for us to say: The Seal of the Prophets, the noblest and wisest of Messengers, the one about whom you have written the most admiring poems, was not aware of the most elementary and humdrum sciences, even the sciences of his day?

You have recounted a Tradition from *Fusus al-Hekam* as follows:

> The noble Prophet used to prohibit the Arabs from interfering in the pollination of palm trees and from transferring pollen from male trees to female trees. Then, when the trees began yielding less fruit, he realized his mistake and said: 'You are better acquainted with this-worldly affairs and I am better acquainted with matters of faith.'

Let me remind you that this Tradition is from *Sahih Muslim*[4] and scholars have raised doubts about it. I have humbly examined it myself in one of my books, which you seem not to have seen. Is the gist of this Tradition really in keeping with the Prophet's life? Let us imagine that the Prophet was neither a prophet nor a scientist. Be that as it may, he grew up in a part of the world where the date was the main crop and

---

[4] *Sahih Muslim* is one of the six canonical collections of Hadith for Sunni Muslims. The Shi'is have their own four canonical collections. [Ed.]

most of the trees were palm trees. Is it conceivable that the Prophet, peace be upon him, did not know about this long-standing divine tradition, which the Arabs of the age of ignorance knew about? This is like saying that someone who has grown up in northern Iran does not know about the ways concerning citrus fruits and rice cultivation.

The Seal of the Prophets and the most noble of beings' top student, the Lord of the Faithful, Ali Ibn Abi Talib, said: "Ask me [your questions] before you lose access to me." And this remark is undoubtedly not just about unseen worlds; it is especially broad. Did Ali, peace be upon him, enjoy such a position in terms of learning whereas his noble master did not?! "What ails you then, how you judge?" (68: 36)

One-dimensional development amounts to a "flaw"

Your remarks about the Prophet's high degree of spiritual development in relation to unseen worlds—if not exaggerated—are effective proof of [his] excellence. He reaches a point where Gabriel cannot keep up with him. In terms of closeness to God, he reaches a stage where the distance was less than people can imagine. How can it be that this Prophet, with this high degree of development on invisible affairs, could have been of the lowest degree on the visible world and that his knowledge of the natural sciences could have been on a par with that of the Arabs of the age of ignorance?

This one-sided development would be like a child whose heart grows but whose brain and other organs remain as they were. If the Prophet's knowledge of the natural world was on a par with that of the Arabs of his time, then what about the knowledge contained in the verses below? Did the Arabs of the day know about the things that these verses are talking about?

1. "And of everything created We two kinds; haply you will remember." (51: 49) Did the Arabs of the age of ignorance know that all natural creatures were pairs or know about every little particle in the world?
2. "Thou shall see the mountains, that thou supposed fixed, passing like clouds—God's handiwork who has created everything very well." (27: 88) This verse is about the movement of mountains in this world, not on Judgment Day. The proof of this lies in the phrase, "has created everything," and it goes without saying that Judgment

Day is not the day of creation, it is the day when the mountains will
tumble and you may have said something about this verse in your
book *The Restless Nature of the Universe*.
3. "I swear by the Lord of the Easts and the Wests." (70: 40) Did the
   Arabs of the age of ignorance know about the number of the easts
   and wests?
4. "He creates you in your mothers' wombs, creation after creation, in
   threefold shadows." (39: 6) Did the Arabs of the age of ignorance
   know about this kind of creation?

Also, Verse 14 of the Mu'minun Sura (23: 14) which speaks of the
creation of human beings in their mothers' wombs.

It isn't possible to explain in full the Qur'an's scientific miraculousness in this letter and I think that your readings so far should suffice
on this subject. But I suggest that you at least read the book entitled
Wind and Rain in the Qur'an by Mr Bazargan,[5] so that it will become
clear how he has used the verses relating to these two phenomena to
prove the Qur'an's scientific miraculousness.

Anything That Comes into Being Is Preceded by Material Potentiality and Time

Reference has been made in your letter to the philosophical principle
that says that any temporal being (*hadeth*) is preceded by material
potentiality and time, and that, since divine revelation is also created
and comes into being, it is not exempt from this principle; so divine
revelation cannot be considered free of these two.

It is very strange to find this remark coming from the distinguished
author of *The Restless Nature of the Universe*.[6] On the testimony of

---

[5] Mehdi Bazargan (1907–1995) is one of the distinguished contemporary Iranian
religious modernists, a freedom fighter and political activist. An engineer by profession, Bazargan tried, in the early phase of his religio-intellectual activities, to reconcile
Islamic/Qur'anic teachings with modern scientific findings. This book was one of his
earliest attempts in this regard. It was published in the 1950s. [Ed.]

[6] In *The Restless Nature of the Universe*, Soroush presents Shirazi's theory of "Substantial
Change" (*al-harakat al-juhariyah*) on the basis of a comparative study with modern philosophical theories about time and change, particularly Einstein's theory of relativity.

The theory of "Substantial Change" was originally suggested by Sadr al-din Shirazi
in the 1700s. In Greek Peripatetic philosophy "change" belonged only to accidents
rather than the substance/essence. Out of the nine accidents only four were subject to

logic, reasoning and the writings of Islam's greatest philosophers, such as Sadr al-din Shirazi and Mulla Hadi Sabzevari,[7] this principle pertains to material creations and is unrelated to incorporeal beings, especially things such as knowledge, and, higher still, divine revelation. How is it that this principle has been applied to incorporeal beings in order to arrive at the desired conclusion?

Inconsistency between the Surface Appearance of the Qur'an and Human Science

One of the subjects that you have raised in your interview and you have also spoken about in your book *The Expansion of Prophetic Experience* is the question of inconsistency between the surface appearance of the Qur'an and human scientific findings. I am very glad to see that you have used the expression "surface appearance of the Qur'an", not the Qur'an itself. And it would have been better if you had said: The inconsistency between our human interpretations of the Qur'an and human findings.

Basically, there cannot be the slightest conflict between science and unerring revelation. If there appears to be a conflict, it is for one of the following two reasons:

1. Human learning is evolving, changing and growing, and it is never constant and 100% correct. Hence, what we view as science today may evolve further tomorrow and change, and the conflict may disappear.

---

change, namely, the accidents of time, place, quality and quantity. Sadr al-din Shirazi added a fifth category, the category of substance. He argued that change in accident cannot occur without a change already happening in the category of substance. In other words, any change in accidental categories is of necessity preconditioned by a change in the category of substance. Therefore, the temporality of nature (i.e. the change in the category of accident of time) means that the nature of the universe is thoroughly restless. *The Restless Nature of the Universe* is one of Soroush's early works, written while he was a student of philosophy of science in London in the late 1970s. It was first published in Iran in 1980 and received approval from several outstanding experts on Sadr al-din Shirazi's philosophy, including Ayatollahs Khomeini and Motahhari. Since then it has been reprinted numerous times and used as a textbook in many university departments of philosophy. [Ed.]

[7] Mullah Hadi Sabzevari is a prominent philosopher in Shirazi's tradition. [Ed.]

2. Our interpretation of revelation is a flawed interpretation and the incorrectness of our understanding has led to the delusion of conflict.

For these two reasons, these two things cannot be deemed to be inconsistent. For example, there was a time when the issue of "Darwinism
and the evolution of species" was raised and it made some people
tremble. They thought to themselves: How can the theory of the evolution of species be compatible with the independent creation of Adam?
Because, according to this theory, all living creatures can be traced back
to a single-cell creature, which turned into various species as a result
of evolution. But, before long, Darwinism turned into neo-Darwinism
and, then, into a third theory known as "the leap" or "mutation". And,
even so, they are all only hypotheses and they have not been proven
scientifically, and they still have a very long way to go!

Now, we will return to the instances that you've cited as examples
of inconsistency and perhaps others before you have also had a similar
view.

a. The issue of the seven skies: Exegetes have written about the expression "the seven skies" that appears in the Qur'an. It has to be borne in
mind that, while the Qur'an speaks of seven skies, it considers everything
that is within human visibility to be the sky of the world. Therefore, the
six other skies are not within the realm of human visibility today. As it
has been stated: "We have adorned the lower heaven with the adornment
of the stars and to preserve against every rebel Satan." (37: 6)

So, as far as the Qur'an is concerned, the other skies are not visible
to us. We hope that human science will advance and tell us something
about them too. This becomes clear in the light of the fact that the
Qur'an considers the world of matter and especially the higher world to
be expanding; in other words, the world's width and length is constantly
increasing although it may not be tangible to us: "And heaven—We
built it with might, and We extend it wide." (51: 47)

In view of these two verses, the fact that science today knows only
one sky does not rule out the existence of other skies.

b. Satan's touch: One of the inconsistencies between the surface appearance of the Qur'an and modern science is that it considers madness
to be caused by Satan's touch. And you have said in this connection:
Ayatollah Taleqani goes even further and, in *Partou'i az Qur'an*, in his

annotation of the verse, "Those who indulge in usury shall not rise again except as he rises, whom Satan has demented by his touch," (2: 276), he says plainly:

> Considering madness as resulting from the touch of and possession by jinn and Satan was a belief of the Arabs of the age of ignorance and the Qur'an has spoken in the language of the people, and this is also the view of some modern Arab exegetes.

First, in his annotation of this verse, the late Taleqani suggested three possibilities: (a) Being possessed and being afflicted with epilepsy and the associated mental disorders; (b) a microbe that penetrates nerve centres; (c) a cause of temptations and delusions.

From these three possibilities, the one that, on the basis of the surface appearance of the words, was acceptable to the late Taleqani was the third possibility, as indicated by the phrases that precede the said possibility. Now, his phrases:

> Since usury is a deviation from the human and natural course, the usurer becomes afflicted with delusions and disorderly thinking...and a tendency towards vindictiveness and paranoia also appears in him...At any rate, he is constantly anxious and muddled and in a state of torment. These states are evident in his words and deeds and the movements of his eyes, hands and feet." (*Partou'i az Qur'an*, Vol. 2, pp. 252–53)

Hence, this is what the phrase "a cause of temptations and delusion," refers to. On the face of it, these phrases indicate that this is the possibility he's opted for. Hence, it is not correct to suggest that the late Taleqani has taken this verse to be in keeping with the culture of the Arabs of the age of ignorance.

Secondly, assuming that Satan and jinn are involved in epilepsy and in nervous and psychological disorders does not conflict with basing them on natural causes, because the effect of non-natural causes on natural events operates at a higher level than natural causes, not on a par with them; just as the effect of God's will in the occurrence of natural events—which is undeniable—operates in the same way.

You are someone who studied with the late Motahhari. Naturally, the following principle about human findings, that is to say, the science that is based on the laboratory and experience, is self evident to you: it has the power to prove things, not the power to disprove things.

Science can say: This or that material cause is involved in madness. But it has no right to say: Some other factor is not involved in madness.

And it cannot by any means be ruled out that, in some types of madness, supernatural causes are also involved. And, in the words of the late Allameh Tabataba'i:

> What this verse indicates is no more than that at least some types of madness are based on the touch of a jinni and basing madness on causes such as Satan does not falsify natural causes; for, non-natural causes operate on a higher level than natural causes, not on a par with them.

Apart from all this, the verse as a whole does not have a very clear meaning, so we cannot consider it incompatible with science or say that divine revelation spoke with the logic of the people of the day.

Chasing Away Devils with Meteors

You said:

> In *Tafsir al-Mizan*, in his annotation of the verses about rebellious devils who try to listen to those on high and are driven away by meteors (37: 1–10), your teacher, the late Allameh Seyyed Mohammad Hossein Tabataba'i, said, with full scholarly forthrightness and sincerity, that the interpretations of all the commentators of the past had been based on ancient astronomy and the surface appearance of the verses. He said that these interpretations were wrong, that their wrongness was now obvious and certain.

I am amazed! What is wrong with this assertion by Allameh Tabataba'i? The only problem is that commentators' interpretation of the verse may be incorrect, because human understanding can never be described as right and stable on all issues.

Moreover, as we said, science has the power to prove things, not the power to disprove things. These kinds of supernatural issues whereby devils are prevented by meteors from entering skies are supernatural, especially where the term *al-mala' al-a'la* (High Council) is used, saying: "…to preserve against every rebel Satan; they listen not to the High Council, for they are pelted from every side." (37: 8)

Without a doubt, this "High Council" is an incorporeal position and superior to matter. Naturally, the meteors that are tasked with driving them away will be in keeping with this position. And Allameh Tabataba'i's interpretation seems correct in view of the fact that he say: "What is meant by sky, on the basis of the analogy (High Council), may be the place where angels reside."

A few fatherly pieces of advice

1. My dear, you have cited more than 40 verses of poetry by Rumi and, occasionally, by others and you've tried to match your intent with the contents of his poems. Would it not have been more appropriate for a graduate of Alavi High School and a student of Motahhari to turn to the Qur'an itself in an examination of the facts about revelation, and to ask these questions of the Qur'an and derive the answers from the verses?

2. If I wrote in my letter that there are elements that are exploiting you, what I meant was that your statements are being raised at a time when the West and Westerners are bent on insulting the Prophet, peace be upon him, and your first and second interview are being aired exactly at a time when Danish newspapers have published the insulting cartoons against the Prophet of Islam and that atheist member of the Dutch parliament is trying to paint the Qur'an in an ugly light with the dissemination of a film.

3. You have said in the letter: When I return to Iran, if possible, I would like to invite you to discuss things face-to-face at a safe and calm venue.

I am much gladdened by this suggestion...But I shun debate in the sense of putting myself on display and showing off. My hope is, rather, that we can continue our scholarly discussion and debate, at a venue of your choice, until the facts are clarified.

4. You have concluded your letter by saying: My conscience bids me to ask you to speak out not just on theoretical matters but also when you see bad actions and unethical behaviour, and not to fall into step with the unjust; and, in this way, to serve as a model to others.

Are these phrases not an unkindness and disrespect to me? When have we ever fallen into step with the unjust?! I am now more than eighty years old. Since the day when I came to know myself, I have occupied myself solely with my pen and with books and teaching and preaching, and I have always reminded people of the Tradition that states: "A nation will not be glorious as long as the rights of the oppressed are not taken from the oppressor fearlessly."

But bear in mind that the injustice that is being done to the Prophet of God and to Muslims today is unprecedented in history. And unjust and usurper governments are, on the one hand, attacking the Prophet and his humane teachings, and, on the other, blatantly trampling on his followers' rights and liberties.

Let us now both pledge that we will proudly side with the wronged in this battle and grapple with the wrongdoer until what has been wrongly taken is rightfully restored.

March 2008

THE PARROT AND THE BEE
SOROUSH'S SECOND RESPONSE TO SOBHANI

To the Esteemed Scholar Ayatollah Ja'far Sobhani,

With hearty greetings and good wishes, I can happily say that your second letter has winged its way to me. I broke the seal as if I was uncorking a bottle of rosewater. I had admired your hardy endeavour and your fatherly tenor earlier; now, I admired it even more.

First. You have shown concern about the "downward curve" of my frames of mind and ideas over the past twenty years; that is to say, since the appearance of *The Contraction and Expansion of Religious Knowledge.*[1] I am glad and grateful that you are tracking my star and charting its good- and ill-omened positions over the years, but it is not entirely clear to me where the observatory stands. It would appear that the astrolabe and plumb line are in your hands, and you are using them to judge the sun's distance and issue rulings about ascending and descending stars. Do as you will! But if it were me, I would weigh up ideas on the scale of reasoning and judge them by their truth, and I would also accord the other side a bit of choice and right to independent reasoning....[2]

What surprises me is that you're scolding someone who has spent a lifetime thinking and humbly formulating reasoned opinions; who has based his views on reason instead of imitation; who is not afraid of orthodoxy's rigid tradition; and who looks upon revelation and its by-products with his God-given power of critical reasoning, confident that "religion" will never be dishonoured in the process.

Now that you have tracked my "downward turn," would that you would also track the "upward turn" of violence, thereby avoiding any suspicion of fellowship with the unjust. Would that you would not sharpen the blade of their viciousness with your silence. Would that you would also say a word or two about the injustices that have been

---

[1] Tehran, 1989. [Ed.]
[2] The omission here is of Soroush's reply to some personal remarks made in Sobhani's Second Letter that were omitted there as well. See footnote 1, p. 303. [Ed.]

perpetrated against me and express outrage at the scandalous conduct, malice and unfairness of the oppressors. Setting me aside, what about that senior cleric of unparalleled distinction?[3] What was his crime to have been tormented as he has been? Why did you and other religious authorities pull your heads into your shells, shuffle into the burrow of silence and raise no objections? The injustice of the house arrest, indignities and ordeals that he was subjected to cannot be referred to any heavenly court; it is a sin that will taint us forever. And there are countless other cases like his.

But where and in whom are our people to find any sensitivity to injustice? How are they expected to believe that, in an Islamic society "the rights of the oppressed can be claimed from the oppressor without fear" (the telling phrase that you cited from Imam Ali's *Nahj al-Balaghah* and which I have treasured and used as my yardstick for years).

Faith Weakening!

You have plaintively said that my "misgivings" weaken young people's faith. Has it not occurred to you that the comfort-seeking conduct and irrational discourse of some of our clerics are much more to blame in this respect? Do you know what destroys faith? Spreading superstition in the name of religion and injustice in the name of God, and being silent in the face of oppression. You can see for yourself that anyone who criticizes the country's Supreme Leader in Iran today is risking life and limb. You pay no heed to this faith-crushing policy but attack me instead and accuse me of weakening people's faith. In the words of Hafez, drinking, roguery and revelry are not half as bad as "employing the Qur'an in duplicitous way". Are our clerics as sensitive to duplicity as they are about exegesis? When and where have our young people

---

[3] Reference is to the grand Ayatollah Hossein Ali Montazeri (1902), the supreme *marja'-e taqlid* (the highest rank of authority in Shi'i Islam). Montazeri, a leading figure of the 1979 Revolution and once designated successor of Ayatollah Khomeini, became critical of the regime, consequently falling out of favor. In the late 1980s, he was subject to mistreatment, due to a combination of factors including his criticism of the regime's treatment of political opponents. After Khomeini's death, he criticized Khomeini's successor and questioned the qualifications of the Leader (*wali-e faqih*). He was then put under house arrest for several years, and has had sever restrictions placed even on his teaching responsibilities. [Ed.]

witnessed "good words, good thoughts and good deeds"[4] from the state clergy? How, then, are these youngsters expected to grow stronger in faith? What have they seen from these "spiritual" leaders other than "corporeality"? How is this expected to enrich our youngsters' spirits? Claiming to have the Hidden Imam's endorsement for sending incompetent individuals to the Parliament; disseminating superstitious and weak ideas from pulpits and from radio and television; raging against critics and stirring up thugs to commit acts of violence; crushing new ideas and calling on thinkers to repent; rousing the novice clergy to express outrage every now and then and to insult a religious authority and distinguished individuals; not even taking pity on Sufi retreats and demolishing them over practitioners' heads; and propagating terror in Friday prayer sermons—does any of this bear any sign of good deeds and good words? Our clergy does not see its own unsavoury role in weakening young people's faith; instead, it peers into every nook and cranny to find some other culprit. In all fairness, I have to add that there is a small minority of pious and righteous clerics who stand apart from the rest. If I believed that the aim of all this philosophical-theological hair-splitting was anything other than the spreading of justice and virtue, I wouldn't talk so much about the misdeeds and mistakes of the country's religious leaders. "If I tell you a bitter tale, it's to cleanse you of all that's bitter."

When—at a time when a film called "Fitna" is being disseminated which is wholly dedicated to demonstrating that Muslims are violent people and that Islam teaches violence—an ungifted *faqih* stands up in Qum and openly advocates murder and assassination, and says, "Muslims must do to Soroush what their duty demands", why do his peers and elders not condemn him and tell him: If this is a *fatwa* (general edict), why do you mention a specific name and if it is a *hukm* (sentence), then, who are you to be issuing sentences when the country is being ruled by a jurist? And by what right are you bringing disgrace upon Muslims? And why are you waving a dagger at reason and asking people to respond to reasoning with violence?

What do you expect from people who are witnessing all of this? Do you expect them to see this uncivilized—nay, anti-civility—behaviour

---

[4] "Good words, Good thoughts and Good Deeds" is a moral/creedal statement of Zoroastrianism, the pre-Islamic religion of Iran. This statement is still widely used in Persian literature and ethical discourse. [Ed.]

and grow stronger in faith? Or, are they more likely to feel ashamed and disgraced as Muslims? Do not forget that, over the past four centuries, although atheists and disbelievers, materialists and naturalists wrote mountain-loads of books rejecting and ridiculing the Church's teachings, what broke and discredited the Church was not these books and words; it was the deal meted out by cardinals to the Galileos. To this day, the Church has not been able to live down that stain, its brow remains branded with the shame; and who knows whether and when it will ultimately shake off the disgrace.

I owe my faith to mystics, not to *faqihs*; so, these cacophonous bellows and threats will not make me tremble in my faith.

You *faqihs* should concern yourselves instead with the youngsters who obtain their faith from you and who entrust themselves to the religion of Muhammad because of you and your colleagues' sermons. Suddenly and unexpectedly, they wake up one day to find that their preachers' words are dripping with blood and violence. Unsurprisingly, this makes them "tremble like willows over their faith".

Learning, Not Sinning

Or, look at Ayatollah Makarem Shirazi, whose own writings are always peppered with the words "ugly" and "hateful" but who is calling on me to repent, without pondering that religion asks us to repent from sin, not from learning. Enlightened indeed are faqihs who breed darkness and rank learning among the sins! What a bad teacher is a faqih who imposes sanctions on thinking, divides ideas into the "permissible" (*halal*) and the "forbidden" (*haram*), and asks thinkers to repent.

In a blatant anachronism you have said that my suggestions coincide and are in line with the publication of insulting cartoons by a Danish paper. Sorry, but my ideas about the word of God and the word of Muhammad, peace be upon him, were first raised in a book entitled *The Expansion of Prophetic Experience* that was published ten years ago in Iran. My interview with the Dutch journalist took place about a year ago. The first preceded by eight years the cartoonists' freedom-crushing action and, the second, occurred two years after it. And, at the time of the cartoons, I wrote a piece in which I notified that one shall not play games with Muhammad's name, because it "is the auspicious banner of the Islamic world's pride, intelligence, aspiration, thought and honour. It is the representative and symbol of all the two worlds' pure and noble spirits. To utter Ahmad's [Muhammad's] name is to utter every prophet's name."

A year and a half ago, I published a detailed piece, criticizing Pope Benedict XVI's remarks in which he had said: "Since Muslims consider the Qur'an to be the word of God, they are not prepared to interpret it." (You can find and read about all of these things on my official website.)[5] So, how can I be suspected of being aligned with foes and scorners?

In sum, neither that infamous newspaper[6] that is devoted to the cult of the Leader and does nothing but sully the truth and sanctify violence and is so offended by the fact that I am a thinker that it accuses me in broad daylight of being in cahoots with Mossad and the CIA (just like that)—and receives no reprimand from you and your cohorts—nor those who urge me to "repent"[7] and call on Muslims to do "what their duty demands"[8] are doing justice, goodness and truth any service. Far from solving any problems with this kind of language, they show that they have no understanding of the problems. Instead of joining in a thoughtful debate and discussion, they use the old weapons of eliminating and silencing those who think "otherwise", and warn them of various punishments in this world and the next. Thanks to their ignorance of the history of other religions and peoples, they repeat their hackneyed mistakes. They shut their eyes to the sun in the hope that it will die and vanish.

Dear Mr Sobhani, breathing fluidity into our musty Islamic theology, returning to the dynamism of pre-orthodoxy times and benefiting from modern learning are necessary if Islam is to endure in the modern world with distinction and pride. This is exactly what makes Islam as a truth richer and more important than Islam as an identity. This is an objective that can only be achieved in a climate of freedom and research. It has no affinity whatsoever with intimidation and excommunication. If our seminaries wish to fall into step with or lead the way in this endeavour, they must act more cautiously and responsibly in their dealings and reactions. If they cannot plant flowers in this field,

---

[5] www.drsoroush.com. It should be noted that this website has been blocked inside Iran since 2007. [Ed.]

[6] Reference is to *Kayhan*, a radically conservative state-run daily paper that is known for publishing accusatory pieces on Soroush. [Ed.]

[7] Reference is to Ayatollah Makarem Shirazi. [Ed.]

[8] Reference is to Ayatollah Nuri Hamadani. [Ed.]

let them not sow thorns, and if they can add nothing to the debate, let them not strangle what there is.

Of course, I am pleased to see that religious authorities and grand ayatollahs have entered the fray and contributed to this debate. And most auspicious of all is the contribution of Grand Ayatollah Montazeri, who is truly the pride of our clergy. I see all this as a sign of seminaries' sensitivity and the subject's importance. What displeases me and disheartens observers is the unsightly language of force and the determination to look for heresy. This must be done away with, intelligently and delicately.

Revelation as a Natural Phenomenon

Secondly. The theory that I have presented seeks to resolve and tackle the questions about "the word of God", offers a rationally defendable mode for God's speaking, and explains and clarifies the worldly and human role (so highlighted in the Qur'an and so neglected by the theory's critics) of Muhammad, peace be upon him, in the process of revelation—no more and no less. This is a theory that has the backing of a vast number of Muslim philosophers and mystics, so I am amazed to see how it is, erroneously or deliberately, being viewed by some as "a negation of the word of God" and an attack on the Qur'an!

My familiarity with the Qur'an is, if not more, then, certainly not less than my familiarity with the *Mathnawi*. And I know by heart all the verses that your distinguished self and some of the other distinguished critics such as Messrs Abdulali Bazargan, Hosseini-Tabataba'i, Ayazi, etc. have cited, and I do not have the slightest difficulty in understanding and accounting for these verses: The fact that the Qur'an was sent down (*anzala*) to the Prophet's heart, that Gabriel was the bearer of the verses, that the Qur'an is "the word of God" (*kalam-u Allah*), that the word (*qol*) "say" occurs countless times within it, that, on occasion, there were delays in the revelation of the verses and that the Prophet sat and waited for them, that the Prophet was told not to rush in reading the Qur'an, that he was not allowed to alter the verses, that people have received the word of God in the form that He wanted them to receive it, that the Qur'an is an extraordinary and miraculous book, and so on. How do these facts contradict the idea that the Qur'an is the product of the human experience of an exceptional man in unveiling the truth (*kashf*); a man who was given a mission by God and enjoyed

His endorsement; whose words were acceptable to God and whose *kashf* was the product of pure and uncommon moments of exalted, mystical union?

I do not know what these critics' interpretation is of phenomena such as death, rain and the growth of fetus. "It is He who forms you in the womb however He wishes." (3: 6) It has been said repeatedly in the Qur'an that it is God who takes people's lives ("God takes the souls at the time of their death"—39: 42) or that the angel of death reclaims souls ("Death's angel, who has been charged with you, shall gather you then to your Lord"—32: 11) or that he sends guardians to take people's souls ("when anyone of you is visited by death, Our messengers take him"—6: 61). Nevertheless, the natural and physical explanation of death [that has been accepted by the orthodoxy] does not seem to be conflicting with the role of God and the angel of death. Is it not also God who "sends down" the rain ("…and have sent down out of the rain-clouds water cascading…"—78: 9)? Do we not even have traditions that tell us that an angel descends with every drop of rain?" But does the natural explanation of rain tie God's hands and force Him off the stage? Do they render meaningless all references to God bringing us rain? Do these references not mean that God is the source of all sources and is hierarchically above secondary causes (not on a par with them), and that everything takes place by His permission and will? If so, then, why should it be the case that any natural and physical explanation of revelation and the "word of God", and highlighting the role played by the Prophet severs its link with God and renders meaningless any references to "God speaking" and "sending down" revelation? Does everything that occurs in nature not have natural causes? So, why should the revelation received by the Prophet be an exception to this rule? Why does nature have to be bypassed and revelation attributed directly to the supernatural?

There are times when it seems to me as if we have returned to the days when some religious people imagined that speaking about the role of the wind, the oceans and the sun in the formation of rain was incompatible with the will of God and they attributed rain directly to God's will. Now, too, the same logic is being used to say that revelation rained down on the Prophet directly, without any link to natural causes (the Prophet's being, his times and society, his knowledge, the language he spoke, etc.). And these causes are thought to conflict with the role of God. The critics cite countless holy verses about revelation being "sent down", but they do not stop to think that this sending

down has also been used in the Qur'an in connection with the wind
and the rain, overlooking that this usage is wholly comprehensible in
a world that is brimming with "His presence" and in which God plays
a part in everything (precisely what was unveiled to Muhammad in
his experience).

How strange that, when it comes to the "word" of God, the orthodoxy
see "sent down" as a metaphor, that is, coming down from the "thick
reality" to the "thin reality". But, when it comes to "word", they take
it in the literal sense. How inconsistent and unmethodical! What is
the logic of taking things half way like this? Either take a metaphorical
view of both "sent down" and "word", so that the problems fall away,
or take both in a literal sense, so that you can meander forever in a
state of confusion.

Hail to the soul of the late, wise master Fakhr al-din al-Razi who said:

> When the Qur'an says that God is the protector of the Qur'an ("It is We
> who have sent down the Remembrance and We watch over it"—15: 9),
> it does not mean anything outlandish and supernatural. The fact that
> Muslims endeavoured to compile the Qur'an and record it means, pre-
> cisely, that God protected it.[9]

And this logic applies to everything else.

Dialogical Nature of the Qur'an

Thirdly. When I say that the Qur'an is the product of the prophetic
discovery of Muhammad Ibn Abdullah, peace be upon him, this does
not, in any way, mean that the discovery is arbitrary so that the Prophet
can alter it or have it revealed to him whenever he wants, and so on
and so forth.

Prophethood aside, even scientific, philosophic or mathematical
discoveries are not arbitrary in this sense. If the theory of gravity is
Newton's human discovery, the fact remains that he had to work hard
for it and sit and wait for the discovery. It was not as if he could formulate it at a moment of his own choosing and in whatever way he liked
and sell it to people in an arbitrary guise. It was exactly the same with
the discovery of the philosophical theory of the principality/facticity of

---

[9] See his *Mafatih al-Ghayb (al-Tafsir al-Kabir)*.

being (*Esalat-e Wujud*). Could Sadr al-din Shirazi overstep the scope of his reasoning and twist definitions and rules to suit his whims? He had to comply with the reasoning; it was not the reasoning that had to comply with him, although his knowledge and his arguments were within the limits of his intellectual capacities. But, can any one break the bounds of his own capacities.

Moving away from science and philosophy, when it comes to composing poetry, too, it is not as if poets can versify at will, that the terminology and imagery are always at their fingertips, that their creative powers are always at exactly the same level, or that poems come to them whenever they want. Quite the reverse, poets are in the sway of their poems, not poems in the sway of the poets. After composing the first volume of the *Mathnawi*, Jalal al-din Rumi waited for two years before his creative powers bubbled up again and the flow of the verses and the wisdom resumed. He said at the time that he had found his creativity and his words "muddied" and had had to wait for them to become "translucent and pleasing".

As for all the instances of "say" in the Qur'an, this, too, has a clear tale. It is a rhetorical technique that the speaker sometimes addresses himself, although, in fact, his audience are other people. We find instances of this in Rumi's poetry. For example, "Say fresh words, so that the two worlds can be refreshed / words that surpass this world's limits and become limitless". What is the difference between this and "Say: 'God is one'," (112: 1) or "Say: 'People of the Book! Come now to a word common between us and you, that we serve none but God," (3: 64) or "Say: 'Call upon God or call upon the Merciful'" (17: 110), etc.

I do not know what Ayatollah Sobhani thinks of the following verse: "So, if thou art in doubt regarding what We have sent down to thee, ask those who recite the Book before thee." (10: 94) Did the Prophet doubt that he was a prophet? Islamic orthodoxy certainly doesn't think so. Or, should it be viewed as another usage of rhetorical techniques and stylistic methods, that is, a phrase may not be directly addressed to the Prophet, but presented in the form of a direct address. Is it not in fact interchangeable in meaning with a phrase that appears elsewhere and is addressed to the people "If you are in doubt concerning what we have sent down to Our servant, then bring a sura like it." (2: 23). The same intent can appear in many different forms. "And many is the time when they are misled by appearances", as Rumi says.

The Qur'an's dialogical character (which I have spoken about at length in the *Expansion of Prophetic Experience* (Tehran, 1998) clearly displays these oratorical techniques and shows how the Prophet's mind and spirit is engaged with the people and the events of his society. This holds true both when the phrase "they will question thee" is used and when it is not [e.g. "they will question thee concerning drinking and gambling. Say: 'In both is heinous sin.'" (2: 219); "they will question thee concerning the new moons. Say: 'They are appointed times for the people, and the Pilgrimage.'" (2: 189)]. In this sense, the Qur'an is a constant, multi-sided dialogue with God and the earthly, natural and historical world in which Muhammad was living. And it is an answer to the questions and quandaries of the time. It was these same quandaries and questions that would sharpen his spirit, fan the flames of need and entreaty within him, and take him to the threshold of discovery, so that he could receive the answers from "the angel of revelation" and convey them to the people in a suitable language.

At times, these entreaties were covert and, at other times, overt. ("We have seen thee turning thy face towards heaven"—2: 144). In any case, it was the effervescence within Muhammad's mind and the tumult within his heart that used to lead him to the experience of unveiling (*kashf*).

Of course, Muhammad was an extraordinary figure. He was a flower in the desert. He was an illiterate orphan, yet produced the "noble" book. And the emergence of that culture-sowing book out of that age of darkness was (in the language of religion) a miracle. The other residents of the Arabian peninsula did not experience any soul-searing challenges, nor did they reach the threshold of receiving solutions, nor did they possess Muhammad's theoretical and practical certainty and courage, nor did they have his talents of articulation and imagination. These were the things that made Muhammad and his book unique and matchless. Miraculous was Muhammad, thus miraculous became his book. Such a wondrous achievement could be expected from a Plato-like person, but certainly not from an illiterate man. It was in this context that, in their interpretation of the verse "if you are in doubt that this book is from God, then produce a similar *sura*" (3: 23) some exegetes have said that it can also mean: produce a sura from a person like Muhammad. (See the *Safi, Al-Mizan* and *Mafatih al-Ghayb*).[10] It was also in this context that some eminent Mu'tazilite and Shi'i figures were of the view that a

---

[10] Feiz al-Kashani, al-*Safi fi Tafsir al-Qur'an*; Tabatabai, *al-Mizan fi Tafsir al-Qur'an*; Fakhr al-din al-Razi, *Mafatih al-Ghayb*.

book similar to the Qur'an could be produced by others but that God does not let it happen.

The Parrot and the Bee

In sum, this matchless figure, with his wakeful heart, insightful eyes, perceptive mind and expressive tongue, was God's creation and everything else was his creation and followed from his discoveries and his artistry. Muhammad was the book that God wrote and when Muhammad read the book of his being it became the Qur'an. And the Qur'an was the word of God. God wrote Muhammad and Muhammad wrote the Qur'an, just as God created the bee and the bee produced honey. And honey was the product of revelation.

Certainly, if we look at our traditions and the holy verses we will find that God speaks ("And unto Moses, God spoke directly"—4: 164), walks ("We shall advance upon what work they have done"—25: 23), gets angry ("when they had angered Us, We took vengeance on them"—43:), sits on a throne ("sat Himself upon the Throne"—20: 5) and experiences doubt ("...I would not have hesitated in the same way as I did in taking [the lives of] my pious worshippers.").[11]

But, if we are looking for the truth, none of these things hold true about Him. The one who is speaking is, in fact, Muhammad whose word has become identical to the word of God because of his closeness to Him. The attribution of speech to God, like the attributions of other human characteristics to Him, is to be taken metaphorically. They are not anthropomorphical.

The model of revelation that considers the Prophet a pure recipient and reporter, posits a speaker-loudspeaker relationship between God and the Prophet. It reduces to zero the relevance and involvement of the Prophet's heart and mind in revelation, sees an angel constantly flitting back and forth between God and the Prophet like a winged messenger. This model replaces closeness with distance (between the Sender and the Sent). It chooses to see the Prophet as Gabriel's mimic. It offers a Sultan-peasant image of God-human relationship. It considers speaking to be as appropriate to God as it is to human beings, and opts for a literal reading of the figurative will. This model will, of course,

---

[11] This is a *hadith qudsi*. [Ed.]

not accept the version suggested by this author. But what guides my understanding is the Qur'anic metaphor of the bee or mystics' metaphor of a tree. The Qur'an teaches us that the bee's biological structure or biochemical factory is exactly like a revelation that is made to it, filling its home with honey.

The Qur'anic verses read:

> And thy Lord revealed unto the bees, saying: 'Take unto yourselves of the mountains, houses, and of the trees, and of what they are building. Then eat of all manner of fruit, and follow the ways of your Lord, easy to go upon.' Then, comes there forth out of their bellies a drink of diverse hues wherein is healing for men. Surely in that is a sign for people who reflect. (16: 68–69)

It goes without saying that the bee is fully relevant to and involved in the honey-making. It is not as if the honey is poured into it at one end and comes out of the other end. Be that as it may, the healing honey is a godly product. And is it not a sign for people who reflect that, instead of speaking about a parrot, the Qur'an speaks about a bee and considers the latter, not the former, to be a symbol of receiving revelation?

As for the metaphor of the tree, it was suggested by Ibn Arabi, who said: "The contemplative pick the fruit of contemplation from the tree of their own being." (*Fusus al-Hekam*, second "fass")

Yes, the bee is a sign for those who reflect and if Ayatollah Sobhani had looked at the bee and the tree instead of the parrot, he would have found a better and more telling image of the relationship between revelation and Muhammad, peace be upon him. How far apart indeed are the mimicking parrot and the productive bee!

And how far indeed are Hafez's words, when he said, "Behind the mirror, I'm parrot-like in a way; I repeat what the eternal master tells me to say," from Rumi's words, when he said: "This one who is the object of 'We have honoured the sons of Adam'[12] and is ever going upward; how should his inspiration be inferior to that of the bee?"

The Formless and the Form

Fourthly. "Do not ever imagine that the Prophet heard the word of God from Gabriel in the same way that you hear the word of the Prophet.

---

[12] Reference is to a Qur'anic verse (*karramna bani adam*). (*Mathnawi*, 5: 1231). [Ed.]

And do not ever imagine that the Prophet imitated Gabriel in the same way that that Islamic nation imitates the Prophet. Immense indeed is the distance between the two! They are two distinct species. And imitation is never authentic knowledge and true cognisance." (Sadr al-din Shirazi, *Asfar al-Arba'ah*, Vol. 7, p. 9, third Journey, seventh station.)

The whole question revolves around the angel of revelation and the nature of its link to the Prophet. Setting aside the literalist theologians, all Islamic philosophers, ranging from al-Farabi to Ibn Sina (Avicenna), from Nasir al-din Tusi to Sadr al-din Shirazi, have considered it impossible for the Prophet to grasp revelation without the involvement of his faculty of imagination. Even if there was a Gabriel, he too would have appeared in the Prophet imagination. And if he did anything it was to "prepare" the Prophet so that he could achieve "authentic knowledge" for himself; not to lecture the Prophet, like a teacher does a student, with the Prophet later merely repeating the lesson to the people. This is the philosophical understanding of revelation, which is, of course, at a great distance from the common understanding of it; much like physicists' "table" which, in Stanley Eddington's words, is very far away from ordinary people's "table". Ordinary people's table is hard and solid, whereas, in physicists' eyes, the same table is full of vacuums and is more like electronic clouds with no definite boundaries. One can only speak about the probability of its being here and there. Therefore, if a saw slices into a table, it is like a cloud grappling with another cloud.

So it is with angels as viewed by ordinary people and by the learned. It has been said in some of the Traditions that Gabriel has six hundred wings or sixty thousand wings and that the Prophet saw him in this guise during the Ascension. And the Qur'an says: "Praise be to God, Originator of the heavens and earth, who appointed the angels to be messengers, having two, three and four pairs of wings." (35: 35) Most commentators and their disciples have taken such phrases at face value and really understood angels to mean winged creatures who flit back and forth between heaven and earth. But Fakhr al-din al-Razi, the 12th century exegete and theologian, wrote cautiously that what might be meant by wings is angels' varied powers and functions, such as providing bounties, reclaiming lives, and so on. In the twentieth century, at the time of the late Tabataba'i, the author of the *al-Mizan*, this view was expressed more boldly and plainly, and he invoked a linguistic-exegetic theory to say plainly that angels are not corporeal beings that can have wings; rather, what is meant by wing is the purposes and functions that are associated with wings; i.e. the tasks that they undertake and the roles that they play. He adds: It is true that, in the Prophet's imagination, angels appeared to have wings, but this was not their true guise; like the angel that appeared to Mary, the fire that appeared to Moses, and other such instances.

In other words, the Qur'an states plainly that there were two-, three- and four-winged angels, but Tabataba'i says that this is not possible; they appeared to the Prophet in this form, but this was not how they really were. Of course it is not only Tabataba'i who was of this view. He was striding within a tradition, following philosophical principles and basing himself on the ideas of philosophers (such as al-Farabi, Nasir al-din Tusi, etc.) that could only lead to this conclusion.

In this tradition and based on this interpretation, the angel's arrival, the delivery of revelation and the like are events that occur within the Prophet's being. Then, this is expressed figuratively and in the language of religion, in a way that suggests that an angel with six hundred wings has appeared in front of the Prophet and spoken to him in Arabic.

To put it more clearly, as far as Tabataba'i is concerned, the correct interpretation and meaning of God speaking about two-, three- and four-winged angels is that the Prophet is saying that he sees them with two, three and four wings. And what's the difference between this and mystics' suggestion that the Prophet used to make Gabriel appear or that Gabriel was, in fact, the Prophet's intellect.

The fact of the matter is that, if we base ourselves on the tradition of philosophers and mystics, we have to say that this was precisely the Prophet's job: to give a form/face to formless/faceless truths. This is the special skill that prophets possess (with mystics and poets, respectively, having it to lesser degrees).

But it is not just wings and flying angels that are creations of the Prophet's power of imagination. "Tablet", "pen" and "throne" are too. They, too, are formless truths, which appear to the Prophet in these guises. And it is exactly the same with, "fire", "houris", "paths", "scales" and so on.[13] These are all images that have been borrowed from the life and environment to which the Prophet was accustomed, and there is not a single unfamiliar image among them.

Of course, this is all the more so when it comes to the language, the words, the terminology and the phrases. These are human vessels into

---

[13] (*lawh*), (*qalam*), (*'arsh*), (*nar*), (*houri*), (*serat*), (*mizan*) are words used throughout the Qur'an. [Ed.]

which revelation is poured and they are all taken from the Prophet's mind and imagination to embrace and encase formless meanings.

The frustration of prophets and, more generally, of mystics has always been due to the fact that the forms have, subsequently, become veils hiding the formless. And husk-peddlers and form/face-worshippers have become besotted with these forms and neglected the formless. More reprehensibly still, they have beaten form/face-shatterers with the stick of excommunication.

I can well understand the linguistic hardship and bitterness experienced by the great master Jalaleddin Rumi (and so much the more so by prophets) when he said that he could neither speak about the Formless nor not speak about it.

> If he (saint) speaks from that, thy foot will stumble,
> and if he speak not of that, Oh, alas foe thee;
> And if he speaks in the likeness of a form,
> thou will stick to that form, O youth.[14]

The Prophet had to perform his task within the confines of two inescapable limitations: first, the limitation of form in conceptualizing his experience of the formless and forcing the placeless into the straitjacket of location; secondly, the limitation of norms and conventions, which tied his justice and politics to the shape and character of his time and place, and forced them into the garb of tribal laws. This is precisely what drives commentators towards philosophical, mystical and cultural translations.

The very fact that God (or the Prophet) speaks in Arabic and endorses the conventions of the Arabs already means that He/he has accepted many limitations. There is absolutely no reason to think that Arabic is the most powerful language conceivable and that it can accommodate the profoundest ideas (as some have claimed). Although the propositions are the Prophet's, the terms and concepts belong to the language and these concepts and terms impose their limitations on his statements. It is the same with the conventions and customs of the Prophet's day which were by no means the best conceivable customs. But most of them were endorsed by the Lawgiver and took on the character of God's precepts.

---

[14] *Mathanwi*, 3: 1276.

The Prophet's revelation is in Arabic. And Arabic is the reflection and synthesis of the Arabs' collective culture and experience. It is the same with any language; 'we have no private language' (Wittgenstein) or, for that matter, celestial language. It is this culture that provides the material for revelation's form and shape. And is the honey bee, which feeds on the flowers and plants in its environment and then puts it all into the form of honey, not the most telling image of prophets, who use the limited material of their time and place, draw on them in their revelational experience?

We do not need to search very hard. Let us be mindful of the two concepts of "sent down" and "human" and let us include them together in earnest and in depth in our understanding of revelation. It has to be seen as "human" through and through. This is exactly what the Qur'an teaches us and guides us to do.

The Prophet's contemporaries used to express surprise at the fact that he ate food and walked through the streets and alleyways just like them. ("They also say, What ails this Messenger that he eats food, and goes to the market?"—25: 7) They thought that a prophet was like an angel; never eating or marrying. And today, our critics say: What sort of Prophet is it that feeds on the culture of his time and strides through the streets and alleyways of history? The logic is the same in both. Both want a Prophet that is super-human. Humanness is historical, linguistic and cultural. You would have to be angel to escape from these things.

Yes, the Prophet was an extraordinary human being. In the language of religion, he was the *wali* (friend) of God. But being a *wali* does not rule out being human. Humanity is an expansive enough vessel to be able to contain *wilayat* and *nubuwwat* (prophethood). The sweetness of his utterances shows that he was paradise's honey bee (not a parrot in paradise's Lote-tree). His prerogatives, too, were expansive. Whatever he thought and said had God's endorsement. Did he not increase the length of the ritual prayers?[15] Did he not say: "If it were not a hardship, I would make it obligatory for people to clean their teeth before every ritual prayer?"[16] Did he not say: "If I tell you to perform the hajj every year, it will become obligatory for you to do so?"[17] And none of these

---

[15] Ahmad Ibn Hanbal, *Musnad*; Horr al-ʿameli, *Wasayel al-Shiʿah*.
[16] Termadi, *Sunan*
[17] Muslim, *Sahih*.

utterances were matters of political expediency or temporary rulings. In effect, although he was fully human, he believed that what he did was approvable by God. And although they were uttered by a human being, the commands he issued took on a divine character.

"The Phenomenon of the Qur'an"

Viewing Islam, religious precepts and the Qur'an in this way, makes it easy to understand the "phenomenon of the Qur'an" and renders unnecessary elaborate and unsound interpretations. It opens up the Qur'an before us like a human-historical text, and it delineates the peaks and troughs of its celestial topography in the light of the peaks and troughs of earthly topography.

Then, we will no longer be amazed by the fact that the Qur'an uses a "lunar calendar" and makes fasting obligatory for everyone on the globe during the lunar month of Ramadan (Ch. 2). Or that it calls on everyone on the globe to reflect on the "camel" in order to see God's powers of creation (Ch. 88). Or that it tells everyone on the globe about the tribe of Quraysh (Ch. 106). Or that it chooses to curse Abu Lahab rather than anyone else (Ch. 111). Or that it sits dark-eyed maidens in Arab tents (Ch. 55). Or that it speaks about the Arab practice of burying unwanted female infants alive (Ch. 81). Or that speaks at length about jinn acquiring faith and declaring their belief in God (Ch. 72). Or, that it talks about the Prophet's wives and their frivolousness (Ch. 66). Or, that it speaks about pagan Arabs' beliefs about the daughters of God (Ch. 53). And so on and so forth. All of these things have an Arab, ethnic and personal tenor and timbre, and are closely associated with the land of Hijaz. And, only a little distance away from there, they may evoke no associations, nor any interest.

We will also no longer be surprised to see that the Qur'an answers some questions that are neither very important in themselves nor of any particular interest to anyone other than the Arabs of the time, such as questions about "new moons", the "two-horned", women's menstrual cycles and the permissibility of fighting wars during specific months; things relating to the mental and historical backdrop of the inhabitants of the Arabian peninsula and their way of life.

Likewise are: the references to "the seven heavens"; or, the idea that semen issues between the loins and the chest; or, the suggestion that nosy devils can be driven away with meteors; or, that our faculty of perception is located in our hearts (not brains); or, other such notions that are in keeping with the underdeveloped science of the time.

And how great the distance between all this and verses such as "And unto God all matters are returned," (35: 4); "God is the light of the heavens and the earth," (24: 35); "He is the First and the Last, the Outward and the Inward," (57: 3); and "Whithersoever you turn, there is the Face of God," (2: 115). Verses that speak of the heady heights of the Prophet's spiritual ascension. How are we to interpret all this contraction and expansion and all these peaks and troughs?

Is it not more correct to see this contraction and expansion as existing within the Prophet himself, who, motivated and given a mission by God, steps into the school of society, like a teacher and a healer of vices (the Qur'an considers education and purification of souls to be the Prophet's two main missions) in order to offer a few lessons (the points of wisdom and the fruits of prophethood that he wanted to share with others because he was so brimming and joyful with them: "to teach them the Book and the Wisdom"—62: 2) and to tackle a few problems (which he was sympathetically concerned about: "grievous to him is your suffering; anxious is he over you, gentle to the believers"—9: 128). And that he sets out to educate the ignorant and to heal the immoralities. His main asset is his pure being, his eventful life, his sympathetic heart and his artistic imagination, which also brings Gabriel (in the language of religion) to the threshold of his mind and lets him see hidden truths and reread life's experiences. He tells people the tale of life and the universe, which have now taken on a different manifestation in his eyes. And, with the utmost joy and eloquence, he speaks about his new discoveries. He says that he sees a world that is filled with light; that it is glaringly obvious to him that the world is not self-standing; that everything is godly; that He is everywhere and, like the sun, is lighting up the horizons. You see Him whichever way you turn. It is He who sends the wind and the rain. It is He who makes the trees and plants grow. It is He who gives life and takes it away. Life is a caravan that has a destination. Human beings have not been created pointlessly. There is an insightful eye that watches over everything and distinguishes right from wrong. Muhammad looks at himself and sees someone who was once a poor and misguided orphan, and who now has a light-filled heart, a rightly-guided soul and a wealthy wife. And he feels that he owes all this to God. ("Did He not find thee an orphan, and shelter thee?"—93: 6) And he believes that the right response to all these blessings is gratitude and good deeds. And he teaches his students thankfulness and obedience. And he complains about his students' disobedience, ingratitude, misguidedness, selfishness and ignorance.

The class becomes riotous. One group denies all his teachings. Another, draws out daggers against him. Another, tests him with unrelated questions. Another submits to his teachings and expresses humility. All these things are reflected in his lectures (which are later written down). The monologue gives way to a dialogue, and the Qur'an is born in the context of this roller-coaster-like, living experience. In step with this vital experience, the teacher-healer becomes more skilled and more of a "prophet" in this school, which is his society. His lessons become richer and more varied. No doubt, if he had lived longer and had even more experiences, his book of lectures would have grown thicker and more colourful. Conversely, if he had continued to live in a cave and in reclusion, he would have left no more in his book of life than a few exalted visions.

Gabriel within the Prophet

Now, it would be difficult to accept that for every single one of these situations and questions, written verses had been drawn up from time immemorial and that God would ask Gabriel to look among the verses, pick the one that was appropriate and take it to the Prophet so that he could read it out to his nation. (This is exactly the image that most ulema—with the exception of the philosophers, who had a philosophical understanding of revelation—had in the past. There are even references in their writings to Gabriel swiftly winging his way back and forth between heaven and earth.)

It would also be erroneous to imagine that, with the occurrence of every event, a new will would be formed in the Almighty and a new verse formulated and conveyed to Gabriel, so that he could, in turn, convey it to the Prophet.

This sort of thing is not even in keeping with the metaphysics of Muslim philosophers (as I will explain below). This conception turns the Prophet's life into a pre-scripted film in which every actor performs their role in a way that matches this or that ready-made verse, leading to the verse being sent down. With the Prophet striding about in each scene, megaphone in hand, repeating his lines. The Prophet could hardly be made more lowly than this.

Would it not be more reasonable and natural to imagine that the Prophet's powerful personality was the determining force: both the discoverer and the teacher, both the speaker and the hearer, both the lawmaker and the lawgiver? In other words, God simply sent the "teacher"; everything else revolved around his experiences and his reactions. This teacher was so well-equipped that he knew exactly what to do and what to say. And, of course, he was human, with all the moods and dispositions that a human being can have. At times, his lessons would be exquisite and, at other times, he would be distracted by mischievous students. At times, he was ecstatic and, at other times, he was despondent. At times, he would pitch his words at a lower level and, at other times, his words would soar. Like a bee, he would feed on everything: on exalted, spiritual experiences; on the mischievous and hostile questions and reactions of his audience; and on his own knowledge. And, of course, all of this could ultimately be traced back to higher sources and, from there, to the Source of all sources and the End of all ends, without whose permission not a single leaf can fall from a single tree and without whose revelation not a single bee can produce honey.

Of course, the Qur'an is the product of special states within the Prophet, but this does not mean that anything that he said at other times necessarily ranked lower than his Qur'anic utterances; is the Abu Lahab verse ("Perish the hands of Abu Lahab and perish he") more eloquent than and superior to all of the Prophet's non-Qur'anic utterances?

At any rate, these are two models for understanding revelation: my model, which is more in keeping with the Prophet's living experience, the metaphysics of Muslim philosophers and the exposition of mystics; and your/orthodoxy's model, which belongs to a mythological world and is in keeping with the perspective of the *ahl al-hadith*. You say that God did everything through Gabriel's mediation. I say that He did everything through the Prophet's mediation and that Gabriel was a part of the Prophet.

Some Metaphysical Considerations

Fifthly. You objected to my use of the metaphysical principle that says that "any temporal being (*hadeth*) is preceded by time and material potentiality," since I said that revelation, too, was preceded by material conditions and, on this basis, concluded that the Prophet's mental and physical conditions paved the way for revelation. Respectfully, I do not think your objection is valid. I think that all your hard work and concentration on *fiqh* [Islamic jurisprudence] may have made you forget that, according to Mulla Sadra's exposition (*Asfar al-Arba'ah*, Vol. 3, p. 55, Chapter 16, seventh stage), this principle does not only apply to form in corporeal bodies and material phenomena (as you seem to think). In fact, it holds true for forms in matter and forms associated with matter (the human soul). It is only the purely immaterial that is not subject to this principle. Let me also remind you that your teacher, the late Tabataba'i, wrote in an annotation on this subject in the *Asfar*, that this principle applies to souls even for the Peripatetics, who hold that souls are non-material from the start; otherwise, this is more clearly the case for Mulla Sadra, who believed that souls are matter first and become spirit later.

To put it more simply, anything associated with matter (whether form or spirit or revelation), is bound to compliance with the above-mentioned principle and the material base is the precondition for its obtainment and presence. And, of course, matter is never an efficient cause, as demonstrated in the First Philosophy.

Let me add that the idea that God can have a changing will is an impossibility. In view of the fact that God is not subject to passing events and does not change, He cannot make decisions on demand, as it were. So, Gabriel's movement between God and the Prophet, carrying messages back and forth, and receiving a specific verse for every specific event and bringing it down to earth is absolutely not in keeping with the metaphysics of Muslim philosophers and theologians, and it is in no way reasonable or justifiable. Of course, it is in keeping with the popular image of a sultan-like God, a winged Gabriel and a Ptolemaic heaven and earth (and this is the image that most Qur'anic commentators offered in pre-modern times.)

Let me also add that, according to Islamic philosophy, God's actions are not preceded and caused by intentions, and it has been demonstrated elsewhere that it is impossible for God to do anything to fulfil an objective or aim. God is not an agent with intentions. The idea that He made a new decision from time to time, and then sent down a new verse in order to achieve an aim or to explain something or to make something happen or to prevent something from happening is absolutely out of the question. Although everything occurs with God's permission, with His knowledge and based on His will, He exercises His will in a different way from human beings.

The solution to all these problems is to see the Prophet's powerful and sanctioned being as the acting agent, the exerciser of intentions, the creator of the verses and the formulator of the precepts; a being who is so powerful that he is God's caliph on earth, his hand is God's hand, and his word is God's word. And the Qur'an is his miracle.

The seamless web of being and the cause-sustainer relationship of God with contingent beings and the course of causality in the skin and pores of all entities leaves no room for a conventional, human Lord-Messenger relationship. God does not govern the world in the way that a king governs a country; God governs the world in the way that a soul governs a body (according to classical natural philosophy). The body works like a self-regulating machine but it is under the soul's pervasive sway. It is not as if the soul is constantly willing things in order for neurons to fire or for hormones to be secreted into the blood, although, in the words of Mulla Sadra, the heart, too, beats by the soul's hidden will. This metaphor and analogy at least shows that, until and unless we have a correct conception of the relationship between God and the world, we will not have correct theories about the Prophet and revelation either. Instead, we will be enslaved by myths which—in order to explain any causal relationship and any function or action—invent a face and a figure, and fill the world with the comings and goings of imaginary personifications.

The above exposition was in line with the philosophy of Islamic philosophers, which is acceptable to your esteemed self. If we were to proceed on the basis of modern philosophy, things would take on a different tenor.

Conflicts of Science and Scripture

Sixthly. As for your remarks about the conflict between the surface appearance of the Qur'an and science, I will not go on at great length about it. I will confine myself to expressing surprise at the fact that Muslim, Shi'i clerics do not seem to be prepared to learn anything from the experiences of the Church, and are repeating exactly the kinds of things that the Church used to say when faced with Copernicus and Galileo. They seem to think that their utterances are as fresh as ever, seemingly oblivious to the fact that their erstwhile advocates have long since abandoned these methods and submitted to vast and awesome twists and turns and contractions and expansions in understanding (hermeneutics) scripture. The Church, too, set its heart for a while on the compatibility of "true science" and "true revelation." Some other time, they entertained denigration of science. For a while, they spoke about not understanding the Speaker's solemn intent. Occasionally, they embarked on outlandish interpretations. But, despite all these clever attempts, they failed. So, they fair-mindedly surrendered and opted for a new path. They reformulated their theology and their theories of religion. They renewed their understanding of God, revelation, scripture and science. And they emerged stronger from that terrifying challenge. The material that has now been written about the conflict between science and revelation can be stacked up as high as the sky. So, I can only be surprised when I see that our share, from this vast array, seems to be little more than a few shreds.

But if the Speaker's solemn intent has yet to become clear, 1,400 years later, then, who do you think is supposed to grasp this intent and when? And if we have to wait for empirical science to make it clear what "the seven heavens" eventually means, then why do we have to be so condescending towards science? And a science that we exploit to prove God on the basis of the argument from design at that. A science, too, that Tabataba'i used in order to change completely the meaning of throwing meteors at devils, issuing a ruling on it that went against the rulings of all other exegetes. And if the Speaker's solemn intent is so difficult and takes so long to grasp on such minor issues as the seven heavens which is unconnected to the fate and felicity of believers, how can we ever be certain that we've grasped the Speaker's solemn intent on more important issues such as "where we've come from and where we're headed"? Will this approach not create irreparable gaps in our understanding of the Qur'an? Will it not spread the dust of doubt and incomprehensibility over everything? Will it not rob us of all confidence and trust in the words of scripture?

Does the Mu'tazilite tradition not show us a better way out to see these incongruous bits of the Qur'an as being in harmony with the beliefs of the Arabs of the time?; regardless of whether such verses are in the Qur'an because of compliance with the language of the Arabs of the time or because of the Prophet's limited knowledge.

You say that if we consider it possible that these kinds of scientific "flaws" found their way into the Qur'an, we will lose our trust and confidence in it, and imagine that there may be other flaws. How strange! Has the division of the Qur'an's verses into those that are clear and those that are ambiguous undermined our confidence in it? Has the idea

that some verses were abrogated by subsequent verses undermined our
confidence in it? Certainly, there will always remain some verses that
cannot be categorized clearly: they may be ambiguous or they may be
clear; they may have been abrogated by other verses and they may not
have been; e.g. "No compulsion is there in religion," (2: 256), which
some commentators believed was abrogated by later verses. It is true
that, if we believe in the idea of abrogation, some verses of the Qur'an
will be rendered useless, but has the notion of abrogation undermined
the Qur'an as a whole? There were, of course, literalists who harboured
such fears and said that, if we accept that some verses are metaphorical,
then, we will have both questioned God's ability to use non-metaphori-
cal language and undermined confidence in the Qur'an, because there
will be cases where we won't be able to decide whether a phrase is
metaphorical or not. But the history of the Qur'an washed away this
fear, although some borderline cases still remain.

Ayatollah Sobhani, the point is not whether Mr Tabataba'i's interpretation of "the meteors and the devils" was right or wrong; the point
is the method he used. The point is that, in his interpretation, he used
both modern science and Greek-o-Islamic metaphysics. In this way,
he rejected the understanding of all the exegetes who had preceded
him. Now, if science has the power to do this and if this is an acceptable thing to do, then, it is acceptable everywhere; even when science
points to something that we dislike it. The important thing is to open
the door to dialogue between revelation and reason, not to subject one
to the other's command.

As to the Tradition about the Prophet having deferred to the knowledge of the cultivators on the pollination of palm trees, it may be
that—as you argue—this is not a very reliable Tradition and is untrue.
There is certainly no shortage of forged Traditions in Shi'i and Sunni
belief after all. But this is not the point. The point is that Muslims and
their leading experts on theology and mysticism have lived for centuries with Traditions of this kind, have believed in them and have not
imagined that they undermined their faith or Muhammad's prophethood in any way. The point is that someone like Ibn Arabi (and there
were many more like him) piously believed that the noble Prophet did
not have total mastery even over the knowledge of his own time (in
medicine, astronomy, botany, etc.), never mind the knowledge of later
times. And they did not think that this belief undermined their faith in
Islam or detracted in the least from the Prophet's stature.

Is it not the case that many theologians (including Al-Ghazali and Rumi) believed in the *Gharaniq* story (that the Prophet received a revelation from Satan)? And have some Shi'i ulema not believed that the Qur'an was tampered with? It may well be that you do not give credence to these ideas. But the fact remains that many Muslims—and great ones, at that—believed them without imagining that they undercut their faith or the Prophet's revelation in any way, and they remained true believers in the Qur'an and Islam. The important thing, too, is that no one was ever excommunicated because they believed that the Qur'an was tampered with or because they believed in the *Gharaniq* story.

Pluralistic Islam versus Monolithic Islam

Finally, let me add that we have to see Islam as precisely this colourful array of beliefs and ideas. Islam is not just what is being taught today in Shi'i seminaries in Iran or in Wahhabi seminaries in Saudi Arabia. Islam is all the understandings and interpretations of it to date (as is Christianity, Judaism, Marxism, etc.).

Had the exposition of Islam been left to chroniclers and faqihs alone, we wouldn't have the rich and colourful Islamic civilization that we have today. If, at a certain point in time, orthodoxy closed the door to fluidity in theology and exegesis, today, seminaries should take the lead in reopening the door and welcoming diverse theological theories and views. They should not try to force ideas into the straitjackets of "fidelity" and "infidelity". They should not succumb to the delusion that they have gone as far as they need to go and that rigidity must now be the order of the day. The only way to ensure that religion survives and endures is to throw open windows and lungs to fresh air. Let them see Islamic culture's multifarious past and Muslims' alacrity and courage in understanding and adopting ideas from China, India, Iran and Greece.

Let them, at least, respect the varied traditions, ways and creeds of Islamic culture and not pray that one lives and the others die. The colourful history of this religion has included exegetes, contemplatives, Sufis, philosophers, chroniclers, literalists and a whole range of schools of exegesis and jurisprudence. They have all existed and have all been Muslims. And, through their disputes, they have lent dynamism to this civilization. If, one day, one of these approaches forcibly overpowers the others and cracks down on them, that will be the day when religiosity will die. Shutting windows is not a skill; let them open new windows if they can.

Muslims today have no option but dialogue. We must use our brief lives to talk with others. And not only with "insiders" but with "outsiders" as well. With scholars, not with the ignorant. And we must do this in order to lend fluidity to worn-out Islamic divinities and to return to the time before orthodoxy set in. Dialogue demands forbearance, open-mindedness, preparedness, humility, the admission of need, an eagerness to learn, the courage to think, a refusal to imitate and a respect for ideas as a sacred effervescence, not as a danger-ground or a sinful assembly. How bad a precedent is set by those who call on scholars to repent, who lock up the bird of the intellect in the cage of *fiqh*, who frighten the deer of thought with the wolf of excommunication, who attach more value to imitation than to reasoning, who rank "parrots" higher than "bees", who make religion a source of enmity and violence, and who sell vinegar instead of honey!

What strength can there be in a *fiqh* that is irrigated with a weak theology? What force can its rulings and *fatwas* carry? And how can a theology that is blocked by *fiqh* achieve new victories? Our *faqihs* are in the grip of a fatal fallacy today. Instead of leaning on theologians and updating their theology and, therefore, their *fiqh*, they shout down theologians. And instead of considering themselves needful of theologians, they want to force it to be the other way around. And this is purely and simply because *fiqh* has become obese and arrogant, and theology has become frail and sickly. Unless and until this is redressed and a balance established, this religion's predicament will remain unresolved.

Abdulkarim Soroush
Washington D.C.
May 2008

BIBLIOGRAPHY

References

Introduction

Abo el Fadl, Khalid. *Conference of the Books.* New York: University Press of America, 2001.
———. *Place of Tolerance in Islam.* Boston: Beacon Press, 2002.
———. *Rebellion and Violence in Islamic Law.* Cambridge: Cambridge University Press, 2001.
———. *Speaking in God's Name: Islamic Law, Authority, and Women.* Oxford: Oneworld, 2001.
———. *The Great Theft: Wrestling Islam From the Extremists.* San Francisco: Harper, 2005.
Alijani, Reza. "M. Shabestari va Roykard-e Wujudi-Fardgara." *Madreseh.* Vol. 2, No. 6. (2007): pp. 67–73.
Abu Zayd, Nasr Hamed. *Mafhum al-Nass: Dirasah fi ʿulum al-Qurʾan.* Cairo: al-hayʾah al-misriyya al-ʿamah al-kitab, 1990.
———. *Naqd al-Khitab al-Dini.* Cairo: Madbuli, 1992.
———. *Rethinking the Qurʾan: Towards a Humanistic Hermeneutics.* Utrecht: Humanistics University Press, 2004.
An-Naʿim, M. Abdullahi. *Toward An Islamic Reformation.* Syracuse: Syracuse University Press, 1990.
Arkoun, Mohammed. *Rethinking Islam.* Translation and Ed., Robert D. Lee. San Francisco: Westview Press, 1994.
Dabbaqh, Soroush. "Mujtahed Shabestari va Iman-e Shurmandaneh." *Madreseh.* Vol. 2, No. 6. (2007): pp. 76–79.
Jahanbakhsh, Forough. *Islam, Democracy and Religious Modernism in Iran (1953–2000): From Bazargan to Soroush.* Leiden: E. J. Brill, 2001.
Kadivar, Mohsen. *Daghdaghehay-e Hokumat-e Dini.* Tehran: Nashr-e Ney, 1379/2000.
———. *Hokumat-e Velaʾi.* Tehran: Nashr-e Ney, 1998.
———. *Nazariyehay-e Doulat dar Fiqh-e Shiʿah.* Tehran: Nashr-e Ney, 1376/1997.
Madreseh. Vol. 2, No. 6. Tehran, July, 2007.
Naraqi, Arash. "Mahiyyat-e Kalam-e Vahyani dar Andishe Mujtahed Shabestari." *Madreseh.* Vol. 2, No. 6. (2007): pp. 63–66.
Rahman, Fazlur. *Islam,* 2nd Ed. Chicago: University of Chicago Press, 1976.
———. *Prophecy in Islam,* 2nd Ed. Chicago: University of Chicago Press, 1979.
Shabestari, Muhammad Mujtahed. *Hermenutiks, Ketab va Sunat.* Tehran: Tarh-e Nou, 1996.
———. "Hermenutiks va Tafsir-e Dini as Jahan." *Madreseh* 2, no. 6 (2007): pp. 84–92.
———. *Iman Va Azadi.* Tehran: Tarh-e Nou, 1997.
———. *Naqdi bar Qaraʾat-e Rasmi az Din.* Tehran: Tarh-e Nou, 2002.
———. "Qaraʾat-e Nabavi az Jahan." *Madreseh* 2, no. 6 (1386/2007): pp. 92–96.
———. *Taʾamulati dar Qaraʾat-e Insani az Din.* Tehran: Tarh-e Nou, 2004.
Soroush, Abdulkarim. *Akhlaq-e Khodayan.* Tehran: Tarh-e Nou, 2001.
———. *Al-Qabd wa al-Bast fi al-shariʿah.* Trans. Dalal Abbas. Beirut: Dar al-Jadid, 2002.

——. *Bast-e Tajrubeh-e Nabavi.* Tehran: Serat, 1999.
——. *Qabz va Bast-e Te'orik-e Shari'at.* 3rd ed. Tehran: Serat, 1996.
——. *Reason, Freedom, and Democracy in Islam: Essential Writings of Abdolkarim Soroush.* Trans and Eds. By Mahmoud Sadri and Ahmad Sadri. Oxford: Oxford University Press, 2002.
——. *Seratha-ye Mostaqim.* Tehran: Serat, 1998.
——. "The Evolution and Devolution of Religious Knowledge." In Charles Kurzman, (ed.) *Liberal Islam: A Sourcebook,* pp. 244–254. Oxford: Oxford University Press, 1999.
Taha, Mahmud Muhammad. *The Second Message of Islam.* Syracuse; Syracuse University Press, 1987.
Wadud, Amina. *Qur'an and Women: Rereading the Sacred Text from a Woman's Perspective.* Oxford: Oxford University Press, 1997.

Chapter One–Appendices

Abi Talib, Ali Ibn. *Nahj al-Balaghah,* (Ed.) Fayd al-Islam.
al-Rida, Ali Ibn Musa. *al-Resalah al-Dhahabiyah al-Ma'rouf be Tibb al-Imam al-Rida.* (ed.) by Muhammad Mehdi Najaf. Qum: Maktabat al-Imam, 1982.
Alusi, Mahmud Ibn Abdullah. *Ruh al-Ma'ani fi Tafsir al-Qur'an.* Beirut: Dar al-Ihya al-Truath, n.d.
Amini, Abdulhossein. *Al-Ghadir.* Tehran: Dar al-Kutub al-Islamiyah, 1952.
'Ameli, Abdulhossein Sharaf al-Din. *al-Muraje'at.* Tehran: Khurasni, 1946.
'Ameli, Horr. *Wasayel al-Shi'ah.* n.p., n.d.
Amoli, Seyyed Heidar, *Asrar al-shari'ah wa Anwar al-traiqha.* Beirut: n.p., n.d.
——. *Jame' al-Asrar va Manba' al-Anwar.* Tehran: Intesharat-e 'Ilmi va Farhangi, 1989.
Berlin, Isaiah. *Four Essays on Liberty.* Oxford: Oxford University Press, 1969.
Eliade, Mircea. *A History of Religious Ideas.* Chicago: Chicago University Press, 1978.
Feiz Kashani, Mullah Mohsen. *Al-Mahajjat al-Bayda fi Tahdib al-Ihya.* Tehran: Maktabat al-Sudouq, 1960.
——. *Al-Safi fi Tafsir al-Qur'an.* Beirut: Mu'asasah al-'alami lil Matbu'at, 1979–1982.
Fukuyama, Francis. *The End of History and the Last Man.* New York: Free Press, 1992.
Ghazali, Abu Hamed. *Al-Munqidh min al-dalal.* Ed. by Farid Jabre. Beirut: Commission Libanaise pour la Traduction de Chefs-d'œuvre, 1969.
——. *Al-Mustasfa.* Beirut: Dar al-Kutub al-'ilmiyah, 1983.
——. *Ihya al-'Ulum al-Din.* Cairo: Mustafa al-Babi al-Halabi, 1951.
——. *Shifa al-Ghalil.* Baghdad: Matba'ah al-Irshad, 1971.
Gilson, Étienne. *Reason and Revelation in the Middle Ages.* New York: C. Scribner's sons, 1966.
Graham, W. A. *Divine Word and Prophetic Word in Early Islam.* The Hauge: Mouton, 1977.
Hafez, *Divan.* Tehran: n.p., n.d.
Hermansen, Marcia K. (Trs.) *The Conclusive Argument from God: Shah Wali Allah of Delhi's Hujjat Allah al-Baligha.* Leiden: Brill, 1996.
Hick, John. *Disputed Questions in Theology and the Philosophy of Religion.* New Haven: Yale University Press, 1993.
Hilli, Ibn al-Mutahhar. *Kashf al-Murad fi Sharh Tajrid al-I'tiqad.* Beirut: Mu'asasah al-'alami lil Matbu'at, 1979.
Ibn Arabi, Muhyi al-Din. *Fusus al-Hekam.* Beirut: n.p., n.d.
——. *Futuhat Makkiyah.* Beirut: Sadir Publications, n.d.

Ibn Babawayh Qumi, Ali. *Al-Imama wa al-Tabsera min al-Heyra.* Beirut: Mu'asasah li al-Hayat al-Turath, 1987.

Ibn Khaldun. *The Muqaddimah: an Introduction to History.* (Trs) Franz Rosenthal. Abridged and edited by N. J. Dawood. London: Routledge and Kegan Paul, 1967.

Iqbal, Muhammad. *The Reconstruction of Religious Thought in Islam.* Lahore: The Ashraf Press, 1958.

Izutsu, Toshihiko, *God and Man in the Koran: Semantics of Koranic Weltanshauung.* Tokyo: The Keio Institute of Cultural and Linguistic Studies, 1964.

Jeffrey, Arthur. *The Foreign Vocabulary of the Qur'an.* Baroda, India: Oriental Institute, 1938.

Kulayni, Muhammad Ibn Ya'qub. *Usul min al-Kafi.* n.p., n.d.

Majlesi, Muhammad Baqir. *Behar al-Anwar.* Beirut: Mu'asesah al-Wafa, 1983.

Mandeville, Bernard. *The Fable of the Bees: Private Vices, Public Benefits.* Ed. E. J. Hudrt. Indianapolis: Hackett Publications, 1997.

Makki, Abu Talib. *Qout al-Qoloub.* Beirut: Dar al-Fikr, 1980.

Modarressi Tabataba'i, Hossein *Crisis and Consolidation in the Formative Period of Shi'ite Islam.* New Jersey: Darwin Press, 1993.

Motahhari, Mortaza. *Barresi Ijmali az Nahzathaye Islami dar Sad Sal-e Akhir.* Tehran: Sadra, 1979.

——. *Imamat va Rahbari.* Qum: Intesharat-e Sadra, 1986.

——. *Khatamiyat.* Qum: Intesharat-e Sadra, 1989.

——. "Khatm-e Nabuvat." In *Muhammad Khatam Payambaran.* Tehran: Hosseinieh Ershad Publications, 1969.

——. *Vahy va Nabuvat.* Qum: Intesharat-e Sadra, 1979.

Movahhed, Muhammad Ali. (Ed.) *Maqalat-e Shams-e Tabrizi.* Tehran: Intesharat-e Daneshgah San'ati, 1978.

——. *Shams Tabrizi.* Tehran: Tarh Nou, 1997.

Nasafi, Aziz al-Din. *Al-Insan al-Kamil.* (Ed.) Marijan Mole. Tehran: Anjuman-e Iran-shenashi Faranceh dar Tehran, 1980.

Qumi, Abbas. *Muntaha al-Amal.* Qum; Mu'aseseh Nashr-e Islami, 1994.

——. *Safinah al-Bihar.* Tehran: lithography, n.p. n.d.

Qushayri, Abolqasim. *al-Risalah al-Qushayriyah fi 'Ilm al-Tasawwuf.* Beirut: Dar al-Jil, 1990.

Razi, Fakhr al-Din Muhammad, *Mafatih al-Ghayb (al-Tafsir al-Kabir).* Beirut: Dar al-Fikr, 1978.

——. *Al-Matalib al-Aliyah.* Ed. Ahmad Hijazi. Beirut: Dar al-Kitab al-Arabi, 1987.

Razi, Najm al-Din. *Mirsad al-'Ibad.* (Ed.) Mohammad Amin-Riyahi, Tehran: Bongah-e Tarjumeh va Nashr-e Ketab, 1352/1974.

Rumi, Jalal al-din. *Kolliyat-e Shams, ya, Divan-e Kabir.* Tehran: Amir Kabir, 1355/1977.

——. *Mathnawi*

Sarraj Tusi, Abu Nasr. *al-Luma' fi al-Tasavvuf.* Cairo: Dar al-Kitab al-Haditha, 1960.

Semnani, Ahmad Ibn Muhammad. *Musannafat-e Farsi 'Ala al-Dawleh Semnani.* (Ed.) Najib Mayel Heravi. Tehran: Mawala Publications, 1989.

Shabestari, Mahmoud. *Golshan-e Raz.* Tehran: Tahuri, 1368/1989.

Shatebi, Ibrahim Ibn Musa. *Al-Muwafaqat fi Usul al-Ahkam.* Cairo, 1969.

Shirazi, Sadr al-Din. *al-Hikma al-Muta'aliya fi al-Asfar al-'aqliyah al-Arba'ah.* Beirut: Dar al-Turath, 1981.

——. *Mafatih al-Ghayb.* (Ed.) M. Khawjavi. Tehran: Mo'aseseh Motale'at-e Farhangi, 1984.

Smith, Wilfred. Cantwell. *Faith and Belief.* Princeton: Princeton University Press, 1979.

——. *The Meaning and End of Religion.* New York: Macmillan, 1963.

Soroush, Abdulkarim. *Akhlaq-e Khodayan.* Tehran: Tarh-e Nou, 2001.

——. *Bast-e Tajrubeh-e Nabavi.* Tehran: Serat, 1999.
——. "Dindari va A'yin Shahriyari." In his *A'yin Shahriyari va Dindari*, pp. 126–146. Tehran: Serat, 2000.
——. "Ihya al-ʿulum al-din." In *Da'erat al-Maʿaref-e Bozorg-e Islami.* Vol. 7, Tehran, 1997.
——. "Jameh-e Tahdib bar tan-e *Ihya*." in his *Qesseh Arbab Maʿrefat*, Tehran: Serat, 1996.
——. *Mathnawi Maʿnawi.* (Ed.) Abdulkarim Soroush, Tehran: Intesharat-e ʿilmi va Farhangi, 1996.
——. *Modara va Modiriyat.* Serat Publications, Tehran, 1996.
——. *Qabz va Bast-e Teʾorik-e Shariʿat.* 3rd ed. Tehran: Serat, 1996.
——. *Qesseh Arbab-e Maʿrefat.* Tehran: Serat, 1996.
——. *Razdani va Rowshanfekri va Dindari.* Tehran: Serat, Tehran, 1998.
——. *Reason, Freedom, and Democracy in Islam: Essential Writings of Abdolkarim Soroush.* Trans and Eds. By Mahmoud Sadri and Ahmad Sadri. Oxford: Oxford University Press, 2002.
——. *Seratha-ye Mostaqim.* Tehran: Serat, 1998.
——. "The Evolution and Devolution of Religious Knowledge." In Charles Kurzman, (ed.) *Liberal Islam: A Sourcebook*, pp. 244–254. Oxford: Oxford University Press, 1999.
Stace, Walter Terence. *Mysticism and Philosophy.* London: MacMillan, 1960.
Swinburne, Richard. *Faith and Reason.* New York: Oxford University Press, 1981.
Tabatabaʾi, Muhammad Hossein. *Maktab-e Tashayuʿ.* Qum: Dar al-Tabligh Islami, 1960.
——. *al-Mizan fi Tafsi al-Qurʾan.* Tehran: Dar al-Kutub al-Islamiyah, 1969–1973.
Tabarsi, Ahmad Ibn Abi Talib. *Kitab al-Ihtijaj.* n.p., n.d.
Tabarsi, Hossein Taqi al-Nuri, *Fasl al-Khitab fi Ithbat-e Tahrif-e Kitab Rabb al-arbab.* Tehran: s.n., 1881.
Taleqani, S. Mahmud. *Partouʾi az Qurʾan.* Tehran: Inteshar, 1971.
Tusi, Muhammad Ibn al-Hasan. *Tamhid fi al-Usul.* Tehran: Anjoman Hekmat va Falsafeh, 1980.
Tusi, Nasir al-Din. *Tajrid al-iʿtiqad.* Qum: Maktabat al-Islam, n.d.
Valad, Baha al-din. *Maʿaref: Majmuʿeh Sokhanan va Mavaʿez-e Baha al-din Valad.* Compiled by Najib Mayel Heravi. Teharn: Mawla Publications, 1987.
Wali Allah al-Dehlawi. *Hujjat Allah al-Baligha.* Cairo: Dar al-Turath, 1976.
——. *al-Tafhimat al-ilahiyah.* Bijnaur: Madinah Barqi Press, 1936.
Zamakhshari, Mahmud Ibn Umar (Jarallah). *Al-Kashshaf.* Beirut: Dar al-Kitab al-ʿarabi, 1947.

INDEX

Abbasids   184, 285
Abd al-Muttalib   87
Abd al-Quddus of Gangoh   5, 66
ʿAbduh, Muhammad   185
Abo El Fadl, Khaled   xlix, xlv, 345
Abraham   4, 28, 86, 136, 297
Abu Dhar   266
Abu Jahl   281, 292
Abu Lahab   71, 80, 292, 335, 338
Abu Sufyan   281
Abu Talib, al-Makki   251, 347
Abu Talib   87
Abu Zayd, Nasr Hamed   xxviii, xxxi,
   xxxii, xxxiii, 271, 345
Accidents
   In religion   83, 90, 173
   and Change   312
Adam   125, 216, 238, 310, 314, 330
Afghani, S. Jamal al-din   33, 185
Ahl al-hadith   338
Aisha   80
Akhbaris   112
Ali, Ibn Abi Talib (Imam Ali)   41, 45,
   50, 56, 82, 90, 105, 108, 110, 117, 142,
   249, 253, 265, 266, 320
Alusi, Mahmoud Ibn Abdullah   299
ʿAmeli, A. Sharaf al-din   246, 346
ʿAmeli, Horr   334, 346
Amoli, S. Heidar   20, 66, 259, 346
Amini, Allameh Abdulhossein   246,
   346
An-Naʿim, Abdullahi, Muhammad
   xliv, 345
Anushiravan   87
anzala   324–325
   see also revelation
Arbery, A.J.   9, 27, 217
Arghun Khan   124
Arkoun, Muhammad   xxviii, xxxi,
   xxxii, xxxiii, xliv, xlv, 271, 345
Aristotle (-ian)   90, 277
Ascension   8, 19, 20, 27, 39, 100, 124,
   206, 221, 248, 249, 256, 290, 291, 331,
   336
   see also miʿraj
Asfar al-arbaʿah (Shirazi, Sadr
   al-din)   108, 331, 339, 347

Ashʿari (-ite)   x, 143, 169, 196, 229,
   274, 290, 295, 299
Augustine   214
Awliya   30, 39, 45, 48–50, 56, 102, 221,
   253, 258
   see also wali Allah

Babawayh, Ali Ibn Qumi   263, 347
Bacon, Francis   159
Bazargan
   Mehdi   312
   Abdulali   324
Bee   125, 126, 159, 330
Behar al-anwar (Majlesi)   79, 246, 347
Bergson, H.   29, 36
Berlin, Isaiah   147, 346
Bible, Hebrew   131
Blasphemy   xxxiv, 128, 129, 255, 287
Boehme, Jacobe   124
Buddhism and Buddhists   68, 300

Canaan   131
Causal
   pluralism   149, 160, 175
   religiosity   182, 185, 187
Causality   340
   principle of   225, 248
   and relativism   160
Cause and reason   156, 158–160
Certitude
   Caused and reasoned   162–165
   and discursive religiosity   237, 241
   and doubt   237
   and experiential religiosity   186,
      190
   and faith   227–228, 232–234
   and religious experience   4, 5, 42,
      150–151
   Revelational   164
Charisma   260
Charismatic personality   xlii, 260
Christian(s)   17, 28, 68, 81, 102, 112,
   131, 133, 140, 143, 149, 165, 166,
   198, 201, 228, 285, 300
Christianity   19, 68, 108, 121, 131,
   132, 149, 165, 166, 184, 228, 343
CIA   323

Compulsion
  of love l, 191
  no in religion 342
Confucius 201
Contemplation 12, 150, 330
Contemplative experience 125, 126
Contemplatives 35, 125, 330, 343
Covenant
  of Adam 238
  of scholars 302
Contingent 17, 123, 194, 197, 203, 307, 340
  absorption in the Necessary 292
Copernicus 340

Danish
  cartoons 317, 322
  media 276
Daquqi, tale in Mathnawi 250
Darwin, theory of 241
Darwinism 314
Dashti, Ali 287
Descartes 160, 220, 294
Divan-e
  Hafez 238, 346
  Kabir (Rumi) 9, 217, 347

Eddington, Stanley 331
Einstein 312
Eliade, Mircea 69, 346
Epilepsy 79, 299, 315
Esalat-e wujud 225, 327
  see also Shirazi, Sadr al-din
Exclusiv(ism) and (-ist) xlix, 140, 171, 201
Excommunication 323, 333, 344
Existentialism 191
Experiential religiosity see religiosity

Farabi, Abu Nasr
  and revelation xxviii, 296, 331, 332
Fars, News Agency 288
Fatwa 111, 321, 344
Fazlur, Rahman xxviii, xxix, xxx
Fetus
  and interpretation of the text 325
Finality xli, 25, 37, 276
  see also khatamiyat
Fiqh
  accidental 83–85
  adequacy of 55–59
  and social developments 107
  (in)complete 58, 100, 101
  minimum necessary 96, 99, 100

Fitrah 28, 54
Foroughi, Bastami 133
Foroughi, M. Ali 278
Formless
  truths 332
  knowledge 229
  meanings 273, 282, 295, 333
  within forms 134
Formless experience xxvi, xxxv, xxxix, 231
  and legal precepts 241–242
  and scripture 241, 243
Foucault, M. 159
Freud 159
Friday prayers 182, 321

Gabriel 12, 218, 253, 281, 290–293, 296, 304, 306, 309, 311, 324, 329–332, 336–339
Galileo 322, 340
Gandhi 201
Ghadir 245–247, 260
Ghadir, al- (Amini) 346
Gharaniq 343
Ghazali, Abu Hamed x, xxiii, xxviii, xxxiv
  and discursive religiosity 237, 240
  and fear of God 229, 230
  and fiqh 83–85, 91, 98–100
  and master disciple 255
  and philosophy 37, 108
  and pride 110, 111
  and religious/prophetic experience 6, 7, 8, 20, 21
  and revelation 292, 300, 343
  and sin 183
  and spiritual guardianship 251
  and theology 188, 236
Gilson, Etienne 228, 346
Greek 60, 71, 77, 145, 277
  philosophy 36, 298, 312, 342

Habermas 159
Hadith
  qudsi 251
  mutawatir 245
Hadid, Surah 300
Halimah 210
Hallaj, Mansour 186
Hanbal, Ahmad Ibn 132, 246, 251, 334
Harakat al-juhariyah 312
  see also Shirazi and Mulla Sadra
haram, (sacred) months 70
hoarding (laws of) 95, 97, 99, 100

Hosseinieh Ershad   32, 34, 347
Hick, John   131–134, 140, 346
Hijaz   77, 99, 295, 335
Hilli, Allameh   55, 346
Houris   70, 71, 310
Hukm   321

Ibn Arabi, Muhyi al-din   x, xxxiv, xli,
    21, 346
    and contemplatives   330
    and prophet and wali   49
    and Khomeini   297
    and the Prophet's knowledge   297,
    342
    influence on H. Amoli and S. Shirazi
    259
Ibn Hanzala   57
Ibn Hisham   210, 211, 218
Ibn Khaldun   8, 10, 80, 297, 347
Ibn Khothaym, Rabi'   265
Ibn Qibah   263
Ibn Sina (Avicenna)   xviii, 96, 108, 141,
    163, 220, 277, 302, 331
Ijtihad   xv, xxii, xxv, xxx, xlii, xliii, 31,
    32, 33, 53, 54, 57, 60, 62, 114
    as cultural translation   xliii, 89, 91
Imam
    Hossein   31, 184, 265
    Baqir   265
    Sadiq   265
    Rida   79, 265, 346
    The Hidden   262, 263, 276, 321
Imamate
    and God's grace   261
Invisible, the   306
Iqbal, Muhammad   xxiii, xli
    and fiqh/ijtihad   31–32
    and finality of prophethood   29–37,
    43–47
    and prophetic experience   5, 66, 124,
    125, 230
    and western philosophy   36, 37
Israel, children of   85, 87, 131
Izutsu, Toshihiko   73, 347

Jabr   191
    see also predestination
Jabri, Mohammed 'Abed al-   60
Jesus   5, 13, 16, 28, 68, 131, 140, 184,
    201, 202, 241
Jews   17, 68, 81, 86, 87, 112, 131, 132,
    140, 149, 162, 163, 166, 249, 308–309
Jihad   xlv, 62, 72, 173, 174, 182
Jinn   73, 79, 299, 315, 335

Jonah   249
Judaism   68, 132, 163, 165, 166, 343
Justice   84, 87, 130, 147, 321
    not being religious   xix, 196
Juwayni   91

Ka'bah   57, 258
Kadivar, Mohsen   xliv, xlv
Kalam
    Allah   324
    e Bari   xxviii, xxix, xxx, 12
    e jadid   x
    e Payambar   xxix, xxxvi
Kant   35, 36, 52, 131, 133, 157, 158,
    175, 294
Kargozaran, Newspaper   288
Kashf   49, 324–325, 328
Khatam al-'urafa (Rumi)   127
Khatam-e payambaran   34
Khatam-e wilayat (Ibn Arabi)   49
Khatami, Muhammad   xi
Khatamiyat   18, 48, 347
    see also finality
Khizr   204, 250, 256
Khorasan   230, 265
Khomeini, Ayatollah   271, 297, 313,
    320
    on revelation and Gabriel   290, 291,
    297
    and Ibn Arabi   297
Khoramshahi, Baha al-din   288
Khums   98, 263
Kulayni, Muhammad Ibn Yaqub   57,
    108, 145, 258, 347
Kumayl   253, 266

Lakatos   x, xliii
Lauh al-mahfuz   xxviii
Limbo, realm of   307
Lote-tree   12, 334
Lubb   xliii, 65
Lutf, principle of   261

Madness   79, 299, 300, 314, 315
Majlesi, Muhammad Baqir   79, 246,
    347
Ma'mun   265
Makarem Shirazi, Ayatollah Naser   322,
    323
Malamatigari   110
Manzelah bayn-e manzelatein   229
Mard-e bateni   125, 190
Mary   5, 6, 332
Marx   152, 159, 201, 202

Marx(ist) and (-ism)   ix, 343
Mawla   246, 260
Maximum possible   xxvi, xlvi, 93, 103
Mesbah Yazdi, Muhammad Taqi   103
Metaphysics
    Greek-o-Islamic   342
    Islamic   ix, 337, 338, 339, 340
    and science   175
    of separation   294
    of presence   294
Meteors   298, 300, 316, 335, 341, 342
Meytham   266
Miqdad   266
Mi'raj   12
    see also ascension
Mongol, army   124
Montazeri, Ayatollah, Hossein
    Ali   xxxiv, 320, 324
Motahhari, Mortaza
    and finality of prophethood   29,
        32–37, 47–48, 54, 55
    and slavery   18
    and fiqh   56, 57, 60, 61
    and Soroush   313, 315, 317
MOSSAD   323
Moses   11, 14, 27, 28, 47, 68, 126–130,
    134, 142, 204, 210, 240, 250, 256, 329,
    332
Mu'ayyad (prophet)   xxxi, 293
Muhkamat   16, 117
Mutashabehat   117
Mulla Sadra   x, xxxiv, 220, 277
    see also Shirazi, Sadr al-din
    and prophetic/religious experience
        27, 253
    on hadeth   339, 340
Muqaddimah (Ibn Khaldun)   8, 10, 80,
    297, 347
Mushaf   xxxiii
Musnad (Ahmad Ibn Hanbal)   132,
    251, 334
Mu'tazilah   xxi, 299
Mu'tazilite(s)   xxi, xxx, 143, 193, 229,
    261, 299
    and principle of lutf   261
    and createdness of the Qur'an
        xxviii, 274, 285
    and accidental verses   300
    and miraculousness of the
        Qur'an   328
    and incongruities in the Qur'an   341

Nahj al-Balaghah   41, 45, 108, 110, 117,
    131, 143, 253, 266, 277, 285, 320, 346

Nass   xxxii, 345
Necessary minimum   xxvi, xlvi, 19, 93,
    94, 113, 145
Neo-rationalism   xx, xxi, xxiii
Newton   7, 326
Nominalism
    and pluralism   168–169
nominalist   xlvii
    definition of religion   68
Noumena and phenomena   131, 133
    Kant and Schopenhauer on   175
Nuri Hamadani, Ayatollah   323

Occultation   259, 262, 263
    see also Imam, Hidden
Orientalists   280, 284, 286, 299
Orthodoxy   ix, xiii
    on revelation and Qur'an   xxiv,
        xxv, xxviii, xxxi, xxxvi, 331–332,
        337–343
    pre-   323, 343
"Ought" versus "Is"   62

Paradoxical
    mission of prophets   37, 211, 216
    mystical statements   252
Parrot   319, 329–330, 334, 344
Perfect Man   148, 249, 250, 253, 258
Peripatetics   339
Peripatetic philosophy   312
Pir   138, 203, 204, 220, 254–256
    Ghazali on   255
    as divine guardian   203
Pluralism
    and essence of religion   168–170
    and principality of quiddity   170
    as manzar/perspective (Rumi)
        127
    causal   149, 161, 174
    epistemological   151, 158, 161
    negative   xlvii, 137–147, 157
    of values and causes   147–149
    positive   xlvii, 119–137
    reasoned   160, 161, 174
Pollination
    Prophetic tradition on   197, 297,
        310, 342
Pope
    Benedict XVI   323
    John Paul II   140
Popper   x, 294
Post-modernism
    and causal pluralism   160
Ptolemaic heaven   78, 339

Ptolemy 229
Predestination 108
Prophet as
  active agent in revelation 295, 304, 306
  contemplative 190, 343
  God's caliph 340
  passive means in revelation 295, 304
Prophet's
  intellect 332
  mu'ayyad personality xxxi, 16, 293
  persona and finality 37–43
  sanctioned being 340
  shakhsiyyat-e haqiqi and huquqi 37–48
  imagination 4, 110, 170, 279, 291, 296, 304, 328, 331–333, 336
Prophet's personality
  and discursive religiosity 204, 219
  and experiential religiosity 204
  and revelation xxiv, xxv, xxvi, xxxvi, xxxviii, 4, 14, 16, 21, 285, 290, 293, 296, 304, 305, 339
  and spiritual guardianship 209
Prophetic
  experience and its dialogical nature xxvi, xl, 13
  experience and its transformative power 217–224
  experience and meaning of expansion xxv, xxvii, 202
  experience and pluralism 134, 169, 230, 231
  experience and formlessness xxvi, xxxv, xxxix, 134, 230, 231, 241–244, 273, 282, 295, 331–333
  mission and change 209, 211–212, 224
Propositions
  indexical 167
  with(out) quantifier 297

Qadar 108
Qadr, night of 14
Qeissari, Dawoud 252, 259
Qeshr xliii, 65
Qiyas 53, 57
Qobad 87
Qol 324
Qur'an
  as discourse xxxii, xxxiii
  created nature of xxx, 274, 275, 285, 312, 329

dialogical nature of 326–327, 338–339
rain in 325
word system of 75–76
Quraysh 70–72, 309, 335
Qurb 12, 251–252, 294
Qunawi, Sadr al-din 252, 259
Qutb, Sayyed 185

Rahner, Karl 140
Ramadan 14, 70, 97, 335
Rationalism
  critical xxii, 156–160, 225
  naïve 156, 160
  and Mu'tazilites xi
  and doubt 151
Rationality
  Instrumental/practical 186, 190
  Theoretical 186, 190
  and hermeneutic 177
Razi
  Fakhr al-din 21, 53, 55, 56, 99, 143, 189, 326, 328, 331, 347
  Najm al-din 124, 347
Reality
  a posteriori view of xlvii
  multi-layered xlvii, 120, 131, 137, 175
  Rumi on 128, 139
  understanding of 157, 158, 175
  thick and thin 326
Relativity
  theory of 7, 312
  of truth and falsehood 144
Relativism 158–160
  ethical 106
  and cause and reason 158–160
Religion
  a priori definition of 68
  a posteriori definition of 68, 76
  perfection of xxvi, 20, 53, 54, 58, 59, 113
Religiousness, meaning of 195–207
Religious experience
  and faith/belief 228–230
  and form/formless 230–232, 241, 244, 282
Religiosity
  discursive xlviii, xlix, 162, 186–191, 218, 234–241, 243
  experiential xxxiv, xlviii, 182, 186, 190–192, 202–207, 220, 234, 235, 239
  pragmatic xlviii, xlix, 162, 182–187, 206, 219, 238, 243

Repentance   72, 129, 215
Resurrection   68, 80, 107, 144, 241,
    253, 256, 257, 300, 307
Revelation
    sending down of   325 (see also
        anzala)
    as natural phenomenon   324–326
    and science
        (Sobhani)   310–315
        (Soroush)   298–301, 340–343
Rumi, Jalal-al-din   ix, x, xi, xxxiv, xxli,
    4, 7, 8, 20, 76, 227, 231, 237, 272, 274,
    283, 290, 292, 327, 330, 341
    and Muhammad's success   3
    and Muhammad's finality   18
    and Muhammad's assension   27,
        248, 249
    as Khatam al-'urafa   127
    and Gabriel   291–293, 296
    and philosophy   37, 236, 294
    and fiqh/shari'ah   65–66, 84
    and revelatory experiences   125
    and religious pluralism   126–130,
        133–138, 140, 170–172
    and discursive religiosity   186, 188
    and experiential religiosity   200,
        215, 217
    and religious experience   231, 233,
        239, 243, 320
    and spiritual guardianship   252–261

Sabzevari, Mulla Hadi   141, 259, 313
Sa'di   170, 173, 175
Saheb al-Zaman   259
    Ibn Arabi on   259
Sahifeh Sajjadieh   285
Sahih
    of Bukhari   251
    of Muslim   132, 310, 334
Salman Farsi   265, 256
Salvation   xii, xxvi, xlvi, xlvii, 122, 129,
    132, 138, 139, 141, 142, 155, 166,
    171–174, 201, 227
Satan   73, 74, 117, 141, 142, 153, 216,
    218, 225, 238, 241, 247, 259, 292, 298,
    299, 314–316, 343
Satanic temptations   292
Schopenhauer   175
Science
    and metaphysics   175
    and revelation (see revelation)
Seal
    of prophecy, the   xxv, xli, 6, 9, 22,
        26–30, 32–34, 37, 40, 45, 52, 169,
        239, 259, 310, 311

see also finality
    of the mystics, the   127
    see also khatam
Secularism(s)
    and types of religiosity see religiosity
    and reason   193–194, 198
    and Neo-rationalism   xx–xxi
Sepehri, Sohrab   128
Semnani, 'Ala al-Dawleh   124, 347
Shabestari
    Muhammad Mujtahed   xxviii,
        xxxv–xxxix, xliv, xlv, 345
    Shaykh Mahmoud   20, 66, 347
Shajarah tayyebah   294
Sharif Mortaza   262
Shah Wali Allah, of Delhi   x, xxxiv,
    31, 47, 82, 85, 86, 88, 346
Shams-e Tabrizi   109, 347
Shatebi   84, 91, 347
Shirazi, Sadr al-din   x, 21, 141, 313,
    347
    see also Mulla Sadra
    esalat-e wujud (principality of
        being)   327
    harakat al-juhariyah   312
    on prophethood   27
    God's knowledge   108
    spiritual guardianship   253
    mysticism and philosophy   259
    hadeth   296, 312
    revelation   331
Skepticism
    Sobhani on   276
Smith, Wilfred Cantwell   67, 228
Sohravardi, Shahab al-din   21
Solomon   176
Spinoza   220
Substantial change, theory of   312
    see also Shirazi, Sadr al-din and
        harakat al-juhariyah
Sultan-peasant (image of God-human)
    292, 329
Sultan Valad   16
Sunan
    Darami   132
    Ibn Majah   132
    Termadi   334
Sunna   xliii, 32, 49, 51, 63, 71, 80, 81,
    109, 117, 144, 242

Tabari   10
Tabataba'i, Mohammad Hossein   48,
    49, 56, 143, 176, 189, 211, 263, 292,
    298–301, 316, 324, 328, 331, 339, 341,
    347

Taha, Mahmoud Muhammad   xliv, 346
Taleqani, S. Mahmoud   299, 300, 301,
    314–315
Temporality
    of nature   313
    of revelation   294–296, 312–313
Tusi
    Abu Nasr Sarraj   251, 347
    Nasir al-din   261, 348
        and principle of lutf   262
        and revelation   296, 330, 331, 332
    Shaykh   55, 261, 348
Two-horned, (interpretation of the
    tale)   18, 80, 81, 309, 335

Ummi   xxvii, 74
Union
    with God   65, 190, 192, 273, 289,
        294, 325
Universals   67
Usul al-fiqh   52, 55–56, 58
Uthman   90

Violence   xlv, 71, 319, 321, 322, 323,
    344, 345
Visible, the   306, 311
Vision
    mystical   7, 8, 49, 124, 219
    prophetic   34, 50, 211, 219, 280, 291,
        337
    sensory   128

Wadud, Amina   xxx
Wahhabi(s)   143, 201, 343
Wahy   xxxv, xxxvi
    see also revelation
Wali Allah/Haqq   42, 253, 257
Wali   49, 50, 191, 205, 247, 250,
    251–254, 257, 266, 334
Wali-e A'zam   250
Wali-e faqih   320
Washington D.C.   xiii, 302, 344
Weber, Max
    and charismatic leadership   xlii, 260
wesal   294
    see also union
wilayat   99, 245, 247, 250
    and nubuwwat   50, 334
    and Imamate   258
wilayat-e
    bateni   202
    Muhammadiyeh   49
    faqih   57, 59, 81, 83, 144
    kuliyyeh ilahiyyeh   289
    tashri'i   46
Wittgenstein   x, 67, 68, 334

Zamakhshari, Jarallah   299, 301
Zayd   16, 26, 80, 81
Zaydis   143
Zoroaster   110
Zoroastrian   127, 149
Zoroastrianism   18, 321